Music in the Elementary School

fifth edition

ROBERT EVANS NYE
VERNICE TROUSDALE NYE
University of Oregon

Prentice-Hall, Inc., Englewood Cliffs, New Jersey 07632

Library of Congress Cataloging in Publication Data

NYE, ROBERT EVANS.
    Music in the elementary school.

    Includes bibliographies and indexes.
    1. School music—Instruction and study—United
States.   I. Nye, Vernice Trousdale.   II. Title.
MT3.U5N94 1985   372.8′7   84-16069
ISBN 0-13-607763-3

Editorial/production supervision and
   interior design: Elizabeth H. Athorn
Manufacturing buyer: Raymond Keating

Printed in the United States of America

10 9 8 7 6 5 4 3 2 1

ISBN 0-13-607763-3   01

Prentice-Hall International, Inc., *London*
Prentice-Hall of Australia Pty. Limited, *Sydney*
Editora Prentice-Hall do Brasil, Ltda., *Rio de Janeiro*
Prentice-Hall Canada Inc., *Toronto*
Prentice-Hall Hispanoamericana, S.A., *Mexico*
Prentice-Hall of India Private Limited, *New Delhi*
Prentice-Hall of Japan, Inc., *Tokyo*
Prentice-Hall of Southeast Asia Pte. Ltd., *Singapore*
Whitehall Books Limited, *Wellington, New Zealand*

Contents

PART 2: From Sound and Tone Qualities to Movement, Rhythm, and Dance

Preface

This edition of *Music in the Elementary School,* like earlier editions, is designed as a text and resource book for the elementary education major, the music education major, the student teacher, and the teacher-in-service. It is a comprehensive book from which college teachers and their students can select problems and activities that are pertinent to their needs. Students can be assigned selected readings and activities in the methods class, and continue to use the book during student teaching and still later in professional teaching.

The authors have chosen to organize Parts 2 and 3 in the general order in which children comprehend and learn music. However, the user of the book is free to use the music chapters in the order that best suits the situation. For example, in a class in which a review of music fundamentals (or the learning of them) is necessary, the college teacher may wish to begin with Chapters 12 and 14, while the teacher who wants a class to begin with an exploratory approach may begin with Chapter 9. Part 1 is essential in that it establishes how children learn music, describes the environment necessary for music learning, discusses individualization of instruction and special learners, and takes up curriculum planning and various types of lesson plans. After this introduction to music teaching, the reader can select from the many activities in Parts 2 and 3 those that are best suited to carry out course objectives.

This edition contains some features not found in the previous edition. The importance of the cognitive process skills (the thinking processes) and the superiority of music as a vehicle to acquire those skills are stressed. Early childhood music and mainstreaming have been incorporated. The Gordon rhythm syllables have been introduced. Sections on student behavior, the computer, the brain, as well as on Dalcroze, Kodály, and Orff are added. Other features include chapters dealing with music and child development, planning curricula, and experimenting with sound and tone qualities; an expanded discussion of individualizing instruction; and a section that deals with copyright law.

The authors are excited about the prospects of improved music instruction and better comprehension of the importance of music in education. They hope that readers will share their enthusiasm as they study and apply the content of this book. We wish to acknowledge the skill and resourcefulness of Elizabeth H. Athorn, production editor, and the contribution of Dr. Sylvia E. Cary, whose experience with individualized instruction enriched Chapter 5.

The best teacher will not be confined to any particular previously laid out plan, but will from the different methods make out one of his own; not indeed one that is stereotyped and unalterable, but one that he may modify and adapt to the varying wants and circumstances of his different classes.

LOWELL MASON
1792–1872

1

Learning, Development, and Planning

chapter one

Introduction

History There has been from the beginnings of music education a cross-fertilization of ideas between the United States and European nations, and now among all nations of the world. The names of leaders from abroad are legion, the most recent major figures being Dalcroze, Orff, Suzuki, and Kodály. In turn, American educators, such as Lowell Mason, Luther Whiting Mason, and many more, influenced music education in other nations. One American movement that attracted the attention of European educators was the Manhattanville Music Curriculum Program, with its emphasis on exploration and improvisation. An earlier distinctly American influence was the school band movement. As events continued to unfold, the strong relationship between music education and education in general became an American distinction. The term *music education* was an invention of the early National Education Association, which expresses the view that music is a part of general education, "music" being the adjective and "education" the noun. This relationship is not as strong in some other nations. The growing emphasis upon how children learn music—the application of learning theory—again illustrates the alliance between music education and general education in the United States. There are other distinctly American contributions, as we shall see.

Music education in the United States is an expression of the needs of the people rather than a product of an artistic elite. Its roots are in the singing school of the early days of the nation when Lowell Mason, William Billings and others responded to the desire of communities that church singing be improved by organized instruction in music fundamentals and note reading.

Among Mason's teaching principles were the following, condensed by the authors:

1. Since students learn by seeing and hearing, and because what they learn should be an evident and logical deduction from well established facts, a teacher guides the pupils to learn by their own powers of reasoning.
2. Educational steps are placed in a logical order that coincides with the natural development of the child, who learns a thing step by step when the necessary skills and background are acquired.
3. The teacher does not depend fully upon books, rules, or formulas, and thus will not teach by merely telling. The teacher depends upon present proof making its appeal to the mind of the pupil.
4. The primary values of music instruction will be social and moral.
5. There will be a strict but loving guidance of the pupil; music should be pleasant and agreeable; the pupil will be actively thinking and learning things constantly; gratification will come from the attainment of knowledge.

Mason's much quoted motto for teachers was:

THINGS BEFORE SIGNS;
PRINCIPLES BEFORE RULES;
PRACTICE BEFORE THEORY.

Elementary school music began to be offered officially in some cities in the 1850s, but it was not until 1864 that music instruction was approved and financed in Boston's primary grades. Luther Whiting Mason joined the Boston music staff, specializing in elementary school music and becoming its dominant figure in that century. He was called upon to assist the music programs of Japan.

Music Methods In 1834 the Boston Academy of Music formed a class for instruction in the methods of teaching music, a short summer lecture course held for a few days in August. Each succeeding year enrollment increased until there were 200 persons from all parts of the nation being instructed in how to improve their teaching in singing schools, private schools, and public schools. As early as 1836 some of these students organized their free time to discuss other matters of concern to music education, church music, and performing groups. Lowell Mason encouraged them, and in 1840 helped to form the National Music Convention to satisfy this demand. Because in those days colleges and universities did not offer course work in music education, other music conventions were organized throughout the country. These were brief, usually from three to five days in length. Their value and popularity created a demand for the *musical normal institutes* held in summers for two to three months duration, forerunners of the present-day summer session.

George Root organized the first institute in New York City in 1853. These continued into the 1920s, when teachers colleges began offering summer courses. One of the most important figures in innovative elementary school music of that day was Mrs. Satis Coleman, Teachers College, Columbia University, who antedated the approach of Carl Orff to some degree.

In the twentieth century music education became an integral part of the teacher education program of the nation, and the four-year degree in it, first introduced at the Oberlin Conservatory, became possible in the teachers colleges of the 1920s. Thus, music education can be traced from the singing school, music convention, and musical normal institute to the teachers college. To repeat: the roots of music education are in the needs of the common man; this is in contrast to other branches of music study, the roots of which can be traced to clerical origins or to aristocratic societies which produced a cultural elite.

More recently, the work in music education of two European composers of stature, Zoltán Kodály and Carl Orff, has tended to increase understanding of and respect for elementary music education in the United States. Another healthy influence has been the interest of private music teachers in applying methods adapted from music education to their studio teaching. Still another positive tendency has come from the almost universal realization that the large majority of music graduates will become teachers, if not in schools, in private studios and in institutions of higher learning. This has resulted in a closer bond among all areas of music because of the importance of teaching to the large majority of students.

In the early days of music education in the United States there were two primary aims of instruction, to read music and to sing acceptably. Later there was additional emphasis on the performance of both vocal and instrumental music. Teachers assumed that by this contact with music, understanding of music and improved social and ethical behavior were somehow absorbed in ways that defied explanation. At any rate, performance became the major criterion of music programs. Still later, appreciation and understanding of music concepts were assigned positions of importance among the goals of instruction. The early attempt to realize these new goals usually resulted in learning facts about music rather than acquiring the ability to discriminate and analyze. A more recent aim has been to achieve musical responsiveness through the study of music as an academic discipline. This is aided by the development of instructional and performance objectives in the cognitive, affective, and psychomotor areas of learning. Music is an *affective* art, based upon feelings that cannot be accurately assessed. Nevertheless, music involves *cognitive* (intellectual) and *psychomotor* (physical) experiences and is learned through the integration of these three areas of learning, since no one of them exists in isolation.

In this decade the general goals include creating a learning environment and using teaching procedures that will develop the musical abilities of the musically gifted, the so-called normal child, and those students with special problems and styles of learning.

Why Music? There are many theories concerning the place of the arts in the schools. In these times of declining public support for education, teachers are called upon to defend the need for music instruction. For example, with all the music in the environment, need we have in the schools that which is so freely available?

In the early days, music in the curriculum was supported by theories about music's utilitarian values in learning cooperation, building character, raising morale, improving physical and mental health, and later, in assisting language arts and social studies. Today some of these theories have been abandoned, others found in need of further research, and a few are admitted to have a degree of merit. Effort is now being made to justify music primarily for its own value.

From the standpoint of how children learn, and the skills and processes involved with learning, there is an answer to our question about the necessity of music in the school. Aesthetic experience, if correctly provided, fosters imagination and feelings in young minds. Art experiences can build a foundation from which cognition (thought), concepts, judgment, and action spring. Developing the imagination will also develop ideas, values, proposals, and theories. Without imagination, both creativity and intelligence are diminished. The teacher might defend music education by saying, "This cannot be left to chance; guidance in school is necessary." Thus arts education is basic in developing thought processes and in organizing and expressing feelings.

The final report of the National Commission on Excellence in Education, *A Nation at Risk: The Imperative for Educational Reform,* April, 1983, contains repeated endorsements of the arts, stating, "A high level of shared education in these Basics (English, mathematics, science, and computer science), together with work in the fine and performing arts and foreign languages, constitutes the mind and spirit of our culture." Arts education on the elementary level is specifically endorsed. The College Board included the arts as one of six areas of basic learning in a report issued the same year. Among recommended skills in the arts are the ability (1) to understand and appreciate the unique qualities of each of the arts, (2) to appreciate how people of various cultures have used the arts to express themselves, and (3) to understand and appreciate different artistic styles and works from representative historical periods and cultures. "College entrants . . . should be able to express themselves in one or more of the arts."

Arts education can enrich experience in ways that other subjects cannot. Arts education gives order and design to feelings and gives them meaning. It provides constant exploration into feelings that extend far beyond everyday experiences. The strange may become familiar and the familiar may become strange. Aesthetic response is indispensable to all experience, and instruction in the aesthetic response is both possible and necessary (Broudy, 1977). Good teaching will improve the sensitivity of the learner to aesthetic qualities in the environment, thus *all* teachers, not only those in the arts, have responsibilities in this area of learning. Aesthetic experience is one of the basics in attaining the state of being educated, thus the school must take serious account of this fact and act upon it. The teacher has the task of providing an environment in which children will respond imaginatively and by being attracted to the arts and coming to terms with them in problem-solving, creation-inspiring situations. If teachers accept this challenge and prepare and plan to provide this environment, the arts will have a permanent and central place in the school and in the lives of children.

As children grow older, they will confront two quite different points of view concerning the arts. Is art good because of the individual learner's personal satisfaction or because of standards established by society or by art "experts"? This interesting intellectual conflict will challenge older children to analyze an experience and to attempt to determine what about it is appealing, less appealing, and not appealing, and why. Children need not agree with the "experts" in these matters, but they should be able to defend their positions with facts about the experience. Children's creativity is more important than models from the past, but such models can be useful to children in their creative activities. The arts add quality to life. Through arts education children learn about themselves, other people, and humanity in general, and it is particularly useful in situations of cultural pluralism, probably being the best medium for understanding other cultures. When music is defined as patterns of sounds and silence, the world of sound is open to exploration and experimentation, and the resulting experiences in the elementary school years should be cognitive, psychomotor, and affective, with mind and body employed in problem-solving processes.

Children find good sense in interdisciplinary experiences, in which social studies, language skills, and literature are combined with the arts. Arts teachers should be competent in more than their areas of specialization. For example, drama and dance are important in good music teaching. Finally, arts education should extend into the community, with adults involved on a lifetime basis.

EXPLORATORY ACTIVITIES

1. From statements in this chapter and elsewhere concerning the purpose and/or justification of music in the schools, prepare a defensible rationale of why music should be in the curriculum.
2. Discuss this statement: "In a world which compels men's minds to invent the machines of destruction, the arts must remind it of the beneficence of beauty and the worth of an individual." (Oleta Benn, in the 57th Yearbook of the National Society for the Study of Education: *Basic Concepts in Music Education,* 1958, p. 355.)
3. Role-play a situation in which a local school board is confronted by some disturbed taxpayers who want art and music eliminated from the educational offerings in order to reduce the local tax burden. Include among the players a music teacher and a parent who want a good music program. The other class members can be the audience at the regular meeting of the board. Later, exchange the roles. Afterwards, identify the ideas that became evident in the performance.
4. It has been said that certain school subjects have to do with *making* a living

while others have to do with the *quality* of living. Discuss whether there is a reasonable priority of importance implied or whether these two aspects of education are equal in importance.

5. Discuss the teaching principles of Lowell Mason listed in this chapter. Are these nineteenth-century ideas applicable today?

6. Identify some nonmusical educational values of music experiences. How significant are they in defending music in the curriculum? The Hoffer reference below will assist you in answering this question.

7. Read and report on the early history of music education in the United States using Birge's book (see References).

References

BIRGE, EDWARD B., *History of Public School Music in the United States.* Philadelphia: Oliver Ditson Co., 1937. Reprinted by the Music Educators National Conference, Reston, Va., 1966.

BROUDY, HARRY S., "How Basic is Aesthetic Education? or Is 'Rt' the Fourth R?" *Educational Leadership,* November 1977, pp. 134–147.

HOFFER, CHARLES, *Introduction to Music Education: Section Two,* pp. 35–54. Belmont, Calif.: Wadsworth Publishing Company, 1983.

HOFFER, CHARLES R., and MARJORIE HOFFER, *Teaching Music in the Elementary Classroom,* pp. 9–10. New York: Harcourt, Brace, Jovanovich, Inc., 1982. Nonmusical values of music.

LeBLANC, ALBERT, "Nation at Risk: Opportunities within the Essentials Report," *Music Educators Journal,* September 1983, pp. 29–31.

LEE, WILLIAM R., "The Snedden–Farnsworth Exchanges of 1917 and 1918 on the Value of Music and Art in Education," *Journal of Research in Music Education,* Fall 1983, pp. 203–213.

Music Educators Journal, March 1983. This issue highlights utilitarian versus aesthetic rationales for arts education.

REIMER, BENNETT, *A Philosophy of Music Education.* Englewood Cliffs, N.J.: Prentice-Hall, Inc., 1970.

REIMER, BENNETT, *Toward an Aesthetic Education.* Reston, Va.: Music Educators National Conference, 1971.

RICHARDS, MARY HELEN, *Aesthetic Foundations for Thinking,* Part II. Portola Valley, Calif.: Richards Institute, 1978.

SMITH, TIM, "The Aesthetic Heart of Education," *Music Educators Journal,* March 1984, pp. 38–40.

TANGLEWOOD SYMPOSIUM REPORT, "Music in American Society," *Music Educators Journal,* November 1967, pp. 49–80.

ZINAR, RUTH, "Highlights of Thought on Music Education Through the Centuries," *American Music Teacher,* February–March 1983, pp. 32–38.

chapter two

Music and Child Development

A child needs the opportunity to participate spontaneously, enthusiastically, and completely in the various aspects of music. No other life experience can bring more thrills and enjoyment, or feelings of individual worth and self-completeness, than experiences in some or all areas of music. With the many occasions it provides for self-involvement and personally initiated activities, music is an effective way for individuals to become acquainted with their unique musical abilities, ways of solving musical problems, and ways of expressing themselves creatively. Self-respect, acceptance, and respect for peers can result from satisfying musical accomplishments.

Seeking and obtaining understanding of how children develop is a prerequisite to becoming a competent teacher. Children learn in any situation as complete personalities. They are the product of everything that has happened to them in the past and of everything that is presently happening to them. Prior experiences of children must be analyzed before one can plan programs for optimum development.

When teachers understand how children grow and learn, they find ways to span the gap between the learner and the subject matter of music. The problem of the teacher's knowing the subject but failing to know the child is a very old one. It has affected all levels of learning. A persistent problem that has disturbed teachers and curriculum planners is how to plan instruction based on knowledge of subject matter *and* children.

As a basis for diagnosing children's levels of development and their instructional level in music, some teachers rely on the sequential stages and characteristics of children as presented by developmental psychologists such as Arnold L. Gesell.

Research by Gesell and his associates resulted in established norms of developmental characteristics by age levels in physical, emotional, social, aesthetic, and cognitive abilities. Research of Piaget and Bruner focused on cognitive processes. Most students pass through the same stages of development, but usually not in identical ways nor at the same ages. There are rather definite stages of the development of intelligence, each carrying with it the embryonic elements of behavior or intelligence required in the succeeding stage. Unless these elements are encouraged to grow, they contribute little or nothing to the next stage, and growth is impeded. The various stages or levels of development have a fixed and sequential order. The time of their appearance varies with the physical development, experience background, and the society or culture of which the individual is a product.

Changes in our view of the world bring with them changes in our view of the child and of man. Today's psychologists are emphasizing the fact that all aspects of development are neither fixed nor necessarily orderly. The concept that development is modifiable is extremely important. Educators once believed that a child at age six would behave in a "six" way, and a child at seven in a "seven" way, and if children did not behave in these specified ways, they were designated as either retarded or gifted. Research indicates that this belief is unsubstantiated. Children grow and learn at different rates and use different styles of learning at each age level. Attitudes toward learning and the rate and amount learned usually result from the types and quality of physical, intellectual, and social stimulation received. Children's learning is further influenced by the amount of positive and emotional support they receive as well as what innate characteristics they inherit.

The concepts of both grade levels and age levels in terms of what children are able to accomplish have been undergoing revision. Individual differences among children are far greater than had once been thought, and it is now known that some children can accomplish feats believed some years ago possible only of older children. Under certain conditions young children can intellectualize at a level thought to be impossible until recently. Children are maturing earlier and educators are learning that even physical characteristics of age groups have undergone change.

What, then, is the value of child development charts where a norm is "established" for various groups of children? Despite the exceptions, they are still useful as general guides for teachers. By knowing general norms, a teacher can judge whether or not a class of a certain age is performing on that level, or if its *mental* age is higher or lower than the norm would indicate. Child development consists of mental, social, emotional, and physical growth. Any child can be above or below the norm for any one of these characteristics. Knowing this, teachers can plan for children's education on the level where they are, and this implies extensive individualization of instruction.

The list of general norms stated below are descriptions of development; they are not limitations or prescriptions and can be expanded and altered. The following chart of general norms may serve as a basis for analyzing a child's level of growth and maturity and as one type of guide for diagnosing, analyzing, and organizing music curricula and daily lesson plans. What are the advantages and disadvantages that may result from using general norms as presented below?

Ages 4 and 5

DEVELOPMENTAL CHARACTERISTICS	SUGGESTED IMPLICATIONS
Large muscles better developed than small muscles; constantly physically active; right- or left-handedness is established.	Physical activities involving large muscles are stressed; walking, running, hopping are related to music; five-year-olds can jump rope; can play simple percussion instruments; movements of animals are imitated; activities include free rhythmic responses to recordings and piano selections that "tell what to do"; creative and spontaneous movement; space is needed for movement because these children are apt to fall.
Language development is limited; speech skills are little developed although both language and speech are improving rapidly; soft palates make pronunciation and enunciation difficult for most.	Chants and calls, singing games and songs with words that are colorful, rhythmic, repetitious and sometimes nonsensical; provisions for much spontaneous and creative response to the sound of words and to music; singing and chanting Mother Goose rhymes and neutral syllables; Latin syllables so-mi, then so-mi-la-so-mi, and finally so-la-so-mi-do can *slowly* be introduced with accompanying pitch levels, arm movements, and hand signals.
Attention span is relatively short, depending on the interest and the activity; most children are very active, affectionate, and aggressive.	Plan music through the day for short periods of time; employ music in other areas of instruction to change the tempo of the day; use a variety of types of songs to relieve tension and fatigue and offer relaxation; include songs involving names, touching objects, and repeating phrases.
Some children are shy and limited in ways of expressing ideas and feelings.	Help children to listen to music in creative ways; encourage dramatizations and imitations of people, animals, and objects.
Usually very self-centered; wants to be involved and motivated; cares little what peers think; is very individualistic; emotions are intense, with brief extremes of happiness, anger, hate.	Give individual help; provide opportunity to sing alone and in small groups; a child will sing cooperatively in large groups only when socially and intellectually mature enough to cooperate in a group; the child needs help in learning to cooperate in singing, taking turns, listening to others; the teacher substitutes the child's name for the name

	in the song and leads in creating calls, chants, and conversational singing which include the child's name.
They have little understanding of ownership.	Create chants such as "This belongs to Mary," (55365–3–) and "The new shoes are Johnny's" (35–365–3–).
Sex roles are not clearly defined.	Use songs and singing games in which each sex has its logical role without being stereotyped.
The harmonic sense is rudimentary.	Emphasize the melodic line and the rhythm, not harmony; songs that require no chord changes in their accompaniment are preferable.
Enjoys the security of repetitious activity.	Repetitive songs, motions, or ideas, and repetitive manipulative experiences with percussion instruments and bells.
Desires to be accepted by adults; needs warmth and security from them; enjoys individual attention.	Teacher and parent sing to the child often, and provide a simple, pleasant, secure environment; they plan activities assuring success; they give encouragement and recognition for children's efforts in music.
Beginning to develop independence; tries to gradually depend less upon adults.	Provide for development of music skills that build self-confidence and independence; song content can aid in adjusting to new or frightening experiences; encourage children to make up new words, chants, songs, motions or rhythms, to play different percussion instruments, and to experiment with sound; encourage discussions and evaluations related to concrete objects and situations; assist social development; opportunities that coincide with their stage of operation are provided for children to assist in planning music activities, to select songs, recordings, appropriate percussion instruments and to decide how to interpret music.
Teeth and bony structures are growing and changing; vigorous action results in fatigue.	A variety of music activities from very active to restful is employed; a *minimum* of twenty minutes of music is distributed throughout the day; action songs and finger plays are used; children listen to many kinds of music including types that encourage rest and relaxation; they are involved in creative body movements and use of percussion instruments.
The beginning of cooperative play in relatively small groups; most learning is nonverbal.	Music activities help children grow in understanding and appreciation of others, as well as the quality of work done; *brief periods* of discussion and evaluation aid in developing their vocabularies, powers of communication, and their ability to relate to and respect others.
Very inquisitive about surroundings; eager to learn and	Provide opportunity to manipulate, experiment with, and use a variety of musical objects to pro-

to respond; very alert; learns primarily through sensorimotor and by reenacting real situations.

duce sound; plan experiences that build sensitivity to beauty of melody, rhythm, and form, and recognition of sad, happy, slow, fast, high, and low; simple imitations and dramatizations are employed; high-low can be equated with right-left on keyboard instruments.

Interested in the "here and now," "what and what for," and in realizing immediate goals.

Provide songs about everyday experiences such as mother and family, playthings, people they know, pets and animals; children need simple directions, demonstrated clearly and explicitly, and musical activities that can be completed in short periods of time; the teacher gives each child opportunities to succeed.

Lives in a world of make-believe and imagination; the child is imitative.

Provide the chance for creative responses in singing, listening, and rhythm; children should create and sing songs about and imitate the movement of animate and inanimate objects and dramatize songs in a simple manner to stimulate imagination, overcome shyness, relieve aggressive feelings and express ideas and personal feelings; songs are taught by rote, thus the teacher's voice and recordings should be good models; teacher's attitudes, skills, appreciations, and enthusiasm are imitated by the children; musical models in the home are very important; the child learns to appreciate the type of music to which he or she is exposed most frequently.

Voices are small; the pitch sense is often underdeveloped.

Many children need help in finding their singing voices; use tone-matching games, calls, chants, and singing conversations to build concepts of up, down, and same in pitch; establish the pitch of songs by means of piano, pitch pipe, or bells; give individual and small group assistance; have children imitate vocally sounds of their environment—train and factory whistles, church bells, chimes, and machines; oral, aural, and visual aids are necessary in building pitch concepts; children have opportunities to play very simple songs or parts of songs on the bells; emphasize listening to singing, then having children imitate the example.

Creative, spontaneous, and uninhibited.

Encourage creating chants, interesting word-rhythms, rhythmic movement and dramatizations; spontaneous singing is encouraged as children play; children dramatize roles of people and animals well known to them; space is provided for children to move freely; percussion instruments, scarves, and balloons can assist creative responses to rhythm.

They work alone or in very small groups.

Individual musical experimentation and small group activities are provided for.

Primary: Ages 5 to 8 (Grades K to 3)

Extend and refine the experiences indicated for five-year-olds. Children in some school systems do not have kindergarten experience and many six-year-olds perform on the level of five-year-olds.

CHARACTERISTICS

IMPLICATIONS

Many children are still unable to sing in tune; most voices are light and high in quality, but some are low and there are usually many different ranges present. The overlapping of ranges at the beginning of the school year will permit about five or six consecutive pitches to be sung by the large majority of the class in unison singing, usually from middle C to the G or A above.

Assist each child in learning to sing in tune; guide children to do individual singing, singing in pairs and in small groups within the large group; help students to experiment with their voices to determine the difference between singing and speaking; students need good models to imitate both in school and at home; begin the year with songs of limited range to assure the largest degree of success; this range is gradually extended; individual singing independent of teacher's voice or recording is encouraged; children use body movements, hand levels, and signals to reveal their comprehension of high and low pitch; children create chants and songs in their vocal ranges.

Large muscles are more developed than small muscles; children tend to move with the entire body as a unit; a lengthening of the limbs.

Free rhythmic movements and fundamental movements such as walking, running, skipping, hopping and galloping are stressed; finger plays develop small muscles; emphasis is given to impersonation of animals, people, and things; keeping perfect time in various tempos is not expected of some younger children because they need to experiment in their own ways to develop muscular control; all are encouraged to improvise rhythmic responses and to take part in activities that lead to improvement in poise, balance, and control in response to rhythmic stimuli; at first the accompaniment follows the response; later the children become able to respond to accompaniments of different tempos; suitable furniture and seating arrangements are provided; they grow in ability to sing with rhythmic accuracy; can repeat rhythmic patterns in body movements and on percussion instruments; become aware of the beat and can demonstrate it in body movements and on percussion instruments; become aware of meter.

Slow growth; children want warm, personal attention.

Employ a small repertory of simple songs well learned and frequently repeated; repetition is essential in learning to hear pitch differences and to match tones; nursery rhymes are reviewed; students are seated near the teacher when they sing; children's names are often substituted for those in songs and are used in question-answer games and singing conversations.

At age six, eye-hand coordination is often poorly developed.

Rote singing and rote playing are emphasized; use is made of large-sized notation on chart paper.

At age seven the heart grows rapidly; muscular development is uneven; motor skills are steadily improving; eye-hand coordination improves; attention span increases.

Time allotted to strenuous physical activity should be brief; active musical activities should be interspersed with quiet responses; singing games and dances can be more complex; there can be greater variety and skill in fundamental movements; percussion instruments are played with more skill and control; some children will play bells, Autoharp, and piano in modest ways; more songs and longer songs can be learned.

Eyes of six-year-olds are not ready for long periods of close work; eyes of seven-year-olds are better developed.

Emphasize a "by ear" approach to music; contour lines are associated with melodic direction; line notation can help in expanding the concept of duration in rhythm patterns; the teacher uses simple notation on large charts, flannel, magnetic, and chalk boards; children observe as teacher notates songs they have created; rote songs are sung from large charts; music textbooks with large clear print are usually introduced in second grade; the teacher sings short songs already familiar to the children while the class does guided observation of aspects of notation in books; children read rhythm notation from large charts and write some of it in simple form on the chalkboard; seven-year-olds can identify similar and different notated patterns, step-wise and skip-wise melodic notation.

Missing front teeth make perfect pronunciation and diction difficult.

Emphasize vowel sounds rather than consonant sounds in simple chants and singing activities; Latin syllables and neutral syllables such as *loo* and *la* can be used; pronunciation and enunciation should not be overstressed.

Six-year-olds are extremely active and constantly on the move; have a relatively short attention span; are easily fatigued; at age seven, children alternate between very active and quiet behavior.

Use music to permit necessary activity and rest and to relieve tensions and fatigue; children need short, frequent, and varied periods of music; listening experiences should be brief; purposes for listening should be explicitly stated; listening skills should be developed gradually.

Eager and anxious to learn.

Involve the child in planning and evaluating a variety of musical experiences compatible with his or her operational stage (see p. 24); gradually introduce and use music vocabulary; expand types of music experiences.

The harmonic sense is largely undeveloped.	Include songs and chants that need no chord changes in accompaniments; complex harmonic accompaniments are avoided; chants and two-part rounds are sung.
Children are highly competitive; they fight with words rather than with fists; six-year-olds are aggressive, egotistical, and often uncooperative.	Give children the chance to perform and to succeed individually; develop social consciousness and social skills by guiding the children to appreciate each other's accomplishments, to help each other, and to appreciate the rewards of cooperative effort.
Children are highly imaginative and enjoy imitating; they are interested in and curious about their environment; they enjoy sounds and sound effects.	Stimulate interest in aesthetic aspects of the environment through use of the senses; in spontaneous and guided dramatizations children imitate sounds and movements of airplanes, missiles, trains, and other machines, the sound of thunder, water, wind, and evidence of its action, people's speech, sounds and movements of animals, and the moods and movements of people; to implement the above, the teacher employs a variety of materials that may include recordings, piano, percussion instruments, bells, pictures, charts, bulletin boards, chalk board, tape recorder, opaque and overhead projectors, slides, filmstrips and movies; experiment with various sound producers to discover the types of sounds resulting from them and the way they are struck to produce them; have children help decide suitable sound effects to enhance their songs and movements; they create accompaniments to songs and recorded music with percussion instruments; they can be sensitive to the suitability of dynamics (loud-soft) in their musical activities.
Rudimentary understanding of time, space, and money values.	Use line notation to show relative length of note values that have been felt through physical action; this is later compared with music notation; begin to teach understanding of simple music design such as the phrase, contrasting sections, tonal and rhythmic patterns, expanded concepts of fast and slow, high and low, and related moods; students learn to comprehend simple note values through identification with rhythmic responses involving the entire body.
Children learn through use of concrete materials, in terms of experience background, and through participation under	Plan time to experiment, to listen, and to participate in learning tone production on wood, metal, skin and other media; relate scale tones to hand signals and the keyboard; step bells are helpful in

wise supervision; limited utilization of the abstract.

developing the scale concept; explore uses of simple instruments, introducing them one at a time, and teach the use of each thoroughly after stimulating interest in what each can do; listen to and watch various types of musical performance; guide listening with a few *specific* purposes; do creative development of music through dramatization, body movement, and the addition of codas, introductions, and instrumental parts; teach songs and music of quality that deal with the here and now, including those that reflect the expanding technological age in which these children live, but on their maturity level; remember that most six-year-olds have been all over the world by means of travel, television, or movies.

Children need encouragement, acceptance, and praise from adults.

See that students develop their special talents and interests in music to the maximum degree; have each child perform acceptably alone and in groups in order to feel success and acceptance from the teacher and peers, and to grow in cooperation, social competencies, and in assuming responsibility; provide a warm, interesting, challenging environment that includes a teacher who knows when and how to give encouragement and feedback; because of children's great need for acceptance by adults, they try to imitate, and thus are susceptible to the teacher's example of enthusiasm, interest, skill, and love for music; offer a music program of quality that sets the stage for greater ability in performance, listening, and appreciation of music.

At age seven, group activities are increasing in popularity; there is some evidence that interests of boys and girls are diverging.

Prepare group singing games, action songs, and percussion instrument experiences; boys and girls should be given some opportunity to select songs and activities in accordance with possible different interests.

At age seven, the concept of right and wrong ways of doing things is beginning to emerge.

Students are ready to evaluate the quality of singing and playing; work with students on ways to improve the sound of their singing and playing, and on the proper care of instruments and other classroom materials.

Early Elementary: Ages 8 to 10 (Grades 3 to 5)

CHARACTERISTICS

IMPLICATIONS

The attention span is expanded.

The music period is extended to as long as thirty minutes, depending on the nature and variety of activities; students can do guided listening to music for longer periods of time; longer songs with greater variety of content and required skills can be taught; two- and three-part song forms and rondo forms can be discovered and identified; obvious cultural characteristics of national or ethnic music can be recognized; there is interest in comparing major and minor tonalities; 2 to 1 and 3 to 1 note value relationships can be comprehended.

Slow steady growth; girls are more mature than boys; this age group has better coordination, is conscious of detail, and is able to devote attention to activities that require control of small muscles of body, hands, feet, and eyes; students are more interested in detailed and intricate work

Provide opportunities to make substantial use of music notation in singing, playing, and creating music; more detailed work is planned in reading music; use of music textbooks is expanded; more complex folk dances can be learned; students can conduct all common meters, with some able to direct music activities of the class; syncopated patterns can be introduced; the Autoharp can be played from chord designations with increasing skill; students reveal their expanding concepts of repetition and contrast in body movement, in creating music, and in exploring musical forms; sequential tonal patterns can be identified in melodies; the teacher guides the consistent progress in establishing specific expectations for musical performance; percussion instruments are played more effectively; recorder-type instruments can be played by nine-year-olds; the teacher gives each student time to develop musical and dramatic skills; individual and group lessons in band and orchestra instruments often begin in fourth grade for the physically mature; lessons on half-sized string instruments are sometimes begun in third grade and for the less physically mature nine-year-olds; there is increasing utilization of the piano and other keyboard instruments by students in music class and at home.

Posture needs attention.

Moving to music and proper singing can aid posture; a variety of music activities can relieve tension and reduce fatigue that cause poor posture.

Vocal chords and lungs are developing rapidly; more control of voice and of breathing; the singing voice of the nine-year-old is better in quality, range, and dependability.

More complex song material of wider ranges can be used; students can study the problem of finding the best places in songs to take breaths.

The harmonic sense is not well developed for eight-year-olds, but a growing number of nine-year-olds possess it.

Select special added parts for students who possess ability to sing harmony; rounds and easy descants are used in working for harmonic development; the Autoharp is employed in listening activities to help students become aware of the necessity for chord changes; simple two-part harmony is achieved during the fourth grade year; I,

IV and V_7 chords can be identified by ear; intervals of thirds and sixths can be recognized by sound and sight; playing Autoharp by ear reveals harmonic comprehension; some can chord piano accompaniments.

Communication skills are now highly developed, including reading skills and a larger vocabulary.

Music reading can be emphasized with the eight-year-old; a useful vocabulary of musical symbols and terms increases; numbers and/or syllables are useful in solving probems in singing and creating music; the functions of meter and key signatures are discovered and applied in creative work; notation of two-part songs is interpreted by nine-year-olds; music textbooks are used more analytically; music is read from books, charts, flannel and magnetic boards and from projections on a screen; the repertoire of songs increases.

Children need encouragement, acceptance, and positive reinforcement from adults; sensitive to criticism; seek positive approval from both peers and teachers.

The implications are the same as for the primary level.

Peers become important; students are better able to cooperate and work in groups; interest in gangs of the same sex and secret codes is strong, particularly at age nine; this is a time of joining groups; eight-year-olds are interested in cowboys and boisterous play; they are prone to accidents.

Plan group exploration, discussion, experimentation, sharing, creating, and evaluating; music clubs and choruses can be organized; use "mystery tunes," notation treated as a code, and songs about Scouts and other groups; permit time for singing, dancing, creating, dramatizing, and playing instruments in and for groups; these activities are planned by the teacher to improve mutual acceptance of students and the individual student's relationship to and status with peers; songs that involve group endeavor and songs of action are emphasized; easy folk dances, play-party games, fun and stunt songs, call-and-response songs are enjoyed; dialogue songs are used in which boys sing one part and girls another.

The age of hero worship begins to emerge at about age nine; students need good adult models; students are interested in patriotism.

Provision is made for reading books written for this age level about composers, musicians, instruments, and the history of music; song material and recordings can relate to musical or historical heroes; dramatizations of the lives of composers, musicians, or heroes are done in musical ways; patriotic songs concerned with great men are stressed.

Interest in other cultures and in the expanding world environment.

Use songs about common problems of the peoples of the world community, with words that mention mechanical progress in production, travel, and communication throughout history; cultural characteristics are identified in terms of specific instruments, rhythm patterns, and dances.

Students enjoy ridiculous humor and the humor in everyday situations; a growing appreciation of imaginary adventure.

Use songs of humor and nonsense; plan listening experiences involving adventure and humor; dramatizations and interpretations include comedy and space age adventure.

Children are rather indiscriminately interested in anything new to them, particularly the eight-year-olds; they are eager to expand their knowledge.

Introduce new and more complex aspects of music notation and vocabulary; a system of note reading can be employed; information about band and orchestra instruments is emphasized; the structure of major and pentatonic scales is explored.

An increasing number of individual differences and abilities appear; a wide range of reading abilities is evident.

Use a variety of techniques to learn the background and level of musical performance of each student: parent-teacher conferences, teacher-pupil conferences, observations, anecdotal records of student performance and attitude, the study of cumulative records and reports, interviews with former teachers, simple and appropriate tests— both standard and teacher-prepared; plan for the development of each student's musical abilities and needs as well as group skills; a music program possessing a variety of activities for the advanced, slow, and average student is necessary; emphasize reading and pronouncing the words of songs.

Rapid development in independence and in work-study habits.

Strive for the development of creative ideas; special class instruction in piano and strings may begin in third grade, in woodwinds and brass in fourth grade; use student leaders in singing and other conducting; guidance is necessary to establish progressive and consistently high expectations and standards of work and performance; provision for independent work is made, such as individual reading of books, playing instruments, composing, bringing from home selected favorite recordings with the stipulation that the student is able to explain to the class the reason for the recording's special worth, and taking music projects home to study and/or complete.

Students need guidance and experience in evaluation of their individual performances and of the performances of others; greater ability in self-evaluation.

Plan successful music activities to build self-confidence; there should be freedom for musical experimentation and invention; guidance is provided in choices and evaluation of related motion pictures, radio and television programs, and recordings; emphasis is given to improving tone quality in singing, more critical listening, and in developing musical discrimination and taste; good standards of musical quality should be provided by the teacher, some of the students, recordings, and films.

Nine-year-olds are very conscious of what is right and what is wrong; they desire to do things correctly; they seek help on specific skills and on mastering information.

Give guidance in evaluating and using music skills and materials; help the uncertain singer; special individual and group work is planned for those who need it and for the specially talented; plan a program of high quality and appeal.

Children continue to learn best through use of varied and concrete materials and through active participation under wise supervision.

Provide varied music activities and materials and opportunity to explore the potentialities of voices and instruments; create words, tunes, ostinati, borduns, introductions, codas, and interludes; plan guided listening with specific purposes; allow for creative interpretation of music, including dramatization and body movement; use music that deals with the present and known.

Children understand concepts of simple fractions, time, and money.

Meter signatures are learned.

Later Elementary and Middle School: Ages 10–13 (Grades 5–8)

A pause in physical growth to be followed by a period of rapid growth; girls mature more rapidly than boys; rapid growth implies an awkward stage.

Rhythmic activities that develop muscular coordination, grace, and poise are employed; some Dalcroze eurythmic exercises are appropriate; activities that reduce awkwardness and self-consciousness; more complex folk dances and formal period dances; the teacher discusses the effects of physical change on the voice and the ability to play certain band and orchestra instruments.

The harmonic sense develops rapidly; the voice range extends in later elementary; the diaphragm is developing and expanding; some sixth-grade boys and most seventh- and eighth-grade boys will encounter the initial stage of the voice change.

I, IV, and V_7 chords in minor can be recognized; polyphonic and harmonic textures can be identified and compared; two- and three-part songs are sung in fifth and sixth grades, with four-part songs in eighth and perhaps seventh if the necessary voices are present; accompanying chords can be determined by ear and by analysis of melodies; the first stage of the changing voice retains the unchanged voice quality, but lowers the range about a fourth; part singing becomes a necessity for boys whose voices have begun to change; write special parts for voices in limited or different ranges that the printed music fails to accommodate; the tape recorder can assist the evaluation of voice qualities and general vocal performance; activities are planned to expand the vocal range; a chorus is organized.

Seeks approval of the peer group; needs to "belong," is

Provide opportunity to work and play together and to share music experiences in group situa-

inclined to be overcritical of self and others; is often prejudiced.

tions; plan for the success of each student in some aspect of music; band, orchestra, and choral groups are offered; provide for the development of appreciation of each individual's unique contributions and skills; emphasize the contributions of all peoples of the world through study of music; invite performers from various racial and ethnic groups to demonstrate their characteristic music and abilities to the class; peer music standards tend to be "rock and roll"; teacher relates selected music of this type to other styles of music that illustrate common characteristics or variations.

The ability to work both independently and with others is more highly developed; the ability and desire to follow leadership of others is present.

Formulate standards or expectations that encourage the best efforts of groups and individuals; aid the student in consistent, sequential, and thoroughly learned activities and give opportunity to analyze, evaluate, and improve music learning; students have opportunity to suggest, plan, organize, create, initiate, and evaluate many types of music activities; improve and perfect needed musical skills, attitudes, and appreciations by working alone with books, instruments, recordings, tape recorders, and learning packages.

Preadolescents often become extremely critical, unpredictable, and defiant; they may mix adultlike behavior with childlike behavior.

To avoid or eliminate this problem, a music lesson should include activities that are made meaningful and purposeful through cooperative selecting, planning, developing, and team evaluation by teacher and students; ask students to assume leadership roles; offer encouragement and praise as it is deserved and needed; activities should be selected in terms of interests, needs, and abilities of each student; high interest is essential to maintain a good climate for learning; the teacher organizes the class with clear goals, rules, and signals.

Students have increased energy; they are interested in activity.

Students must be involved in cognitive processes and physically active performance; various dance steps relate to music, social studies, or physical education; improvise dance steps and action routines.

A wide range of abilities.

Analyze every student in terms of abilities, capabilities, level of performance, and needs; the teacher uses knowledge of the content and performance levels of prior grades to organize a music program that meets these individual differences; provides opportunity for every student, including the specially talented, to progress at his or her own rate; when necessary the teacher seeks assistance from guidance personnel, parents,

	other teachers including private music teachers in the community; the school must have a wide variety of types and levels of instructional materials.
Interests of boys and girls are usually divergent.	Include activities in which boys and girls sing in turn or have separate parts, and in which dance partners change frequently; select songs and rhythmic responses that appeal to both boys and girls; encourage creating according to individual interests.
Teasing and hostility between some boys and girls.	Attempt to offset this through carefully selected activities that involve both sexes in participation and evaluation; feelings and relationships are discussed.
Listless at times, but highly active generally.	Plan both quiet and active types of music including listening purposefully to recordings; listening to performances of others; quiet songs, action songs, rhythmic responses, dramatizations, and playing instruments; when possible, intersperse music throughout the day as it is needed to relieve emotional tensions or fatigue and to supply variety.
Resentment of any kind of attention or activity that appears to cause an individual to lose status with the group; seeks to conform to standards exemplified by student leaders in the group and by the majority of peers.	Teacher refrains from types of criticism and overpraise that would cause an individual to lose status with the group; encouragement, praise, and correction are often given privately; the teacher uses student "leaders" to establish standards and expectations of performance and behavior.
Students desire the approval and understanding of adults even though they are attempting to become more independent of them.	Provide opportunities for students to assume more responsibility for their actions and ideas, to pursue their own interests, to explore, to experiment, and to create.
Students are often silly; they giggle unnecessarily, are loud, rough, and like to joke.	Use songs, rhythmic responses, and instrumental activities that help self-understanding and provide for release of energy and release from emotional tension.
Attracted to adults who possess humor, understanding, and warmth, and who are constructive, mature, and positive in their approach.	Show interest, confidence, and enthusiasm; reveal appreciation of appropriate humor; be considerate and appreciative of each student's efforts; respect each student's personality and use constructive, positive criticism.
Interested in music, concerned with adventure, mystery, humor, work, transportation, inventions, outer space, family life, non-Western music.	Include these topics in music selected for study; variety of music content should be sought; music of Asia and Africa can be explored.

Wants to know why as well as how; inquisitive about scientific reasons that support facts, situations, and theories.

Study of accoustics is introduced; the scientific foundations of tone production, including characteristic vocal-instrumental types and qualities, are explored; harmonic principles related to chord structure can be studied; the causes of the voice change are defined; music structure in songs and larger vocal and instrumental forms is studied.

Interest in and increased understanding of an expanding environment including time and number concepts; more complete understanding of the contributions of past achievements to present-day culture.

Emphasis is given to understanding various cultures of the world through music that reflects history, customs, religious, scientific, and social problems; students create, notate, and invent appropriate music as an outgrowth of their knowledge of these topics; include opportunity to understand and appreciate the history of Western music and the musical contributions of all peoples; the learner can recognize scales, modes, tone rows, all common intervals, and unusual meters.

Possess the background for understanding and enjoying fantasy.

Plan for creative composition and dramatization inspired by fantasy; music having fantasy content is used in listening activities; the ways musical tones communicate stories are explored and analyzed.

Sustained and intense interest in activities that hold meaning and purpose to them.

Music period can be lengthened; students can plan special programs as well as participating in band, orchestra, chorus, composition, reading books about music and musicians; time is provided for the students to perfect the activity; creative activities are highly important and can include inventing and composing in "new" scales, experimenting with tape loops, the synthesizer, and exploring aspects of experimental music.

Along with peer identification, students begin to develop a sense of self-importance and identity; begin to display characteristics that will continue into adulthood.

Some students enjoy solo performance with instrument or voice when they believe they have sufficient skill; dramatic performance is enjoyed by many, which implies class-organized and produced stage productions.

Sense of self often leads to a need for more privacy; may be seriously concerned about futures and possible careers.

Carrels in which to study privately are provided; the many types of careers in music and those related to music are studied, demonstrated, and visited.

Many wish to appear adult.

At upper middle school level there is an inclination to reject a songbook approach as childish, and to prefer self-initiated or special interest projects.

The preceding chart of developmental characteristics is not only an explanation of children's growth stages; its implications provide in large part a sequential school music program, bases for daily lesson plans, general expectations, and suggestions to decrease behavior problems. Thus, it is meant to be useful to the college student who is making plans to teach music, and should be referred to as the reader continues through this book.

Cognitive-Interactionist Theory

The cognitive-interactionist theory states that children's behavior changes and develops as they interact with their environment freely in exploratory and experimental ways, with adults in the position of facilitators, guides, questioners, observers, analyzers, environment-planners—in other words, interacting with children. The learner is viewed as being dependent on both external and internal stimulation for learning. The leading cognitive-interactionists are Benjamin Bloom, Jerome Bruner, J. McVickar Hunt, and Jean Piaget.

According to Piaget and recent brain research, learning must be viewed as a long, cumulative process, not a response to one or a few learning encounters, and the brain must be conceived as a growing and developing organ that is influenced by both environmental experiences and heredity. This research is bringing to light data that is expanding present-day knowledge about the unique functioning of individual brains. It has also emphasized the importance of building programs and using teaching methods that stress individual learning styles, giving more emphasis to school organizational practices that provide for these styles. In their theories of learning, both Piaget and Bruner, along with many other present-day authorities, convey the idea that students learn in different ways at different stages, as stated in the explanations of their designated stages, soon to follow.

Jean Piaget *(1896–1980)* Jean Piaget, a Swiss, and originally a biologist, has emerged as a dominant figure in today's early childhood education. He is the leading advocate of the cognitive-development theory. According to him, intelligence has a biological base in that all organisms respond and adjust in relation to environmental stimuli. This interaction with the environment takes place on both physical and mental levels. In common with other cognitive psychologists, Piaget believed that the human mind is endowed with an intuitive and self-seeking urge to learn. His theory centers mostly on the nature and development of cognition. He said that an individual could not be given knowledge, but must obtain it through personal discovery and structuring in an environment rich in appropriate encounters where learning is not rushed or forced.

Piaget engaged in extensive observation of very young children, following them longitudinally from birth through adulthood. From these observations and research evolved his processes and stages of intellectual development.

Adaptation Processes. Piaget designates three interrelated processes that children use to construct experiences into structures or patterns that facilitate the development of thought processes and problem-solving abilities. These processes are assimilation, accommodation, and equilibration.

1. *Assimilation* is the process where new data or experiences are fused into present cognitive structures or patterns. For example, the child who comes in contact with a mallet for a bell set and identifies it as a hammer is attempting to assimilate or use a previously designed structure or pattern. The second process of accommodation is then called into play.

2. *Accommodation* is when an existing structure is altered because of new incoming data or experiences. These new data and/or experiences are then absorbed and related to previously processed data or experiences to create novel and higher level structures or patterns, e.g. as the children experience using the mallet to play the bells, and hear the musical sounds resulting from this method of striking an object, their concept of hammer as an implement used for striking or hitting is extended to include other types of striking implements and the effects resulting from each. If children do not possess appropriate assimilated and stored data to relate and add meaning to incoming data, it cannot be accommodated. The child does not have sufficient background information to understand what the teacher is attempting to teach.

3. *Equilibration,* the third process, entails the balance between the inflow of new information and experience and one's capability to incorporate it into existing knowledge. *Adaptation* is being able to use knowledge acquired from assimilated and accommodated data and experiences. Cognitive processes are acquired and expanded as the individual keeps a balance between these processes.

Piaget's Stages of Cognitive Development

The following stages are an outgrowth of Piaget's cognitive development theory, in which he emphasized that all organisms adjust and respond in relation to environmental stimuli. This interaction with the environment influences both physical and mental development.

Sensorimotor or Preverbal Stage—Birth to 2 Years. During this span of time children engage in numerous interactions with objects, situations, and people in their immediate environment through use of the senses: they listen, look, smell, taste, touch, grasp, feel textures, pound, manipulate, suck, and experiment with objects. Thus their evolving mental development and structures are altered to accommodate the new data. At this stage infants' thinking centers around use of their sensory and psychomotor behaviors. They are usually unable to use representational thought processes and of necessity must act out what is contained in their minds. The sensorimotor stage is prior to use of formalized language development.

Preoperational Stage—Ages 2-7. During the preoperational years the child must span the gap between the sensorimotor activities of the infant and the internal mental activities of the school-aged child. Language and mental images are gradually substituted for the sensorimotor activities of infancy. Instead of grasping, things are requested. The mother is thought of even though she is not visible. Make-believe play and dramatic movement are very important because through them the children are assimilating symbolically the experiences, roles, and ideas of their immediate environment. Simultaneously, assimilation is being balanced by accommodation, which is the primary function of imitation. Through imitation young children are able to accommodate different experiences, thus expanding their concepts.

This phase of development is designated as preoperational because most children are unable to engage in thought that involves operations on data. Characteristic of most children at this level is their inability to combine parts into a whole, to arrange parts in different ways, and to reverse operations or processes. Some children can begin to classify objects with obviously common attributes. They also begin to place things in a series. Mental pictures or symbolic representations are being formed; children usually function intuitively, not logically, based on their immediate experience and perception. Symbols are used to represent objects, and labels and names are acquired for experiences, a type of concept formation.

Concrete Operations Stage—Ages 7–11. The term *concrete operations* means that children can now operate in thought on concrete objects or their representations. They can serialize, extend, subdivide, differentiate, or combine existing structures into new relationships or groupings. They now think logically about things rather than accepting surface appearances.

As children acquire and assimilate knowledge and data from their actions, and then accommodate or adjust their mental structures to the new data and knowledge, thinking processes are altered. Even though most children at this stage of cognition can usually employ logic, their thinking has its basis in the concrete rather than the abstract. The mental ability necessary for the combining of various elements is developed usually toward the end of this stage. The combining of operations is used to discover the concept of a hierarchy. Learners discover that they can combine parts of a whole in many different ways and still not alter the total. They learn to classify, order, number, use concepts of space and time, conservation and reversibility, and to discriminate in increasing degrees of exactness.

Conservation of knowledge results from the repeated experiencing of a concept or situation under varying conditions until it is mastered to the degree that it can be transferred mentally to a new experience, thus proving that learning has taken place. For example, a class has had many and varied experiences with 2/4, 3/4, and 4/4 meters, and has been accumulating comprehensions of meter that will eventually reveal to the teacher whether or not conservation has taken place. This test will come when the class is confronted with listening to a recorded composition that has 5/4 meter, a new experience. The prior experiences with meter will assist the class in finding accents that determine meter. They may find either a 3 + 2 or a 2 + 3 pattern of beats. Discovering that every fifth beat is the stronger one, they will be able to theorize 5/4 meter, thus making the transfer from their previous experiences. The teacher then knows that conservation and transfer have taken place, and that learning has been accomplished.

Stage of Formal Operations—Ages 11–12 through Adulthood. This period of cognition usually appears in early adolescence. Children can now reason on the basis of hypothesis and the abstract, not just on the basis of objects or the concrete. They construct new operations, attain new structures and grouping of structures, and develop relationships between and among ideas. In other words, learners are operating on operations, which means they are capable not only of thinking about concrete things and situations but can think about and analyze the thoughts of others and they can identify variables in problems and analyze them critically. This is the highest level of intellectual thought.

Obviously, children must develop mental processes in order to be able to assimilate, to accommodate, to act, to think, and to reorganize and reclassify information. For instance, until young children have learned to control pitch, at least to some degree, with their singing voices, they cannot sing a recognizable tune or learn a new one. The *spiral* concept of the curriculum is considered to be a series of encounters with ideas or situations in which the children successfully accommodate themselves.

Piaget states that the principal goal of education is to create people who are capable of doing new things—who are creative, inventive, and discoverers who do not simply repeat what other generations have done. His second goal of education is to form minds that can be critical, can verify, and will not accept everything they are offered. Today's society is bombarded with slogans, media opinions, and even ready-made commercially promoted types of music. We need to be able to distinguish between what is proved and what is not. We need students who are able to find out for themselves, who can verify rather than accept casually the ideas that come to them.

J. McVickar Hunt* (1906–) Hunt wrote in 1961, "It is no longer unreasonable to consider that it might be feasible to discover ways to govern encounters that children have with their environments, especially during the early years of their development, to achieve a substantially faster rate of intellectual development and a substantially higher adult level of intellectual capacity." (J. McVickar Hunt, 1961) Implications from Hunt's studies are impressive:

1. Because the most rapid growth of intellectual development takes place before age eight, both enriched home environments and earlier schooling should be considered.
2. Intelligence is not fixed; while heredity sets limits, the environment governs to what extent those limits are reached.
3. Children whose environment is lacking in various enrichments may be handicapped throughout life, while children whose home enrichment is intellectually stimulating are very likely to do well in the classroom.
4. The greatest need for an enriched environment, including good nutrition, is during the early years of rapid growth.

Hunt's well-known "problem of the match" poses the following task for teachers. Diagnose the child's level of performance, then plan and present

* The following discussions of J. McVickar Hunt and Jerome Bruner are reprinted from Vernice Trousdale Nye, *Music for Young Children,* 3d. ed. © 1975, 1979, 1983 Wm. C. Brown Publishers, Dubuque, Iowa. All rights reserved. Reprinted by permission.

challenging new experiences only slightly more difficult than had been accommodated at that performance level. This is the "match." Relate these new experiences to earlier ones, and continue the process of the match. Children will advance in their learning as they make generalizations, and build relationships between concepts by transferring the information previously accommodated to new situations.

Jerome Bruner (1915–) Like Piaget, Bruner theorizes that children have an innate urge to learn and that learning can be its own reward. He stresses the power of spontaneous learning that supplies reinforcement in its own activities.

The goal of teaching is to promote the general understanding of a subject matter. Bruner would have the child grasp the structure (conceptual organization) of music in order to relate its parts to the whole and to each other, stressing the idea that learning based on structure has meaning and therefore is remembered. (See Chapter Three.)

Bruner formulated a theory of instruction that has become popular with many music educators. His theory consists of four parts adapted here to relate to music:

1. *Motivation.* Motivation originates from within the individual and nurtures the urge to learn. Motivation is composed of the interest and the desire to acquire proficiency as well as the need to associate and to work with others. Motivation can be learned, but is influenced by maturation.

   Children's curiosity and interest in music are enhanced when they are aware of the goals and are involved in worthwhile and relevant musical experiences.

2. *Structure.* Music concepts can be introduced to the child at the child's cognitive level. The structure of the body of musical knowledge can also be learned by young children when adapted to their level of cognitive development and understanding. Bruner presents three levels of development that serve as a substitute for the theories postulated by Piaget.

   a. *Enactive representation level.* The young child learns music best through action and the senses—touching, manipulating, visually examining, counting, playing musical instruments, using the body and its muscles in rhythmic interpretations, by chanting and singing, and by creating music.

   b. *Iconic representation level.* Young children conceptualize at the iconic (image) level. They learn music from imitating sounds, moods, movements of animals, people, machines, and plants.

   c. *Symbolic representation level.* The child at this stage is able to use language to explain and interpret experiences. Words can be used to represent songs, rhymes, poems, and to describe musical experiences. Children can use simple notation at this stage.

3. *Sequence.* Musical percepts, concepts, and skills should be taught in sequence. Bruner suggests that teachers begin with enactive representation if possible and move progressively up to the symbolic. Children would first be actively involved in singing, rhythms, or playing instruments prior to the use of words to explain the learning experience.

4. *Reinforcement.* Teachers must encourage and reinforce children's musical efforts. Children need to know of their progress in order to advance to increas-

ingly higher levels of performance. Feedback should be administered astutely; timing is crucial. If feedback is given prematurely it hampers the learning, if too late, the learner may assimilate incorrect data or skills.

Bruner's major point of emphasis is on discovery learning. Most young children come to school with an enthusiasm for, and high interest in, music and movement. They want to become actively involved in experimenting and discovering musical concepts and skills. This can occur only in an environment rich in varied types of materials with a teacher who frees children to explore on their own but who knows when to intercede and facilitate their learning; time for such exploration and experimentation must be made available. Children's spontaneous, original, and creative activity is directed from within and holds relevance and purpose for the learner. Concepts experienced for themselves in a discovery-exploratory environment are readily retained and used to learn higher level concepts than those learned through rote learning. While the discovery method is not the only instructional method, the teacher can use discovery skills to create an exciting and interesting environment for learning music.

According to Bruner, language is a major factor in young children's cognitive development. Research indicates that children's cognitive understandings are significantly improved when correct labels are supplied to objects and activities at the appropriate time by the teacher. Children can sort instruments by size, color, and shapes such as triangle, round (drum), and rectangle (woodblocks); they need their high, low, fast, slow experiences named and described as they sense these with their bodies. As they listen to musical recordings or sing songs, they need to be involved in discussions which follow the activity to verbally express how the music made them feel (sad, happy, angry, etc.); if it were loud, soft, fast, slow; how different sounds can be made on instruments; how one instrument, one song, or one recording can be compared with another, noting likenesses and differences.

Children need guidance in using words in varied contexts and for various purposes. The fact that language usage correlates highly with children's maturational levels is widely accepted. It is also believed that the stimulation supplied by home, school, peers, and community increases the quantity and quality of language and music.

Programs following the cognitive-interactionist theory are usually based upon the following ideas. A belief that:

1. Children's behaviors change and develop as they interact freely with their environment.
2. The role of the teacher/adult is that of a facilitator, guide, questioner, observer, analyzer, and environment-planner.
3. Children possess an intuitive and self-seeking urge to learn, and are responsive to external stimulation.
4. Children learn best through personal discovery and process learning.
5. Conceptual learning is basic to the development of intellectual thought.
6. Learning cannot be rushed or forced.

Brain Research Many psychologists, educators, and scientists are pursuing research associated with the functions and operations of the brain. Much interest has been shown in the hypothesis that the two hemispheres of the brain perform unique functions. Data concerning ways in which the brain processes perceptual information and how the brain controls and affects memory and motivation have stimulated increased interest in the biological and neurological structure of the brain and the entire neurological system.

Early research caused some to conclude that the right hemisphere of the brain controlled creativity and that rationality was dominated by the left hemisphere. This was later found to be incorrect. More recently researchers report that while the two hemispheres have different perceptual functions, both are engaged in learning music and art. Both are involved in thinking and organized reasoning. The right hemisphere has more to do with emotion, and the left with discriminating and time relationships in music, while memory for single chords is stronger in the right hemisphere. It is found that there are individual variances in the way students use the parts and the entirety of the brain, thus implying different learning styles. An individual's highest achievements result from using the complete powers of both hemispheres simultaneously. This field of research is in its infancy, and promises to produce findings that will assist educators to better understand the mental processes of learners.

Applications to Music Teaching To apply this chapter to music teaching, we must translate Piaget's admonition that the young learner manipulate objects in acquiring concepts, into that learner's acquiring concepts of pitch, duration, dynamics, and other elements of music that are aural, not concrete in a physical sense. It would seem that the answer lies in making these aural abstractions as concrete as possible by relating them to visual (charts, pictures, drawings, films) and hands-on physical relationships such as body movements and playing instruments. The content of young children's music should include their identity, their bodies, and their feelings because of their egocentric nature. We should teach one thing at a time, clearly portrayed. The teacher provides opportunity to manipulate, experiment with, and use a variety of musical objects—but normally one object at a time. Impersonations and dramatizations assist learning. Teachers and parents should be good models to be imitated. Creative and improvisatory activities are encouraged because of their vital importance in learning; they demand personal involvement. Visual aids are employed. Notation (as rhythm and pitch symbols) is introduced slowly through movement, drawings, and the keyboard, which serves as a physical picture of tonal relationships. Experimenting with various sound-producers assists development of listening skills. Hand signals may assist comprehension of pitch differences. Step bells tend to make concrete the rising and falling of scale pitches. From this type of foundation, learned concepts can be transferred to more complex musical knowledge and skills. Without it, optimal musical growth is questionable. In later elementary years students should be able to learn rapidly; they should be able to accomplish logical thinking and reasoning, along with other aspects of intellectual thought. However, at all levels is found the necessity for working and experimenting with the concrete as a foundation for being better able to think in the abstract.

EXPLORATORY ACTIVITIES

1. Observe children at various age levels to find how many have the characteristics described by the norms for those age levels.
2. Stage a mock debate in which one or more classmates defend developmental norms and an equal number claim that they have little application in teaching today's students.
3. Select a cognitive-interactionist psychologist for investigation. Try to make application to music teaching of the theories of one of the following: Benjamin Bloom, Jerome Bruner, J. McVickar Hunt, or Jean Piaget.
4. Review the developmental stages stated by Bruner and Piaget and compare them. Observe a grade level of your choice to find examples of students operating in those stages in a real-life situation. Are the students at one stage only or do you find evidences of other stages also? How do your findings influence the learning environments you would plan for those students?
5. If a student is operating at Piaget's stage two, and the teacher is making him or her try to function at stage three, what happens to the student's cognitive learning? affective learning? psychomotor learning?

References

BLOOM, BENJAMIN, *Stability and Change in Human Characteristics*. New York: John Wiley, 1964.

BRUNER, JEROME S., *The Process of Education*. Cambridge, Mass.: Harvard University Press, 1966. Also see *Toward a Theory of Instruction* (Cambridge, Mass.: Harvard University Press, 1966).

FRANKLIN, ELDA, and A. DAVID, "The Brain Research Bandwagon: Proceed with Caution," *Music Educators Journal,*. February 1970, p. 49. Also see "Letters to the Editor," October 1977, pp. 7–15.

GESELL, ARNOLD L., et al., *The Child from Five to Ten*. New York, N.Y.: Harper & Brothers, 1946.

HUNT, J. MCVICKAR, *Intelligence and Experience*. New York: Ronald, 1961.

NYE, VERNICE TROUSDALE, *Music for Young Children,* 3rd ed., Chapter Two, "An Introduction to Learning Theory." Dubuque, Iowa: Wm. C. Brown Publishers, 1983.

O'BRIEN, JAMES P., "How Conceptual Learning Takes Place," *Music Educators Journal,* September 1971, p. 34.

PHILLIPS, J. JR., *The Origins of the Intellect: Piaget's Theory*. San Francisco: W. H. Freeman Company, 1975.

PILLSBURY FOUNDATION STUDIES, *Music of Young Children*. Santa Barbara, Calif.: Pillsbury Foundation for the Advancement of Music Education, 1978.

SPRINTHALL, RICHARD C., and NORMAN A., *Educational Psychology: A Developmental Approach,* 2nd ed., pp. 121–124. Reading, Mass.: Addison-Wesley, 1977.

ZIMMERMAN, MARILYN P., *Musical Characteristics of Children.* Reston, Va.: Music Educators National Conference, 1971.

———, "Percept and Concept: Implications of Piaget," *Music Educators Journal,* February 1970, p. 49.

chapter three

How Children Learn:
A Basis for Teaching

One of the most important considerations in planning any music curriculum is the recognition of how students acquire, amass, and retain percepts and concepts, and employ knowledge and understanding at the various stages of development. Teachers of music must continually search for validated theories postulated by educational psychologists. These theories must be carefully assessed before choosing those most pertinent to guide the special growth and learning needs of a particular group of students. Concepts and skills to be learned must be sequentially ordered and introduced at carefully chosen times for the development of optimum learning. For example, multiple and repeated experiences are necessary for young students to develop skills and knowledge on how to order visually and aurally. They must have many encounters with cause and effect relationships before they can grasp a simple understanding of logical sequence. Therefore, at the preoperational and concrete operational levels, major emphasis must be placed on manipulative and exploratory experiences with the concrete.

Research has shown that the amount and quality of learning is in direct proportion to experiences. Another way of saying this is if students lack certain experiences they cannot learn. One of the most encouraging and optimistic beliefs of our time is that intelligence is *something that can be changed* to an important degree by improving the quality and amount of experiencing. This belief serves as the foundation for the processes of inquiry and discovery in today's education.

Teaching and Learning

Teaching and learning are different operations. Teaching consists of actions intended to induce learning, and learning consists of acquiring knowledges, skills, and feelings by means of perceptions and concepts resulting from the stimulation of the senses. Learning can take place without teaching. In the school environment it is assumed that learning occurs as a result of interactions between teacher and learner, although this may or may not be true. Teachers and learners engage in verbal and nonverbal cognitive operations such as defining, examining, contrasting, interpreting, classifying, designating, applying, analyzing, demonstrating, synthesizing, and evaluating. They also practice psychomotor skills such as musical performance and body movement in relation to musical stimuli, and affective reactions of a nonverbal nature that indicate values, feelings, intentions, and ideas.

Learning to Think Musically

Percepts and Concepts

Music is an aural art, and the stimuli that bring forth musical responses are musical structures varying from a single percept of a sound source to highly complex sources. When musical perception takes place, the learner's mind becomes aware of aspects, organizations, and relationships of the music being experienced; a percept is the mental residue of this sense perception. Repeated and related percepts can result in concepts, and concepts in turn influence new and old perception.

Musical responses can be either observable (overt) or unobservable (covert), the latter taking place within the mind. Overt responses can be any form of observable performance such as moving, singing, playing, writing, and conducting. Covert responses include sensations, feelings, and thoughts. Percepts, when combined, become the musical concepts of the learner; obviously these concepts are outgrowths of personal experiences and percepts, and are discovered and processed by the learner. Because each person's experiences and mental processes are different from those of any other person, and because the same is true of musical experiences and physiological and mental inheritance, concepts therefore differ from person to person. Concepts are very complex and are continually being developed and modified. They cannot be communicated verbally with precision because the one who attempts the communication is speaking from a personal interpretation of the relevant concepts. Verbal communication of music concepts can improve to the extent that those exchanging information happen to hold approximately the same version of the concepts. Many of the covert responses cannot be verbally communicated.

To think conceptually, one progresses from the level of perception of objects, situations, and events, to making associations, to forming concepts, to grouping two or more concepts to form a generalization, to applying the generalization to solve related or new problems. Previously formed concepts and generalizations can be considered to be part of the data used to form the learner's personal new and expanded concepts and generalizations.

Implied in the above paragraphs are three major types of *thought processes,* or levels of *associative thinking.* They are listed below as a summary with illustrative approaches provided as guides for developing each type of thought.

1. *Perceptual-cognitive memory.* This form of thought involves simple recognition of facts, rote memory, and recall. The learner associates a present experience with past encounters and meanings in an automatic, routine, uncritical manner, making a one-to-one match of incidents, situations, and occurrences without questioning or analyzing the reasons why. This is the most simple form of thinking.

> What is the name of . . .?
> Who is . . .?
> Where is the . . .?
> What is the meaning of . . .?
> Describe . . .?
> What is a . . .?

2. *Deductive-convergent thinking.* This level of associative thinking is more complex than the cognitive memory type. Facts (percepts) and previously stated concepts and generalizations are presented to students as data for them to analyze and to organize by using deductive thought. The resulting newly expanded and formed concepts and generalizations are usually not characterized by creative and personal thought. To develop this type of thinking, the student must be guided in

> identifying what information is to be studied.
> exploring relationships within the given data.
> forming inferences by contrasting and comparing within the confines of the teacher-supplied data

Thus, students can deduce from prepared sources and remembered data the logical, acceptable answers, conclusions and/or generalizations desired by the teacher. Questions to further this type of thinking include:

> Explain how this could happen.
> Tell why you think so.
> Give your reasons for such a judgment.
> How did you reach that conclusion?
> Why is it called . . .?
> What conclusion have you reached?

Perceptual and associative thinking as presented above are necessary bases for later inductive and conceptual thinking. Both are important, but should not be used to the neglect of other types of thinking.

3. *Conceptual-inductive thinking.* When thinking inductively, learners begin with their identified problems, plan for solutions of the problems, collect relevant

data, and analyze and organize them into concepts which in turn are summarized as concluding statements or generalizations, and then assess their endeavors. It is the reverse of deductive-convergent thinking. Students, usually not the teacher, provide the data, and the process encourages creative and personally valued thought. This type of thinking includes associative and conceptual thinking, thus there is interrelatedness of processes in practice.

Approaches to use that induce conceptual-inductive thinking include:

What would happen if . . .?
How many ways can you . . .?
Give all the reasons you can think of for. . . .
Present as many possible solutions to the problem as you can.

As students become involved through the use of questions related to all of these types of thinking, they become more adept in their use of cognitive inquiry process skills and in their ability to direct their own learning.

Alice S. Beer implies that the creative-inquiry approach is synonymous with the conceptual inductive approach. In an article in *Baltimore Public Schools Bulletin of Education,* XLII, No. 4, she wrote:

Children are learning more about music by creating music themselves. In effect, children are acting as composers and by composing are acquiring a first-hand understanding of the process of composing. In trying to create music, children find a need to learn a great deal about the nature of music, its composition, structure, balance, unity, variety, beauty, tone color, expression, dynamics, tension and release, scales, harmony, rhythm, melody, and of course, its notation.

As the children evaluate their own compositions, they feel a need to refine, rework, and improve. This is essentially the conceptual approach to learning rather than the imposition of a pre-established set of ideas. In the process of creativity, students learn through discovery—discovery of their own need for knowledge that can be immediately put to use.

She describes children's dramatizations of "The Three Billy Goats Gruff," in which they experimented with telling the story by selecting a rhythm instrument for each character. They added a cymbal to provide tension and heighten the dramatic effect of the fight between the Troll and Billy Goat Gruff. This experience helped children discover how sound and music can tell a story. An intermediate grade utilized a tone row as a backdrop for sounds of instruments and other classroom resources in working out a musical description of a busy city street. This led to a better understanding of how Gershwin accomplished this in *An American in Paris.* Other classes explored composition approached through words—using children's names to create a rondo, using old sayings, original poetry, television commercials, names of birds, etc. Some children developed compositions based upon exploring terms such as *theme* and *variation* which they had found applied to a number of compositions. In writing their variations they learned much about how a composer works. Others learned how composers add descants, ostinatos, and counter-melodies, and still others learned more about using chords and tone clusters, adding and subtracting instruments, and how composers end compositions. She concluded:

> The conceptual approach promises an effective way of presenting music to children, more effective perhaps than memorizing a certain number of songs and rote-learning certain musical facts. Like other educational innovations, creative approaches to music education place the student in the center of a learning process. Thus, the student's music education emanates from capacity and skill in musical expression and response, and leads to understanding and maturity in performance and musical literacy.

The creative process is necessary for self-fulfillment. It seems that students respond to learning whenever they can become personally involved in this process, regardless of aptitude or socio-economic background. To be creative is to think in new and different ways.

It is commonly said that children need to be "free" in order to create, and this has led to much misunderstanding. Some have mistakenly believed that children must not be restricted. In the first place, there must be certain restrictions to make it possible to have a classroom situation in which creativity can flourish. At the beginning of the process, to give children the confidence that they can produce their own music, many music teachers restrict these children to using only a few tones of the pentatonic scale on metalophones and xylophones. This restriction frees them to create because they are protected from the complexities of the complete major scale with its leading tones. Conformity to basic rules, such as how and when to play instruments, the care and storage of equipment, the distribution of various music materials and their collection, and taking turns in class discussion, are necessary routine matters. Such things get in the way only when they become ends in themselves instead of being functional.

Critical-Evaluative Thinking

This type of thinking is a matter of using judgment. Critical thinking makes evaluations in accordance with a set of either intrinsic or extrinsic criteria. Students will examine music, symbols, or processes in order to deduce the extent to which the criteria are met. In order to do this, the underlying concepts must be well understood, what is being evaluated must be clearly perceived, and feelings must be restrained to avoid interference with the appraisal.

In music there is much critical examination of performance and recordings in terms of pitch, tone qualities, tempo, dynamics, articulation, tension and release, form, and the balance of musical elements. When evaluating a song, the relation of the words and the melody is also under scrutiny. Questions involved could be: "Listen to the song we just sang as I play it back to you on the tape recorder. Have we utilized all appropriate ways for singing it expressively?" "Is the form of this recorded composition logical in terms of what the composer has named it? He called it 'Theme and Variations'." "Which percussion instruments are most suitable to accompany this music? Why?" "Does this melody make good sense in terms of what the words are communicating? Why or why not?" Such questions cannot be answered by a simple *yes* or *no:* they always imply a logical defense of a *yes* or *no* in terms of criteria derived from past experience or from current class determination of them—standards which are recorded in writing or are understood. The teacher will see to it that opinions and facts are not confused.

When concerts are presented in elementary schools, it is necessary to set up standards for how to act when one is at a concert. When children and teachers plan together for such events, their criteria would be appropriate standards of behavior they would expect, both as members of the visiting performance group and as members of an audience. Against these criteria they would plan their behavior critically. After the concert the students would evaluate the behavior of the performers and themselves in terms of their stated criteria.

This type of thinking involves value judgments and beliefs. As the learners reflect, refine, and test their beliefs they should become more able to defend them on factual grounds rather than on an emotional basis. In this way values and beliefs acquire additional meaning and significance. The student develops the ability to make value judgments, to act on the basis of hypothetical propositions, to test, prove, and seek new data if needed, and to prize values.

The following assists teachers in guiding critical and evaluative listening.

> Listen for musical elements or ideas related to questions and problems under consideration.
>
> The criteria to assist judgment are either listed or commonly understood.
>
> Listen for musical ideas which act as cues to guide the listener to answer the question or solve the problem.
>
> If the music is program music, listen for the musical means the composer utilizes to communicate the story or description, and evaluate their effectiveness.
>
> If the music is pure music, listen for the interrelation of the musical elements under consideration, and evaluate its effectiveness.
>
> If tone color is under appraisal, instrument identification is of importance when considered in light of the choice of the composer in the type of tone qualities necessary for communication, either of program music or of pure music. Evaluate its suitability.

When young children examine a bell set, they feel it, may attempt to taste it, look at its shiny smooth surface, eventually discover that it can produce sound, and experiment with this characteristic; they may form a mental image (percept) of a bell set which is stored in the mind and retrieved when needed. Later, when they relate this percept to other types of keyboard instruments, they have made an association based on the common elements of the appearance of the keyboard and the fact that it can produce pitches on the different instruments. Through this series of experiences students gain concepts of keyboard instruments. Their concepts continue to expand as they acquire progressively more experiences, and these become a part of their thinking processes. For example, when students first see a celesta, they will want to find out what new manner of keyboard instrument it is, what it is used for in the orchestra, how the sound is produced, and why it sounds different from other keyboard instruments they know. The ability to do this results from the acquisition of a concept that is useful and transferable when learners are confronted with a problem concerning keyboard instruments. The more that is known about the construction of such instruments, what produces the sound, and what makes the tone qualities differ, and the more understandable data are available for easy transfer, the greater will be the ability to think conceptually and act in terms of keyboard instruments.

The lesson for the teacher implied from the above is that students should have an accurate and clear perception of any aspect of music under study because they cannot develop precise associations and meanings unless they can differentiate between the characteristics of what is being studied—in this instance, the bell set. The teacher seeks ways to set up purposes in the minds of students and assists them in their observations, discussions, and in summarizing or evaluating the outcomes of their experiences. Student-produced data should be listed, interpreted, grouped, labeled, analyzed, and related whenever possible. This entire process may be initiated with questions such as "What is it?" "How do people use it?" Is it like any other instrument?" and "How is it different from other instruments?" In order for students to function on gradually higher symbolic levels, appropriate labels and vocabulary are introduced and used. An example follows.

Miss Ferrens brings a two-tone (two drums of different pitch) bongo drum into her classroom. The drum remains on the music table for a week while the children respond with curiosity to Miss Ferrens' invitation that they examine the drum to find out how much they can learn about it. She suggests from time to time that they perform simple experiments with it to see what types of sounds come from it, under what conditions the most resonant sounds can be made, why there is a difference in pitch, and how the drum might be struck to produce what the children believe are the best results. After a few days she asks: "In what different ways do people play drums?" The children theorize that drums can be played by hitting with some kind of stick and with the hands. One boy who had observed a dance band drummer says that some drums can be struck by using the foot on a mechanical striker. The children are then urged to observe drumming whenever they can on television and in rehearsals of the school band and orchestra in order to test their theories resulting from the restated question: "How are drums best played, and in how many different ways?" Later Miss Ferrens brings in other drums; the snare drum, hand drum, and conga drum. The children play them and compare their characteristics and study them to find out how each was made. Eventually the tambourine is added to be compared with the drums, and the children try to find more drums of different kinds.

Analysis: Miss Ferrens first planned for a common set of experiences for all the children with the one drum. As the children experimented with it, they produced additional experiences for themselves. They were freed for *action* through which their experiences took place and which made those experiences more meaningful because they were self-involving. The children drew on prior experiences with pitch, with tone qualities, and with ways of striking objects. After experiences with the other drums (such as the snare) they were able to discover common characteristics as well as differences. The bringing in of the tambourine was an interesting *discrepant event* whereby the children discovered that its sound was different and its construction varied in one respect from the concept of the membrane drum: it had metal jingles on it, and this made its tone quality different in a special way. To gather more data a field trip was made to a music store which had many drums on display; later the class visited the band rehearsal room where the drummers played the different drums and answered questions. Inferences were made about the functions of drums in the world.

Compare all of this with a lecture given by a teacher during which pictures of drums are displayed, then a recording of the sound of a number of drums is heard. Contrast this with Miss Ferrens' approach in terms of experiences, data, inferences, and action. How much decision making by the children took place?

Higher Level Abstract Concepts Some musical concepts are highly abstract, such as the interdependence of the various elements of music. The inception of this concept takes place when students find that recognizable melody cannot take place without some form of rhythm. This concept is gradually acquired through repeated experiences with a number of melodies and rhythms. For instance, "Happy Birthday to You" and "The Star-Spangled Banner" are completely different melodies, but there is a rhythm pattern common to both. The student should discover that the first parts of these two songs have identical rhythm and that "Joy to the World" utilizes the major scale in its beginning measures, but it is the rhythm that clearly distinguishes it from the way the major scale is commonly played. The students can try to invent a melody without rhythm to find that rhythmic feeling may be reduced but cannot be eliminated. Out of these experiences grows the generalization that "the interdependence of pitch and rhythm produces melody." Later on, harmony and other musical elements will expand the generalization of the interdependence of these elements in producing various types of music, and the students will use this principle in creating their own music.

Unless the teacher plans the lesson in such a way that the students know what they are listening for in melody and rhythm, they might conclude that they are simply singing a song or clapping a rhythm becuse the teacher told them to do it. The teacher must bring the focus of the lesson clearly to the attention of the students. This is done by planning some type of activity that reveals to the teacher what the students already know about the content of the lesson, or one which connects with the students' past experiences. Then the focusing of the lesson may be brought about through questioning or class discussion of the problem before it, and writing important points on the chalkboard. In class discussions there should be references to past experience, to possible future activities, and the problem should be defined and clarified. Unless the purpose for the activity is made clear in the thinking of the students, little goal-directed learning results.

"Musical understanding may be approached fundamentally by grasping combinations of sounds and the succesion of patterns by which these sounds become interrelated. Isolated tones become meaningful when associated with other tones. Problems in the perception of rhythm, harmonic progression, texture, and formal design require similar modes of studied relationships. Habits of concentrated attention to stimulate memory and frequent comparisons to motivate critical attitudes are then essential to the task of coordinating the intellect with sense perception." (Schwadron, 1967)

Questions, a Stimulus for Conceptual Learning

The term *question* can be used to mean any intellectual stimulus that calls for a response. Questions, problems, and tasks have always had a prominent place in pedagogy, but currently they are planned to encourage various forms of thinking rather than being used in random and sometimes confusing ways.

Research substantiates the fact that the quality and type of questions employed in any learning situation by either the teacher or the students, or both, greatly improves the student's ability to do cognitive thinking.

In the musical environmental setting of the classroom, questions asked by both teachers and students form some of the most important stimuli that motivate and spark creative performance and learning. Adults' provocative questions influence students to organize and express their questions similarly. Students need repeated encounters and practice to develop the skill of asking and using appropriately varied types of questions that stimulate independent inquiry.

There are simple and complex questions which can be useful with very young children, slow learners, and average and gifted learners at all levels. Teachers should not assume that special learners with mental and emotional impairments should be asked only simple, data-level questions and that the advanced student be asked only high-level process questions; all learners should have opportunity to respond to every type of question—matched to their optimal operational level of performance.

Teachers need to construct key questions and sequence them prior to use with a lesson or an activity. An attempt should be made to attain a proper balance of questions that pertain to all three domains—cognitive, psychomotor (skills), and affective—even though none of the domains are completely independent of the others.

Questioning Strategies and Cognitive Process Skills

As stated earlier, in developing cognitive thought processes, the teacher begins by providing learners with data-collecting experiences by means of which concepts can be derived. Degrees of expansion and complexity of these concepts yield an increasing mental ability to interpret and to make generalizations. From there the process moves to a higher level at which learners have practice in analyzing and synthesizing data, evaluating and judging as required by the experience or problem, and they then have an opportunity to make application of this knowledge in solving new problems. It is important that in music learning, thinking abilities that call for music skills are emphasized.

In preparing questions and using them to teach cognitive understandings, skills, and competencies, the task is clarified when a model is detailed and used as a guide to assure balance, depth, and appropriateness of questions. One such model containing three categories follows. (Notice the types of questions under each category.)

COGNITIVE PROCESS SKILLS

I. *Concept Formation* (*collecting and organizing data*). Concept formation is basic to other cognitive processes and is the necessary foundation for formulating generalizations.

   A. Identifying and enumerating through use of the ear, eye, and body various musical characteristics, elements, objects, and events such as pitch, rhythm, instruments, and concerts. What did you hear? See? Feel? (Identify. List. Examine. Compare.)

   B. Grouping in accordance with common qualities, uses, and other characteristics. For example, type of chords, even and uneven meters, types of phrases, and classifications of instruments. How can we group these most logically? If we don't know, what can we do or where can we go to find out?

   C. Discriminating between the features of these and abstracting common characteristics or elements, like the instances of 4/4, 5/4, 6/8, and 7/8 meters being different, yet containing the same note values or possibly using the same tempos. How are they alike? What names should we give to these categories?

II. *Interpreting Data and Generalizing.* After data have been assembled and ordered, and after an understanding of the relevant concepts has been achieved, it is possible to relate concepts and use them to form generalizations.

   A. Examining the same aspect of music in several different compositions.
   Example: What are the outstanding rhythm patterns in each of these songs?

   B. Comparing the same aspect of music in several different compositions.
   Example: Contrast these rhythm patterns: How are they the same; how are they different?

   C. Generalizing.
   Example: This type of song tends to have a rhythm pattern characteristic of Latin American music.

   D. Explaining.
   Example: The characteristic rhythm pattern is the result of each song's relationship to the same national dance.

III. *Application of Data, Concepts, and Generalizations.* Concepts and generalizations can be used to

   A. Compare objects, performances, activities, or phenomena.
   Example: How can we use the concept of a stage work in comparing a stage play with an opera? A ballet with a musical comedy?

   B. Predict possibilities.
   Example: What do you think would happen if there were no woodwinds in symphony orchestras? If there were no percussion section? What would happen if there were no symbols to depict accidentals in music?

C. Supporting predictions.

Example: Why do you believe the woodwinds are needed in symphony orchestras? What evidence can you give to prove that the percussion section is important? How do you know that it would not sound *better* if all accidentals were abandoned?

D. Verifying.

Example: How can we find out if instrumental music in Asia includes woodwinds? Are drums in Africa more or less important than drums in our music? Where can we find evidence to answer these questions?

When asking questions, be alert to the following:

1. Observe the type of thinking your questions stimulate. Some students may respond to a simple data question with a high level of thought.
2. All types of questions can be useful at all stages of mental operations. Learners at preoperational and concrete operational stages can analyze and make applications when they are working with concrete objects and situations. The more mature and gifted students can respond to questions requiring a greater measure of abstract thinking.
3. Distribute representative questions so that they will involve each student at his or her operational level of thinking.
4. Be sure to provide time for students to answer questions that call for interpretation, analysis, and application. Higher level thinking requires time, and if insufficient time is provided, frustration can result. Silence is a powerful motivator of thought when used with discretion and at the appropriate time. Be patient and wait.
5. Refrain from interrupting the learner's thought by repeating the original question too soon or by altering it. This confuses, disturbs, and hampers effective thinking and learning.

Motivation and Learning

The problem with motivation in the past has been that too often students become active in the learning process to please the teacher or to conform to the peer group (extrinsic motivation) instead of becoming active in learning because they wanted to find out something for themselves (intrinsic motivation, also inquiry). Suchman (1966) presents three levels of motivation. One is the *visceral,* in which the learner is motivated by body needs and the urge to survive. Another is the *social-ego* level, in which the learner seeks to be accepted by peers and adults. Teachers frequently employ this level to bring pressures to bear on students; grades are usually included among the status symbols. The third is the *cognitive* level. Suchman emphasizes at least three kinds of cognitive motivations: *Closure,* when the learner is faced with a situation with which his or her knowledge is not adequate to cope and desires a solution, answer, or explanation; *Curiosity,* when learners actively enjoy the process of finding answers to questions (these learners may not accept the five-line staff without wondering why it has five lines and not three or seven); and *Power,* when learners realize that knowledge gives them control over their environment and they want the security and confidence this can bring them.

The type of motivation affects the way learners are apt to behave. Visceral motivation, which implies physical danger or discomfort, is not a type that permits much sifting of ideas or theorizing; the student thinks only of what will work to get him or her out of a very uncomfortable situation. Since productive reflection demands security, visceral motivation denies such reflection at the outset, and the individual who is afraid, overtired, or hungry is regularly not a good learner. The pressures of social-ego motivation can generate worries about failure or nonacceptance. Students under these pressures are apt to think about themselves rather than about the world outside of them. In both of these types of motivation the vital process of inquiry is defeated. The mind is hemmed in by external pressures that prevent its being occupied with creative matching and ordering of experiences, which is necessary for inquiry to take place. Contrast the following two approaches to motivation.

Mr. Sperry asks his class a question concerning a piece of music the class knows well: "Why has Bach's 'Air for the G String' become a universal favorite?" All are free to contribute their thoughts. One student says she believes it is because of the calm and flowing style of the composition. Another believes that the interesting combination of a leading melody with polyphonic texture has made the piece appealing. Another says that if Bach's name had not appeared as the composer, the music would probably be unknown today. The class listens to each theory, discusses and examines it. New evidence is given to assist in evaluating the theories. No final answers result, and there are no right or wrong answers. The class is motivated by the thrill of thinking, gathering data, and then of more thinking.

Compare this with another class in which "Air for the G String" has been studied. The teacher's motive is to try to find out how much the class knows about the music by asking one question of each student in turn. After the class has been questioned in this way, the teacher gives a short lecture in which she states specifically why this music has become a universal favorite. The class takes notes part of the time. Some of the students take no notes; they furtively draw pictures or look out of the window. How has social-ego pressure been used? How much creativity can there be in this class? In which class will there be more anxiety?

The first of the above two examples is one of inquiry learning, which is learning that may be teacher-planned but is learner-directed and controlled as it unfolds. The teacher promotes learner growth by knowing how and when to get out of the way of the developing learner and how to continually motivate development by giving positive, appropriate, and well-timed reinforcement, feedback, and needed assistance. When the classroom environment promotes intrinsic motivation, it has set free one of the most powerful stimuli for learning. The learner then works toward a goal that he or she wants to achieve; thus the goal is a personal matter, not an extrinsic stimulus such as doing what the teacher tells the student to do.

The Structure of the Subject The current philosophy of learning emphasizes that beneficial and purposeful learning can be attained and used if it is acquired through a program organized around the basic structure of a subject. In other words, the student must understand the subject of music, including all of the related parts that comprise its structure. The teacher must be concerned with the relevance of the content of the structure to the student's interest and abilities and select those parts appropriate for study by students who differ in maturity, learning styles, and musical capacity. Structure consists of organized concepts and generalizations that collectively define a subject area. The structure of music as a subject of study consists of the concepts and generalizations of the elements that comprise music: dynamics, duration (rhythm), pitch (melody, harmony, polyphony), tone quality (timbre), texture, and form. When these concepts and generalizations have been selected and translated, experiences are planned that allow students to discover them. Research indicates that there is a need to organize a logical sequence of experiences for developing concepts (see pages 103–112).

A program organized in a logical, sequential format provides continuity of experiences. In preprimary and primary grades the music program is often a random assortment of unrelated activities. Even though students are exposed to a variety of experiences in this type of situation, they may not perceive the structure of music or its methods of inquiry. In a sequentially developed program, students should explore data and develop concepts commensurate with their operational levels and learning styles. This consideration prevents teachers from operating at a conceptual level that is too difficult for the majority of students. When students learn the component parts of music in relation to a meaningful structure, musical content is more readily understood and its details remembered for longer periods of time. As students employ structure, they can use it in their future research and organization of knowledge, thus making it possible for them to conserve and transfer knowledge from one learning experience to another.

Weakness in a conceptually structured music program results primarily from failure to include current musical events and problems that evolve within any school or home environment. Time must be provided for students to experiment and explore music on their own. In competent teaching, structure, content, and creative processes are combined into a meaningful pattern.

Principles of Learning   As is evident in this and the preceding chapter, any discussion of the teaching of music requires attention to the new concepts concerning acceptable theories of learning that contemporary research has introduced. Today's teachers must develop some directional criteria for improving their students' intellectual development. These should not attempt to project upon students learning for which they have insufficient background, nor should learning be delayed past the optimum time to satisfactorily master it. Research data pertaining to learning are almost constantly undergoing revision. The teacher has little choice but to seek out the most recent pertinent research findings that can aid in revising and updating the principles of learning used to guide more effective and efficient mastering of music. Such principles are invaluable for teachers when used as implications and criteria for forming a personal philosophy, identifying goals and objectives, designing learning environments, selecting types and varying levels of difficulty in materials of instruction, planning programs, lessons, and activities, selecting teaching strategies, and choosing ways to evaluate all aspects of growth and learning. Each of these aspects should be constantly examined and made compatible with the principles which follow.

Learning is facilitated when:

1. Music activities are selected that are on the student's physical, intellectual, and social maturity levels.
2. The teacher has obvious confidence in the student's ability to learn music, and expects and makes it possible for each to operate at his or her optimal level.
3. The teacher employs a variety of activities and materials for individual, small-group, and large-group activities through which the students develop favorable self-concepts.
4. The teacher arranges for musical problems to be solved by the students.
5. The students have musical experience that are satisfying and enjoyable to them.
6. The students have good models with which to identify (other children, parents, teachers, other adults).
7. There is a planned, sequential, but flexible program of music instruction from level to level.
8. Students are provided with individualized, specific, frequent, sequential, varied, and appropriately spaced practice.
9. Teachers and parents work together to help students learn music; the musical and cultural environment influences to a significant degree students' musical perceptions and values.
10. Learning styles, levels of proficiency, and aptitude are recognized, studied, and accommodated.
11. The students see meaning and relevance in what they are doing as they make immediate functional applications of skills and procedures, as they become involved in establishing objectives, selecting appropriate activities and materials, and assessing the degree to which the objectives have been realized.
12. Teachers are able to select and state what they are going to teach and the subsequent pupil learning behaviors (objectives), how they are going to accomplish this (methods and materials), and then determine how well they have taught it (evaluation).
13. Students are taught the skill of asking different types of questions and are encouraged and given time and opportunity to employ this skill.
14. The teacher is an active facilitator for learning, a co-learner, and a resource person who shares in class activities.
15. The students' musical activities are successful for them. The teacher plans activities in which children can be successful, in which they are interested, and through which they can progress in learning music.
16. The student is intrinsically motivated, thus personally involved in what is to be learned.
17. Students experience music through a combination of senses—touching, manipulating, visually examining, hearing, and using the body and muscles in rhythmic interpretation.
18. Students experience music actively by singing, moving, listening, improvising, and playing instruments before being taught verbally and symbolically.
19. Students have environments that are rich and varied in types of materials, and teachers who encourage them to explore and experiment on their own, but who know when to intercede and facilitate learning.

20. Musical percepts and concepts are presented in meaningful settings and in sequential order.
21. Learners are free to explore, discover, question, and profit from making mistakes.
22. Feedback and reinforcement assist by verifying progress and correcting errors; generally, early correction benefits productive learning.
23. There is consistent teacher-student evaluation and positive reinforcement by teacher and peers.
24. It is recognized as a long, cumulative process that is attained through repeated, meaningful activities.
25. The structure of the body of musical knowledge is adapted to the learner's level of cognitive development and understanding.
26. Students experience concepts for themselves in a discovery/exploratory environment, thus more readily retaining and transferring them to higher level concepts than those experienced through rote methods.
27. The classroom environment is structured appropriately to permit creativity.
28. Democratic and autocratic teaching methods are used appropriately, depending upon what is being taught at the time.
29. Students' command of the tools for learning music makes possible their becoming independent learners.
30. Previously learned concepts are associated and combined with new ones.
31. Students are allowed to discover what they already know about music, and progress from there.
32. Teacher planning takes into account that students learn in different ways at different stages of mental operation.
33. Students have attainable, but expanding, goals.
34. Students experience wholesome social and emotional relationships with their peers and with their teachers.
35. Students respond to new situations (stimuli) in terms of successful performances used formerly under different settings or within different contexts (transfer and application).
36. The teacher recognizes that conceptual learning is basic to intellectual thought, and plans accordingly.
37. Students have experience working in more than one type of class organization; they need to work in both structured and open-creative types of organizations.
38. Students understand clearly what is to be learned, how it is to be learned, and how the learning will be evaluated.
39. Students learn by progressing from the concrete to the abstract.
40. The classroom is free of the use of music activities or their denial as threats or punishment.
41. The teacher knows that individuals have different learning styles, ways of processing data and forming concepts, and learning skills, thus uses instructional organization practices that make it possible for each student to learn in terms of his or her own style.
42. The teacher views an individual's brain as a unique, growing, developing organ that is influenced by both environmental factors and heredity.
43. Active participation and discovery are recognized and used as producers of the most effective learning.
44. It is neither rushed nor forced.

EXPLORATORY ACTIVITIES

1. What are the implications of the statement that most learning takes place outside of school? How should this affect the content of music lessons in school? How important do you think the home environment is in education, and what can teachers do about it?

2. Be able to explain the sequence of mental processing from percept to concept to generalization. Relate this to helping students to comprehend music.

3. Listening has been claimed to be the basic musical activity. Prove this by speaking from the examples of classroom music in this chapter.

4. Select a song, identify the concepts to be taught, and prepare a list of different types of questions appropriate to teaching your chosen concepts to students. Sequence the questions in a logical order and label each type of question.

5. What is generally the best way for students to be motivated to learn? How can teachers try to make this possible?

6. Explain what is meant by "the structure of music." Indicate the educational value of structure. What are its disadvantages?

7. Observe a music class at the level of your choice and answer the following questions: How was the class motivated to learn? Did the students have genuine musical experiences or did they talk about music most of the time? Did the teacher ask questions of different types? Were all students participating at their individual levels? Was the focus of the lesson applied to other musical situations? Did the students have the musical background to understand what they were to learn? Were the students involved in planning, suggesting, or experimenting? What was the possibility of continuing some of the activities at home? What suggestions do you have for improving the conduct of the lesson?

8. Listen to a teacher in action before a class. Analyze the types of questions used (data, interpretive, analysis, application, evaluative). Was sufficient time allowed to answer questions, and to what extent were they distributed among the students? Did the teacher do all the questioning or were students encouraged to phrase their own?

9. Identify cognitive, affective, and psychomotor learning. Explain them with musical examples.

10. From the list of commonly accepted principles of learning, select three to five and explain how you would apply them when teaching music at a level of your choice.

References

AUSUBEL, DAVID P., *Educational Psychology: A Cognitive View.* New York: Holt, Rinehart and Winston, 1968.

BOWER, G. H., and E. R. HILGARD, *Theories of Learning, 5th ed.* Englewood Cliffs, N.J.: Prentice-Hall, Inc., 1981.

FOWLER, CHARLES B., "Discovery: One of the Best Ways to Teach a Musical Concept," *Music Educators Journal,* September 1970, p. 38.

HUNKINS, FRANCES P., *Questioning Strategies and Techniques.* Boston: Allyn and Bacon, Inc., 1972.

Music Educators National Conference, The Ann Arbor Symposium Session III, *Motivation and Creativity.* Reston, Va.: The Conference, 1983.

NYE, VERNICE TROUSDALE, *Music for Young Children,* 3rd ed., chapter two. Dubuque, Iowa: Wm. C. Brown, 1983.

RYAN, FRANK, and ARTHUR K. ELLIS, *Instructional Implications of Inquiry.* Englewood Cliffs, N.J.: Prentice-Hall, Inc., 1975.

SANDERS, NORRIS M., *Classroom Questions: What Kinds?* New York: Harper and Row, Pub., 1966.

SCHWADRON, ABRAHAM A., *Aesthetics: Dimensions for Music Education,* p. 95. Reston, Va.: Music Educators National Conference, 1967.

SUCHMAN, J. RICHARD, "Motivation," *The Instructor,* December 1966.

chapter four

The Learning Environment
and Implementing Instruction

The most decisive influence on the learning process is the quality and use of the music environment. Each teacher must pause to ask, "What factors must I consider as I design challenging and stimulating climates in which each student can learn all aspects of music to his or her optimum level?" To address this pertinent question, constant attention must be directed to the interaction or interplay among such factors as the learning stages and styles of the student, teaching strategies, type and nature of the music content, necessary skills to be developed, and the physical environment. The number of students to be taught, the number of mainstreamed learners present, the musical philosophy of the school faculty, music consultants, and teachers of music combined with qualified music aides or assistants all influence the nature and type of climate for teaching music.

The Teaching Staff The best musical environment for students is one in which both the classroom teacher and music specialist are involved in music teaching. Even if there is a music room to which students go to enjoy instruction from a specialist, students need the stimulation for and approval of music in their lives from the homeroom teacher. The roles of music specialist and classroom teacher are somewhat different, in that the specialist is acknowledged to be the primary musical resource, the leading planner, the writer of long-term objectives and, above all, one who helps the classroom teacher in his or her efforts to teach music. The classroom teacher has a marked advantage in being with the students nearly all of the time, knowing them well, and thus being the major influence in the total education of the students. Because of this, there is a very strong need for the two teachers to work closely together in the interests of a balanced program of instruction for all students. The classroom teacher can use music in social studies and history learning and for physiologically and psychologically necessary changes in routine. Music can improve the possibilities for general learning in any classroom. Many music specialists are not given sufficient time with students, thus have difficulty in achieving objectives without assistance from the classroom teacher and/or teacher aides and assistants. The ideal music program needs additional staff—aides and other types of assistants, including parent volunteers—as well as adequate time in which to help students learn music.

The use of music specialists to provide a break in the day for classroom teachers is a highly questionable practice. While all teachers need some relaxation during the day, this should not be done at the expense of a good educational program for students. In some situations there are no specialists, and the entire music program is the responsibility of classroom teachers. In such instances there may be one teacher who is accepted as a leader in working with all to establish objectives, order materials, and act as chairperson of music for that building. In such situations there is usually increased dependence on the music series books as a dependable source of at least a minimal music program. They provide a sequential plan, songs and other materials, simple accompaniments, questions to ask, use of classroom instruments, pronunciation guides for foreign language songs, excellent recordings of singing and of instrumental music for listening, some Orff and Kodály methodology, related art and other enrichments, suggestions for teaching special learners, other individualized instruction, and special units of work called "satellites" or "modules."

The following example of a work module is taken from *Spectrum of Music,* Book Two, Teacher's Annotated Edition, by Mary Val Marsh, Carroll Rinehart, and Edith Savage.*

Imitating Animal Sounds

Purpose: To explore the use of the voice for making sounds of animals

Materials: Textbook, recording, resonator bells C, D, E, MusicCenter 6, 7.

Motivation: Talk with children about pets. Read a story about animals. Display pictures of animals. Talk about where they live. Ask the children to imitate animal sounds. Ask them to tell stories about their favorite pet or animal.

Exploration: Have the children
1. Listen to the song and follow the words and the notation. Observe that parts of the song are repeated.

* Reprinted with permission of Macmillan Publishing Company from *Spectrum of Music,* Book 2, Teacher's Annotated Edition, by Mary Val Marsh, Carroll Rinehart, and Edith Savage. Copyright © 1983 Macmillan Publishing Co., Inc.

2. Sing the song. Begin with "Cat goes fiddle-i-fee." After repeated singing of this phrase, sing the whole song.
3. Add the name and sounds of other animals to extend the song.
4. Divide into groups, with each group singing the name of an animal and its sound. (This will help to emphasize the structure of the music.) Move their hands with the direction of the animal's song.

Extension: On another day, play the animal names and sounds on resonator bells: "Cat goes fid-dle-i-fee" (C, C, E, E, D, C), "Duck goes quack, quack" (C, C, E, E).

Desired Responses: The children should demonstrate: Greater skill in singing and more accurate matching of pitch. More skill and enjoyment in creating new verses for the song.

Mainstreaming Disabilities:

Auditory: Memory (naming animals and their song) Motivation, 1, 2, 3, 4. Auditory-Motor Integration (playing patterns; showing pitch direction with hands) 4, Extension.

Visual: Memory (finding repeated animal's song, in notation) 1. Visual-Motor Integration (playing patterns) Extension.

Motor: Gross (showing pitch direction) 4. Extension.

Curriculum Correlation: Can the children find the word "yonder" in this song? Have them put their fingers on the word. How many times do they see it in the song? [*3*] What does the word "yonder" mean? [*Over there*]

BARNYARD SONG

Kentucky Folk Song

Movement: After the children have practiced singing the names of different animals and their sounds, have them play a movement game. Have them form a circle.

Choose a child to stand in the middle as the Cat, miming its actions at the appropriate point in the song. The Cat may choose the Hen, who will choose the next animal. More animals may be added to the song and game.

Technically, a *music supervisor* has authority over a music program and its teachers, if that person desires to exercise it. Most classroom teachers have expressed their preference for a *music consultant* who acts as helper and resource person when called upon by teachers. In practice, classroom teachers who are competent in music teaching request the most assistance, while those neglecting music or preferring not to teach it fail to contact the consultant. Thus, the problem of authority in music programs is sometimes avoided, or is obscure, being said to rest with the principal. The environment for music learning may be inadequate unless the principal acts to ensure a good program.

Organizational Plans
The educational philosophy of the school administrative staff, the entire school faculty, and especially the classroom teacher and music specialist will guide the designing of different types of instructional plans. Each plan and its specific philosophy will necessitate a different climate or setting for learning. Therefore, no one type of environmental climate or plan will suffice for all types of organizational plans and philosophies concerning what music students should learn, why they should learn it, when they should learn it, and how.

Teachers should be prepared to work in several types of school organizations, including the expedient "plan" of fitting X number of students into the space available in the existing school plant. A plan that has become widely accepted is the 6-3-3 plan—elementary school, junior high school, and senior high school. A later plan that has grown in popularity is the 4-4-4 organization—primary, middle, and high school. (A variant 5-4-4 plan includes kindergarten with the primary school.) The later plan came about in part because the junior high school became more of an imitation of senior high school than an institution that clearly served its age group. Also, earlier maturity of many students led to rethinking the organizational plan. Recently there has been a move toward grouping students of ages 5–8 as Division One, ages 8–10 as Division Two, and ages 10–13 as Division Three. This plan has an overlapping of ages to provide for varying individual growth stages. For example, an immature 10-year-old would be in Division Two while an advanced 10-year-old would go to Division Three.

Alternative schools are organized to meet the demands of the community, segments of the community, and some educators. They indicate dissatisfaction with the established system of education. By means of these schools, special needs are met, and the educational program is assumed to be more relevant to the learners. Such schools range from traditional schools in which "the basics" are emphasized, to experimental schools of many types. Alternative programs can include an entire school, some age levels within the school, or only one group of students. An attractive example was the IMPACT project, in which the arts formed the core of the curriculum and the other subjects were planned in accordance with this concept (Wenner, 1973).

The *self-contained classroom* is a type of curricular organization in which a group of students is in contact with one teacher for a major portion of the school day. It is in contrast to the *departmental* organization which divides the day into as many time periods as there are subjects, with each subject taught by a different teacher who specializes in it. Historically, there are three different concepts of the self-contained classroom: (1) all subjects taught by one teacher (with occasional assistance), (2) all subjects except music, art, and physical education taught by one teacher, and (3) all subjects in the primary school taught by one teacher, with varying degrees of departmentalization in the middle school. Art, music, and physical education were introduced into the curriculum as special subjects, taught by specialists, and they are identified in educational history as the traditionally specialized subjects. Even so, history also reveals several reversals of opinion that have at times assigned basic responsibility for music teaching to classroom teachers through sixth grade. The seventh and eighth grades were usually departmentalized. The amount of time allocated to music teaching is often determined by the type of organization employed within a school or within a class. The organization also influences the space needed, the learning materials and equipment, and the number and qualifications of personnel.

In order for students to become involved in the excitement and process of learning, they must have access to a learning environment that makes it possible for them to explore their interests and problems in all of the above types of organizational environments.

A *middle school* that consists of from two to four of the fifth through eighth grades constitutes a major trend in today's organizational plans. Earlier maturation has speeded acceptance of a school designed specifically for preadolescents who need the relative security of their own developmental group. (See Developmental Characteristics, ages 10–13, pp. 19–22.) This age group is highly interesting, and teachers who understand it find the work most rewarding. One opinion has it that these students are often in a "jungle of self-doubt and anxiety," and the teacher's task is to bring them through this period of growth with self-confidence and a rational basis for value judgments. Obviously there is a great need for college music courses designed to prepare teachers for this age group; it is essential that these teachers understand the interests and learning problems of this volatile, critical, and often emotionally explosive age and the implications of these behaviors for designing programs, managing learning situations, and teaching this developmental level. Music requirements for upper middle school vary among the states, with most requiring 90 to 100 minutes per week for music instruction, with general music daily for one semester of the seventh and eighth years for those not enrolled for the full year in vocal or instrumental groups.

There should be a balance between group instruction and individual instruction. While most students want and need the security and conformity that large groups provide, they also want and need small group and individualized study because of the wide range of individual differences that exist. There should be exploratory creative types of programs with related special interest activities or modules (units of concentration) through which students seek what in this puzzling world is real, true, and relevant. The environment should be arranged as a musical laboratory. "Modules" or "satellites" are offered by series publishers, written by teachers, and designed cooperatively by teachers and students. Titles may include American Music, Guitar, Professional Autoharp Techniques, Rock Music, Jazz, African Drum Rhythms, Electronic Music, Music Our Parents Liked, Let's Produce an Opera, and many more. Two textbook publishers that provide these modular studies or miniunits are:

Macmillan Publishing Company, Inc., Front and Brown Streets, Riverside, N.J. 08370

Silver Burdett Company, 250 James Street, Morristown, N.J. 07960

Another publisher, Cherry Lane Publisher, P.O. Box 430, Port Chester, N.Y. 10573, provides units based on popular music of the day.

For some years teachers have had to cope with the notion that rock music is the voice of this age group, and the fact that the group identifies with it. All music has common elements, and bringing rock and popular music into the classroom means that it will not only be examined for its own qualities, but aspects of it will be studied and compared with the same features found in other types of music—melody, rhythm, tempo, tone quality, harmony, texture, and form, as well as musical components such as call-and-response, ostinato, polyrhythms, and improvisation (cadenza). Rock or disco adaptations of classics can provide an adventure in comparisons, such as "Fifth of Beethoven" (Millennium Records) and his *Fifth Symphony,* and, at Halloween, "Night on Disco Mountain" and Mussorgsky's *Night on Bald Mountain.* The history of popular music from rhythm and blues to rock is often of interest, as is the history of jazz. One way to examine popular favorites is with the following criteria: (1) To what degree is it original? (2) How well is it performed? (3) What does it communicate? How well does it do it? (4) Will it live or have a short life? Why do you think so? The teacher will urge the students to share their knowledge of the music, knowledge that is sometimes greater than the teacher's. After all, the teacher's place is to help students discover the relationship of all types of music, and to be able to do so, the teacher must know and understand today's music.

Contemporary textbooks provide opportunities for musical stage productions, which many students will enjoy organizing and performing. Parents can be of assistance as resource persons, tutors, or general volunteers at appropriate times. Guest performers from the community can demonstrate, and field trips into the community can be made. See pages 65–71 for information about classroom management.

The teacher's success depends upon (1) planning a logical sequence of subject matter and concept building, (2) long-term goals selected for the term or year, (3) instructional goals and objectives as guides to units, modules, daily lessons, materials, and selection and specification of activities, (4) knowledge of the students, and (5) his or her enthusiasm and open attitude toward learning. A list of references and resources especially for this age group may be found at the end of this chapter (pp. 71–72).

Environments Necessary for Specific Types of Learning

If learning is experiencing in meaningful and relevant ways, then attention must be focused on providing environments productive and appropriate for each student to experience and advance in the spectrum of music. The activities pursued in any one of the types of learning environments presented below will influence any one or all the others since cognitive (intellectual), psychomotor (skills, muscular), and affective (feelings, values, and attitudes) aspects of students' learning are closely related and in many ways inseparable.

1. Social and Affective Learning. Knowledge alone is insufficient as a goal of any form of education. Unless constructive attitudes and values accompany it, knowledge is at least neutralized and is even dangerous on occasion. Any music experiences in which students engage should be those that provide aesthetic qualities as an integral part of each encounter. Since social acceptance, attitudes, and feelings are related, the affective atmosphere of the classroom must be one that furthers positive emotional and social growth.

When the environment frustrates students by failing to meet social and emotional needs, there is little to contribute to the development of wholesome attitudes and values in music. A learning environment that permits destructive, negative opinions of any student's music or of people tends to further negative attitudes and values.

There is general belief that feelings and emotions cannot be taught in a direct manner. For example, the importance or beauty of a musical selection is not taught by a teacher telling students how important or beautiful it is, or by the students merely verbalizing. Students must *internalize* the importance and beauty to such an extent that their conduct toward the selection, and their response to and understanding of other music are affected.

Attitudes, emotions, and values, whether good or bad, will be developed in the classroom; it is the teacher's responsibility that they be healthy and constructive. Raths, Harmin, and Simon (Raths et al., 1966) suggest that teachers plan for this by using the following adapted steps in teaching valuing processes:

> Encourage students to make musical choices and to make them freely.
>
> Help them discover and examine available alternatives when faced with choices.
>
> Help students weigh alternatives thoughtfully, reflecting on the consequences of each.
>
> Encourage students to consider what it is in the music they prize and cherish.
>
> Give them opportunities to make public affirmation of their choices of music.
>
> Encourage them to act, behave, live in accordance with their choices.
>
> Help them to examine repeated behaviors or patterns in their own lives.

Students' attitudes and values regarding music may reflect the attitudes of both the peer group and those of high status adults. Thus it is possible that a student's attitudes and values can be weakened by contradictory musical influences emanating from adults and peers (radio, television, and recordings). Since students' musical backgrounds and experiences differ, teachers should not strive nor expect to have all children acquire the same set of musical values.

The positive attitudes and values of teachers are highly important in the instructional process. The chance remark of a teacher might have a lasting infuence on a student. The teacher's attitude toward music, with its great variety of values and uses in human life, will usually affect children's attitudes.

Different types of music affect people differently. Therefore, the teacher should work toward a classroom environment in which the varied opinions of students toward works of music are listened to with interest, valued, defended with musical knowledge when necessary. (Why did you like or dislike this music?) Such an environment permits disagreements that can be expressed in ways that permit personal differences while arguing intellectual points in support of positions taken. Musical values and attitudes toward music cannot be separated entirely from respect, concern for the feelings of others, and the acknowledgment that people can hold differing values—especially in a classroom situation in which there is neither hostility nor aggression. An intellectually sound position for a music teacher to take is one that attempts to judge "good" music in accordance with how well it performs its function, and to operate in a climate of openness that admits the exploration of every type of music to attempt to find out what it is used for, how it is constructed, and how good it is in its category. In this atmosphere every facet of music from Renaissance to jazz and electronic has a place, and their values are to be discovered by students in their personal learning of music.

2. The Creative-Exploratory Approach (open-informal environment) is based on the assumption that if students' learning, including sensitivity to aesthetic experience, is to be fully developed, there must be time for exploring such learning in a relaxed, encouraging, and enjoyable environment. For creative involvement to occur, teachers must plan for it; the teacher's responsibility is to nurture and encourage the creative spontaneity of every student. This creative/exploratory setting frees all students to explore, observe, and test their ideas. The school day is integrated, not segmented, and learners can pursue problems of their choice in depth, unhampered by traditional subject barriers. Some group instruction takes place, but the focus is on the individual learner and freedom to learn.

The content of the curriculum is determined by student interests and needs; there are few restrictions on use of time and space, and students are free to interact with each other in order to learn from peers. The teacher's role is that of resource person, diagnostician, and designer of the environment. The teacher observes students' responses to environmental stimuli, determines students' future needs as derived from that observation, and redesigns the environment to accommodate further learning. Open-ended questions dominate the teacher's queries, and he or she intervenes at appropriate times to assist learning with questions and other stimuli. Evaluation emphasizes the process of learning rather than the final product of the experiences.

3. Two Direct Instruction Approaches (autocratic environment). In the *teacher-directed* approach teachers are dominant figures who determine instructional goals and objectives, select and present course content, and make decisions. Interaction between teacher and students is limited because the teacher does most of the talking, discussing, and demonstrating. A formal environment is arranged to reflect this, often with seats in straight rows. The teacher decides what types of behavior expectations are acceptable for the class and usually demands and attempts to enforce these. Students speak, sing, and otherwise perform in ways the teacher indicates, and there is little interaction permitted among them although a team spirit is hoped for. Such an environment as described above often results from inadequate time and/or space.

The teaching is primarily textbook or workbook centered. Large group (class) instruction is emphasized; there is ordinarily an absence of small group and individual teaching. The expectations of the teacher are focused on the average learner, thus discipline problems are found more frequently in this approach because the gifted are bored and the slow learners are frustrated. Closed-end questions dominate and are usually directed at the average and above-average students to the neglect of the slow learner. The above refers to the general music class, but is characteristic of many bands, orchestras, and choruses.

The *direct instruction* approach is a well-planned, highly structured procedure emphasizing behavioral objectives. Teachers establish and articulate the learning goals, actively assess student progress, and frequently make class presentations illustrating how to do assigned work. Learning is closely directed, supervised, and controlled by teachers, and students have little if any influence over instruction and their own learning. In both of these approaches, teachers employ primarily data-level one-answer-type questions. The large classroom organizational plan serves as the setting for both teacher-directed learning and direct instruction.

How does direct instruction function? This approach involves the identification of music topics or skills within music curriculum areas and the development of objectives that test learners' *mastery* of each of these topics or skills. The student involvement aspect includes a mastery test, a series of lessons that teach the material assessed in the mastery test, and a series of diagnostic instruments to be administered at frequent intervals while instruction proceeds, a process often called "mastery learning." The diagnostic tests are vital to the process since they provide teachers with the feedback required for them to determine the success of the instruction. As a result of the tests, students are moved to corrective work if they have not mastered the material or skill, or to extension activities if they have.

Direct instruction uses the large group plan of teaching or environmental setting as does the teacher-directed approach. However, direct instruction provides through its diagnostic-corrective-extension activities a high degree of individualization. Because it is based upon group instruction, it is easier for the average teacher to manage than some of the more detailed individualized classroom procedures. In direct instruction much class time is devoted to textbook teaching and responses on a simple recall level. Current critics of public education claim that teachers should develop more student activities that involve critical thinking skills.

The effectiveness of direct instruction depends on the type of student being taught. Students who are less able to control their own thinking do best with this approach, but the more individualistic, creative thinkers do less well. Similarly, high ability students have been found to do better in small group plans than in large groups followed by paper work done individually. Low ability students usually need the greater direction and help provided by the teacher in the large group direct instruction method.

The choice of a teaching approach should depend on the musical objective a teacher wants to attain most effectively and efficiently. Thus, if teachers want to teach inquiry skills they should seldom use direct instruction. If, on the other hand, teachers want to teach basic music skills, direct instruction would be appropriate as one way to do it. Effective teaching involves the considered selection of a teaching approach to attain a specific desired educational outcome with a particular type of learner.

4. The Conceptual-Process Approach to Learning. In this environment, students are freely engaged in attempting to solve musical problems by exploring, questioning, discussing, performing, interpreting, generalizing, analyzing, synthesizing, evaluating, and valuing. In a musical environment that is conducive to the development of these cognitive and inquiry skills, students are guided in focusing their attention upon problems that have no single solution.

The comments of both students and teachers are accepted because of their pertinence to the solution of the problem being investigated. All students, as well as the teacher, are given equal freedom to engage in the above intellectual processes.

The teacher functions by asking questions that challenge the learners to seek more significant and penetrating answers and solutions as well as to stimulate more research and discussion among students and between teacher and learners. Students question each other and freely discuss alternate solutions as they pertain to musical problems and to a concept or hypothesis which gives the discussion focus. The problem outlines the general direction of pursuit. The teacher employs all types of thinking and questioning, which are used as needed to develop musical attitudes, values, concepts, generalizations, or skills.

Proper questions in music class are based upon music activities, directed toward musical concept learnings, and follow the activity as well as precede it. They stimulate better listening, better singing, better rhythmic responses, better playing of instruments, more creativity, more use of notation, and better understanding of all components of music and various musical concepts.

When students are involved in a conceptual process approach, they need an environment constructed as a laboratory which contains music materials and media of varied types and levels of difficulty that build and expand musical concepts. Freedom of movement and opportunity to work cooperatively, and to share with peers and teachers within that environment is a necessity. For a more detailed description of cognitive-process thinking and learning see pages 112–122.

The Physical Environment

Learning is difficult when attempted in impure air, uncomfortable temperatures, and improper lighting. The busy teacher who is in the same classroom all day will sometimes fail to notice insufficient ventilation, unhealthy temperatures, and faulty lighting because of gradual changes as the day progresses. Classroom committees can be established to give students experience in assuming responsibilities and to relieve the teacher of part of this routine task.

The arrangement of the furniture reflects the type of learning that can take place. Classroom seating should be arranged to make it possible for students to take part in discussion as well as in individual and group work, and to provide opportunity for listening effectively and courteously to any class member who is speaking, singing, or playing an instrument. Seating on the floor is best for some activities. Chairs and desks should be selected for the varying sizes of students so that all can be comfortably seated.

The varied activities in music make moveable furniture a necessity. Seating (or temporary standing) will be changed at times for singing in large or small groups, playing instruments, creative interpretations, rhythmic responses, individualized instruction, and dance. Special seating may be needed if some of the students have difficulty hearing or seeing. The manner in which students move from one activity to another is established by clear instruction from the teacher and by teacher-pupil planning. The teacher's well-designed questions stimulate learners to plan and take responsibility for this part of classroom routine. Ways of leaving and entering a music room, going to and from a music or assembly room, and moving books, instruments, and other materials are additional aspects of classroom routine.

Visual aids, displayed at eye level, commonly include a drawing of the keyboard, pictures of instruments and musicians, charts of hand signals, rhythm syllables, and note values. Cue cards for listening experiences can be useful visual aids. In listening-analysis activities the mood of a recorded composition can be heightened by drawing shades, turning lights on or dimming them, by employing color or placing objects in ways to reinforce the aural effect.

When instruments and equipment are selected, the teacher chooses those that produce excellent tone quality, are durable, attractive, and easy to store, and are suitable for the students. When songs are selected, the teacher looks for simplicity and variety in the melody, repeated parts that assist rapid learning, content interesting to the age group, proper range for the voices, appropriate length for the maturity level, rhythmic appeal, the desired mood, and a suitable, attractive accompaniment. A song is examined to find what teaching purpose it can serve. Is it worth learning? Is it a worthy art, folk, or popular song? Does it contribute to the realization of the stated objectives?

Every school should provide each student over age seven with copies of two music textbooks (basal series) and access to a variety of supplementary books and materials. Currently published music series are:

Comprehensive Musicianship Through Classroom Music (1972). Addison-Wesley Publishing Company, 2725 Sand Hill Rd., Menlo Park, Calif. 94025

The Music Book. Holt, Rinehart and Winston, Inc., 383 Madison Ave., New York, N.Y. 10017.

The Spectrum of Music. The Macmillan Publishing Co., Inc., 100F Brown Street, Riverside, N.J. 08370.

Silver Burdett Music. Silver Burdett, 250 James Street. Morristown, N.J. 07960.

Recordings and teachers' books accompanying the textbooks should also be available. When series books are selected, the teacher considers print, size, clarity of notation, a good grade of paper that is free from eye-straining gloss, ease of handling by students, color, illustrations, absence of clutter, general attractiveness, well-organized and comprehensive indices, content that appeals to the age group, quality of content, general durability, quality of cover, simplicity and musicality of accompaniments, helpfulness of teachers' books, and quality and usefulness of recordings.

Each school building should contain a learning resource center or laboratory that provides not only books about music but recordings, videotape equipment, computers, films, filmstrips, transparencies, projectors, and programed and self-instructional materials. The following instruments are expected to be in each basically equipped classroom: various drums of high and low pitches, six pairs of rhythm sticks, sandblocks, woodblocks, maracas, claves, cymbals, finger cymbals, tambourines, triangles, cowbell, five sets of melody bells, one set of resonator bells, jingle bells, jingle clogs, gong, four soprano recorders, assorted xylophone-type instruments, four Autoharps, one ukulele, and one guitar. There should be easy access to an overhead projector, opaque projector, screen, film projector, record player, two tape recorders, television set, radio, and a metronome. Orff-designed instruments should be included. While programed materials are in conflict with the creative and discovery approaches, they may be suited to the learning styles of some students and have values for all students in the area of music skills and for reinforcing the learning of both skills and concepts. The crucial issue is how well these materials assist in the realization of the identified objectives (see pp. 73–88).

A system for distributing materials and collecting them should be planned with the students, who should know where and how to store them. If small plastic wind instruments are used, each should be labled with the student's name and be placed in a container to keep it clean. For sanitary reasons, instruments should not be exchanged, but if this is necessary, a disinfectant suitable for plastic must be used. The instruments must be cleaned periodically with disinfectant applied with a small brush or cotton swab.

Criteria must be established, preferably with the students, for proper use of the room in viewing films and television, listening to radio programs, and using the computer, music learning center, or stations. A classified card file of recordings should be part of the teacher's equipment.

The physical environment necessary for individualized instruction is one in which the customary rows of desks are absent. Instead, students work at tables, on the floor, at wall displays, at chalkboards and charts, and at learning centers. Hallways, closets, booths, and alcoves are used to provide space for many types of activities. There is a variety of borrowed, inexpensive, and free materials and objects with which to experiment. The usual music equipment is present: melody instruments, music books and books related to music, percussion instruments, chording instruments, recordings, pictures, puzzles and games, and flash cards. The sound center recommended by the Manhattanville Music Curriculum Program should be included, and there might be a science-of-sound center, a multimedia center, an electronic music center, and an instrument construction center. Care is taken that students are not confused by an overly rich environment; teachers need to arrange one that challenges and interests but does not overwhelm.

A music learning center can be located in a part of the room which is relatively secluded, yet accessible. It may be in a booth off the main classroom or it may consist of one large table or several smaller ones upon which can be placed materials and interesting directions or challenging suggestions as to what to do with them. The center could contain bulletin boards on which can be mounted information about community musical events, composers, recommended radio and television programs, musical achievements of students, charts, musical symbols, cartoons, jackets from books about music and from recordings, newspaper and magazine clippings, notation of unnamed familiar songs (which can be identified by studying this notation), favorite songs, rhythm patterns, and pictures relating to musical subjects. However, the bulletin board must be arranged attractively and changed frequently if it is to accomplish its mission of attracting maximum interest. Soft mallets for bells, and headsets with record players can eliminate or reduce interference with other activities in the room. By teacher-pupil planning, criteria for the use of the materials and equipment are established. These criteria should include also when and how students are to work in the music learning center or laboratory.

Music teachers today use cultural resources in the community to enrich learning. The expansion of the learning environment makes it necessary for the teacher to become familiar with all areas and facilities of the school plant and community that can be useful for music instruction. When students explore the musical resources of the community, and when parents and other community resource people contribute to the music program, the physical boundaries for music learning are thereby expanded. Students can plan contributions to the community by sharing their music and dance skills with senior citizens and other adults. In turn, adults may contribute bits of musical history and information on music of other cultures, which students may obtain permission to preserve on tape and present to the class.

Organizing for Instruction

In an effort to make instruction in all areas of music more effective and to provide opportunities for students to learn in varied and unique ways, the teacher uses, when appropriate, organizational plans consisting of large and small groups and individualized plans. All students should at times be involved in all of the above-mentioned plans.

Large Class Groups The teacher should ask, "Which aspects of the lesson or activity can be accomplished most effectively and efficiently in the large group?" In the total group the teacher may:

Introduce a music concept or skill to be learned.

Introduce one or more problems related to the concept or skill.

Review a musical skill.

Clarify and plan with the students the activities to be pursued in small groups.

Identify and group students who can work well together in smaller groups.

Make general plans for small group work by establishing objectives; indicate places for working (areas of the room, station or lab center); establish time limits and criteria for working in small groups; designate the signal for returning to the large group to share small group accomplishments when appropriate.

The large group serves as a stimulus and place for sharing the musical ideas, learnings, and performances of both small groups and individuals. The presentation of large musical group performances when they involve the combined efforts and contributions of smaller groups and individuals becomes an exhilarating experience and a motivator for improving small group and individual conceptual and skills learning. The musical stage production is an example.

In contrast to the current emphasis on individualization, the Orff-Schulwerk emphasizes that students can, through music, develop the total personality by actively and creatively sharing learning experiences within a large group, and by cooperating rather than competing. According to Orff, the student can act as an individual and as a member of a small group within the social context of the large group. As an individual, the learner can speak, conduct, improvise, suggest arrangements of voices and instruments, suggest new approaches and activities, play, dance, or sing a solo part; as a member of a small group the student can speak, sing, play, or respond with movement or dance, all as a cooperating member of the class group. Thus the Schulwerk claims to operate in a manner in which the social values of large group contacts are not lost. The teacher is a member of the group who serves as guide, facilitator, stimulator, and co-worker. After all, music is a social, gregarious activity in which musical performance is shared with others.

Small Groups In an effort to make provision for unique ways of learning, varied stages of development rates, and interests of students, teachers employ small groups. These operate in designated areas within the room, or in the library, conference room, music laboratory, or other nearby places. Activities in which small groups may engage include practicing a music skill from a tape or computer lesson, composing music within stated limits, planning accompaniments, learning to play ukulele or guitar from taped lessons, listening to and analyzing a recorded musical selection, planning a musical performance or related dramatization, and learning songs from recordings. While small groups can be used at any level, they can be more effectively employed at the later primary, elementary, and middle school levels. When students have not participated in small group work, the teacher should begin by organizing one group while the remainder of the students work as a class or as individuals. The teacher then *gradually* organizes additional groups until the time when most or all of the class can be involved in this manner.

There are limitations as well as values of small group work that teachers should know. *First,* small group work should be limited to some purpose that members of the group can share. *Second,* groups should be limited to activities in which the students possess or can be taught the skills needed to develop the activities. *Third,* groups should be limited to activities in which cooperative action is required to achieve stated purposes. If an activity can be completed by an individual or by several individuals working independently, there is no need to organize a group. *Fourth,* groups should be limited to activities in which effective working relationships can be maintained. If interpersonal conflicts and differences in points of view cannot be reconciled, progress cannot be made by forcing individuals to work in a group.

In small groups, students:

Adhere to a cooperatively developed list of expected behaviors.

Clarify their objectives.

Decide upon a tentative plan.

Identify the responsibilities of each individual.

Do research and processing.

Evaluate and make value judgments.

Decide if and how they will share their ideas, learned concepts and skills, and created performance with the large class group.

In the total class group, the members of small groups:

Report to and/or perform for the large group.

Answer questions asked by classmates.

Receive suggestions from peers and teachers as to ways to improve.

Record data from all small groups and analyze and interpret the information; draw conclusions.

Evaluate in terms of purposes.

The teacher circulates among the groups, giving assistance. Close supervision is usually necessary for productive learning to take place. Some groups need only a minimum amount of supervision, whereas others need considerable guidance. The teacher's role is to offer suggestions, ask questions, commend students for good work, be a co-inquirer and resource person when needed. If the teacher finds that some students lack skills to complete a task, skills groups may be organized to help them master these skills as tools before they return to the original small group.

Individualization   Another organizational plan is individualized instruction. In this plan teachers provide experiences for students working individually, sometimes without direct teacher supervision. Individualizing instruction is an attempt to actualize the educational principle of accepting students "where they are" in musical responsiveness and permitting them to progress as far as they are capable. In such a program there are both teacher-directed and student-selected activities. This plan will be detailed in Chapter Five.

Today's teachers face far more complex problems in classroom management than those of their predecessors, resulting from pronounced sociological and educational changes. In the past, students were in the classroom because they and their parents wanted them to be there; today's compulsory attendance laws force them there. In former years, students were apt to be culturally similar; today's students represent various national and world cultures. According to surveys, in a group of thirty students, 50–75 percent will be cooperative and willing, 10–15 percent will be above average to bright and need challenging tasks to prevent boredom, and 15–25 percent will be underachievers who need more individualized attention. One survey states that 10 percent need special help and have minor emotional problems.

Nationally, one-third of the students do not live with their natural parents; there are now more than seven million single-parent families. More than 65 percent of mothers of school students work outside the home, making the school a substitute parent, at least in part. Despite the above, it is heartening to find that most students want to do well, be accepted, obey rules, and will respond reasonably to competent teachers.

Acceptable classroom conduct is something that has to be worked on over extended periods of time with understanding and patience. Discipline problems are too often approached with immediate and forced correction rather than seeking the causes of disruptive behavior and finding ways to prevent it.

Many suburban schools have become increasingly culturally and racially diverse, including black, Hispanic, Vietnamese and other ethnic groups. Forced busing, an example of using public schools as agencies of social change, has been an influence whereby students have found themselves in unfamiliar social relationships charged with anxiety and concern. Uneasiness and apprehension can often be observed. Uncertain human relationships and the lack of flexible space in which to expand instructional programs have combined to result in major behavioral problems. Furthermore, parental resentment of other cultural and ethnic students can aggravate problems. (The authors urge the reader to have faith; this bleak recital presents problems to which you can find solutions, for solutions must and will be found.)

A major problem exists in the teacher's reaction to minority students. Many teachers are carriers of invalid information and preconceived ideas about these students that they reveal unconsciously and that result in adverse relations between student and teacher. In other words, teachers' unconscious prejudices, revealed to students in ways often indirect and subtle but understood by students, can culminate in a threatening and suspicious atmosphere that can have disastrous effects on instruction and discipline. A good exercise for teachers is to draw up a list of questions to use to assess the effect they as teachers may have on students. The following list may be revised and expanded:

1. Do I place derogatory labels on students such as "culturally and economically deprived," or "learning impaired"?

2. Do I use body language that communicates negative reactions? (Do I avoid touching, eye contact, or listening to students? Why? What harm am I doing by this?)

3. Do I use descriptive words—dumb, lazy, slow—and stereotyped racial slurs that show disgust and nonacceptance?

4. Do I allow the student(s) to become isolated or ignored in class?

5. Do I correct their language too often and in improper ways?

6. Do I select relevant and significant content when studying music of ethnic groups?

7. Do I select and use music content, skills, behavioral objectives, teaching procedures, and student activities compatible with the ethnically different and special learners' learning styles, abilities, and past cultural experiences?

8. Do I give all learners an equal chance to participate at their levels of performance?

9. Do I give minorities and special learners appropriate time to reply to questions during the entire music period?

10. Do I have minority students perform meaningless menial tasks?

11. Am I overly solicitous for their attention to win favor and acceptance from them because I don't know what else to do?

Encouraging Self-Control

Class control is a complicated process, involving many different personalities, each unique. There are no specific solutions that will apply in all situations. Every teacher is different, and each must determine what techniques function best in terms of his or her personality and those of the students. In order for learning to take place, there must be appropriate order and control. The nature of the activity determines to some extent the type of order and control. Positive behavior is furthered through teacher-pupil planning in which students have a major part in defining the conditions necessary to learn most effectively and deciding how to achieve them. The feeling is developed that the classroom is the *students'* classroom and that each student has a definite responsibility in helping establish and maintain the standards by which it functions. In such a classroom the teacher helps develop the importance of the individual, a sense of respect for others, and a maximum of self-control. Since self-control develops slowly, and students regress from time to time, teachers and students evaluate the established standards for each activity, their success in maintaining these standards, and what they need to do next time to improve. Standards for a listening activity will obviously be different from those for a singing activity. After standards are well established and incorporated into the behavior of most students, teachers work with individuals having difficulty, analyzing behavior and planning ways of modifying it. A factor that helps greatly to alleviate behavior problems is found within music itself. Music can provide a variety of activities from which can be selected those suited to each student's interest and ability.

There are many factors that influence students' behavior. Most misbehavior is the direct result of conditions in the learning environment. The misbehavior might have been prevented had the teacher given proper consideration to the following:

Physical Comfort. Children who are too cold, too warm, too crowded, who must breathe stale air, who cannot see or hear what is going on, who are not comfortably seated, have been seated too long, or have been physically active for too long, often misbehave. Students should be seated in ways to facilitate their participation in, and concentration on, the activity at hand.

Organization and Proper Routine. Teachers who are well prepared, and who have made provision for proper directions and routine, usually project a feeling of confidence and security that is reflected in the behavior of students. Students sense insecurity in teachers and are disturbed by it. Therefore, teachers must make careful plans for learning activities, and assemble all materials needed in developing them. They must also give attention to such details as how to begin and conclude the lesson, how to keep it progressing steadily and thoroughly toward realization of the intended purposes, how to seat or group students for specific activities, how to distribute and collect materials, when to change or alternate activities, and how to evaluate and summarize with students the accomplishments of the day.

There is no substitute for clearly defined and enforced policies of performance and behavior that have been created through the combined efforts of staff, students, and parents. Ordinarily, classroom rules should be drawn up by teacher-student efforts, reviewed often, and revised when necessary. When students have a part in making logical rules of class management and conduct, they understand them and are much more apt to observe them.

Challenging Every Child. Students who are engaged in activities that are interesting and worthwhile to them are normally well behaved. Those who fail to find interest and purpose in what they are asked to do become bored and often disturb others.

The Teacher. Teachers know that students reflect their enthusiasm, interest, and confidence. This confidence is based upon the knowledge that what they are doing is significant to the physical, social, emotional, aesthetic, and intellectual development of students. Teachers should be happy, well-adjusted, and truly want to teach. They assist students in solving their own behavior problems, but when unable to do this in specific cases, will seek assistance. Teachers know that prestige will be lost if they repeatedly send students to the principal, and do this only as a last resort. Teachers' behavior is consistent, understanding, and firm, and reflects sincere interest in every student. They have a good sense of humor, see humor in many situations, and know that humor, when properly used, can help in the solution of behavior problems. Teachers refrain from using ridicule and sarcasm and are mature in their behavior. As adults, they are objective, not overly friendly or emotionally attached to children, and if they are in error, or do not know answers to problems, they admit it. Teachers retain self-control and are dependable adults in whom students can have confidence and faith. As much as possible, individual students' behavior problems are solved privately, since this is usually more effective and less disturbing to both the troublemaker and the class. The class is not made to suffer for what one or two students may do. Teachers are generous with positive reinforcement whenever it is deserved. Their speaking voices are pleasant and vary in pitch and intensity. They know that a tense voice disturbs students. Their singing voices are natural, sincere, and pleasing. Teachers approach difficult situations calmly. In order to accomplish these things they tend to their own physical and mental health by getting sufficient rest and wholesome recreation. Their personal appearance is such that it increases the students' respect and serves to remind them to be neat, clean, and orderly.

Teachers know students' names in a well-behaved class. Books and materials are distributed after directions for an activity have been determined, or after standards for the activity have been reviewed. Teachers anticipate possible problems and plan ways to offset them. They intersperse appropriate music throughout the day or period to relieve tensions and unify the group. Through thoughtful selection of music a teacher can calm or stimulate the students as desired. Small difficulties can be avoided by simple actions. For example, if a teacher sees a student about to trip another in rhythmic movement, or about to throw an eraser, he or she can ask the student a direct question that will bring him or her back into the group activity at once. The teacher keeps eye contact with the various members of the class at all times. Attention cannot be focused on notation in a music book or on piano accompaniments so exclusively that the class cannot be seen; this necessitates complete familiarity with the song being taught and its accompaniment. The division of the class at times into several groups, one singing, one accompanying, and the third evaluating the musical performance of others, is conducive to class control because it gives every student something specific to do. Other purposeful ways to involve students include tending the record player, pressing the chord bars of an Autoharp, playing the bells, conducting, or interpreting music creatively through body movement or dramatization. The teacher usually refuses to talk when students are talking, and when he or she begins to speak, does so in a low-pitched, calm, positive, soft, but easily heard voice.

All behavior is goal-centered and has specific causes. Teachers must continually collect information about students in order to understand the motives for their behavior and to attempt to deal with the causes of it. When a student must be corrected, this should be done with due consideration for cultural and family background and motives. Because every student is different, the manner of rebuke appropriate for one may not be appropriate for another.

When the teacher shows consistently, and over time, that each student is recognized, respected, and possesses dignity and personal worth, many will be motivated to perform school tasks that far exceed normal expectations. Effective teachers must be optimists, and will by their actions consistently reveal insights, knowledge, and understandings that convince students that each one has something unique, and possibly great, to offer. The teacher should make a constant effort to see every favorable aspect of a student, recognizing it and reinforcing it, thus giving that student a feeling of success and accomplishment. The ultimate goal of the teacher is to assist the student in developing the ability and desire to assume responsibility for his or her own behavior.

At times a student's behavior may originate in situations beyond the control of the music teacher, as implied in the following questions:

Did the student encounter an unpleasant situation in the previous class?

Did the student's parents exhibit serious conflicts, disagreements, and arguments this morning?

Did one of the parents desert the family?

Does the student feel unaccepted and unwanted at home?

Did a close family member or friend suffer a serious accident, illness, or death?

Was the safety or health of the student felt to be in jeopardy?

Did the student lose the attention and support of a friend?

Teachers who care about each student seek an understanding of the abilities, family, special interests, and special problems of that student. They will demonstrate this caring in scores of specific, tangible acts. As a result they will have the ingredients of a well-disciplined classroom, one where learning can take place in a friendly and accepting atmosphere. Success should be planned for each student, remembering the old saying, "Nothing succeeds like success." When nothing seems to solve a discipline problem, don't give up. Remember that some students function best in a setting where interaction with peers is limited. The teacher may need to isolate a student in a part of the classroom temporarily until he or she feels able to become positively involved in the class.

Remember that students need to know the purpose of assigned tasks and the boundaries of permissible behavior. Madsen and Madsen (1974) offer the following guidelines for establishing classroom rules:

1. Involve the students in developing the rules.
2. Keep rules brief and to the point.
3. Phrase rules, when possible, in a positive way (e.g., "Sit quietly while I work with the clarinets," instead of "Don't talk, band.")
4. Remind the class of rules at times *other* than when someone has misbehaved.
5. Post rules and review them regularly.

Some additional suggestions for managing student behavior follow:

1. Be fair, firm, consistent, and professional in all relationships with students.
2. Have a few realizable rules and enforce them with firmness.
3. Consider student reactions to your facial expressions, body language, and movements. Be sure that they reflect sincerity, personal warmth, and lack of prejudice.
4. Try removing the disruptive student from the site of the disturbance for a short time (2–5 minutes).

5. Conduct student-teacher conferences to explore reasons for misbehavior and to determine what student and teacher can do to correct it.

6. Disassociate the misbehavior from the offender, showing that while you may abhor the behavior, you continue to respect and like the culprit.

7. Use visual aids to help students know what is expected of them. For example, print the order of activities, page numbers, etc., on the chalkboard or show it on an overhead projector so all students know the sequence of what is planned.

8. Minimize nonmusical tasks; emphasize the musical ones.

9. Prior to the arrival of students at the music room, arrange the room and have all materials ready and easily available.

10. Anticipate arrival of students in the music room. Have a smile and greeting ready, conveying that you are happy to see them. Know each one by name as soon as possible and use names when addressing students.

11. Try planning to give every student something to do the instant he or she enters the music room. For example, in a chorus rehearsal, the first student will go to the piano and sound the beginning pitch of the song placed there. He or she and the second student will begin singing their parts, and all other students will go to their places, find their music, and join in as soon as possible.

12. Always begin class promptly so that students will know that this is the established pattern in your room.

13. Be certain that every student, including the less capable and the gifted, is actively involved. Remember that students are naturally active, and unless they are active in ways you have planned, they will be active in unpredictable ways. So, keep them busy!

14. Be imaginative and operate the class in a way that, although all understand the established routines, you will manage to vary your approach just enough to "keep them guessing." Add interesting chords or rhythm patterns to drills. Plan a surprise dramatization. Change the furniture, wall charts, or bulletin boards. Make your room and class an interesting and challenging experience.

15. Make your enthusiasm contagious. Show it in your movements, facial expressions and voice.

16. When speaking, use proper diction, appropriate volume, and good voice projection. Speak in short sentences. Speaking too fast can disrupt communication and cause misunderstandings that create discipline problems. From time to time, tape your voice in class and study how you might make it more effective.

17. Avoid competing with extraneous noise.

18. Refrain from presenting too many ideas, concepts, or activities all at once or too rapidly. Simplify by teaching a few things thoroughly rather than many things superficially.

19. Do your best to eliminate interruptions.

20. Capitalize on student interest and enthusiasm; use it, don't squelch it!

21. Learners tend to develop discipline problems when they are not challenged, so be sure that your lesson is arranged to be a challenge to every student at his or her individual performance and interest level.

22. Avoid talking too much; make music instead.

23. Let the class assume some of the responsibility for aspects of the lesson.

24. Give students an opportunity to discuss and share musical discoveries, questions, and performances with peers.

25. Close each lesson on a challenging, pleasant, and positive note. At intervals, ask the class what they now know or can do that they did not know or could not do a week, month, or semester ago. They should be able to discover their gains in musical knowledges and skills, thereby building pride and improving morale (evaluation). Then ask if they think there are things they could learn or might perform better (planning for the future).

EXPLORATORY ACTIVITIES

1. What are your arguments in favor of having music specialists teach all the music in a school? What are the disadvantages of this?
2. What are your arguments for having classroom teachers responsible for all music teaching in a school? What are disadvantages of this?
3. What can be said in favor of plans in which specialists and classroom teachers share responsibility for teaching music? Are there disadvantages, and if so, what are they?
4. What is the difference between a music supervisor and a music consultant?
5. Study the example from a music series book (pp. 50–51). In how many ways might a music series assist teachers of music? What are series books unable to provide? When does a teacher need a variety of instructional materials?
6. Design a music center for your ideal classroom. Detail your expectations or standards for students who are to work in the center.
7. Describe the music program in a local school. Who teaches music? How much time is allotted for music instruction? Does the school have a usable and helpful curriculum guide? What music series or other materials are used? What equipment is available? If a specialist is employed, what space is provided, how many schools does the specialist service, and how many students does that person teach each week? Does the specialist assist classroom teachers?
8. Interview a classroom teacher or a music specialist. Ask that person to identify strengths and weaknesses of music instruction in his or her school.
9. Observe a school music class to find out how behavior problems are handled. If you find few such problems, account for that situation.
10. In your observation (question 9), did you find the physical arrangement of the classroom appropriate for the activities? What organizational plans were employed, and were they best for the tasks involved? Was the teacher's behavior appropriate for the type of learning taking place? Was the instruction teacher-directed? direct instruction? conceptual-process learning? creative-exploratory? individualized? large group? small group? a combination of two or more of the above?

References and Materials

General BOLIN, MARY JANE, "Building an ARC in New York City," *Music Educators Journal,* October 1978, pp. 42–49. About an arts resource center.

EPSTEIN, CHARLOTTE, *Classroom Management and Teaching: Persistent Problems and Rational Solutions.* Reston, Va.: Reston Publishing Co., Inc., 1979. A behavior modification approach.

GEERDES, ARNOLD P., *Planning and Equipping Educational Music Facilities.* Reston, Va.: Music Educators National Conference, 1975.

MADSEN, CHARLES H., and CLIFFORD K. MADSEN, *Teaching/Discipline: A Positive Approach for Educational Development*. Boston: Allyn and Bacon, Inc., 1974.

Music Educators Journal, Music in Open Education Issue, April 1974.

RATHS, LOUIS E., et al., *Values and Teaching: Working with Values in the Classroom*. Columbus, Ohio: Charles E. Merrill Books, Inc., 1966.

STRADLEY, WILLIAM E., and RICHARD D. ASPINALL, *Discipline in the Middle School*. New York: The Center for Applied Research in Education, Inc., 1975.

WENNER, GENE C., et al., "IMPACT," *Music Educators Journal,* January 1973.

Resources for Middle School

ATHEY, MARGARET, and GWEN HOTCHKISS, *Galaxy of Games for the Music Class*. West Nyack, N.Y.: Parker Publications, 1975.

———, *Treasury of Individual Activities for the Music Class*. West Nyack, N.Y.: Parker Publications, 1977.

BEETHOVEN, JANE, and CARMEN MOORE, *Rock It*. Sherman Oaks, Calif.: Alfred Publishing Co., 1984. Textbook, workbook, recordings, and teacher's manual concerned with popular music and rock.

BENNETT, MICHAEL, "Pop Listening Guide," Memphis: Michael Bennett, 3149 Southern Avenue, Memphis, Tenn. 38111.

———, "Make the Top 40 Work for You," *Music Educators Journal,* January 1975. pp 32–34.

Keyboard Publications, 1346 Chapel Street, New Haven, Conn. 06511. Electronic music and many other subjects. Recordings.

KONOWITZ, BERT, *Jazz Classroom Activities*. Syosset, N.Y.: Plans Ahead, Inc., 12 Hemlock Drive.

———, *Vocal Improvisation Method*. Sherman Oaks, Calif.: Alfred Publishing Company.

METZ, DONALD, *Teaching General Music in Grades 6–9*. Columbus, Ohio: Charles E. Merrill Publishing Company, 1980.

MONSOUR, SALLY, and MARGARET PERRY, *A Junior High School Music Handbook,* 2nd ed. Englewood Cliffs, N.J.: Prentice-Hall, Inc., 1970.

Playing the Guitar. A satellite for individual study. Morristown, N.J.: Silver Burdett Company, 1975.

SNYDER, JERRY, *Basic Guitar Instructor,* Vol 1. New York: Charles Hansen, 1974.

THOMPSON, DICK, "Plugging into Pop at the Junior High Level," *Music Educators Journal,* December 1977, pp. 54–59.

VULLIAMY, GRAHAM and LEE, eds., *Pop Music in School*. Cambridge: Cambridge University Press, 1976.

chapter five

Individualization of Instruction*
and Special Learners

Individualized instruction is the practice of planning a program based upon an individual's learning style, developmental level, cultural background, and past achievements, in order to make possible that student's optimum growth in cognitive, psychomotor, and affective learning. This is in marked contrast to an approach in which students are continually drilled on skills and facts in order to bring them to the same performance level of the other students in a class. The authors believe that individualized learning can take place when each student is planned for as a unique human being, whether the student is in a large group or a small group, is one of a pair of peer learners, is in a one-to-one relationship with a teacher, or is working alone. The musical needs of each student are met when (1) musical experiences begin where the student presently is (a teacher should not assume that all students of the same age have identical musical backgrounds), (2) the curriculum is

---

* The authors are indebted to Dr. Sylvia Cary for much of the following discussion of individualization of instruction, including the charts and drawings. The information was reproduced or adapted from her unpublished dissertation, "Individualized Music Instruction—Traditional Music Instruction: Relationships of Music Achievement, Music Performance, Music Attitude, Music Aptitude, and Reading in Classes of Fifth Grade Students," doctoral dissertation, University of Oregon, 1981, Dissertation Abstracts International, 1981, Vol. 42, Number 10 (Order Number DA8201812), Copyright © 1981 by Sylvia Estes Cary.

diversified through a wide variety of learning alternatives that are offered concurrently rather than consecutively, (3) planning is made for continual progress by each individual, and (4) continuous assessment and feedback are given. Since grouping has been discussed before, this chapter will concentrate largely upon ways to teach individuals apart from group instruction.

When today's teachers examine the make-up of school classes, they may find results of Public Law 94-142, which made mandatory the "mainstreaming" of many students with special problems. They may also find gifted students, another category of learners with special needs. Thus, today's teachers view the classroom quite differently from the way most teachers of earlier times viewed it. Students are now helped to regard themselves as unique persons who need not necessarily be able to conform to the standards of developmental levels or to those of other students. However, teachers find norms useful in the process of analyzing, comparing, and diagnosing individual students, a process necessary in planning for a learning growth based upon accepting them "where they are" in musical responsiveness. Many teachers now plan so that each student will progress as far as he or she is capable. Extensive planning and meticulous records are required in an individualized program. Public Law 94-142 demands that a personal program (Individualized Education Program or I.E.P.) be planned for each mainstreamer and that records be kept. However, this is a logical approach for every student, not just for the special learner.

The reader has probably already sensed that the fact that students study by themselves is only an indication that individualized instruction *might* be present. Unless the teacher has studied each learner from a diagnostic view and a program for each learner has been planned, there are only individuals studying; true individualized instruction is not yet in place. It is obvious, then, that a teacher is unable to institute individualized learning in the educational sense in a short time.

The Informal Classroom

The informal classroom represents a distinct change in beliefs and techniques. While it consists of teacher-directed activities, the teacher addresses the entire class infrequently. The classroom is arranged into learning stations (centers, laboratories, studios, computers) and each contains an activity of challenge and interest. During most of the school day individuals and small groups move from station to station. Many directions for each activity are in written and printed form. Some directions are on tapes or recordings; some are given directly by the teacher. The activities are created by imaginative and resourceful teachers and students to match the maturity, learning style, needs, and interests of each learner. Students are free to learn from each other and in all areas of the curriculum, because learning is not compartmentalized into discrete areas. An elementary classroom may have as few as one or two music stations, while a music room could have thirty. Individualized instruction per se does not dictate a particular school or method of instruction. The techniques can operate along a continuum of choices from behavioristic to humanistic, conservative to radical, and strictly structured to loosely structured.

In addition to the usual equipment for music study, the music stations require teacher preparation of various types of meaningful materials in the form of direction sheet, booklet, learning packet, chart, manipulative instrument or object. Some of these are housed in boxes.

Flexibility of the environment, sound and sight control, and careful storage planning are essential if the concomitant needs of flexibility in the areas of instructional size (from individual to total group), communication modes, instructional content, rate and depth of learning, assessment, and psychological needs of all students are to be met. One plan developed by Cary leaves a large circle-type seating area in the middle of the room that can be used for whole class activities. This also provides an area in which easily movable materials can be temporarily placed. At the same time there are permanently established areas for storage, materials, instruments, and stations. The hallway outside the music room or classroom, storage closets, and the library can be used. Figures 5.1 and 5.2 show diagrams of the music room, storage, and hallway that illustrate the physical implementation of flexibility, sight and sound control, and storage.

The sound-producing equipment should generate balanced sounds, with no sound source conspicuous by being distinctly louder than others. Some can be pointed away from the rest; some sounds can be absorbed in part by drapes and acoustically treated walls; others can be muted by sound-absorbent partitions. The floor should be carpeted, if possible, to absorb more sound. The entire area demands acoustical study to balance and soften the many sounds that characterize individual and small group instruction. The use of closets, hallways, and vacant rooms helps to reduce the problem of undesirable sounds interfering with learning. Sounds that seem cacophonous can in reality be harmonious if the students are intensely involved in what they are doing. The attitude of the music teacher, other teachers in the building, students, and administration must be one of acceptance of a certain level of sound.

Sight barriers are important psychologically, especially at the beginning of new individualized experiences. Many students are more distracted by what they see than by what they hear. Not only do sight barriers aid in concentration, the dividers also mark off perimeters of learning stations. These boundaries, in terms of classroom control, help to avoid disputes that arise when one person interferes with another. Later in the experience, often just the hint of a sight barrier is enough to keep order.

Being able to store equipment, instruments, files, and materials, but still having instant access to them, is another difficult demand. One teacher's plan and diary follows:

The music room for the individualized instruction group had built-in storage shelves along most of the two long walls. It also had two movable book cabinets

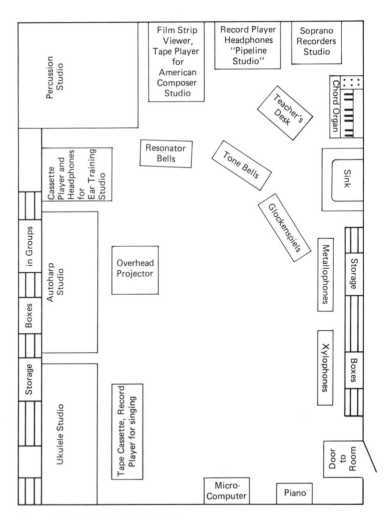

Figure 5.1. MUSIC ROOM PLAN

that served as dividers. The phonograph recordings were kept in the portable book shelves and on some of the built-in shelving. Other equipment was kept on carts and tables in the places designated for its use. These included film-strip projector and cassette player for the American composers station, record player and headphones for "Pipeline," the cassette player and headphones for Ear Training Concepts, the overhead projector, the reel-to-reel tape recorder, and the cassettes and record player for the singing station.

An initial problem in setting up this equipment was the lack of sufficient electrical outlets. This was solved by purchasing several three-way plugs. Many extension cords had to be taped (and often retaped) to the floor to avoid hazards.

The musical instruments were kept or stored basically where they were used. In the percussion area the bass and snare drums and roto toms were on stands. The hand drums, cow bells, maracas, gongs, etc., were in shelves or counter-tops. The ukuleles and Autoharps were on the countertops of the built-in

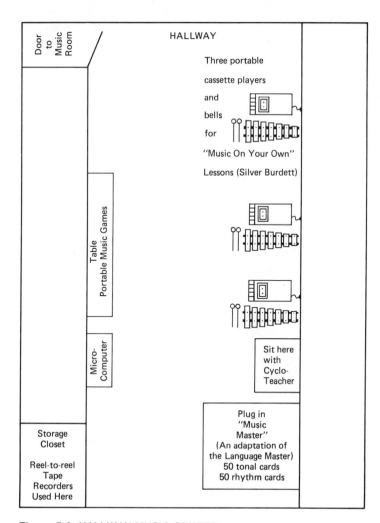

Figure 5.2. HALLWAY MUSIC CENTER

shelves. Soprano recorders were in special boxes with divided compartments in the recorder area. Resonator and tone bells and glockenspiels were on table tops; these tables had open shelves underneath where mallets were kept. The xylophones, metallophones, piano, and chord organs remained in their permanent places.

A most difficult problem was how and where to keep each student's files and materials. Most of the time approximately seventy students were in the program. Carrying their materials and records of progress back and forth from their home rooms was not a good idea. The music teacher collected thirty-five large, identical ski boot boxes and labelled each for two students. The first week of the project these were stacked in one area and the classroom managers called out students' names to come to get their boxes. This took far too much time but was not quite as disastrous as having all students grabbing at once for their files. The second week a better plan was implemented, and by the third week the students could get their boxes immediately with no problems. This successful plan scattered the boxes in permanent places all around the room. Then, as the students entered the room they could simultaneously, quickly, and quietly get their materials. [See Figure 5.1.]

The Master File of all the instructional materials was kept in open cardboard boxes, color coded and alphabetized. Through trial and error it was decided that only the teacher and the daily classroom managers had permission to get into this file to distribute material.

Teachers' Responsibilities in Individualized Instruction

Individualized instruction places heavy responsibility on the teacher to diagnose each student's musical background, capabilities, needs, and interests, to prescribe for and with each student performance objectives and sequenced learning activities to realize these objectives, and to provide the necessary instructional resources. The teacher must further assume the responsibility for establishing reasonable time limits for each task. Upon completion of the task, the teacher and student assess the degree of progress made and then move forward through the cycle described above, hopefully at a higher and more challenging level. The teacher who uses these procedures must not only plan and equip learning centers but must also keep detailed records on each student. In a class of thirty or more students and one teacher, it is obvious that this teacher must extend him- or herself by means of aides, programmed instruction, modules, student tutors, and a variety of instructional materials.

The teacher's major focus should be on developing intellectual processes, though not to the point of excluding outcomes. Students should learn facts, but these facts are normally those acquired painlessly through the pursuit of an interest. More importantly, students should develop self-confidence in ability to achieve, and to acquire skills that satisfy their curiosity. If an objective is to prepare students to enjoy music throughout their lives, teachers must assist them in developing appropriate skills that can be applied to the solution of all types of musical problems and that will increase their sensitivity to an appreciation of music. To have at one's command the process of seeking knowledge is to have gained a basis for security in a changing world.

Classroom Management Concepts of classroom management originate and evolve from all areas of individualized instruction and in turn influence all components of individualization. Individualized instruction may be a variety of opportunities, but without workable techniques of classroom management it can become a variety of disasters. (See classroom management, pp. 65–71.) A common misconception among music teachers is that an individualized classroom is one in which all the students are quietly plugged into headphones, listening to music and perhaps writing. A few students may be doing this, but most of these learning alternatives are sound-filled interactions between the student and music.

Classroom management is implemented through transition from traditional classrooms, discipline and ground rules, grouping, scheduling and time management, matching learners and stations (assessment and prescribing), labeling stations, and through the instructional materials—both teacher-made and commercial. The transition period from a traditional music classroom to an individualized program must be carefully planned for both the teacher and the students. The teacher must be one who strongly desires to move toward individualization. This attitude correlates with the teacher whose personal job satisfaction does not depend upon continual direct teaching of the authoritarian type. Student readiness for transition is vitally important. The transition can begin on a small scale, with one, then two and more learning stations added to the customary class group instruction until, if desired, a complete transition has taken place. A second way is to change to a fully individualized program at once. A third is for the entire school curriculum to be organized around the informal or open classroom concept. Following are some ideas that were used to implement the students' transition into individualized instruction.

1. Positive attitudes were developed by discussing the fact that everyone works differently and could do different things at different times if classroom activities and behavior were appropriately managed.
2. A plan was discussed and developed as follows: first, one small group would work on something different during the main group activity; second, when this was successful, two small groups could work concurrently with the main group; third, the class could function with all small groups; and fourth, as students were ready, individual work could occur simultaneously with small group work.
3. Students were involved in the physical demands. They manipulated materials and moved equipment during the transition phase so that they helped decide where best to place everything. The final room plan was derived through this trial-and-error process.
4. As students experienced moving around the room, the hallway, and out of doors, they gradually made a transition from a seated classroom to a moving classroom.
5. Students discussed and helped establish working rules such as the following: "Put your materials in your file box when finished." "Play your instruments softly." "When you enter the room, look at the sign that tells you either to be seated as a group in the central area or to go to your current individualized area."
6. New studios were introduced one by one and explained to the entire class. For example, the Music Master machine was demonstrated to the whole class; then it became a studio to be assigned. The American Composers filmstrip, recording, and reading and writing materials were demonstrated and used as an entire class strategy; then it also became a studio to be assigned.
7. Students' responsibilities in record keeping were introduced. Each form was explained to the class, and the students began to use it before the next form was introduced.

In establishing discipline and ground rules, students should have both the freedom and the responsibility to operate within defined perimeters. A simple set of necessary and clearly stated ground rules make a program manageable, and if the teacher involves the students in establishing them, the students are usually more cooperative.

Signals other than verbal are useful because of the level of sound that can exist and because students are working in different areas of the room. A most effective signal is the flicking of the lights for instant quiet. The teacher or student managers can then proceed with announcements. Overhead projectors can be used for messages following the flicking lights.

Students can make large charts listing rules as they become necessary. Examples are: "Work within your studio area." "Do your record keeping." "Do not keep anyone else from learning." "Only the teacher and the managers get materials from the master file."

Individualized music instruction has some specific psychological issues that the teacher can address:

1. Analyze quickly which sounds at the stations are productive and which are not. Then intervene in a positive way with those that are not.
2. Group students carefully. Be aware of people who behave negatively when put in close proximity.
3. Calmly accept some lack of order and messiness. A certain amount of it is inevitable.
4. Be aware of students needing help and guidance and step in before they become so frustrated as to become disruptive.
5. Establish the idea that the students are becoming more independent and will not be constantly watched. At the same time, however, establish that it is easy to notice those who are preventing others from learning and that they will be disciplined.

Grouping Grouping needs to be examined because the emphasis on the individual learner is sometimes confusing to those seeking to understand informal types of class organization.

> The motivation for learning often comes from interaction with others. A music classroom where all activities are conducted in small groups or individually will eventually lose the satisfaction that comes from combining efforts toward a common musical goal or from receiving evidence of successful achievements through peer response. The teacher must plan a regular time when students can share the skills and understandings they have gained while working independently. The connection between individualized tasks and classroom musical activities must be clearly understood by the individual student. Without this motivation for learning, the individualized atmosphere can become as sterile and as non-productive as some feel the traditional music classroom has been. (Meske and Rinehart, 1975)

Scheduling and Time Management Scheduling and time management are the teacher's responsibility. Instructional timing is as vital to the individualized structure as it is for the traditional approach. After initial guidance of students into the program and after observation of their responses, learners' needs and interests dictate their individual, small-group, and large-group involvements with music, and a schedule is planned from this practical base. Many types of schedules can be found.

The short- and long-range plans are taken from the overall time plan of the year. In daily planning the teacher has to plan for the beginning, middle, and end of each session. Sometimes the class functions as a total group at the beginning of a lesson, then changes to a different mode of working. At other times the class can spend the last few minutes all together. Sometimes both the beginning and end are total group work. There are many other combinations such as three weeks of single and small-group work and then two weeks of full-group work, or a month working on a program, then back to an individualized mode. In any case, the teacher has to plan enough time at the end of each class period for everything to be recorded and put away so that students are ready to leave exactly at the time scheduled.

Individual time assignment is somewhat built into the learning materials—single tasks or contracts to full packets. There still has to be flexibility for pacing; a single task might take one student less than one music period to complete whereas another student might require two music periods to finish.

Matching Learners and Stations Matching learners and stations involves assessing the student's progress and deciding (usually with the student) what learning and station should be next. Before students are assigned to or select a station or project, the teacher must know whether or not each learner is able to complete the task successfully. A correct diagnosis is paramount to the outcome. What musical knowledges, skills, and experiences are necessary as prerequisites? A station could require, for example, singing ability, note-reading level, or Autoharp experience. What other knowledges and skills might be necessary? (Do students have the vocabulary needed in order to follow direction? Can they operate a tape recorder?) How can the teacher answer the above questions?

An ideal diagnostic process would assess as many aspects of the student's skills and traits as possible. These could include reading level, learning style (visual, auditory, kinesthetic, mixed), cognitive style (concrete, abstract), need for structure, mode of instruction, social style preference (from alone to large group), family history, and peer relationships. In music, performance levels in moving to music, listening, singing, playing, reading, writing, and creating, and cognitive understandings of the elements and structure of music would be included.

The following are possible means that can be used in both pre- and post-diagnosing: standardized tests, teacher-made diagnostic tests, aptitude tests, demonstrations of skills or performances, observation of student behavior, anecdotal records, sociograms, personal journals, questionnaires, and role playing.

Assigning the learning station or project is next in the process. This prescribing and the student's success in following it is the heart of individualized instruction. A major difficulty for the music teacher is finding the time to do it. Students must be conferred with and individually assigned on the basis of the individual need. Some teachers use aides, volunteers, or older students to free themselves for individual conferencing. A teacher can con-fer with each student quietly while the whole class is watching a film or doing other work that would free the teacher. The teacher and student can also make next assignment and station decisions while individualized work is taking place during regular class time. Sometimes the teacher manages to have a "free" period during the day when students can come in to discuss their progress and next assignment. Developing project and assignment charts that match the equipment and materials of the room is a must for classroom management. Figure 5.3 is *only part* of a chart, but it illustrates how to list materials in the room and match names with them.

Labeling Stations and Materials   There are many types of stations from which teachers can select to serve learning situations. They usually bear descriptive titles although some teachers give numbers or letters to theirs. Many are named from musical elements to be studied: Rhythm, Melody, Harmony, Form, Tone Qualities, Dynamics, Tempo, and sometimes Music Fundamentals or Theory. Others may be Guitar, Autoharp, Ukulele, Keyboard Lab, Electronic Lab, Filmstrip, or Programmed Materials. Many teachers invent titles that amuse learners, such as Make and Play, Drums Away, Fun and Games, Keyboard Capers, Read All About It, Play that Tune, Listen! Composer's Corner, and Make a Tone Row.

Examples of activities are adding an Autoharp* accompaniment to a new song learned from tape recording and/or notation; creating an original melody on the bells and notating it; comparing the rhythm patterns of three different songs; creating a melody on piano black keys with the right hand and adding an accompaniment on black keys played by the left hand; transposing a tune one can play on a xylophone to another key; and exploring the synthesizer. There are endless possibilities of this nature that teachers can arrange for students. Some should be available without specific instructions so that students can explore them according to their own interests. Assistance can come from commercial sources such as the music textbook companies. For example, the Macmillan *MusicCenter* activity cards, Silver Burdett's *On Your Own,* with tapes and printed material, and Holt, Rinehart and Winston's *Individualized Music Program,* with tapes and printed materials. Educational Record Sales, 157 Chambers St., New York City 10007, offers recordings for individual and small group singing: "Johnny Can Sing Too," vols. 1, 2, 3, "Song Dramatization for Children," "Song Rhythms"; for rhythmic activities: "Exploring the Rhythm Instruments," "Introducing the Rhythm Instruments," and "Our First Rhythm Band," vols 1, 2; and for listening: "Listening to a Recording." New materials are constantly becoming available and are frequently exhibited at conventions of music educators. Computer-controlled games are available from Milton Bradley, Parker Brothers, Tandy (Radio Shack) and other companies. Currently popular games are *Simon, Super-Simon, Merlin,* and *Electronic Repeat.*

* A source of learning station activities for Autoharp is *Teaching Music with the Autoharp* (Northbrook, Ill.: Music Education Group.)

| | Week_____ | | Week_____ | |
	First Day (Name)	Second Day (Name)	First Day (Name)	Second Day (Name)
Classroom Management Conductor	1.			
	2.			
	3.			
Ear Training Concepts (cassette tape recorder)	1.			
	2.			
Singing (record playing bells, cassette tape recorder)	1.			
	2.			
Ukulele	1.			
	2.			
	3.			
	4.			
	5.			
	6.			
	7.			
	8.			
Autoharp	1.			
	2.			
	3.			
	4.			
Chord Organ	1.			
Piano	1.			
Music Master Cards	1.			
American Composers (filmstrip viewer, record player)	1.			
	2.			
Microcomputer	1.			

Figure 5.3. **STATION ASSIGNMENT CHART.** The number of blanks indicates quantity of equipment.

Designing and Labeling Materials Designing and labeling materials are perhaps more difficult than setting up stations. To be truly individualized, the activities and materials at the stations have to provide for, include, and label the following:

> Social style (from one person to a full ensemble)
> Rate and length of learning (from single task to full packet)

Cognitive, skill, and affective areas (cognitive: melody, harmony, rhythm, etc.; skill: moving, singing, playing instruments, etc.; affective: valuing and related areas.)

Difficulty level (I, II, III, etc.)

Communication mode (instruction on tape, through reading, directly from teacher, or other)

Place of work (station name)

Content labeled with course goals and objectives

It is possible to plan a materials structure that provides for all of these criteria. For several years a fully individualized program was planned, implemented, described, and the results presented in research by Sylvia Cary, who developed a structure that allowed for and labeled all of the above criteria. The materials were labeled and color coded in a way that helped both students and teacher. The following list explains the color coding in five areas across the top of all materials.

1. Number of people
    solo—black
    duet—blue
    trio—green
    quartet—purple
    ensemble—yellow
2. Lessons in packet
    single task—black
    minipacket—pink
    full packet—green
3. Difficulty level
    level I—blue
    level II—blue (all levels in blue)
4. Station
    singing—orange
    musicology—brown
    percussion—purple
    movement—pink
    listening—orange
    ukuleles—green
    etc.
5. Elements/Concepts
    melody—red
    harmony—red (all concepts in red)

A specific example of labeling is:

Trio   Minipacket   Level III   Melody   Recorder Station

Under this would be the goal, objectives, and activities in the cognitive, psychomotor, and affective domains.

If a long yellow line across the top of the packet preceded all of the rest of the information, it indicated that the main idea was coordinated with other studios. This plan allows the teacher occasionally to assign a coordinated main idea to many. For practical reasons it was decided to put all of the teacher-made resources on ditto paper even though more attractive materials could be used. In this way additional sheets could be made as necessary from the ditto masters. The color coding was added with pens. The Master File contained everything in color-coded folders made from large sheets of construction paper. Commercial materials and learning packages were helpful additions. A listing of them was color coded, labeled, and included in the Master File. Examples I through IV are some of the developed materials.

EXAMPLE I: Solo   Single Lesson   Level I   Metronome   Percussion Studio

Goal: To understand the purpose of a metronome and play with a metronome

Objectives: Play various percussion instruments at different speeds with a metronome. Read and play rhythm patterns using ♩ ♫ ♩ 𝅗𝅥

Domains: Cognitive, Psychomotor

My name is: _____

You will need the metronome and various percussion instruments.

1. Set the metronome at 90. Listen.

2. Strike a drum with each click. Try other instruments.
   Is it a steady beat? _____

3. Set the metronome at 120 and play along.
   Was it faster or slower? _____

4. Pick your own setting and play.
   What setting did you choose? _____

5. Put the three settings in order from slowest to fastest.

   _____ _____ _____

6. Practice playing the rhythms below at different settings.

♩	♩	♫	♩		♩	♩	𝅗𝅥
1	1	1 &	1		1	1	1, 2
or Step,	Step,	Run-ning,	Step		or Step,	Step,	Step-bend

I played these rhythms. _____Yes _____Not Yet

Put your instruments away. Fill out your progress chart and leave it and this task sheet in your storage box.

Extensional Activities:
1. Look up Metronome in Music Dictionary.
2. Look up the words on the metronome such as Allegro—Adagio, etc.
3. Make up new rhythms and play them with the metronome.

Goals: Understanding and reading the treble clef
Understanding and reading the bass clef
Identifying notes and rests
Understanding and reading time values
Understanding and reading time signatures

Obectives: A student will: identify all pitches on either the treble or bass staff, recognize and identify the kinds of notes and rests used, read time signatures, tell how many beats there are in each measure, correctly identify the kind of note that gets one count within a time signature.

Domain: Cognitive

Lesson Number One:

My name is: _____

First, open the cyclo-teacher by lifting from the bottom edge, then turn the wheel counter-clockwise until the arrows line up at "start."

Place the TREBLE CLEF learning cycle in the cyclo-teacher with side 1 up, fitting the learning cycle over the raised center of the cyclo-teacher wheel.

Next, place a clean answer wheel over the learning cycle and close the cover.

Read each question carefully and write your answer in the space provided. Slide the lever at the bottom of the cyclo-teacher to the right to check your answer and bring the next question into view, then return the lever to the left. Mark your correct answers with a "C" and your wrong answers with an "X."

After you have answered all the questions on this side lift the cover and see if you missed any of the questions marked "Key." If you did, place another clean answer wheel over the learning cycle and answer the questions again. When you can answer all the questions marked "Key" correctly, turn the learning cycle over to side 2 and repeat the above steps.

When all questions on both sides marked "Key" have been answered correctly you are ready for Lesson 2.

Return the cyclo-teacher and put this packet† in your storage box.

Lesson Number Two:

Get the cyclo-teacher.

Proceed as in Lesson One *except* use the BASS CLEF learning cycle.

Lesson Number Three:

Use the NOTES AND RESTS learning cycle.

Remember, at the end of class time, put everything away.

Lesson Number Four:

Hang in there!

Use the TIME VALUES learning cycle.

* Field Enterprises Corporation
† Packet ideas by Don Wolf (college student)

Lesson Number Five:

Horray! You are still here!!

Use the TIME SIGNATURES learning cycle.

When all questions on both sides marked "Key" have been answered correctly ask your teacher to quiz you on one of the songs that you have been singing in class. See if you can identify the treble and bass clefs, name the pitches, the note values and rests that are used, and the time signature.

Put the cyclo-teacher away, mark your progress chart and put it and this packet in your storage box.

EXAMPLE III: Solo   Minipacket   Level II   Valuing   Listening Studio

---

Goal: To understand that music is expression; that music communicates feelings.

Objective: Listen to music; write answers about communicating feelings; listen again; reevaluate with additional information; extensional activities.

Domain: Affective

Mini Lesson One:

My name is: _____

Take out cassette tape number 5. Also get a pencil and blank white paper.

Listen to the excerpt of the music that is on the tape.

Check the feeling that is the *closest* to how you felt as you listened.

      _____ anxious   _____ sleepy   _____ unhappy

      _____ serene   _____ jazzy   _____ happy

Listen to the tape again and as you listen *draw* on the paper the mental feeling that it gives to you.

Do you like this feeling? _____ yes _____ no

Should music communicate feelings? ____ always ____ sometimes ____ never

Do you value feelings? ____ always ____ sometimes ____ never

If you have a little time left you may listen again and draw another picture. Or . . . you may choose to get started on your next lesson.

Put tape 5 away and leave this minipacket in your storage box.

Evaluation   Learning stations, classroom management, materials, and student progress should be constantly evaluated. The old adage "By his works ye shall know him" applies when evaluating the learner's progress. Teacher aides or classroom helpers are often useful in the task of keeping individualized instruction in successful operation. Teachers must develop record keeping that is appropriate to each unique situation, and students can keep behavior and progress records also, as shown in Figure 5.4 and 5.5.

     Transposing instructional theory into instructional reality is an open-ended task that often appears impossible. Music specialists are responsible for large numbers of students in many different classes, and many know

Figure 5.4. MUSIC STUDIO REPORT

MY NAME IS_____

I have completed (if not completed-explain) the following music job cards:

_____

_____

_____

_____

Figure 5.5. STUDENT PROGRESS CHART

MY NAME IS_____

This week I worked on:	Grade (If Appropriate)	I had mature behavior:
Sept. 27		
Oct. 4		
Oct. 11		
Oct. 18		

only the techniques of mass instruction. Few materials are individualized for music, and simultaneous sounds constitute a continuing problem. Even though the ideal will never be reached, music teachers are making continuous strides in that direction. Through long range planning and progress along a continuum of small increments, the implementation of individualized instruction can be attained. If each child is to have full opportunity to realize his or her own unique potential, each must feel, work, and be guided as an individual.

The federal law mandating mainstreaming for those students able to profit from attending regular classes contains the following definition of learning disability: a disorder in one or more of the basic psychological processes involved in understanding or using language, spoken or written, which may manifest itself in an imperfect ability to listen, think, speak, read, write, spell, or do mathematical calculations.

Teachers should be cautioned that there are many variables in intelligence. Some special learners who are handicapped in some areas are in the genius category in others such as piano skills, mathematical calculations, and memory. Some students classified as special learners may function normally in most music activities while many others require special consideration. Some receive additional resource room instruction to better assist their areas of deficiency and are in regular classrooms the remainder of the day. Still others have part-time special class instruction. Thus there are three general levels for special learners: (1) those in regular classes with or without supportive services, (2) those in regular classes with supplementary and resource services, and (3) those who are in special classes part time. A mainstreamed class should have no more than fifteen students. The goals of music instruction are the same as for the normal student.

An ancillary staff is essential for mainstreaming to succeed. Such a staff includes some or all of the following: special education teacher and/or consultant, hearing clinician, speech clinician, school nurse, school psychologist, school social worker, school media director, principal, guidance counselor, and perhaps others. The media specialist can assist with construction of uncomplicated charts, music notation, and drawings that can be clearly comprehended by all students, particularly the special learners. Schools should train teachers to utilize this ancillary staff. With this training, teachers should be able to:

1. Plan course content, teaching strategies, class procedures, and evaluation methods.
2. Recognize sociological, psychological, and cultural characteristics of mildly disabled students.
3. Design and implement a curriculum for the individual special learner.
4. Identify learning styles and the resultant instructional strategies and devices, and construct reinforcement media and materials for the mainstreamed student.
5. Create means of evaluation appropriate to measure both classroom progress and student achievement.

The Students and Their Problems

Because of many individual differences, it is not possible to generalize on the problems of special students. Brains operate differently. For example, students with hearing difficulties may compensate for this visually; some need to have musical responses translated into sensorimotor experience to comprehend them. The teacher must deduce the learning style of each student and construct plans based on that knowledge. All students have needs; special learners differ only in that they have more of them.

Obviously, adjustments will have to be made to accommodate special learners in a mainstreamed class. If most of the instructional goals, objectives, activities, and evaluative criteria involve skills and conceptual development beyond their capabilities, special learners will fail to achieve them, and their self-esteem and confidence may be irreparably damaged. Music is a subject in which mainstreaming can be successful because music provides more flexibility in levels of accomplishment than other subject areas at both concrete and abstract levels, and it serves cognitive, affective, and psychomotor development levels. A variety of responses can be planned, with some of them within the capabilities of special students. Music also serves some nonmusical goals, such as those requiring nonverbal responses, social acceptance, team play, and muscular coordination. Individualization of instruction is essential, thus the teacher will obtain all possible information about each special student, observe that student carefully to assess strengths and weaknesses, and from such information and observation find instructional solutions that will advance that student in musical responsiveness and success, no matter how small some of the steps might be.

When placed in the regular classroom, the exceptional student will first want to observe others, a normal reaction for anyone in a new environment. Should the special student fail to respond, opportunity to experiment with or play an Orff keyboard instrument will usually result in participation, with mallet held with hand (or teeth when necessary). The teacher should do nothing for a student that he or she can do without assistance because special students normally want to be self-sufficient and take care of themselves without help unless absolutely necessary.

Some students have auditory problems and have difficulty in distinguishing different instrumental sounds, different rhythms, and contrasting sections of music. Some have trouble with letter and word direction in reading, such as confusing *rat* and *tar* or d, b, and g, that may spill over into failure to distinguish between ♩♩♩ and ♩♩♩ . Some may be confused when asked to respond to a situation where both auditory and visual perception are needed. Such a student will be troubled when trying to read and respond to rudimentary notation such as the Kodály abbreviations. Other learning-disabled students have trouble coordinating any two or three senses. Some cannot distinguish details from general configurations, thus music textbooks can be disastrously confusing because of the wealth of information on some of the pages. Sometimes this can be remedied by constructing cardboard frames that eliminate from the page all things extraneous to what is to be studied. Multiple verses printed for a song can confuse a student who is trying to center attention on one of them, thus that verse might be reproduced on a chart or shown from an overhead projector. There are students unable to understand teachers' directions that contain several different commands, such as, "Listen to the recording, find the beat, and show me with your body that you feel the tempo." In this instance the teacher may need to demonstrate the activity, specify the part of the body that is to react to it, or actively help the student find the beat. Some may be unable to read Autoharp chord symbols and respond to them by stroking the instrument in time with the class's singing. They may have a reading problem or trouble with integrating the visual and the psychomotor. Perhaps a fellow student can help by stroking while the first student presses the chord bars. The teacher's task is to make possible some kind of success despite all of these difficulties. A resource teacher may assist by helping a student with the activity before music class. Materials may have to be adapted in some way in order for individual students to find success. When construction of materials takes time, ancillary personnel are needed to assist the teacher (Atterbury, 1983). Some of the students may bring tape recorders to class so that they may take their musical experiences home to review and study; thus the teacher should speak in a manner the recorder will pick up clearly. The more recent music series offer suggestions which may be suitable for, or can be altered to assist, the special learner in the mainstreamed classroom.

Parents and the Mainstreamed Class

The cooperation of parents is indispensable to the mainstreamed class. Many parents of special learners are concerned about their children's acceptance by teachers and other students, and they may fear the comparison of their child to the "normal" students. They often have pressing needs of their own in relation to their handicapped children, and teachers usually find a need for telephone calls, conferences, and discussion and support groups. Parents are usually aided by being able to talk and work with other parents of special learners. The teacher must be prepared to talk with parents about the goals for the class and about short-term objectives for each student, and may save time by having these posted where parents can read them. Some teachers find that having student notebooks that travel from school to home and back, and in which teacher and parent can write information for each other is helpful. Parents should be assisted in helping their children with music at home, and instruments, tapes, recordings, learning packages, and other materials should be available for home use. Home visits are often essential in learning how best to assist the special learner; the teacher needs to know the family setting in order to plan for the student. As with every student, community and home influences on the musical attitudes of students are extremely important to a music program. Is the student encouraged to move to music, sing, play instruments, create? Does anyone sing to and with the student? Do family members play instruments, sing, listen to music? Do parents understand the significance of music in the physical, affective, and cognitive growth of children? Do parents know how to give positive feedback to their children, and do they understand the need for freedom from dependence on them by their children? The teacher and parent need to know that each can be helpful to the other in assisting the special learner. Parents can help at times in the music class; they should visit class frequently and become involved in it when appropriate.

The Orthopedically Handicapped

One aim of the teacher is to develop the physical responses of these students to the limits of their physical handicaps. Their eagerness to try can be a good example for others. Substitute motions are required in many instances, such as hands in the air for walking, and tapping a resonant part of a wheelchair in time with the movements of others. Bobbing heads can do this too, and students should be encouraged to create their own responses. Percussion instruments can be strapped to a hand or foot when necessary. Orff mallet instruments can be played with the mallet held in the mouth. When one is improvising or composing, the pentatonic bar arrangement on Orff instruments and resonator bells assures degrees of success. These students need ample time in which to perform physically, thus the teacher needs to have patience. Singing can help spastic students relax their throat muscles by making singing a more flowing response than their speaking. Singing in a chorus can be enjoyed from a musical standpoint and result in the satisfaction of being a full participant in a large group. Words of songs should not call attention to physical abnormalities. For example, a song about five fingers is not suitable for classes in which some have more or fewer than five.

The Visually Impaired

The blind and the near-blind students are capable of singing, playing instruments, composing, and even dancing. Their supposedly keen sense of hearing has been exaggerated, although it is possible that dependence upon listening may have sharpened it a bit. In general, however, listening skills must be learned. The National Library Service for the Blind and Physically Handicapped, Library of Congress, now provides songs for the blind in braille notation, and publishes *A Dictionary of Braille Music Signs*. The symbols sensed by touch have multiple uses; they have different meanings in mathematics and in reading literature. Autoharp bars can be marked with these textured dots. Tapes can be prepared for the blind to assist their learning of musical concepts. Large print and up-front seating is advised for the visually impaired; special music stands for holding materials close to some eyes are necessary. Teachers can produce music for the blind on a braille-writer or a braille slate where they are available. Blind students need to be helped with their comprehension of space; they have a normal fear of falling, and need to know their way around. Songs and musical games can be helpful in increasing their feelings of security and accomplishment; studying blind musicians is a good idea. Bill Evans, Stevie Wonder, and Ray Charles are examples.

The Hearing Impaired

Completely deaf students are usually not found in mainstreamed rooms, but those with hearing impairments attend classes with or without hearing aids. They can hear low pitches better than high ones. The partially deaf often suffer from muscular tension, speech disorders, and language deficiencies. However, improved and new types of hearing aids have assisted many students; pitched vibrations can be felt through the skin, muscles, and head bones and translated into musical sense. Through feeling vibrations these students are able to sense rhythmic sound, thus floors made of materials that vibrate serve to bring them into contact with music; they enjoy echo-type rhythm games this way. Hardwood floors and amplification enable these students to dance and to sense variations in dynamics. When partially deaf students have the ability to hear, though at subnormal levels, they can learn to match tones, hear scales, and to concentrate on listening to music. This is helpful in improving speech because accents and syllabic duration can be explained in musical sound and rhythm patterns. Some songs provide rhythmic bases for speech improvement.

Hearing-impaired students learn to read lips; thus they should be no farther from the teacher than six or eight feet and placed at an angle from which they can easily see the teacher's lip and tongue movements. These students' learning style usually leans heavily on the visual, so visual demonstrations are helpful. Tapping the beat or pattern on the shoulder and placing the hard-of-hearing between good singers are also of aid to these special learners. Color coding keys on bell sets and tone bars and on Autoharp chord bars has been helpful. The hearing-impaired students should be encouraged to invent rhythm patterns, songs, and instrumental pieces because they are often deficient in creative experience. Recent research has found that some deaf persons can hear or sense the ups and downs of melody lines; they can hear the sound of a gong but not that of a triangle; some can hear a guitar if it is held close to the ear; and low-pitched Orff instruments can be heard, but not the high-pitched glockenspiel.

The Educable Retarded These students operate at a lower level of competency than the so-called normal child, thus are not able to conceptualize and generalize at higher levels of thought. Initiative and curiosity are frequently lacking, thus exploratory and process learning are hampered. Most of these students operate at Piaget's earlier stages of learning, the equivalent of children aged two to seven. This means that teachers may expect short attention spans, difficulty in using abstractions, difficulty or failure in comprehending similarities and differences and cause and effect, poor verbal communication, excessive emotional reactions to confusing situations, poor memory, oversensitivity, and reluctance to act in new situations or activities. A slower pace for learning is necessary, with more structure, routines, and direction, combined with frequent changes of activities. Concrete stimuli are needed. When suitable materials and visual aids are supplied, these students can clarify music concepts (abstractions). The concept *same-different* can be acquired through musical experiences. Sequencing of learning in small steps is important to the success of these students, and hand puppets, visual aids, words of songs, and body movements can improve vocabulary and communication skills. Open-ended questions can assist this process. Clear and precise directions can reduce occurrences of excessive emotional reactions, as can the teacher's purposeful ignorance of some of them. Carefully sequenced activities can help remedy poor memory, stressing one element at a time with much repetition. These students usually enjoy music and songs that are rhythmic and inspire interpretations by body movements. As do young children, these students enjoy singing throughout the day as they relate to or express their reactions to their daily activities in song. They can learn to operate tape recorders.

The Learning Disabled or Perceptually Handicapped

There are students who appear to be normal with the exception of a malfunction or immaturity of the central nervous system. These children suffer various cognitive inabilities such as incapacity to organize, classify, assimilate, perceive, and to transmit information. The implications to the teacher of these conditions include simple repetition of enjoyable music activities; varied approaches to learning that require more than one sense; use of short, repetitious, interesting songs, recordings, and instrumental pieces; simple imitations, such as in echo-type songs and echo-clapping; and body responses with both large and small muscles for those who lack muscular coordination. The teacher's directions should be brief and explicit. Finger plays, action songs, easy games, and songs that state directions in their lyrics are good for those whose minds do not process details well. Calming music is used with hyperactive children, and stimulating music for lethargic ones. Rhythmic rhymes and words can assist those who have difficulty remembering words.

The Culturally and Economically Different

Some students may be quite normal when they are in their home and neighborhood environment, but are at some disadvantage when they are placed in a classroom where most of the students are English-speaking, middle class Americans. They should be considered *different* rather than disadvantaged, which has acquired some derogatory implications. Also in this category are slow learners (due to socially and educationally deprived environments), who initially require some of the same attention received by the learning disabled and the educable retarded.

To bring unity to a classroom that includes these students, music can speak to subjects they all know: home, family, work, play, food, clothing, country, special days, travel, dance, and the emotions all humans share. Music of subject matter interest and rhythmic and/or melodic appeal should encourage the class to make music together and render differences of little importance except to add interest to some music when students tell about it. These students need a warm, friendly teacher and positive interaction and social relations with classmates. When friends are made, it may be possible to assign a student to be a "big brother" or "big sister" who helps the culturally or economically different student. Music should provide experiences in which the English language becomes increasingly comprehensible and in which a larger vocabulary assists cognitive abilities. Parents and members of the community from other cultures can be invited to dress in native costume and to perform (and possibly teach) their songs and dances. Parents can teach their children songs to sing for the class, or tape them at home for a student to bring. The teacher should select music that places the different culture in the most favorable light, and should be certain that authentic music is presented, free from stereotypes.*

* The third edition of this book (1970) has an extended discussion of this type of special learner, pp. 567–573.

The Gifted Gifted students are recognized as an important national resource to be nurtured. Giftedness has been unduly equated with high intelligence, but it is now known that giftedness is not always bestowed in horizontal fashion, but very often vertically. For example, a person can be extremely talented musically while being rather average in other respects, and other talents may be similarly isolated. Errors have been made in assuming that a high I.Q. student who is "good at everything" in school will be an excellent musician. That student will probably be a good, but not a great musician, and if pushed into music performance as a career may someday decide that he or she would prefer to be a stockbroker because that person *knows* that being only "good" in music performance is not good enough. The reverse of this can happen, as when a young university professor of political science, who had been guided into that occupation by family pressure, suddenly resigned his position at a leading university to try to become the musician he had always wanted to be. So in dealing with the gifted, the search should be for those of outstanding talent in a subject area or skill as well as selecting those of high intelligence.

These students need a balanced program of cognitive, affective, and psychomotor education, but with additional work in creativity and in the area of their special talent. As in any individual's education, the teacher identifies the student's talent, interests, persistence, and limitations, and designs a learning environment for that student's optimum growth. Interest and persistence are vital; there are numerous examples of extremely talented students who lack the interest and persistence necessary to develop their talents into anything worthwhile. Gifted students are usually in the regular classroom for most of the day in order to continue to develop normal social relationships.

As with other students, the teacher works to assist these special learners to build musical percepts, concepts, and relationships at their capacity levels, with emphasis on problems that stimulate creative thinking and process learning. Many opportunities should be provided to exercise initiative, to develop the skills of working independently while at the same time to be accepted by peers, to become emotionally secure and socially adept. The teacher provides enrichment activities and experiences, special materials and sources of information. There will be higher level performing on instruments or voice, composing music, and devising unique dance movements. The music specialist, classroom teacher, and parent will find it necessary to work together for the gifted just as they do for the handicapped learner.

EXPLORATORY ACTIVITIES

1. Observe school classes at a level of your choice to look for evidences of individualization of instruction. To what extent is it taking place? Identify problems; observe how problems are met.

2. Select one of the special issues of the *Music Educators Journal* listed in References for study. Notice the many ways the Music Educators National Conference assists those who teach music.

References

ATTERBURY, BETTY W., "Success Strategies for Learning-Disabled Students." *Music Educators Journal,* April 1983, 29–31.

CHADWICK, D. M., and C. A. CLARK, "Adapting Music Instruments for the Physically Handicapped." *Music Educators Journal,* November 1980, 56–59.

The Gifted and the Talented: Their Education and Development, National Society for the Study of Education 78th Yearbook, Part One. Chicago, Ill.: University of Chicago Press, 1979.

GILBERT, JANET P., "Mainstreaming in Your Classroom: What to Expect," *Music Educators Journal,* February 1977, 64–68.

GRAHAM, R. M., and A. S. BEER, *Teaching Music to the Exceptional Child.* Englewood Cliffs, N.J.: Prentice-Hall, Inc., 1980.

HOTCHKISS, GWEN, and MARGARET ATHEY, *Treasury of Individualized Activities for the Music Class.* West Nyack, N.Y.: Parker Publishing Company, Inc., 1977.

JANKOWSKI, PAUL, and FRANCES JANKOWSKI, *Accelerated Programs for the Gifted Student.* West Nyack, N.Y.: Parker Publishing Company, 1976.

MESKE, EUNICE B., and CARROLL RINEHART, *Individualized Instruction in Music.* Reston, Va.: Music Educators National Conference, 1975.

Music Educators Journal, Special Issues: Music in Special Education, April 1972; Individualization in Music, November 1972; Music in Open Education, April 1974; Teaching Special Students, April 1982.

Oregon Music Materials, 2535 Charnelton St., Eugene, OR. A source of games and learning activities students can do without the teacher.

SCHMIDT, CHARLES P., "Cognitive Styles Research: Implications for Music Teaching and Learning," *Update,* Spring 1984, 18–21.

chapter six

Planning Curricula

To be concerned with curricula once meant to be concerned almost exclusively with organizing content into a logical sequence to fit whatever time was available. The differences among individual students and the intellectual and psychological changes they experienced as they developed toward maturity received slight attention. Today the importance of organizing content and teaching procedures to accommodate differences among individual students has become recognized. Concern with the curriculum cannot be separated from concern with knowledge about typical and atypical human development, nor can it be isolated from what students have already experienced and know. In planning a curriculum one should begin with what students have already mastered, and sequentially and gradually expand and organize music content by involving students in challenging, relevant, and varied learning experiences at increasingly higher levels.

A music curriculum is a planned and sequenced guide for the teaching of musical content at both system and school levels and in the classroom. The way such curricula are implemented determines the degree of success attained by the students. Curriculum guides are effective when those who will use them are directly involved in developing them. They are apt to fail when they are imposed on teachers who had no part in constructing them.

The major responsibility of a curriculum planning committee at the district and/or school level is to determine the general overall instructional goals of a music program. The planning is done cooperatively by the principal, music supervisor, consultant, music specialists, classroom teachers, and possibly a college professor or two, students at the middle school and secondary levels, and members of the community. The first action of a planning committee at the system level is to agree upon and develop a philosophy concerning music education, because the long-term goals grow from this. Such a philosophic statement expresses belief concerning the importance of music education. Two examples follow:

> Music education is part of aesthetic education; aesthetic education is part of the general education of the child. Through experiences with music, the learner will be increasingly capable of feeling, creating, discovering, performing, learning, and thinking.

> Through music, people can live more full and complete lives because of their sensitivity to the world of sound. Such persons will know music's language, its symbols, and be able to form concepts concerning the elements that comprise music—concepts that will serve as tools to find meaning and to add to their knowledge of music and the human experiences of which it is a part.

Such statements should give direction to music teaching in the district or school, in the classroom, and for an individual. They should enable a teacher of music to make clear the value of music in the lives of students. The committee for the system or school next develops *long-range goals* that relate to the stated philosophy. These goals are general and fairly abstract because they apply to a school district K–12, or an entire school. The Oregon Department of Education's *Music Education Guide,* p. 17, lists these long-range goals:

Students will:

Know the basic elements and structure of music.

Be able to use notational systems.

Be able to improvise and create music.

Demonstrate performing skills.

Know the implications of music in our society, with respect to music careers, its avocational and leisure uses and, as consumers, know about musical products.

Value ethnic music and the American musical heritage.

Value music as an avenue of communication for the exchange of feelings and emotions.

Respond overtly and covertly to the inherent esthetic qualities of music.

Develop acute auditory discrimination.

After writing long-range goals, the system or school committee writes *instructional objectives* based upon them. These objectives are more specific, particularly in terms of the cognitive, psychomotor, and affective domains. They are sometimes written in general behavioral terms such as, "By the end of the year the students will demonstrate comprehension of _____ by

_____." They describe the desired outcomes of a general comprehensive musical program.

The teacher works from the above goals and objectives when planning instruction, translating and rewriting the instructional objectives into terms that apply to large or small units of work and time spans for a particular class, group of students, or an individual student. From the revised instructional objectives the teacher writes the *specific behavioral objectives* that will be used in lesson plans.

Writing Behavioral Objectives

Specific behavioral objectives are stated in terms of precise behavior to be manifested by the students, the learning to be attained, and the conditions under which learning occurs. In other words, a well-written behavioral objective states *what the students are expected to do, under what conditions they are expected to do it,* and *to what extent (how well) they are expected to do it.* A behavioral objective is precise and limited, such as, "After listening to these (specific) recordings, the students will identify the dominant woodwind instruments by writing their names in the spaces provided on the worksheet." The objective states something the students can do after an educational experience.

The three parts of a behavioral objective were stated above as (1) what the learners will do, (2) under what conditions they will do it, and (3) how well they are expected to perform. What the learners will do should be identified by an "observable verb." Part two of a behavioral objective, the conditions section, should not have a time limit unless time is an essential part of the objective, and this is seldom the case. Part three, how well the learners are expected to perform, is best expressed by using the phrase "at least" when numerical criteria are desired. It is permissible to use two, three, or more sentences if these are needed to state an objective fully. It is also permissible to use pictorial means when these contribute to communicating the objective clearly. The words "correctly" and "will be able" are often redundant in stated objectives. For example, "The learner will name the wind instruments of the orchestra" is a better statement than "The learner will correctly name the wind instruments of the orchestra." Objectives should apply to the individual student rather than state that "at least 85 percent of the students" will accomplish what the objective asks. Although there may be some pupil failures, it is not necessary to predict this on a class basis. When percents are applied to quantities, such quantities are only those that are expressed in numbers. For example, if there are ten items in a test, 90 percent can be used when referring to nine of the ten questions.

There may be subobjectives related to the major objective. For example, a subobjective related to the behavioral objective immediately above might be, "After listening to this (specific) recording, the student will identify the clarinet as the solo woodwind instrument by writing its name in the space provided in the worksheet." A subobjective is written in the same manner as the major objective, but is subordinate in relation to the major objective within this educational goal.

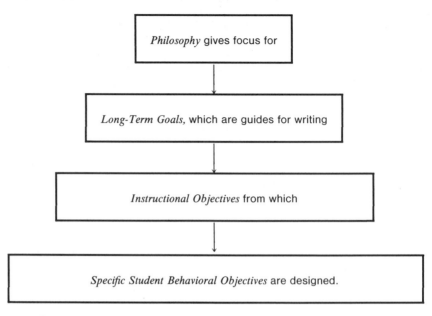

Figure 6.1. MODEL FOR CURRICULUM DESIGN

The model for curriculum design shown in Figure 6.1 can be used to design district, school, or classroom program guides for a year, a specified reporting period, a week, or for a group or individual daily lesson.

Designing Instructional Programs

Teachers use long-term goals, instructional objectives, and student behavioral objectives as a foundation for planning music programs for the entire year. They study state and local curriculum guides, obtain information from the principal and fellow teachers, and study appropriate records of each learner to find out his or her musical background and level of competency. They then formulate the major goals to be attained in the year immediately ahead. They consider local, state, and national events, seasons, holidays, and special days to determine to what extent these special events can be related to the year's program. They locate all available music materials and examine them to see which can be used. They incorporate flexibility into the details of planning so that students can make some decisions and choices. They realize that there should be continuous planning that progresses from week to week and from one day to the next within the framework of the plan for the year.

In order to design curricular programs, it is necessary to know the amount of time allocated to teaching music. Minimum time allotments vary among states and among school districts. Obviously it is difficult to designate specific time allotments in self-contained classrooms where the teacher, in addition to scheduled time for music, integrates it when appropriate into all areas of the curriculum throughout the school day. This is especially true in nursery school, kindergarten, and first grade.

Types of plans also vary in accordance with the philosophy and objectives of the teacher and of the school, the size of class, number of aides, and type of classroom organization. The use of objectives as a basis for sound program planning will be discussed below.

Content Areas and Objectives In order to develop musical learning in the fullest sense, it will be necessary for the teacher to select and develop objectives in four major areas:

1. Music knowledges or content (data, concepts, and generalizations).
2. Cognitive process skills.
3. Music skills.
4. Music attitudes and values.

While the teacher may choose to emphasize any one of the four areas in any given daily lesson or unit plan, it is likely that elements of all four will be present in most plans. The four areas of objectives are outlined below.

I. Music Knowledges or Content (data, concepts, generalizations)
   A. The Subject Matter Content of Music
      1. Expressive Elements
         a. tone qualities
         b. tempo
         c. dynamics
      2. Constituent Elements
         a. rhythm (duration)
         b. melody (pitch)
         c. harmony
         d. form
   B. The Structure of Music (concepts, generalizations)

II. Cognitive Process Skills Applied to Music
   A. Observing
   B. Comparing
   C. Classifying
   D. Collecting and Organizing Data
   E. Summarizing
   F. Generalizing
   G. Creative Thinking (synthesizing)
   H. Inferring from Data and Interpreting Data
   I. Hypothesizing
   J. Analyzing
   K. Evaluating
   L. Applying

III. Music Skills
   A. Listening
   B. Moving to Music

C. Singing
D. Playing Instruments
E. Reading Music
F. Creative Skills
IV. Musical Attitudes and Values
A. Choosing
B. Prizing
C. Acting on Decisions

The Four Major Curricular Components drawing (Fig. 6.2) indicates the four major categories of music teaching: the components of music as a discipline (content); cognitive process skills; music skills; and attitudes, values, and behaviors. These form the framework from which the teacher selects justifiable objectives, then plans learning experiences which serve to promote them.

Selecting Program Content The program content should be selected according to the capabilities the learner must acquire to satisfy the instructional objectives. Such content will be selected and adapted from the structure of musical knowledge, which is included in this chapter, and will be appropriate for the experiences and ac-

Figure 6.2. FOUR MAJOR CURRICULAR COMPONENTS

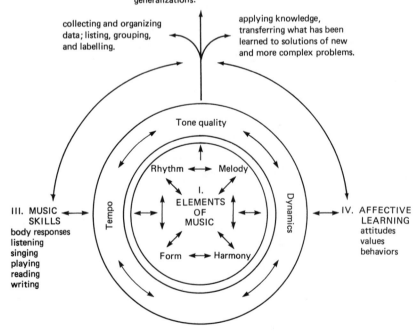

tivities through which the musical elements are experienced—movement, improvisation, musical performance, composition, and analysis of music. The capabilities and learning styles of each student must be considered in order to select content that is appropriate. Music content consists of data, concepts, and generalizations, which Jerome Bruner calls the *structure* of a discipline. These three categories of knowledge are explained below.

Data refer to particulars rather than to universals. They are propositions or statements that include things or situations of the present or of the past. Data can be tested and proved to be true or false.

Examples of musical data (facts) are:

Bach died in 1750.

A sharp placed before a note raises its pitch one half step.

In the same meter, a quarter note has the same duration as two eighth notes.

Some teachers place major emphasis on the learning of facts as ends within themselves. They fail to see the importance of using them as a foundation for organizing information into higher levels of knowledge. As a result, they may emphasize information of only minor import. Whether or not a fact is important to learn is usully determined by the context in which it is used. It is therefore important that students participate in learning experiences that help them tie together the facts they acquire to form more meaningful relationships.

If teachers wish to help students understand music more fully, they must do more than merely help them learn facts; they must also help them use facts to acquire a further understanding of knowledge at higher levels of conceptualization such as exist in concepts and generalizations.

Concepts. Fraenkel (1973) states that concepts, unlike facts, "are definitional in nature. They represent those characteristics that are common to a group of experiences. Concepts do not exist in reality; they represent our attempts to give order to reality—to order that information from our environment that we receive through our senses. We attempt to bring order to this sensory input by attaching symbols (word-labels) to certain similarities we perceive in our experience. . . . Notice, however, that concepts are invented rather than discovered. . . . Concepts thus are mental constructions devised by man to describe the characteristics that are common to a number of experiences," which include those with musical phenomena heard, seen, and felt. "They facilitate understanding, for they make communication easier," thus reducing the complexity of the musical environment into manageable proportions.

All concepts are not indicated verbally. Verbal or aural dimensions may lead one to experience a particular emotion or feeling that, although unnamed, is a concept. Perhaps later on the learner (perhaps a music listener) can analyze a reaction and name it, thus forming a concept that is more accessible and usable. Since concepts are inventions of the mind, they are personal creations of individuals, thus may not always be as alike as teachers may wish them to be. Each learner develops his or her mental constructs, which we call concepts. These result from many experiences in which data become organized into meaningful abstractions.

Generalizations are statements that contain two or more concepts and that show relationships among concepts. Like facts, generalizations can be substantiated or disproved by referring to concrete or obvious evidence. Both concepts and generalizations aid students in organizing and seeing relationships and meaning in music.

Generalizations offer insights into the way music is produced and into the ways it affects the life of man. They not only describe facts (data) and concepts but give structure to them. Careful consideration must be given by the music teacher in the selection of valid and significant content objectives, which include the processing and mastery of relevant and worthy data, concepts, and generalizations.

The following Conceptual Structure of Music outline is highly condensed and can easily be expanded. The generalizations stated in formal, adult language may be used by teachers in planning programs, courses of study, instructional objectives, and lessons. They are rarely recited or presented to students. The same concept or generalization may be sought and explored at very rudimentary levels, progressing in spiral fashion to ever higher levels as students grow in musical knowledge. *Most generalizations are tentative;* they will be tested and refined further. For example, young students learn that "sound and silence have duration," but this generalization will be expanded, refined, and made more specific as students enlarge and improve their experiences in music.

The spiral-type curriculum reflects the development and expansion of musical skills, concepts, generalizations and their relationships in students' minds. For example, meter (as an aspect of rhythm) becomes an increasingly complex concept as a student has experiences with it over years of schooling. Thus, the same basic musical concepts are taught at all levels in a from-simple-to-complex sequence. Lasting understandings and attitudes are acquired sequentially as a result of many related experiences and encounters with the same core concept. At first the student has only a hazy awareness of concepts involving rhythm or melody. Next come perceptions, then reinforcing experiences to test these early perceptions, and finally growth and understanding until the student has developed mature concepts (Oregon Department of Education, *Music Education Guide,* p. 17).

The outline describes in conceptual terms a world of music from which teachers can select and prepare content objectives suitable for an individual, a class, a level of accomplishment, a course of study, or a complete music curriculum. The Conceptual Structure of Music outline portrays music as a broad content area from which only a small part would be selected by the teacher for implementation within the boundaries of a music lesson or a year's course of study.

The complete sentences are generalizations (conclusions, principles, summarized ideas, main ideas). Following most generalizations are concepts from which they were constructed.

A Conceptual Structure of Music

Tempo
- Tempo (degrees of fast and slow) is found in all organized music.

lento	slow	*presto*	very fast
largo	broad and slow	*a tempo*	in original tempo
andante	moderately slow	*accelerando*	gradually faster
allegretto	moderately fast	*rallentando*	gradually slower
allegro	lively	*ritardando*	gradually slower
vivace	spirited		

Dynamics
- Dynamics (degrees of loud and soft) add interest and variety to expressive musical performance.

accent	> ∧	more than usual stress
pianissimo	*pp*	very soft
piano	*p*	soft
mezzo piano	*mp*	medium soft
mezzo forte	*mf*	medium loud
forte	*f*	loud
fortissimo	*ff*	very loud
sforzato or *sforzando*	*sf*	heavy accent
crescendo	cresc.	gradually increasing loudness
decrescendo ▭	decresc.	gradually decreasing loudness
diminuendo ▭	dim.	gradually decreasing loudness

Rhythm
- Rhythm in music is a grouping of sounds and silences of varying duration, usually controlled by a regular beat.

beat	dotted notes
equal divisions of the beat	rests
unequal divisions of the beat	speech-rhythm
one-to-two relation of note values	notated speech-rhythm
one-to-three relation of note values	articulation such as staccato and legato
one-to-four relation of note values	fermata ⌒
notated rhythm	

- Accent or lack of accent governs types of rhythm.

metrical rhythm	free rhythm
meter, bar line, measure, up-beat (anacrusis), downbeat, meter signature, duple meter, triple meter, primary accent, secondary accent, rhythm pattern	rallentando (rall.)
	accelerando (accel.)
	rubato
asymmetrical rhythm (5/4, 7/8, etc.)	no common metrical beat (such as some Oriental, Indian, and Hungarian music that cannot be expressed in traditional notation)
"measured" rhythm (no regular recurring beat, such as in Gregorian chant)	syncopation as a disturbance of the normal pulse of meter, accent, and rhythm

- Musical sound has duration and pitch.

word-rhythms related to duration
word-rhythms related to duration and pitch
notation of word-rhythms
notation of melody

- Devices related to rhythm are used by composers to add interest and variety to their compositions.

rhythm patterns   canonic imitation
rhythmic ostinati   polyrhythm
augmentation   free rhythm (rit., rall., accel., rubato)
diminution   syncopation

- There are rhythms that are characteristic of peoples and nations.

distinctive rhythms in national songs
distinctive rhythms in national dances
   (minuet, waltz, polka, schottische, square dance, etc.)
distinctive rhythms associated with ethnic groups

- Rhythm is universal and has meanings beyond music.

the seasons	architecture	day and night
waves of the ocean	painting	life cycles of plants and animals
the grain of wood	the heartbeat	the speech and movement of man

Melody

- A melody is a linear succession of tones that are rhythmically controlled and are perceived by the human ear as a meaningful grouping of tones. (Children might say, "A melody is a line of tones in rhythm that sounds right.")

- Melodies have direction: The successive tones of a melody may go up, go down, or remain on the same pitch.

pitch and vibration   notation of pitch (staff, note, clef,
high and low   numerals, and syllables to
contour   identify pitches)
relation to tension, climax, and release

- The tones of a melody have duration: Melodies are formed by a union of pitch and rhythm.

relation of song melodies to word rhythms
note values (see Rhythm)
rhythm patterns in, or related to, melodies

- The tones of a melody may have adjacent (scale-line) pitches or skips (chord-line pitches).

scale (major, minor, diatonic, modal,   home tone
   pentatonic, chromatic, tone row derived   key
   from the chromatic, wholetone, ethnic,   key signature
   invented)   accidental

passive and active scale tones (tension
  and release)
tonal centers
intervals
relation to chords (see Harmony)

- Melodies have form: They are usually formed of distinct parts or sections.

phrase
phrase arrangement (repetition and contrast;
  unary, binary, and ternary song forms)
sequence
tonal patterns and their alterations

- Melodies can be manipulated through various devices. (Children might say, "Melodies can be changed in different ways.")

transposition	melodic variation
diminution	rhythmic variation
augmentation	harmonic variation
inversion	octave displacement
retrograde	

Harmony, Polyphony, and Texture

- Harmony pertains to the vertical aspect of music, the successions of chords and the relationships among them. (Children might say, "Harmony means chords and their changes.")

- Texture, a term derived from weaving, pertains to vertical and horizontal elements ("threads") in music which produce such effects as light, heavy, thick, and thin, and which include styles of composition such as homophonic and polyphonic.

- Homophonic music consists of one melody with an accompaniment.

accompanied song
accompanied instrumental solo
music of the nineteenth century
harmony suggested by chord tones in melodies

- Polyphonic music has two or more melodic lines sounding at the same time; these melodic lines are connected in tonal music by harmonic relationships.

round, canon	music of Palestrina and J. S. Bach
counterpoint	harmony suggested by chord tones in melodies
contrary motion	descriptive terms: contrapuntal, imitative,
fugue	canonic, fugal, atonal polyphony
fugal entry	

- A chord is any simultaneous combination of three or more pitches; some may be more agreeable to the ear than others. (Children might say, "A chord is three or more notes sounded together.")

Chord construction—3rds, 4ths, 5ths,   relation to melody
  clusters, contrived chords   harmonizing a tune
inversions   chord tones
relation to key centers   passing tones
  triad   consonance
  scale   dissonance
  major   primary and secondary chords
  minor   chording
  question and answer (V–I)   chords relating to no tonal center
  cadence: full, half, plagal   atonality
parallel chords   chords as conjunctions of melodic
    lines

- Identical harmonies can be sounded at different pitch levels.

transposition
key signatures

- Harmonies can be combined.

bitonality
polytonality

Sounds and Tone Qualities

- Some kind of sound can be produced by almost every object in the environment.

- Tone quality (timbre, tone color) is the difference between tones of the same pitch produced by different voices and instruments; it distinguishes the sound of one voice or instrument from another.

- Sounds, voices, and instruments can be classified according to tone quality, range, characteristics, and the means employed to produce them.
Conventional sound sources

voices	instruments
soprano	strings
alto	plucked
tenor	stroked
bass	bowed
	keyboard
	woodwinds
	flue
	reed
	percussion
	brass
	organ
	electronic

Unconventional sound sources

paper	wood	food	other
rubber	metal	materials found in nature	
glass	plastic	body sounds	

- Instruments can be played in ways that produce a variety of sounds.

legato	vibrato
staccato	use of extreme ranges of high or low
spiccato, as concerns bowing	stop, as concerns the organ
mute, as concerns strings,	glissando, as concerns the harp, keyboard,
trumpet, French horn,	and other instruments
trombone	experimental ways

- Voices and instruments may be combined to produce an infinite variety of tone qualities: Composers and arrangers select different voices, instruments, and tone qualities for specific reasons.

- The difference in tone qualities can be explained scientifically: It results from the proportion in which the fundamental tone is combined with the harmonics or overtones.

resonance	partials
harmonics	vibrato
overtone series	oscilloscope

Form

- Musical forms are similar to plans of construction made by architects.

- Melodies may be divided into parts

motive
phrase
period

- Melodies can be extended and altered

introduction	repetition	retrograde
coda	section	thematic development
interlude	diminution	augmentation
sequence	inversion	

- Most musical form is based on the principle of repetition-contrast (same-different, unity-variety).

a a	rondo:
a b	A B A C A; or
a b a	A B A C A B A
A B A sections	variation

- Some forms can be classified as contrapuntal.

round   canon   fugue

- A compound form comes into being when several movements are combined to form a complete musical composition.

instrumental compound forms	movement (of a larger work)
sonata	suite
concerto	of classical dances
symphony	of folksongs
overture	for the ballet

An example of using this Structure of Music at elementary and middle school levels follows. The teacher has abstracted a generalization from the outline, "The family of reed instruments includes the oboe, bassoon, clarinet, and saxophone." In developing this generalization, concepts of each of these instruments must be formed. When considering the bassoon, data such as these will be learned by the students.

Data	a long tube which doubles back on itself
	a double reed made of cane
	a conical bore
	a tone of cavernous quality
	a bass instrument
	a very wide range of pitches
Concept	the standard bassoon
Generalization	(assuming concepts of the four instruments have developed) The family of reed instruments includes the oboe, bassoon, clarinet, and saxophone.

Notice where the generalization originates in the Structure of Music. What might be termed a subconcept in the Tone Quality section was restated as a generalization. Find the source. It is the word "reed."

Thus far, the ways students learn have been emphasized; attention will now be given to the bases from which teachers plan. When students *learn,* they begin with facts (data), but when teachers *plan,* they begin with generalizations (see Figure 6.3).

Despite the reverse appearance of the two columns, it should be obvious by now that the teacher's planning will reflect the learning process. The first step in learning is *perceptual.* Students learn facts by means of the

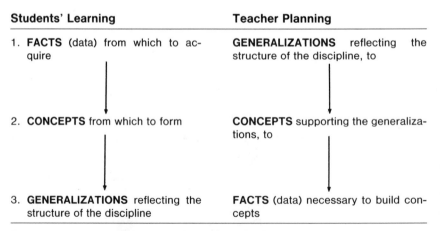

Students' Learning	Teacher Planning
1. **FACTS** (data) from which to acquire	**GENERALIZATIONS** reflecting the structure of the discipline, to
2. **CONCEPTS** from which to form	**CONCEPTS** supporting the generalizations, to
3. **GENERALIZATIONS** reflecting the structure of the discipline	**FACTS** (data) necessary to build concepts

Figure 6.3. THE LEARNING–PLANNING SEQUENCES

senses, and the effective teacher plans to encourage their use of every appropriate sense.

The second step in students' learning requires *associative-process thinking* in that the images and data are retrieved from mental storage, reexamined, explored, and organized so that concepts may be formed from them. The third step has to do with *forming generalizations* based on experience with concepts, and applying these generalizations in new situations to test them and to change and refine them.

This generalization may later be refined and expanded if the teacher chooses. For example, the discovery of the *metal* reed could be planned as a *discrepant event* which would bring the attention of students to the function of reeds in the accordion, harmonica, and reed organ. Then the concept of the "family of reed instruments" will expand and the concept of "reed" will grow. Students can discover that each metal reed is constructed to produce a definite pitch, while each cane reed must in some way accommodate difference in pitch. Thus discovery grows out of discovery as the teacher guides the process in a helpful but unobtrusive way. Students are guided to discuss their findings and problems as they work with the tone qualities, range, appearance, and mechanical features of reed instruments. Such study as this is ordinarily *only a part* of a lesson plan which includes a variety of musical activities.

In developing concepts, students may listen to music, perform music, compose it, write it, analyze it, and discuss it. The aim is to clarify the mental image of the aspect of music under study.

Organizing for Conceptual Learning

Teachers of music have a logical plan to follow when they begin to organize their teaching efforts. They will:

1. Know, understand, and be able to describe each broad generalization upon which the structure of music is based. — *generalizations*

2. Know and understand each concept upon which the comprehension of each generalization rests. — *concepts*

3. State in their plans the behavioral changes that will result from experiences planned to achieve this. — *objectives (behavioral)*

4. Choose the music experiences and music literature that will help the learner to develop each concept and realize each objective. — *experiences*

5. Select or develop evaluative techniques to measure the effectiveness of the musical experiences used to assist the learner in building concepts that in turn lead to the formation of generalizations. — *evaluation*

Students should be helped to formulate a definition of music. They should know that it is sound which is intended to be music taking place in time, and that it may be very simple or very complex. In its more simple forms music will contain only some type of sound in some type of pattern; in its more complex forms it may involve all of the elements of music.

Students work with musical facts, concepts, and generalizations in two ways: (1) listening to music and (2) performing and composing music. Habits, attitudes, and values are influenced by these processes, the type of classroom environment (both physical and social), and the example set either consciously or unconsciously by peers', teachers', and parents' attitudes toward music.

The selection of materials of instruction that most clearly reveal the essentials of a lesson is vital and poses another important task for the teacher. All of the above is necessary to relate the learning process to the teaching process.

Another major task of the teacher is to engage in a type of questioning that guides conceptual learning through discussion, assists students in their comprehension of pertinent aspects of the subject matter at hand, helps them relate the parts to the whole, and encourages them to explore, theorize, interpret, experiment, analyze, synthesize, and evaluate. Students should be encouraged to verbalize their experiences. A balance of questions involving the various types of thinking are used by teacher and student as they assemble data and seek solutions to problems. In the exploration and building of musical understandings students usually begin at the data level, move to the concept level, and then to the generalization level (see pp. 110–111). The teacher should pose questions that move student thinking from data to concept to generalization. Examples follow:

Cognitive-memory Questions
"What is meant by this term or symbol?"

Divergent Questions (open-ended)
"What would happen if there were no terms or symbols?"

Convergent Questions (closed)
"Under what conditions are musical terms and symbols used?"

Evaluative Questions
"Are these the most appropriate terms and symbols for the best communication of this song's message?"

Cognitive Process Skills

Cognitive process skills necessary for conceptual learning include (1) collecting and organizing data—listing, grouping and labeling, (2) generalizing and making inferences from data—comparing and contrasting (differentiating); interpreting data; making inferences; developing generalizations, and (3) applications of knowledge—using what has been learned in new and different ways.

Examples of cognitive behavioral objectives to develop the above process skills are:

CATEGORY OF LEARNING

BEHAVIORAL OBJECTIVE

Knowledge

The students will identify eight instruments of the orchestra as they listen to each of them from a specially prepared tape.

CATEGORY OF LEARNING	BEHAVIORAL OBJECTIVE *(cont.)*
Comprehension	The students will differentiate 2/4, 3/4, and 4/4 meters by demonstrating the conducting pattern of each meter as they listen to musical examples of each of them from a prepared tape.
Application	Given an eight-measure chord sequence, the students will provide a melody consonant with the chords in a meter of their choice. Three or fewer errors in notation will be considered satisfactory.
Analysis	Given the score of an unfamiliar song from a music series book, the student will identify sequence, ostinato, repeat sign, rhythm pattern, melody pattern, the key, and the scale tone that initiates the melody. Two or three omissions will be considered satisfactory.
Generalization	After analyzing notation of several selected melodies, the students, in response to the question, "In how many ways do melody pitches move?" will conclude that *pitches move in three ways:* they repeat, follow scale lines (adjacent pitches), or move in skips, often following chord lines.
Synthesis	Given the melody with its accompanying chords, the students will create a classroom orchestra score involving voices, piano, bells, Autoharp, and percussion of their choice.
Evaluation	Students will listen to the singing of the class while they observe the score of the song. They will then judge the performance in terms of intonation, pronunciation, appropriate tone quality, and rhythmic accuracy.

For assistance in using cognitive process skills in lesson plans, refer to the plan in Chapter Seven, pp. 135–136 (Example III).

Psychomotor Objectives. The term psychomotor unites mind and movement; it describes mental processes that have movements as the end result, thus including musical performance. There are a number of categories of psychomotor skills. At the lowest level is perception that eventually calls for a physical action, then follows the "set," which implies a readiness to act, the guided responses (an observable reaction), a learned response of habitual nature, a more complex overt response such as the automatic fingering on an instrument, then the advanced control of motions that results in adaptations or improvements, and finally, the ability to originate or develop new skills.

Musical performance requires cognitive processes, and this combination of mental processes with the resulting physical responses is called psychomotor learning. Such consequences can be evaluated in terms of observable performance. Ways of doing this include the use of behaviorally stated objectives that refer to individual and group musical performance or other body movement and certain creative activities. Checklists and rating scales can be used to evaluate the performance of individuals. Checklists for evaluation can be constructed, using such titles as Musical Skills, Instrumental Performance, Vocal Performance, Improvisation Skills, and Conducting Skills.

If students are to engage successfully in music learning activities they will need to become involved in a variety of psychomotor musical skills that will assist them in their growing understanding of music. Appropriate objectives should be developed in the following areas of music skills:

1. *Listening.* Listening is the basic music skill, because learning the skills of singing, playing, and moving to music is dependent on the learner's ability to listen to, analyze, and appreciate music. The most productive learning situations in music involve listening: matching a given pitch, discriminating between pitches; creating and improvising rhythms, melodies, harmonies, and movement to music; analyzing musical form; and improving performance skills. All sensory musical experiences contribute to the development of the student's listening skills.

2. *Moving to Music.* Students learn music by moving their bodies to its salient characteristics as they listen to it. They need to experiment with free interpretation, characterization, dramatization, fundamental movements, singing games, and dances.

3. *Singing.* Singing is one of the most satisfying of human activities. Students need to be able to sing on pitch with a tone quality suitable to the meaning of the words they sing. By the time they leave the elementary school they should possess the ability to improvise vocally and to sing independent parts of songs such as parts of a round, chants, and descants, and those necessary for harmonic part singing.

4. *Playing Instruments.* The desire to manipulate musical instruments seems universal; students ordinarily find great pleasure in playing instruments. Through performing on percussion instruments, bells, xylophone, and recorder, they can contribute to their understanding of rhythm, pitch, form, dynamics, tempo, and melody. By chording on the Autoharp and piano they can learn much about harmony and chord construction. Improvisation and composition are related skills.

5. *Reading Music.* This skill relates to all the other skills in that music notation symbolizes what is heard and what is performed. There are music symbols for pitch, duration, meter, tempo, dynamics, and harmonization.

A plan for teaching skills is found in Chapter Seven, p. 137.

Affective Content and Objectives are concerned with feelings, attitudes, appreciations, and values. When working in this area, teachers must remember not to indoctrinate learners, but to help them acquire information upon which to act and make judgments with increasing independence. Also, since such acts and judgments are often highly personal, the learner's privacy should not be threatened. When students are reacting positively to music— that is, with personal enjoyment, it can be assumed that they are finding satisfaction in the experience in which they are involved, that they desire to hear more of this kind of music, that they identify with it, and that they desire to evaluate it. Since such personal responses are often covert (not observable), the behavioral objective may appear to be not applicable, or at least more difficult to construct, because of a lack of definite criteria to measure performance. In contrast to the observable and measurable verbs typical of cognitive objectives, nonobservable and nonmeasurable verbs such as the following are appropriate for long-term affective goals: appreciate, love, desire, choose, like, dislike. However, under each of these long-term affective goals must be listed and sequenced specific and measurable instructional teaching and student behavioral objectives that indicate specifically what students will do to reveal that they appreciate, love, desire, enjoy, like, or dislike.

Four learning categories to use as guides when constructing affective behavioral objectives for elementary schools have been identified, according to the Krathwohl-Bloom *Taxonomy* (1964):

1. *Receiving*   Being receptive is made known by observable awareness, willingness, or attentiveness.

2. *Responding*   Active desire for an experience, voluntary action, lack of resistance.

3. *Valuing*   Forming personal preferences, developing firm convictions, recognizing traditional values, acting in accordance with convictions.

4. *Organization*   Comparing, relating, and synthesizing values; developing a personal hierarchy of values.

In the affective domain, teachers should commit themselves to the task of creatively devising ways for students to express covert (internal) learnings in overt ways. There are many overt ways in which pupils reveal their individual appreciations, attitudes, habits, values, and interests. See the examples which follow:

Affective Behavioral Objectives

CATEGORY OF LEARNING (covert activity)	BEHAVIORAL OBJECTIVE (observable and measurable)
Receiving (being receptive)	After several successful experiences in accompanying with the Autoharp, the student, at the teacher's suggestion, takes the instrument to a practice booth on his or her own time to work with a learning package concerning the Autoharp.
Responding	When given the opportunity to choose to participate or not participate in several types of group activities, the student chooses to join a recorder group.

CATEGORY OF LEARNING (covert activity)	BEHAVIORAL OBJECTIVE (*cont.*) (observable and measurable)
Valuing	After attending a school concert of the local symphony orchestra, the student voluntarily writes to the conductor, urging him or her to bring the orchestra to school for another concert.
Organization (of a personal hierarchy of values)	When provided time to listen to phonograph recordings, the student arranges them in order of his or her preference.

Research indicates that children's attitudes and values regarding music may reflect the attitudes of both the peer group and those of high-status adults. Thus it is possible that a child's music attitudes and values can be affected by contradictory musical influences emanating from adults and peers, and from radio, television, and recordings. At the same time, music teachers should not strive for or expect that all students acquire the same set of musical values.

The teacher's personal attitudes toward music will usually affect students' valuing more than formal class presentations on learning to value. The chance remark of a teacher might have a lasting influence on a child.

Teachers should work toward a classroom environment in which the varied opinions of students toward the many different types of music are listened to with interest and defended with musical knowledge when necessary. (Why did you like or dislike this music?) Such an environment permits disagreements that can be expressed in ways that permit personal differences while arguing intellectual points in support of positions taken. Musical values and attitudes toward music cannot be separated entirely from respect, concern for the feelings of others, and the acknowledgment that people can hold differing views—especially in a classroom situation in which there is neither hostility nor aggression. An intellectually sound position for a teacher to take is one that attempts to judge "good" music in accordance with how well it performs its function, and to operate in a climate of openness that admits the exploration of every type of music to attempt to find out what it is used for, how it is constructed, what values are reflected in it, and how good it is in its category.

The students' feelings about and interest in a learning experience determine to a significant degree what they learn about a subject cognitively. What a person learns cognitively and affectively *cannot be separated.* The affective domain influences every part of the learning and evaluation process.

While behavioral objectives are acknowledged to give precise direction to teaching and learning, they become controversial when used rigidly, stifling individuality. As stated above, they are somewhat difficult in the affective domain because many affective responses are not observable, thereby ruling out the clear evaluation typical of cognitive responses. Perhaps the matter can be summarized by saying that any good idea can be weakened by those who use it poorly, and that the teacher's judgment must prevail over rigidity of any kind in the human experience we call education.

Teachers should ponder the warning of Charles Leonhard not to over-emphasize the intellectual aspects of music: "We should exercise caution in abandoning the goals we have worked toward under the often vague term appreciation. One danger that I see in the current emphasis on concepts and structured learning is that we may become so involved in the specifics and minutia of music that we forget that the musical experience is basically an affective experience. Whatever else it may achieve, music loses its value when it fails to touch the heart and stir the feeling of people."* Those words urge teachers to consider students' appreciative responses to music and to realize that these are often nonverbal in character. This is part of affective learning—the feelings and emotions aspect. Music is always a reflection of humanity; the technical aspects of music are only a means of communication. *Music is an aesthetic experience and a social language before it is an intellectual experience,* and competent teachers never forget this when they plan the music lesson.

Creative-Exploratory Objectives. There are objectives that are open-ended, therefore not as exact in nature, being focused upon experiences rather than on precise outcomes. These free students to venture into what are to them uncharted avenues of music learning. When students are engaged in music experiences of this type, there are certain characteristics in their efforts to learn. They are:

> Seeking individual fulfillment through a musical experience.
>
> Freely experimenting, exploring, and testing their own ideas.
>
> Disclosing their imagination in creative ways.
>
> Operating on hypotheses and intuition to create new musical sounds, forms, and interpretations.
>
> Employing analytical thought processes to seek musical meanings and results.

Musical exploration and creativity can take many forms: improvisation, movement, composition, conducting, interpretation, and experiments with sounds and instrumentation. Creative-exploratory objectives should encourage students to find new ways that involve inductive and intuitive thought processes. The Manhattanville Music Curriculum Program (pp. 152–163) provides examples of this.

When initiating a creative-exploratory approach, students begin with music familiar to and accepted by them. Questions designed to cause them to analyze and explore the structure of known music serve as an understandable and secure base from which to expand questions of the same type

* Excerpt from address by Charles Leonhard at the Conference to Improve the Effectiveness of Music Education in Oregon Elementary Schools, Gearhart, Oregon, April 27–28, 1967. State Department of Education, Salem, Oregon.

to apply to new types of music later. Questions such as the following might be used:

Why are sharps used in some songs and flats in other songs?

What would these songs sound like if there were no sharps or flats? Let's try them and find out.

Why do we need the staff, notes, and rests? Try some other way to notate this song.

How are songs composed? Tell us how you do it.

How does notation control sound? How accurately do you think notation does this?

How and what does music communicate?

What effect does a composer's cultural background have on the types of music he or she composes?

The above types of questions call for answers that learners can discover rather than memorize. Creative-exploratory learning requires active involvement and interdisciplinary thinking. Students can apply and test their musical knowledge as they search for answers to problems that become personal musical experiences. In the creative-exploratory process students explore their own ideas through the use of a variety of types of media and instructional materials. As they seek answers they make additional musical discoveries. Music becomes a specific affective and socially pleasant experience.

Such involvement promotes the desire to learn form, style, and notation, to listen analytically, and to understand how music is constructed and why, rather than simply identifying isolated aspects of music. It leads to a positive attitude toward music. In such an approach, facts and skills are not neglected but are taught as tools of learning so that students progress to a stage when they can control and direct their own learning.

When complete, the curriculum will consist of four major components: (1) musical content (data, concepts, generalizations), (2) cognitive process skills, (3) music skills (psychomotor), and (4) affective aspects. When long-term goals and instructional objectives are clearly delineated, they implement learning in all these areas, and an effective and sequentially developed program results.

Music Learning Activities, the Essential Ingredient

The curriculum plan is nothing more than a design on paper until students become actively involved in learning both music content and processes. Content and processes are best learned concurrently. The selection and organization of music content form a means whereby knowledge is transmitted. The selection and ordering of learning experiences promotes the application of knowledge; therefore the teacher's judgment and management skills are crucial to successful learning. The teacher has always been the most important single influence in education.

To review, the learning experiences planned for the purpose of realizing specific goals and objectives should deal with musical encounters that call for problem solving and decision making by students and which provide for individual differences in interest, learning styles, and capabilities. It is through musical learning activities that students become both observers and participators in the world of music, thus acquiring the competencies to assimilate, understand, and work with the knowledge they obtain. Teachers should consider not only what they expect students to learn, but also how they expect them to learn it. Music knowledge taught as an end in itself fails to encourage students to think, does not alter attitudes, and fails to further the mastery of skills.

Learning Experiences Learning experiences are activities designed to engage students with aspects of musical subject matter, skills, and attitudes. The purpose of such involvement is to motivate students to think about and use music content, to achieve optimal music learning, and to stimulate their interest so that later they can learn more successfully in self-directed ways.

The appropriate learning activity is determined by the nature of the subject matter and the objectives the teacher and students desire to attain. At times the most suitable activities will be student behaviors such as interviewing, describing, discussing, explaining, and performing. In other cases the most relevant activities will be the creation and development of composition, musical arrangements, dance, and drama. In still other instances experiences such as viewing a film and attending a concert will be more suitable.

Teachers must decide what behaviors, products, or experiences might promote the insight they desire and will serve to realize learning in all areas of the music curriculum. Will it suffice if students simply read about tempo or see a film about the way individuals physically interpret the rhythm in a musical selection? Should the students make inferences based on the movement and tempo shown in the film? About how tempo expresses feelings? Maybe they should discuss how the tempo in the selection makes them feel. They could dramatize their interpretation of what a composer is attempting to communicate or how the music as a whole makes them feel. Then, too, they may be encouraged to interpret a musical selection through creative movement and dance; they may discuss their impressions while moving creatively and interpreting the rhythm, melody, or harmonic changes of the selection.

Not All Learning Activities Serve the Same Purpose Some activities provide for *input* of information. Activities of this kind include reading, observing, interviewing, listening to live performers or recorded music or viewing films. These kinds of activities are essential for students, since they must have information or data to work with or think about before they can be expected to engage in intelligent action. In other words, they must work with data before they can transpose it into concepts and generalizations. These data must be organized and internalized in expectation of being used, thus the necessity for a second type of learning activity which fosters *structuring* of information (cognitive process skills). Such activities help students to organize and make sense out of the materials to which they have been exposed. A third type of learning activity helps students to *demonstrate* what they have learned: how best to perform a phrase of music, how to interpret a selection through movement and dance, or how to dramatize the feeling and mood of a particular selection. Students need to show the skills they have mastered, to show how effectively they can think. Their ability to summarize and form concepts and generalizations is evidence of a mastery of content and skills as well as an indication that they understand the behaviors, performance, problems and feelings of others.

A fourth type of learning activity encourages students to express themselves by *exploring-creating* or producing an original product. This type of learning activity includes composing, improvising, altering music in various ways, writing new verses to songs, interpreting music through performance and movement, conducting, arranging, and accompanying. Although there are similarities and overlap between the processes of demonstrating and creating, demonstrative experiences provide an opportunity for students to show the degree to which they understand data that they earlier acquired and ordered, whereas creative activity encourages students to use their newly acquired understanding of data to produce a new or different product or to present an original performance.

An understanding that varied types of learning experiences serve different purposes should help a teacher design learning activities that assist students to learn in diverse ways. Often, students are engaged for the most part in the same kind of activity every day—listening to the teacher talk (most teachers talk far too much). It is necessary that teachers talk. But students have unique learning styles, and many do not learn music well by talk or the teacher's singing, or by printed song material. These students need to be more directly involved. It is for this reason that direct and relevant activity such as attending a community music program, interpreting a song by dramatizing, role-playing, performing music in active ways, illustrating it pictorially, dancing and movement is significant and effective. *Active* learning is needed. Obviously, students need to learn from textbooks and supplementary books as well as from other printed music literature, but for students to learn conceptually there must be a variety of levels and types of materials and activities.

Some students can learn through reading; others learn best kinesthetically, through observing, hearing, or touching musical instruments or other objects which they are exploring. Some can work best by themselves while others prefer group participation. Most understand more clearly if they can demonstrate at once by some overt means what they have assimilated. Others grasp the relationship more clearly when they organize music data into concepts and generalizations, or through an outline or chart format.

Students should be provided the opportunity to learn by participating in four major categories of learning experience (see Table 6.1):

1. Sensory intake
2. Structuring—organizing

Table 6.1. Categorized Learning Activities

	Sensory Intake	Structuring-Organizing	Expressive-Demonstrative	Exploratory-Creative
READING	song books articles songs magazines duplicated materials charts posters bulletin boards	outlining chart making illustrating arranging music question answering question stating summarizing writing identifying	dramatizing role playing discussing writing illustrating reporting explaining forming questions analyzing	solving problems inventing composing improvising arranging music role playing miming painting questioning
OBSERVING	musical experiments films slides filmstrips pictures drawings illustrations paintings photographs musical instruments rhythmic movement performers television	choosing recording experimenting ordering sorting	generalizing singing playing instruments dancing movement conducting describing reacting preparing charts drawing murals choosing notating	hypothesizing predicting singing playing instruments drawing movement dancing forming questions making instruments illustrating discussing
HEARING	recordings lectures discussions radio music community music school programs classroom music			
TOUCHING	musical instruments sound producing objects			

An activity may appear in more than one category according to its use.

3. Expressive—demonstrative
4. Creative—exploratory

Curriculum designs must therefore include not only long-term goals, specific instructional objectives, and behavioral objectives, but must also incorporate appropriate experiences for the realization of these goals and objectives.

Summary

Teachers of music who are competent in designing and implementing a comprehensive curriculum for students

1. Must possess a rationale or philosophy which incorporates the following: Why teach music? How should music be taught? When should it be taught and under what conditions? What can music do for students that no other subject can do as well?
2. Understand how students develop physically, emotionally, aesthetically, socially, and cognitively (intellectually): How do students learn? How may teachers diagnose the musical capabilities, learning styles, and interests of each student?
3. Know accepted learning research and theories and are able to apply them in program construction and lesson planning.
4. Are knowledgeable of what should be taught: data, concepts, and generalizations, process skills, music skills, and attitudes.
5. Are able to write appropriate and clearly stated goals (long-term), instructional objectives, and behavioral objectives for the teaching of the major components in a curriculum as stated in item four above.
6. Select, sequence, and use a variety of appropriate learning experiences and materials to realize the stated objectives.
7. Use questions that foster different levels of thought processes.
8. Develop appropriate teaching strategies for directing the learning activities for individuals and the class.
9. Evaluate the success of the music program for individuals and the class and sometimes for the school and community.
10. Possess enthusiasm, a positive outlook, and faith in students' ability to learn.
11. Continue to seek, study, and analyze recent trends, materials, media, and equipment.
12. Work cooperatively with other classroom and music teachers, specialists, and consultants in revising and keeping music programs updated.
13. Voluntarily attend workshops, conferences, and conventions to observe the performance of competent teachers of music to obtain knowledge of how to better organize and implement the music program.

EXPLORATORY ACTIVITIES

1. Define goals, instructional objectives, and behavioral objectives; explain the relationship among them and the purpose and use of each in planning instructional programs and lessons.

2. What music activities are basic to the elementary and middle school music program?
3. Identify and present in class long-term goals to be furthered in a comprehensive elementary and middle school music program.
4. Make a list of musical goals to be realized in a year's program. Write them in the form of behaviorally stated instructional objectives.
5. Explain the advantages and disadvantages of long-term planned programs and curriculum guides.
6. Evaluate this statement: "We have a wonderful music teaching guide in our school; it tells the teacher exactly what to do each day."
7. Suppose that there is a national curriculum in music. What might its advantages and disadvantages be?
8. Give reasons why a sequence of music study that is well organized in terms of subject matter might fail to be sequential for a learner?
9. Demonstrate the difference between a fact, a concept, and a generalization in music.
10. Design a structure of the subject of music for a level of your choice.
11. Plan what you believe to be an appropriate and desirable music program for ages 5–8. Consider all the elements of music. Discuss your formulated program with others.
12. Examine the music curriculum guides used in a school system near you and appraise the suggested music learnings for each age and performance level. Compare these suggested learnings with those in a guide from another school system.
13. Examine a music course of study used in a nearby school system to answer the following questions: What musical content, facts, concepts, and generalizations are stated or suggested? Do you find serious omissions? If so, what are they? What suggestions are made for the spiral development of concepts and generalizations? Are student objectives stated in behavioral terms? What teaching procedures, types of questions, and methods of inquiry are listed? What musical attitudes, appreciations, habits, and values are encouraged?
14. Relate the approach presented in *The Study of Music in the Elementary School: A Conceptual Approach* (MENC, 1967) with the Structure of Music Outline in this chapter.
15. Analyze the Structure of Music Outline and revise it to suit your purposes. Add or delete generalizations, instructional objectives, and concepts, or reword them. Determine how you will use this suggested structure in teaching the elements of music.
16. In the history of music education in the United States, whenever teachers have concentrated exclusively on facts about music rather than on the beauty and satisfactions of music, students' appreciation of the subject has declined. How can teachers prevent this negative development and still use a conceptual approach?

References

BOYLE, DAVID, compiler, *Instructional Objectives in Music: Resources for Planning Instruction and Evaluating Achievement,* Chapter 6. Reston, Va.: Music Educators National Conference, 1974.

BRUNER, JEROME S., *The Process of Education,* p. 7. Cambridge, Mass.: Harvard University Press, 1960.

————, *Toward a Theory of Instruction.* New York: W. W. Norton and Company, Inc., 1966. The spiral curriculum and discovery learning.

COMBS, ARTHUR, *Educational Accountability Beyond Behavioral Objectives.* Washington, D.C.: Association for Supervision and Curriculum Development, 1972.

FRAENKEL, JACK R., *Helping Students Think and Value,* pp. 94–96. Englewood Cliffs, N.J.: Prentice-Hall, Inc., 1973.

FYFE, JOAN Z., *Personalizing Music Instruction: A Plan for Implementation.* Sherman Oaks, Calif.: Alfred Publishing Company, 1978.

HOLT, DENNIS M., "Competency Based Music Teacher Education: Is Systematic Accountability Worth the Effort?" *Council for Research in Music Education,* Bulletin No. 40 (Winter 1974), pp. 1–6.

KRATHWOHL, DAVID R., BENJAMIN BLOOM, and B. B. MASIA, *Taxonomy of Educational Objectives: Handbook II: The Affective Domain.* New York: David McKay Company, Inc., 1964. Adapted.

RADOCY, RUDOLPH E., "Behavioral Objectives in Music: Shall We Continue?" *Music Educators Journal,* March 1974, pp. 38–40.

REGELSKI, THOMAS A., *Principles and Problems of Music Education.* Englewood Cliffs, N.J.: Prentice-Hall, Inc., 1975.

"You Can Build a Comprehensive Music Curriculum," *Music Educators Journal,* November 1974, pp. 42–45.

chapter seven

Planning for Teaching

The teacher's knowledge of the competencies of students at the beginning of the year serves as a base for developing annual music programs, units, or lessons. A model to use as a guide for the optimum learning of each student at the class and individual levels is given on page 126.

To learn about students and their musical abilities the teacher can use information from the following sources: health records, cumulative records, checklists, tape recordings of performances, interviews with former teachers (including private music teachers), anecdotal records, student-teacher conferences, observations, class discussions, and parent-teacher conferences.

The First Plans A primary consideration when planning lessons is the prerequisite knowledge of the students. As the old saying goes, "You can't come from where you haven't been." The teacher should plan to extend and expand student knowledge of music and must know where those students are musically in order to begin such planning. The initial lessons for the beginning of the school year are usually quite simple and in large part exploratory, in that the teacher is assessing the musical competencies and interests of the students. These plans might center around pleasurable singing and getting acquainted.

First Day	Try some echo-clapping.
	What are your favorite songs from past years?
	What did you learn to sing at camp last summer?
	Can someone help us learn a good one?
	Common repertoire songs. Plan to do something different with one or more of them.
Second Day	Review familiar songs; try to add something new to them.
	Discover or invent a rhythm pattern to be used with percussion instruments with a song.
	Teach a new song.
	Begin to use songs or parts of songs for individual and group tone matching; use echo-type songs.
Third Day	Review well-liked songs.
	Make up a tune for a short poem.
	Introduce a recording for listening related to known songs; create appropriate rhythmic responses.

Lesson plans vary in complexity from the extremely simple to the highly intricate. However, plans that are simple in design can be intricate in their implementation. A plan in which one song, one recording, or one

Figure 7.1. MODEL FOR DIAGNOSING AND PLANNING FOR LEARNING

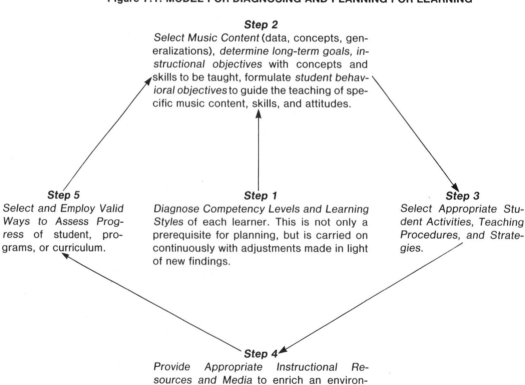

Step 2
Select Music Content (data, concepts, generalizations), *determine long-term goals, instructional objectives* with concepts and skills to be taught, formulate *student behavioral objectives* to guide the teaching of specific music content, skills, and attitudes.

Step 5
Select and Employ Valid Ways to Assess Progress of student, programs, or curriculum.

Step 1
Diagnose Competency Levels and Learning Styles of each learner. This is not only a prerequisite for planning, but is carried on continuously with adjustments made in light of new findings.

Step 3
Select Appropriate Student Activities, Teaching Procedures, and Strategies.

Step 4
Provide Appropriate Instructional Resources and Media to enrich an environment conducive to realizing the objectives.

rhythmic response appears may be too brief or too monotonous because of the many repetitions of the single musical experience. It is also possible that individual differences cannot be well accommodated in such a plan. Experienced teachers have learned that it is essential to a functional plan that more than one music activity be employed in order for students to respond to and analyze music in different ways. Many college teachers do not accept one-idea plans although some do when it is the initial attempt of a college student. However, it is understood that as later plans are designed, they will reflect an ability to organize more complex plans in which several objectives and music skills may appear. Furthermore, when more complex and detailed plans are written, it should be acknowledged that they cannot be read by the teacher during the teaching process. They are memorized in part, and the teacher follows a short list of planned activities including key questions. Experienced teachers regularly use such lists, often on 3 × 5 cards.

There are many different possibilities for planning, and the teacher normally chooses experiences and strategies suited both to the children under instruction and to his or her personality. No teacher will operate exactly like any other teacher; each is a unique personality. Thus the planning of the lesson will be a reflection of the particular teacher who prepares it, showing how that teacher's strengths are employed and how possible weaknesses are accommodated. Such plans may be for a daily lesson, a week's work, or a more lengthy unit. A sample lesson plan that may be used as a guide for devising a teacher's own plan follows:

An Instructional Plan

The experience (the nature of the experience and the plan for conducting it):

Designed for: Large Group _____ Small Group _____ Individual _____
                 Other _____
Time span needed for completion:
Materials needed:

Objective(s) (state in performance terms the observable behavior of the learner, the conditions under which this takes place, and the extent of learning expected):
Cognitive _____

_____

Affective _____

_____

Psychomotor _____

_____

Prior knowledge required (competencies needed by the learner for the task):

Evaluation:

___

In the above Instructional Plan *the experience* is to be stated in descriptive terms. The teacher lists special *materials necessary* in the conduct of the experience, and composes an *objective* or objectives in behavioral terms that spell out what observable activity or activities the learner will perform as a result of the experience. The *prior knowledge required* section causes the teacher to reconsider the learning sequence to be certain that the learners have the necessary prerequisities to enable them to profit from the experience. When many such plans are assembled and sequenced, they could be the equivalent of a course of study.

Detailed Lesson Plans

There are aspects common to all detailed lesson plans. One is determination of prerequisites of knowledge for the lesson. Another is the formation of instructional and behavioral objectives. (The writing of these was stressed in Chapter Six.) When they are properly written, they state the behavior by which the student evidences comprehension of a concept or generalization, under what conditions, and to what degree. A third aspect is the selection of activities through which the student can engage in mental, physical, and affective processes that best assist forming concepts and generalizations. An important principle is to plan for a variety of activities that keep learners involved, interested, happy, and provide for individual learning styles and competencies. This requires that these activities be suited to abilities of each student so that he or she can experience success after due effort. A fourth aspect is the selection of materials and media to use for the activities. In music education the term *materials* means all the musical, mechanical, and literary items needed. Songs and recordings of worth should be chosen. All materials should be assembled and prepared in advance of the lesson to avoid confusion and loss of time. The *procedure* is the fifth common item. Sometimes this is stated in the activities section. This is the learning sequence and includes appropriate key questions. An example of such a sequence is:

1. A review of a favorite song, rhythmic response, or both that recall earlier learnings. Always try to add something new to review experiences.
2. A new problem activity usually related to or an outgrowth of the review.
3. Application of the problem in a new situation, such as in a different song, or on a different recording. This is done to evaluate the success of the children in

achieving the objective of the plan. From this the teacher will have clues indicating how to plan for the next lesson.

4. Close the lesson by singing a well-liked, familiar song.

A sixth aspect is summarizing what has been learned in the form of a generalization. A seventh is evaluation. This part of the plan may be incorporated into the procedure. The test regarding where it should be placed is, "Where can it be treated adequately?" It could conceivably appear in all parts of a plan. Did the learners achieve the behavioral objectives? Were they challenged and satisfied with the experience? Which aspects of the plan were successful and which were not? Which students need more assistance? What are the implications for the next music lesson?

The following suggested plan can accommodate all of the information discussed in Chapter Six relating to associating objectives with the structure of music, using data, forming concepts and (eventual) generalizations by students, behavioral objectives, learning activities, and teaching procedures that include questioning strategies.

EXAMPLE I. Model Daily Lesson Plan Outline

Name _____

Date _____ Level _____ Time _____

Concept(s) to be taught:

Instructional objective(s):

Student behavioral objective(s):

Materials and media needed:

Teaching strategies or procedures:
A. Beginning and motivating activities (setting the stage for learning).
   1. Planning activities with students.
   2. List possible types of questions and their probable sequence.
B. Student developmental activities. Plan at least three different types for each lesson to accommodate individual learning styles and to realize instructional and behaviorally stated objectives written above.
C. Conclusion in the form of a generalized statement (generalization or principle).
D. Evaluation.
   1. By students and teacher.
   2. By teacher to adjust the teaching of the next lesson.
Please use back of sheet for comments by student teacher and/or supervising teacher for evaluation, follow-up questions, etc.

Explanation of the Daily Lesson Plan

Concepts to be Taught. This refers to any aspect of the elements of music (see Figure 6.2, page 102, or A Conceptual Structure of Music, pp. 105–109).

Instructional Objective. This states the purpose of the lesson from the standpoint of the teacher. *Example:* To expand knowledge of tonic-dominant chord changes. Notice how behavioral objectives relate to this instructional objective.

Behavioral Objective. This identifies what will happen from the standpoint of the students. *Example:* After singing and accompanying with the Autoharp several (specific) familiar songs, some of which can be harmonized by (1) one chord, and (2) two chords, the learners will identify the tonic and dominant chords in these songs when the teacher plays them on the piano, the Autoharp, and from recordings. They will identify the tonic chord by raising one finger, and the dominant chord by raising five fingers, and will do this with their eyes closed.

Remember that behavioral objectives call for students to behave or perform in a variety of ways, such as (Nye, 1970):

Identifying a musical instrument, term, symbol, or aspect of notation by picking it up, pointing to it, touching it, or communicating it verbally.

Naming an instrument, form, term, symbol, or relationship.

Arranging three or more phrases, terms, symbols, measures, or events in order based on a stated plan.

Describing properties sufficient to identify a type of song, phrase, term, symbol, or relationship.

Selecting an object, term, symbol, or phrase from two or more which might be confused.

Composing or *constructing* music, accompaniments, musical instruments, a drawing, and written or verbal statements which indicate ability to infer, hypothesize, and evaluate.

Demonstrating the sequence of operations necessary to carry out a musical procedure.

Deriving an answer to a musical problem by employing the behaviors stated above, and organizing these into various types of data derived from such behaviors into a musical concept or generalization to be applied in the solution of other musical problems.

Performing or *conducting* music in a manner that proves comprehension of a concept or acquisition of a skill.

Materials. List all media and/or materials needed for the lesson—projectors, films, slides, transparencies, tapes, recordings, charts, maps, books, songs, paper, instruments, objects, and resource persons if they are needed to assist. Teachers should be specific when listing sources; state the title of a book, with publisher and page numbers; state the manufacturer of a recording and the record number.

Teaching Procedures and Learning Experiences. This is the "how to do it" part of the plan. What the teacher does and what the students are doing in each activity is included here, as are the teacher's questions. The teacher tries to use as many different types of questions as are logically appropriate in exploring an idea or concept—knowledge, interpretation, application, analysis, synthesis, and evaluative types of questions. (See "Questions, a Stimulus for Conceptual Learning," pp. 40–42.) This section can be divided into two distinct parts: (1) Introduction, which may include a review of a previous lesson, building readiness for the lesson of the day, and establishing objectives, and (2) Developmental strategies, the work-study-game activities the students will engage in to realize the objectives of the lesson.

Conclusion(s) in the Form of a Generalized Statement. This results when students construct their own conclusion or generalization derived from their guided involvement in a variety of developmental activities used in the lesson to realize the objectives of the plan as focused upon the concepts to be taught.

Evaluation. Evaluation consists of specific techniques to determine if the behavioral objectives have been realized by the close of the lesson. Teacher and students summarize and generalize what has been accomplished or learned, what they planned to do but did not complete, how well they did what they did, where they could improve, as well as what they need to continue to work on in the next lesson.

The above plan will help beginning teachers become skillful in organizing a lesson. Less detailed plans are used by experienced teachers because they know many of the details and procedures and do not need to write them.

Inexperienced teachers may feel that a great many things must be packed into a lesson in order to accomplish the year's objectives, and they may err by striving to cover too much in a teaching plan. The fear of omitting something of importance can cause the acquisition of knowledge to become an objective rather than a process that nurtures the capacity to pursue profitable learnings. Such an approach negates the idea of conceptual learning because in order for concepts to grow and generalizations to be formed, main ideas should be approached through the use of a variety of data and all appropriate senses. This is quite different from a random acquisition-of-information approach.

The best lesson plan is just a guide; it is not a law. Regardless of how well designed lesson plans may be, in "real life" they are often altered in midstream, and sometimes even abandoned. Teachers find that they must be flexible in using lesson plans. An unexpected event in the classroom may alter the steps planned to lead to the objective or emphasize a different concept or objective, or an occurrence outside the classroom may interrupt the sequence. Unless the teacher is able to keep the students in the center of the process despite unexpected happenings, a breakdown will result. *Teaching is an art,* not a science.

There may be a series of lessons emphasizing one concept. A common error is to include too many objectives. However, read the *Comments* at the end of Example II on page 134 to find out how a teacher might touch upon many objectives while emphasizing one.

The lesson plan for second or third grade given in Example II includes some of the possible teacher-pupil interactions which obviously would not be written in a teacher's plan. It will be successful only if the students have previously mastered the concepts listed.

EXAMPLE II. Lesson Plan for Second or Third Grade (30 minutes)

Generalization: The tones of melodies may have adjacent (scale-line) pitches or skips (chord-line pitches).

Instructional objective: Some melodies move in skips or steps.

Prior knowledge necessary:

Concepts	Data
high	line
low	space
skip	measure
step	
scale	
melodic line	
chord	

Behavioral objective: The children will differentiate between parts of selected melodies which move chord-wise and parts which move scale-wise by demonstrating with their hands and/or bodies and by identifying such parts in notation.

Pacing Teaching Strategies (expanded here for illustrative purposes):

A. INTRODUCTION (5 minutes)

> *Teacher:* What do we remember about the song "Taps"?

Teacher writes major points on chalkboard as children state them.

> *Child:* We sang "Taps" last.
> *Teacher:* Why did we sing it last?
> *Child:* Because it is a song to end with; it begins, "Day is done."
> *Teacher:* Today we are going to do more with this song. Let's sing it again. Each of you think of a way to show the high and low pitches. Try to remember how the tune goes. Can you hear it in your head without singing it?

Children demonstrate with hands.

> *Teacher:* Where did you begin?
> *Child:* Low

Teacher establishes the pitch and the class sings the song.

B. DEVELOPMENT (20 minutes)

Teacher directs students to sing "Planting Cabbages," and says, "Sing it as you did last week, with part of the class singing measures one and two, five and six, and the rest singing measures three and four, seven and eight." The teacher has assigned the more difficult chord-line measures to good singers, and the less difficult scale-line measures to the less certain singers.

PLANTING CABBAGES

2. *You can plant it with your feet. . . .*

3. *You can plant it with your hands. . . .*

TAPS

Restfully   U.S. Army Bugle Call

Day is done,   gone the sun,   From the lake, from the hill   from the

sky.   All   is   well,   safe - ly   rest,   God   is   nigh.

The class sings the song as directed.

> *Teacher:* Now comes the puzzle: In what way are these songs alike? (*pause*)
> *Child:* Could we sing the songs again?

The class sings the songs again.

> *Sally:* The tunes are different.
> *Fred:* The rhythm is not the same.
> *Marie:* The way we sing "Can you plant the cabbage so" is a little like "Day is done, gone the sun."
> *Teacher:* Why do you think they are alike, Marie?
> *Marie:* The tune in both places skips instead of going in steps.

The teacher produces charts of the notation of each song and asks Marie to explain what she means by pointing to the measures.

> *Teacher:* Does anyone have another theory? Let's sing these songs again, watch the notes, and think how it sounds when the melody skips lines and spaces.

The class sings the songs again.

> *Teacher:* Was there any part of these two songs that didn't skip lines and spaces?
> *Bob:* The part I sing in "Planting Cabbages" doesn't skip.
> *Teacher:* I see that you have examined this song carefully, Bob. Look at the chart and show us the part that you think doesn't skip.

Bob points to measures three and four.

> *Teacher:* Play those measures on the bells, Pete. (*He does.*) What did you discover?
> *Pete:* The notes were all next to each other; there were no skips.
> *Teacher:* Play measure seven and eight. (*He does.*) What do you find there?
> *Pete:* There is a skip in measure seven.
> *Teacher:* Can you change the song so there isn't a skip there, Pete?

Pete experiments and adds an E between notes D and F to eliminate the skip. The teacher writes the E into the chart by making D and E eighth notes that are slurred on the word "same." Pete plays measures seven and eight as revised.

> *Teacher:* Let's all sing measures seven and eight to see if we like them this way.

The class sings the measures and likes the change. Pete volunteers that it is easier to play on the bells this way.

> *Teacher:* Can we analyze the melody of "Taps"? The teacher holds up the chart of "Taps."
> *Child:* It's all skips; it has some repeated notes.
> *Child:* There are dotted notes.
> *Teacher:* Let's examine "Planting Cabbages." Can you use the chart to explain what you find?
> *Children:* It's half skips and half steps; measures one and two, five and six are

skips, and measures three and four and seven and eight are steps; it's in 6/8 meter.

Teacher: Everyone sing the measures that skip along chord lines and let Pete play the measures that step along scale lines.

The class does as directed. The teacher next tests the class on its comprehension of chord lines and scale lines by the following process:

1. A familiar song is sung as the children move to show skips and steps as they hear them in the melody.
2. The class decides if skips or steps are present and states where they are found in the song.
3. The teacher shows a transparency of the notation on the screen to enable the class to verify its decision.

The children will find:

"A Hunting We Will Go"	to be	all steps
"Merrily We Roll Along"	to be	all steps except one skip at the end of the first phrase
"Little Tom Tinker"	to be	all skips and repeated notes until steps in the last measure
"Bow Belinda"	to be	a skip pattern one step lower, then one step higher, with steps in the last measure.

C. CONCLUDING THE LESSON (5 minutes)

Teacher: Let's see if we can state in one sentence all the important things we learned about melodies today.

Class: Some melodies move in steps, some move in skips, and some move in steps and skips. (Notice how the children summarized the day's lesson by stating their findings in the form of a generalization.)

The concluding activity is the singing of "Bow, Belinda" and clapping the beat while volunteer pairs of children improvise dances in turn.

Materials:
Chalkboard
Songs the children know. Source: *Basic Music,* 5th ed., Nye and Bergethon, Prentice-Hall, Inc., 1981.
Charts of the notation of "Taps," p. 63, and "Planting Cabbages," p. 63.
Transparencies of "Merrily We Roll Along," p. 1, "A Hunting We Will Go," p. 85, "Little Tom Tinker," p. 153 and "Bow, Belinda," p. 68.

Comments: Notice that the teacher plans to work toward many more goals than stated in the focus of the lesson. Besides working toward the generalization and behavioral objective stated, this teacher will give attention to:
Tonal memory (Can you hear it in your head without singing it?)
High and low pitch
Body movement in relation to high and low in pitch
Grouping children in accordance with their degree of ability to sing accurately on pitch
Using notation to solve musical problems
Playing an instrument (Why do you think the teacher chose Pete to play the bells?)
Manipulating a melody by changing it
Comparing measures seven and eight with the changed version to judge if the new version is acceptable
Emphasizing listening skills

A concluding activity which involves body movement in dance improvisation (creative), clapping the beat (rhythm), and which may involve "pure enjoyment" as well as possible application of melodic skips and steps and repeated notes to dance movements.

At this time the teacher does not plan to relate chord lines to chords; this is reserved for a later lesson. There may be question as to whether the teacher should have used the terms "chord line" and "scale line." Either the class has sufficient background so that no student would question the use of the terms or the teacher is using them in the hope that some student might ask about them; then a study of these would be proposed as a suggestion that came from the class. The teacher did not plan to develop the reference by the children to repeated notes or repeated note groups; the class was guided in activities that emphasized skips and steps—the stated objective of the plan.

The closing activity can be questioned if it leaves the children in an emotional state that would make their learning in a following subject difficult. It would be assumed that it will not, or if it did, this teacher would follow it with another concluding activity to quiet the children, or that the class is followed by dismissal for the day or for recess or physical education.

The lesson plan in Example III illustrates the use of various cognitive process skills. Teachers should not attempt to pattern all of their lesson plans after every step listed here, for some objectives do not lend themselves to all of the processes. They should, however, include all that are applicable to the realization of the stated objectives. The plan is appropriate for eight- or nine-year-olds, depending upon their musical maturity.

EXAMPLE III. A Lesson on Cognitive Process Skills

Materials: drum, chalk and chalkboard, (specific) music book, recordings.

Teacher's instructional objective: To teach the generalization that "regular accent determines meter."

Concepts to support the generalization: beat, accent, meter signature (or time signature).

Situation: Asking the class to listen and observe, the teacher plays a drum or claps hands with steady beat, sounding no accent. "Now do it with me, stopping when I stop." The class responds.

Observing: "How would you describe what you heard?" "Could you tell what the meter (time signature) might be?" "Why not?"

Comparing: The teacher now repeats the performance except that he or she accents every other beat. "Now you do it." The class responds. "How would you compare what you just heard with what you first heard?" "What is the musical term for the stress I placed on some of the beats?" (*Answer:* accent) "How often did I accent the beats?" (*Answer:* every other beat) The teacher repeats the performance, but accents every third beat. "Compare what I did this time with what you heard the other times." (We have now heard no accent, an accent on every other beat, and an accent on every third beat.)

The teacher writes what he or she did the first time on the chalkboard. At teacher's signal, class claps what is written.

| | | | | · | | | | | | | |

A child is asked to draw a short line either above or below the note stem as the teacher plays the example again, stressing every other beat:

The class claps what is written. The teacher again writes the series of note stems on the chalkboard and asks another child to come forward to notate accents. He or she plays an accent on every third note.

| | | | | | | | | | | |

Classifying: "How many kinds of accents do we now have?" (*Answer:* three—no accent, an accent every other beat, and an accent every third beat) The teacher now asks a child to draw a barline before each accented note. "What meter signatures can we place in front of these examples? (*Answer:* none for the first, 2/4—or 2/2 or 2/8—for the second, and 3/4—or 3/2 or 3/8—for the third) "What names can we say that conform to these two-beat and three-beat meters?" (*Answer:* Ma-ry, John-ny, Jack-son, Ok-la-ho-ma for two-beat meters; Me-lo-dy, Ros-a-lie, Jon-a-than for three-beat meters) The class repeats each name a number of times while clapping or stamping the accent. Children suggest and experiment with other names.

Collecting and organizing data: The children open their music books and search for meters with two and three beats to the measure. These are listed on the chalkboard under each category.

Summarizing statement: When a meter contains two beats, the numeral two appears high in the meter signature; when a meter contains three beats, the numeral three appears high in the meter signature. (An exception is fast 6/8, which will be dealt with later.)

Recognizing assumptions: The teacher says, "Some people say that all music 'swings' in twos or threes. How can this be when some of the meter signatures you saw in your books were 4/4 and 6/8 and perhaps others?" At this point, the books are opened again, and the children are helped to find that 4/4 can be considered to be 2 plus 2, and 6/8 to be 3 plus 3. The latter meter should be closely examined in the music, for 6/8 meter is almost always written in such a manner that the measure can be divided to illustrate that 3-plus-3 characteristic (rather than a mathematically possible 2 plus 2 plus 2). Meters such as 5/4 and 7/8 should probably be reserved for study at a future date when this information becomes necessary.

Creative thinking: The teacher suggests that the class invent meters up to six beats in a measure. The class invents and labels a number of meters by placing regular accents at different intervals by clapping, stamping, or using percussion instruments.

Inferring from the data: Students state in their own words: Accent determines meter; regular accents result in meter; there are many meters.

Analyzing: The teacher plays recordings of short selections that clearly denote 2/4 and 3/4 meters. The children are asked to "feel" the beats and accents, and determine the meter of the selections.

Application: The children find songs they like in their books and sing them with a "feel" for the meter; they also conduct the meters. This will lead them to discover that some songs are more heavily accented than others, and that the strength of the accent is sometimes a matter of musical taste rather than a matter of musical mechanics. "Love Somebody" has a strong accent while "America" needs almost none.

EXAMPLE IV. Lesson Plan for Teaching Skills

The specific skill to be developed:

Behavioral objective(s) to be realized:

1. *Description and Demonstration*
   The skill is demonstrated or otherwise made known to the learners.
   a. The specific skill action is described.
   b. The skill may be demonstrated by a performer (such as the teacher or a skilled student) or by audiovisual means.
2. *Trial to Assess Degree of Skill and Need for Improvement*
   The learners are led to try out their present degree of skill in order that the teacher or the learners identify common errors or the general need for improvement.
3. *Practice for Mastery*
   The practice of the skill, how this is arranged for, and a listing of varied drill activities. Remember that these are sometimes in the form of games.
4. *Application or Assignment*
   The use of the new skill in other settings, for variety, practical application, meaning, and for measurement of the degree of mastery of the skill by the learners.

Relationship of Concepts in Lesson Plans

We have focused attention on lesson plans that typically emphasize a few concepts and generalizations. These plans may appear to limit student activities to experiences with relatively few mental constructs. However, it is important to realize that concepts having to do with one aspect of music relate inevitably to numerous other musical concepts that operate on the periphery of a lesson plan and may not be mentioned in it. For example, activities designed to expand concepts of rhythm may include relationships with concepts of melody, tempo, texture, dynamics, tone quality, form, and note reading. Singing experiences may relate naturally to concepts of rhythm, tempo, texture, dynamics, notation, pitch, harmony, tone qualities, and form. Experiences with instruments may involve all of the above at times. These relationships are good, and many music concepts not mentioned in lesson plans may be expanded incidentally in the stated activities. The most interesting and fruitful plans contain materials and activities that touch many more music concepts than mentioned in the plan.

In the chapters to follow, the reader will find a similar interrelationship of concepts. There will be chapters concerned with sound, rhythm, singing, and playing instruments. Keep in mind that these will include concepts relating to all of the musical elements, despite the stress on one primary element in a chapter. Listening, the basic music activity, pervades every chapter. Watch for activities that require purposeful listening.

Criteria for Use in Designing Lesson Plans

While there are always exceptions, most lesson plans can be evaluated by applying the following criteria:

1. The teacher's instructional objectives are clearly stated. They are drawn from one or more of the four major curricular components: elements of music, cognitive process skills, music skills, and attitudes-appreciations-values.
2. Behavioral objectives are stated in specific terms which incorporate evaluation directly into the objective.
3. The teacher plans challenging and interesting ways to motivate interest in the lesson.
4. The teacher presents a variety of activities in logical sequence that employ all appropriate senses—the ear, eye, and muscular response.
5. The teacher balances activities in terms of intake types (such as viewing and reading), and expressive types (such as performing and creating).
6. The teacher accommodates individual differences including individual learning types.
7. The teacher states key and varied questions.
8. The teacher presents a concept in two or three different contexts.
9. The students are kept active mentally and/or physically during the entire lesson.
10. The teacher selects each activity to assist in the realization of a specific objective.
11. The teacher designs plans that contain general expectations such as what all participants are to do when students or teacher enter and leave the classroom. Distributing books, finding pages in books, getting instruments ready to play, and sounding the first pitch are some of the aspects to be planned. For example, if song titles and page numbers are on the chalkboard or transparency, both time and the teacher's voice can be saved.
12. The teacher lists all necessary materials of instruction needed.

After teaching a lesson, a teacher might ask (for the parts of the lesson where appropriate):

1. Did I encourage student inquiry and discovery of concepts rather than tell them in lecture style?
2. Did I encourage student creativity?
3. Did I keep the students active and interested by providing timely and appropriate feedback?
4. Did I select appropriate activities and materials for the realization of the objectives? Were activities logically and effectively sequenced?
5. Were questions formulated to progress from simple to more complex thinking? Were they varied to suit different learning styles?
6. Did the students and I evaluate the lesson in terms of the stated objectives?

The range of musical interests, aptitudes, skills, and knowledge is so extensive at any given grade level or age that nongraded plans of school organization present few difficulties to teachers who have been aware of students' individual differences and have provided for them in their previous organizational plans. Also, an accurate concept of team teaching is one in which the classroom teacher and the music specialist plan and work together for the good of the students.

The checklist in Fig. 7.2 is an instrument to evaluate an instructional plan.

		Weak	Below Average	Average	Strong	Superior
Clarity of Instructional Objectives	The objectives of the lesson are clear.					
Appropriateness of Objectives	The objectives are neither too easy nor too difficult for the students.					
Organization of the Lesson	The individual parts of the lesson are clearly related to each other in an appropriate way. The total organization facilitates what is to be learned.					
Selection of Content	The content is appropriate for the objectives of the lesson, the level of the class, and the teaching procedures.					
Selection of Materials	The specific instructional materials and human resources used are clearly related to the content of the lesson and complement the selected method of instruction.					
Beginning the Lesson	The students come quickly to attention.					
Clarity of Presentation	The content of the lesson is presented so that it is understandable to the students. Different points of view and specific illustrations are used when appropriate.					
Pacing of the Lesson	The teacher "stays with the class" and adjusts the tempo accordingly.					
Student Participation and Attention	The class is attentive. When appropriate the students actively participate in the lesson					
Ending the Lesson	The lesson is ended when the students have achieved the objectives of the lesson. There is a deliberate attempt to tie together the planned and chance events of the lesson and relate them to the immediate and long range goals of instruction.					
Teacher-Student Rapport	The personal relationships between students and the teacher are harmonious and positive.					

Figure 7.2. CHECKLIST FOR AN INSTRUCTIONAL PLAN

Practical The songs to follow are presented to assist the college student in designing a
Application lesson plan. Whether the plan should be written at this time, or following
study of Parts Two and Three is a matter for the instructor of the class to
decide. However, some preliminary thought about lesson plans could be of
value. Professional teachers will select for use the song or songs that best
lead to a realization of stated objectives. Songs, or any other materials of instruction, are analyzed by teachers to find whether or not they are suitable
for their purposes.

In this chapter, a number of principles for planning lessons were stated,
most of which will not be repeated here. Using all appropriate senses (eye,
ear, body) was one. Thinking in terms of cognitive, affective, and psychomotor learnings was another. Planning in terms of helping learners form
concepts about or relating to the elements of music was an important principle. The conceptual structure of music can stimulate formulation of objectives. How to write instructional and behavioral objectives was discussed in
Chapter Six. We suggest here some ways to use the songs in lesson plans,
realizing that the competent and creative teacher will think of many more.

Songs for Lesson Plans

SONG	RELATED CONCEPTS AND ACTIVITIES
Little Ducklings	melodic contour; scale tones; perform tune on bells
Jennie Jenkins	tempo (fast); contour (disjunct melody line); chord roots; two-part form; improvise a chant on scale tones 5–6 (*so-la*); questions and answers in text suggest two groups of singers or solo and chorus
The Sow Took the Mea-sles	form; ¢ and 2/2 meters; chord tones in the melody (disjunct); experiment with *ritard* to better communicate the meaning of the text; chord roots to play and/or sing; tonic-dominant harmony
This Train	provision for high and low voice ranges; the beat (marching); selection of appropriate percussion instruments to improvise an accompaniment; possible dramatization; syncopation; related recording for analysis
Kum Ba Yah	part singing; improvising harmony; singing in thirds; I–V₇–IV harmony; adding a chord root part (middle C, low F and G)

THE DUCKLINGS

Heads be - neath the wa - ter, tails up in the air.
Now they're right side up, and now they're up - side down.

JENNIE JENKINS

American Folksong

1. Oh, will you wear white, oh, my dear, oh my dear? Oh,
2. Oh, will you wear blue, oh my dear, oh my dear? Oh,

will you wear white___ Jen - nie Jen - - kins? I
will you wear blue___ Jen - nie Jen - - kins? I

won't wear white, for the col - or's too bright, I'll___
won't wear blue, for the col - or's too true,

buy me a fol - dy rol - dy, til - dy dol - ly, seek - a - dou - ble,

Roll,_____ Jen - nie Jen - kins, roll!_____

3. *Will you wear red—I won't wear red, it's the color of my head.*
4. *Will you wear green?—I won't wear green, it's a shame to be seen.*
5. *Will you wear purple?—I won't wear purple, it's the color of a turtle.*

(More verses can be created describing different colors.)

THE SOW TOOK THE MEASLES

American Frontier Song

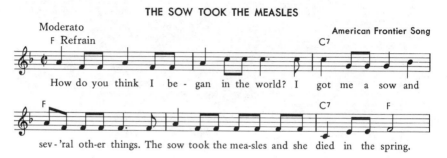

How do you think I be - gan in the world? I got me a sow and

sev - 'ral oth - er things. The sow took the mea-sles and she died in the spring.

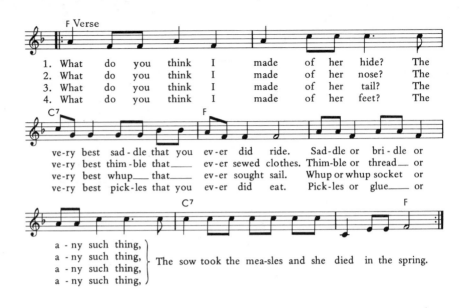

1. What do you think I made of her hide? The
2. What do you think I made of her nose? The
3. What do you think I made of her tail? The
4. What do you think I made of her feet? The

ve-ry best sad-dle that you ev-er did ride. Sad-dle or bri-dle or
ve-ry best thim-ble that____ ev-er sewed clothes. Thim-ble or thread__ or
ve-ry best whup__ that____ ev-er sought sail. Whup or whup socket or
ve-ry best pick-les that you ev-er did eat. Pick-les or glue__ or

a - ny such thing,
a - ny such thing,
a - ny such thing, } The sow took the mea-sles and she died in the spring.
a - ny such thing,

THIS TRAIN

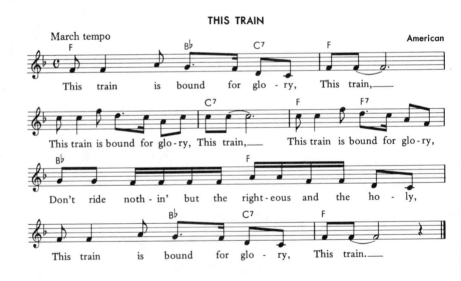

March tempo   American

This train is bound for glo - ry, This train,____
This train is bound for glo-ry, This train,____ This train is bound for glo-ry,
Don't ride noth-in' but the right-eous and the ho - ly,
This train is bound for glo - ry, This train.____

This train is built for speed now, etc.
Fastest train you ever did see,
This train is bound for glory, this train.

This train don't carry no liars, etc.
No hypocrites and no high flyers,
This train is bound for glory, this train.

KUM BA YAH

Afro-American Spiritual

2. *Someone's crying, Lord, Kum ba yah!*
3. *Someone's singing, Lord, Kum ba yah!*
4. *Someone's praying, Lord, Kum ba yah!*

EXPLORATORY ACTIVITY

> When working on assignments to write lesson plans, remember that the current music series textbooks offer assistance.

References

NYE, ROBERT E., et al., *Singing With Children* 2nd ed., Introduction. Belmont, Calif.: Wadsworth Publishing Company, Inc., 1970.
See also references for Chapter Six.

chapter eight

Evaluation

The final step in developing a music curriculum is to establish means of evaluation. Evaluation is a process of assessing to what degree objectives and goals have been attained. Specific and immediate student objectives, teacher instructional objectives, as well as long-term program goals serve as criteria that guide evaluation at all levels of teaching and learning. Evaluation in music consists of assembling, interpreting, and using data to measure three aspects of the curriculum: student achievement, teaching success, and program adequacy. Assessment of student achievement is determined by the use of various tests and evaluative techniques. These devices are employed to determine the amount, relevancy, and quality of the learner's behavior as measured by long-term program goals and the precisely stated performance objectives. When objectives are clearly stated, they yield specific levels of performance from which criteria for student achievement can be established.

Evaluation is not an end within itself; it is a continuous process that is a useful tool in *adjusting* learning goals, objectives, and experiences. The major purpose of evaluation is to ascertain at various points the degree of progress achieved, and, when appropriate, to assist in the adjustment of plans and in the improvement of instructional activities and procedures. It is not presented here as an activity to be employed exclusively at the conclusion of a program or any aspect of a program, but as an integral part of each of these. Therefore the subject will be developed in some detail.

There are music educators who deny that there is adequate means of measurement of musical growth because music is rooted in the affective domain, thus not easily measurable. Music teachers take three different positions concerning measurement by observable behavior: some deny that meaningful appraisal is possible; others believe that ways can be found to evaluate all music experience; some believe that while the result of most musical experiences can be measured, the result of some which are covert will remain difficult to assess until creative teachers are ingenious in preparing performance objectives that will indicate externally what students have internalized. Some experiences may continue to be impossible to appraise.

Evaluation can disclose the need for instructional provision for individual differences in both musical aptitude and learning styles. It can also disclose what aspects of the program need revision and refinement. A realistic evaluation of student achievement can lay the foundation for evaluating teacher success.

Evaluation data can seldom be accepted at face value; they must be studied and interpreted. Perfection is not attainable, but music teachers must strive to provide the most effective program possible under existing conditions, and evaluation should help to attain this goal. "Existing conditions" can refer to space, scheduling, equipment and supplies, which are also in need of appraisal, revision, and improvement as they relate to the learning process.

Suggested Guidelines

Any effective program of evaluation should be guided by several specific and significant criteria:

Evaluation should be made in terms of behavioral objectives. Examples of this type of objective are: The students indicate their understanding of the relationship between vertical and horizontal chord tones by successfully arranging the horizontal chord tones found in selected melodies vertically, finding and playing chord tones on keyboard instruments, and singing chord tones to accompany songs; the students demonstrate their understanding of the structure of the major scale by performing major scales without notation on the bells from several different pitches; the students reveal positive attitudes by listening with interest at home to the televised Young People's Concerts, as demonstrated by their class discussion. The value in stating objectives behaviorally is that they are described in simple, direct, observable, and realizable *performance* terms that incorporate evaluation.

Everyone concerned with learning in the music program should be involved in evaluation. Learning is facilitated when a receptive environment for performance, composition, and analysis of music exists. Bringing about such an environment necessitates the formulation of a basic point of view, establishment of objectives and ways to realize them, and use of diverse techniques to appraise the degree to which the objectives have been attained. Administrators, parents, other adults in the community, teachers, and students should work together in this process. Teachers have the leading role, serving as guides and facilitators in this process. Questions the teachers might ask include: Do the learners understand the objectives? Are they of personal importance to individual learners? How can I help individuals to identify and analyze the various aspects of objectives and the difficulties entailed? What procedures can I use to help students become conscious of the next steps needed? How can I assist them to discover other meanings and possibilities related to the problem?

Students learn best when they are given opportunities to identify what they need to learn, have some choice in what they are to learn, plan how they are going to learn it, and appraise how well they have done so. Questions the learners might ask themselves include: What do I already know about this problem? What does the problem entail? What do I need to know? Where do I begin? What resources do I need? What is my next step? As a result of each bit of evaluation data collected, the student should become more secure and certain of what next steps should be taken.

Evaluation should be recognized as necessary feedback and put to use. Students require feedback in order that they may adjust to their world, find reason to reorder or change the world about them, and to build their self-concepts. The school should provide realistic, unbiased, and valid feedback to learners so that they perceive their condition accurately and become better able to set objectives and plan procedures to achieve them. Learners must be able to analyze, assess, and know results of their attempts to learn; if they do not have this feedback they do not understand how to modify and improve their learning.

Records for furthering the quality of student learning should evolve from the various means of evaluation used. Grading is seen increasingly as a report of doubtful accuracy created more for the benefit of parents and academic bookkeeping than for the teacher-learning process. The reason a grade symbol has little meaning is that it is rarely supported by an explanation of how it was determined. In order for it to have meaning, one must state objectives, the type of evidence which indicates attainment of the objectives, and the analysis of the evidence. Most of what teachers are continually evaluating in their work in the classroom either cannot be summarized into a grade, or can be summarized only with extreme difficulty. Also, subjective influences such as personality, effort, and apparent interest may interfere with teachers' efforts to assess certain types of accomplishment accurately. In music there are many factors to consider. There can be goals and objectives of progress in understanding and using the elements of music, the skills of the program, types of thinking, and musical attitudes and behaviors. Even though a teacher analyzes each of these in relation to a specific student, the grade symbol may be as much a rating of the effectiveness of the teacher's procedures as it is of the learner's progress.

An important principle to be remembered is that when grades must be given, the student and parent should know the basis for and meaning of the grade. What students want to know in music is the evidence of their progress in one or more of the many facets of the study; a grade of C, B, or A generally does not communicate specific meaning.

When students transfer from one school to another, their new teachers should receive records of their progress in music. Also, there is a need to communicate student progress through some form of record to their parents. Records do not need to be exhaustive; they should include only necessary and pertinent data. Records and data can be valuable in helping students to become more self-directed and exacting in their learning, if these records are organized into meaningful feedback that serves as a guide for students in making decisions and seeking information on their own.

Tests comprise only one type of evaluation; they serve primarily as an instrument of measurement. They have a place when they are used in conjunction with other evaluative devices to help students assess their progress and when they are used by teachers as *one way* of evaluating.

Many different types of evaluation are used. If learning in the three domains—cognitive, affective, and psychomotor—is to be assessed, then the appropriate evaluative techniques must be employed. Some possible means of evaluation follow:

Observation	Inventories	Case studies
Discussion	Samples of creative work	Tape recordings
Checklists	Teacher-made tests	Evaluative criteria
Diaries	Standardized tests	Cumulative records
Questionnaires	Group-made tests	Activity records
Charts	Anecdotal records	Attitude scales
Logs	Sociometric tests	Evaluative questions
	Musical performance	

Children practice self-evaluation by means of: group discussions, folders containing samples of work such as compositions, tapes made of performances, verbal feedback from teachers and peers, criteria decided upon by the group, checklists, and diaries.

Teachers decide what combinations of devices they need to use in accordance with the types of evidence desired. Tests used to measure and assess accurately should have the following characteristics:

Validity. They measure what they profess to measure.

Reliability. They measure accurately and consistently.

Appropriateness. They are designed in accordance with the type of learning and the capabilities of the individual or group to which they will be applied.

Practicality. They are easy to use and are not unduly costly in terms of time or money.

Objectivity. They can be used by different persons with the same results.

Usefulness. They will reveal data that can be used.

Behaviorally descriptive. They reveal data related to behavioral objectives and actions of the students.

Evaluative Devices Described

One of the many devices used in evaluation is the essentially simple checklist or checksheet. For example, the 1974 MENC Standards include lists of general standards, such as "Each elementary school provides two current basal series for each classroom." Such standards can be quickly useful in determining whether or not a school music program adheres to them by checking either a *no* column or a *yes* column opposite the standard. A checklist that appraises programs in more detail can be constructed with points under major headings such as Activities and Strategies in the Classroom, Measurement of the Child's Musical Growth, and The Teacher. These headings and points are at the left of the sheet, with columns to their right. Lines are drawn to provide spaces in which to check either *yes, partially, no, and plans for improvement?* (See Figure 8.1.)

	yes	partially	no	plans for improvement?
The elementary music program has a sequentially organized program has a well-qualified staff has adequate materials of instruction				

Figure 8.1. PROGRAM EVALUATION

The same principle can be adapted for use with individuals. A checksheet can be constructed to reveal pupil responses to certain musical concepts, such as loud-soft, fast-slow, high-low, crescendo-decrescendo, woodwind, brass, and percussion. These can be listed under the heading *Behaviors,* with vertical columns to the right indicating the type of musical activities in which pupil recognition or use of these concepts took place, such as singing, composing, moving, playing, listening. (See Figure. 8.2.) Another device can be constructed to record the current level of competency attained in the mastery of a particular skill, such as playing a ukulele. The assessment should reveal what abilities the student possesses or lacks, such as naming the strings, tuning the instrument, and performing specific chords and accompaniments.

When written tests are constructed, the teacher should provide the learners with a very easy way to respond to the questions. Because most tests should be in the context of a musical experience, such as listening to music, the pupils should concentrate on the music, unhindered by possible struggles with writing at the same time. If writing is to be done, it should occur after the musical experience is concluded. Normally, the questions are likely

BEHAVIORS by means of:	SINGING	PLAYING	LISTENING	MOVING	COMPOSING
Recognition of: loud-soft					
fast-slow					
high-low					
cresc.-decresc.					
woodwinds					
brasses					
percussion					

Figure 8.2. STUDENT PROGRESS EVALUATION

to be of multiple choice or other type in which the students simply circle or check the answer. See Figure 8.3 for sample test items.

A simple type of written test can be used before young children understand the staff. For example, if teachers' purposes have included expanding concepts of how pitches move in scale-line patterns, they can use the first three notes of "Three Blind Mice"and similar repeated patterns in songs the children have come to know well. Written correctly, this particular pattern could be drawn:

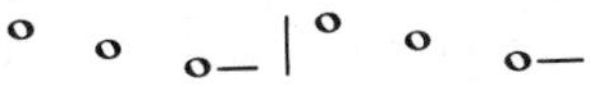

o o o— | o o o—

On the test paper, it might appear with one misplaced note, and the children would be asked to find and circle the error:

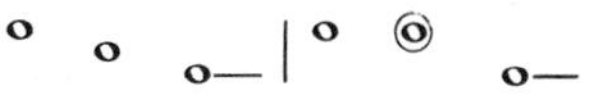

o o o— | o ⊚ o—

Figure 8.3. SAMPLE WRITTEN TEST

> *Instructions:* Listen carefully, then circle the best answer.
>
> 1. The contour of the melody is like: 
>
> 2. The tempo is:
>   fast   moderate   slow
>
> 3. The form of the piece is:
>   A A   A B A   A B A C A
>
> 4. The added part is a:
>   descant   ostinato   harmony part in thirds

The Teacher's Self-Evaluation

One of the best ways for teachers to evaluate their classroom performance is to tape an entire music period or, better yet, videotape it. Then one can play it back and make judgments as to his or her effectiveness. That teacher may discover surprising things and make corrections and improvements before a supervisor suggests them. If a videotape is used, the viewer can judge general appearance including body language, expressions used, various movements, and determine if these are satisfactorily employed or should be changed.

The Tuckman Teacher Feedback Form, published by Hyman in 1975, is an instrument for measuring classroom and rehearsal climate by means of behaviorally stated characteristics. Teachers can use this for self-evaluation or have a colleague make the assessment.

Other Instruments for Evaluation

While our discussion has centered largely on teacher-made evaluative devices, those from other sources should be recognized. The music series publishers are currently offering assistance to teachers in evaluation. For example, Holt, Rinehart and Winston offers "Student Progress Reports" and includes charts that provide student evaluation forms. Silver Burdett has Competency Tests for grades one through six, and "What Do You Hear?" answer sheets for use when students listen to recordings. State Departments of Education often publish useful evaluative instruments and are a source that should be investigated. There are various published tests; selected ones are listed at the end of the reference section. They are used frequently in research.

EXPLORATORY ACTIVITIES

1. Examine courses of study in music published by city, county, and state education departments to learn what provisions are suggested for evaluation and to what extent evaluations are made in terms of purposes and needs.
2. Indicate practical ways in which each of the criteria in this chapter may be used in music teaching. Which ones do you believe should receive more attention? Which do you think are the most difficult to employ?
3. How can you aid children in using self-evaluation in the lessons and units of work you plan? Design a checksheet for a specific lesson.
4. Arrange to observe a class in music and discuss with the teacher the evaluative techniques used. Share this with the college class.
5. Examine a cumulative record form used in a local school system. What music data are recorded? What additional entries, if any, are needed? Why?
6. Prepare a sample checklist, a guide for an observation, a questionnaire, and a chart that can be used in a music unit you plan to teach.
7. How can you use discussion as an evaluative technique in a unit or lesson you

are teaching? Anecdotal records? Tape recordings? Open-ended questions? Musical performance? Logs and diaries? Tests? Discuss these techniques critically with other students and with your teacher.

8. Formulate a lesson plan on the basis of pertinent objectives. Then devise ways to evaluate the success of the plan in terms of achieving these objectives.

References and Materials

General COLWELL, RICHARD, *The Evaluation of Music Teaching and Learning.* Englewood Cliffs, N.J.: Prentice-Hall, Inc., 1970.

————. "Musical Achievement: Difficulties and Directions in Evaluation." *Music Educators Journal,* April 1971, pp. 41–43, 79–83.

LEHMAN, PAUL R., *Tests and Measurements in Music.* Englewood Cliffs, N.J.: Prentice-Hall, Inc., 1968.

The School Music Program: Description and Standards. Reston, Va.: Music Educators National Conference, 1974.

WHYBREW, W. E., *Measurement and Evaluation in Music.* Dubuque, Iowa: Wm. C. Brown Company Publishers, 1971.

WILHELMS, FRED T., ed., *Evaluation as Feedback and Guide* (1967). Association for Supervision and Curriculum Development, 1201 Sixteenth St. N.W., Washington, D.C. 20036.

Tests BENTLEY, ARNOLD, *Measures of Musical Abilities.* London: George G. Harrap & Co. Ltd., 1966.

COLWELL, RICHARD, *Music Achievement Tests.* Urbana, Ill.: School of Music, University of Illinois, 1970.

GORDON, EDWIN, *Iowa Tests of Music Literacy.* Iowa City: Bureau of Educational Research and Service, University of Iowa, 1971.

———— *Musical Aptitude Profile.* Boston: Houghton Mifflin, 1965.

———— *Primary Measures of Music Audiation.* Chicago: G.I.A. Publications, Inc., 1979.

WING, H. D., *Wing Standardized Tests of Musical Intelligence.* Quebec: Institute of Psychological Research, 1961.

2

From Sound and Tone Qualities to Movement, Rhythm, and Dance

chapter nine

Experimenting with Sound and Tone Qualities

Many ideas for teaching music will be presented here. The college student is not expected to absorb all of them at this time, but should seek beginning points from which to expand her or his musical and pedagogical knowledge. When people learn music, the general order of this learning is from sound (tone qualities) to movement (rhythm), pitch (melody), and harmony. Music is presented here in this general sequence. However, the college teacher may choose to alter this at any time to best accommodate the needs of the class.

Sound Sources and Qualities
When discussing the subject of musical sound, it is important to realize that the sense of hearing is fully developed in the newborn infant. When a beautiful tone is produced, a baby may lie perfectly still, concentrating attention on that sound. When a harsh, threatening sound is heard, the infant may respond by crying. Because of this, experiences with qualities of sound form the early foundations for musical growth. Children need many opportunities to explore and experiment with sounds. The Manhattanville Music Curriculum Program (MMCP) listed the many possible unconventional sound sources that children can discover, if given the opportunity to explore them (see Table 9.1).

Maria Montessori, in her work in early childhood education, planned exploratory experiences for children in the following order: finding sound sources that produced the same sound, finding sound sources that produced

Table 9.1. Unconventional Sound Sources

Paper	Rubber	Wood	Metal	Outdoor Materials
construction paper	bands	ruler	sheet metal	dirt
wax paper	balloons	spatula	saws	pebbles
tissue paper	hose horn	yard stick	tools	stones
newspaper	balls	bowls	can tops	leaves
light-weight cardboard	inner tubes	bamboo sticks	pie plates	grass
brown, bag paper	tires	tongue depressors	oven shelves	snow
white stationery paper	toys	pencils	wire	rain
sandpaper		blocks	cans	twigs
cardboard strips	**Glass**	whistles	pails	branches
napkins	soda bottles	toys	baking pans	pine cones
magazines	jugs	tables	cookie sheets	eucalyptus pods
cardboard dividers		chairs	pipes	water
foils	**Plastic**	clothespins	strips	
cardboard boxes	funnel (horns)	poles	whistles	**Other**
paper balls	ruler	popsicle sticks	toys	string
old books	straws	broom handles	tables	rope
egg crates	food containers	kitchen utensils	chairs	twine
cardboard cylinders	bottles	containers	washtub	flower pots
toilet tissue cylinders	sprayers	strips	nails	calfskin
paper towel cylinders	toys		screws	chamois
carpet cylinders	brushes	**Food**	washers	
material cylinders	buttons	condiments	bottle caps	
corrugated cardboard	combs	seeds	paper clips	
fruit crates	old records	kernels	funnels	
straws	plastic strips	rice	scissors	
milk containers	boxes	coffee	bolts	
papier mâché	tools	sugar	foils	
toys	cups	corn flakes	kitchen utensils	
paint buckets		bread crumbs	waste basket	
ice cream containers		grains	springs	
cigar boxes		macaroni	machines	
cups		coconut shells		

Source: MMCP Interaction

contrasting sounds, and finding scale-line pitch arrangements by ordering a series of bells of identical appearance. Montessori's procedure can be of use to teachers when they assess the level of musical development of young children. MMCP recommends a classroom arrangement that includes a sound materials center as a learning laboratory for individual and small group use. The walls, ceiling, and floor of such a center should be lined with sound-absorbent materials. Available for placement in the center should be one tape recorder of good quality and a record player with multiple headsets, in addition to sound sources that would include some of the commonly used percussion instruments.

By the time children enter kindergarten they are five years old. Most should be able to hear and match pitches with their voices and bells or psaltery, and adjust their vocal pitches to correct errors. They are usually able, or soon will be able, to listen to music of various types and to play a simple percussion instrument as an accompaniment. The teacher plans experiences in listening to songs and recordings, including recordings that sound the tone qualities of various common standard instruments. Young children can learn to identify these. Selected recordings of ethnic and contemporary music are good to use, as well as music of the Viennese classical composers, because Viennese classical music has clearly recognizable melodies that children can comprehend. Community and school resources can be employed, including older children and adults performing music for the children. Children can be guided to associate concepts of loud, soft, heavy, light, fast, slow, happy, and sad with different types of sounds and music.

There is an order to experiences with sound that is helpful to teachers. The first phase is exploratory-based, in which children discover types of sounds made by voices and objects. The second phase is the employment of sounds to describe experiences or to evoke feelings. The association of these classroom sounds with nature, poems, stories, and feelings is an interesting part of the study of sound imagery. Following this is the third phase, in which children study duration, dynamics, pitch, and tone qualities, often in improvisatory ways. This phase differs from the previous ones in that comprehension of the elements of sound become more specific and definable. Identifying *same* and *different* can lead to discovery of the phrase and other components of musical form. The fourth phase is the composing of music along with inventing, discovering, or selecting the means to record it, if it should be preserved for later use (Tait, 1977).

The use of *improvising and composing* in music education is a part of the revolt against an older type of music teaching that consisted primarily of singing songs from books and some listening experience. It was found that as children grew, they resented this simple approach and that, finally, many teachers as well as children seemed to suffer boredom and frustration. Critics of the former method claimed that a better way to music learning should include children's engaging in basic musicianly activities. They should:

discover musical sounds and how they are produced.

improvise and compose music.

use their voices, bodies, and abilities to play instruments to perform music they create.

interpret and evaluate what they create.

be able to notate what they create.

More precisely, they should learn music by acting out the roles of the musician—singing, playing, improvising, composing, listening, conducting, interpreting, and evaluating music. Those who promoted these theories believed that learners must *produce* music as well as *receive* music from others. The learners were to come to realize that music is a continuously evolving art; thus they would be actively involved with contemporary music as well as with the art, ethnic, and folk music of the past. These learners were to be adventurers, explorers, and innovators in music who would be free to take risks in their creative endeavors.

Early promulgators of these ideas were the American composers Henry Brandt and Lionel Nowak. Following their pioneering efforts, the Contemporary Music Project (CMP), an outgrowth of a young composers in residence program that began in 1958, was in operation from 1963 to 1969, financed by the Ford Foundation. This project included seminars and workshops for music educators and pilot programs in elementary and secondary schools to study methods of presenting contemporary music and to explore music learning by means of creative experiences. The results of three pilot programs appeared in *Experiments in Musical Creativity,* a 1966 publication of the Project and MENC. A conclusion made by the San Diego pilot program was, "Activities related to contemporary music, such as composition for percussion instruments, synthetic scales, and new sound sources provide a unique medium for creativity. The student with little or no background . . . can 'create' with enthusiasm and success, thus gain a first-hand contact with music that he might otherwise miss" (p. 61). CMP did much to make these ideas known, but the most powerful thrust toward new methods of instruction was made in 1965–1970 by the Manhattanville Music Curriculum Program (MMCP), USOE V-008 and USOE 6-1999.

Perhaps the reader will encounter middle school classes to which improvisation and composition comprise the *only* acceptable pathway for them; in most classes these activities may be an important *part* of a music program. A music textbook series that exemplifies this is *Comprehensive Musicianship Through Classroom Music,* published in 1972 by Addison-Wesley. This series resulted from the Hawaii Music Program, a state-financed project. Each elementary level teacher's book contains a Table of Contents Scope and Sequence Chart that includes the concepts to be learned, the songs and recordings that may assist this learning, and the musicianly roles to be assumed by the students. In the "musicianly roles" column the reader can quickly discern how improvisation and composition are integrated with the other activities that comprise a balanced program of music instruction.

What is the sequence of activities that lead learners toward composing music? There is logic in the young child's attempting to imitate what is heard, taking steps to explore the sound-producing possibilities of the environment, evaluating these sounds, then using them to improvise, and finally to compose. Understanding the term improvisation requires some thought, because when an improvisation has been notated, it becomes a composition. By definition, improvisation is the production of music without the aid of notation or memory. While this is true of percussion music of indefinite pitch, it does not explain that in more complex melodic music, memory of the underlying harmony is often a part of improvisation, notably jazz improvisation, in which performers invent their own melodic variations based upon a remembered succession of chords. Bach, Beethoven, and Handel were as renowned in their day for their improvisations as for their compositions. But children in our classrooms are not famous composers, they are only young people who can be fascinated by working with sounds. MMCP has made composing possible for them by a definition that defines music as *some kind of organization of sounds and silences intended to be music.* This places composition in reach of everyone.

The Manhattanville Music Curriculum Program

The Manhattanville Music Curriculum Program is an approach easy to initiate and can be adapted to any age group. Like all methods, it requires some years to develop its full potential. Aspects of it should be experimented with in the methods class in order that the college student may understand how musical learning takes place when the learners are actively involved in making their own music. For a complete explanation of this approach to music teaching of young children aged 3 through 8 read *MMCP Interaction: Early Childhood Music Curriculum,* Bellingham, Washington: Americole, 1979. The following is a list of concepts that children from the ages of three to eight acquire preparatory to the MMCP program through the learning experiences described.

Sounds are everywhere. While in the classroom or on a short field trip have children listen to and describe sounds of the environment. "Are they high, low, soft, loud, dull, short, steady, rumbling, . . . ?" Vocabulary is needed in order to discuss sound and tone qualities.

Sounds have pitch. Search the classroom for objects that can produce sounds. Classify these into those producing definite and indefinite pitch.

Our bodies can be used to make sounds. Have children explore the many sounds that can be made with the body. These will include clapping hands, slapping thighs, snapping fingers, rubbing palms, stamping feet, clicking tongue, hissing, "shh," and others. Ask that several of these be organized into a short composition. When it has been practiced it can be tape-recorded and played for the children's evaluation.

We can imitate the sounds we hear. Children can imitate sounds better than many adults. Have them imitate sounds from their environment such as fire sirens, police cars, birds, garbage trucks, and jet planes. Develop a repertory of sounds to draw upon later. Try to avoid the stereotyped sounds adults have built into the child's world such as "oink, oink" and "cock-a-doodle-doo" because these are not authentic imitations of animal sounds. Let the children create their own.

Objects can produce different kinds of sounds or tone qualities. In order to increase sensitivity to tone qualities, ask young children to identify sources of sounds in listening games. The teacher might use a cardboard screen to hide the sound source. Suggestions of such sources might include those such as an egg beater, air escaping from a balloon, pouring water, crinkling paper, as well as more conventional sounds.

Sound has vibration. After children know the game, they can be assigned in pairs to develop sounds they can challenge the class to identify. Later on the teacher can make the game more complex by producing somewhat different sounds from the same object. Children might discover that some percussion instruments should normally be held in a way in which they are free to vibrate.

We can analyze instrument sounds. With young children select, for example, a tambourine and make sounds with it. Ask questions such as "Can it sing a song?" (no) "Can it play softly?" (yes) "Can it play loudly?" (yes) "Does it make jingling sounds?" "Can it make a short sound?" "Can it make a long sound?" After this, find uses for the tambourine in a song or as a sound effect in a story. Do the same with other instruments.

Percussion instruments can be classified in many ways. Young children can classify percussion instruments in accordance with the type of sound. Which instruments click? ring? jingle? swish? rattle? boom? Which instruments have sounds that are light? heavy? medium? This activity can relate to the functions of instrument tone qualities in accompanying songs and recordings. Older children might use adult classifications and decide to group percussion instruments under headings such as membrane, hollow, solid, and keyboard. Let children suggest other possible classifications; there are many more.

Sounds can be the same or different. The teacher prepares a number of sound producers *in pairs* to assist young children to recognize similarities and differences in sounds. There may be identical-sized jars or cans or plastic containers with the same and different numbers of peas or beans in them. Some could contain pebbles or marbles or beads. The task is to shake them, listen to them, and classify the pairs that sound alike.

Tone qualities relate to sound effects. Young children can decide upon the suitability of specific instruments or other sound sources for sound effects. They can select them to correspond with characters in stories such as The Three Bears, Three Billy Goats Gruff, and Three Little Pigs. (Older children can create stories in sound such as "My Day," "A Storm in the Mountains," "A Day at the Seashore," "A Haunted House, "Halloween Night," "Space Journey," and "Little Red Riding Hood.")

Every voice sounds different. Plan for young children to listen to different speaking voices in the class. With eyes closed, can these voices be identified? Plan such listening games, emphasizing the uniqueness in the vocal sounds of each person. Encourage children to classify the speaking voices in terms of low, medium, and high. Children can relate these to choric reading that emphasizes differences in the tone qualities of the speaking voice.

The material to follow explains in brief the strategies involved in the Manhattanville Music Curriculum Program for children aged 3 through 8.

Music consists of sounds and silences presented in some organized manner.
There are many kinds of sounds. Sounds can be classified.

The free exploration of sound sources (paper, metal, body, rubber, plastic, glass,
and materials from nature) is recommended. This comprises the first of a series
of steps that lead to experiences with every component of music. The second
step is *guided exploration,* in which the teacher encourages the children to find
additional sounds, to find more ways to produce sounds (this involves skills), to
label new sounds (this involves vocabulary), to classify new sounds in various
ways, to listen and react to sounds produced by other children and by the
teacher, and to learn to respect the efforts of others. The purpose of evaluation
is not to point out failure, but to clarify and extend children's ideas and judgments. The teacher assists the children's learning by such actions as presenting
clues and examples, presenting words, asking questions, showing pictures and
other types of illustrative material, and presenting musical examples. Contrasting words (walking-running, crawling-skipping) suggest different movements
in time; those such as whispering and shouting suggest different dynamic levels
and different ways of producing sounds.

Sounds can be organized and related.
Two or three people may produce more varied music than only one person.
We can compose music as individuals or in small groups.

Step three is *exploratory improvisation.* The child is encouraged to repeat
sounds he or she enjoys and to relate them to other sounds. This relationship
might be contrasting sounds, through which the child may learn that contrast
can heighten the expressive implications of sounds, or it might be that by combining two or more sounds a new and different effect can be achieved.

Step four is *planned improvisation.* In this phase children are to be gaining
performance and memory skills necessary to produce compositions that are
aesthetically satisfying. They are guided by the teacher to organize groups of
sounds into meaningful music ideas, to identify the ways these sounds are arranged, to criticize constructively the arrangement of the sounds, and to use
this experience to suggest other ways of improvising their own music.

The teacher accepts and works with whatever the child produces, regardless
of its quality, remembering that these exploratory experiences are important
and real to the child, and that the type of learning is basically intrinsic, not dictated by the teacher. After a trial run of a student composition, teachers might
ask questions such as: "How do you know when to start and stop?" (This helps
them to discover the need for a conductor if they do not have one.) "Do you
have a leader?" "Did you hear a change of tempo?" "What kinds of sounds did
you hear?" "Did it sound the way you wanted it to sound?" "Would you want
to change this piece if you had a chance to do it over?" "Are you satisfied with
it?" The composing and performing of a composition can bring into focus
problems in duration, pitch, tone quality, dynamics, and tempo, and teach
compositional techniques such as the *ostinato,* a repeated rhythm or tonal pattern, in a practical setting that is honest and logical to the child.

The fifth step is *reapplication.* As children continue to compose their own music, they will discover and find need for all the component elements of music as well as skills in musical notation. First they will find a need to save their compositions, and will invent notation for this purpose. Eventually standard notation will be necessary for them to do what they want to do with their musical ideas. When children are trying to invent their own notation, teachers ask questions such as: "What if you wanted to show a thin texture in your music?" (Use a thin symbol.) "What if you wanted to show a thick texture?" (Use a thick symbol.) "What if you wanted to show low?" ((Use the bottom of the page.) "High?" (Use the top of the page.) "Short?" (Use a short symbol.) "Long?" (Use a long symbol.) "Rising pitch?" (Use a rising symbol.) "Silence?" (Use a blank space or a circle.) "Falling pitch?" (Use a descending symbol.)

This same type of beginning in musical learning can be used by the older children also. Even the middle school student can enjoy the thrill of experimenting freely with music.

There are immediate problems with this approach, one of which is the noise factor. MMCP calls this "creative fallout." As the group work expands, there must be space for the children to work, and in many schools this is not easily found. However, many teachers have discovered that children are able to concentrate in group composition while all groups are in the same classroom, one group in each of the four corners while others occupy the center area. The size of the group will vary in accordance with the assigned task. It can be from two to six, with four and five commonplace.

MMCP Interaction suggests that the teacher can organize the activity so that at a given time the class will explore sounds coming from paper, metal, or the voice. Other possibilities include those made by rubber, glass, plastic, outdoor materials, and other sound sources. It states possible questions the teacher might ask to simulate interest and creativity.

The following example is reproduced from *MMCP Interaction*.

ALTERNATE SERIES: METAL ENCOUNTERS

Phase I—Free Exploration

Instructional Objective: To explore a wide variety of sounds using metal sound sources.

Procedure:
1. Place a variety of metal objects, such as old kitchen utensils, large nails, horseshoes, pipes of varying sizes and lengths, metal bars, keys on a key ring, pans, pan lids, tea trays, empty coffee cans, etc., in a place designated as the sound materials center.
2. Encourage pupils to select and explore the objects for sounds. This may be done on an individual basis during the course of the school day, or pupils may select metal objects and share sounds in groups.
3. After adequate time for initial sound explorations, the following questions may serve to stimulate discussions of the sounds:
   Were any sounds alike? If so, how were they alike?
   Why were some sounds different? Could the differences be described?
   Pupils will identify the differences and similarities in sounds in many different ways, including the physical techniques involved in performing them, relating sounds to personal experiences, and their acoustical characteristics, i.e., timbre, pitch, duration, volume.

4. Suggest that pupils find other metal objects, metal toys, pie plates, paint cans, etc., to add to the sound materials center.
5. All new objects should be explored for the variety of sounds they can produce.

Phase II—Guided Exploration

Instructional Objective: To explore a wide variety of metallic sounds and sound-producing techniques.

Procedure:
1. Invite pupils, as a class or in small groups, to find two very different or contrasting sounds with the metal objects they have selected from the sound materials center.
2. Allow an appropriate amount of time for exploration.
3. After individual pupils perform their sounds, other group members or the entire class should attempt to imitate the two contrasting sounds on other metal objects.
4. Discussion during and after performance and imitations may deal with the following:
   How was the sound made? Did the beater make a difference?
   Can the sound be made in any other way? Are any imitations exactly the same?
   Note: A few minutes of exploration may be desirable before volunteers are ready to imitate a performed sound.
5. Pupils should be given two or three minutes of exploration time to investigate each of the following questions posed by the teacher:
   What kind of sounds can you find that remind you of a clock ticking; water dripping; a baby walking; a father's heavy footsteps; a ball bouncing; teeth clattering; a horse galloping; a snake crawling?
6. After each question and a period (two or three minutes) of pupil exploration, volunteers can be invited to perform their sounds.
7. After all sounds have been performed and taped, listen to the tape and try to identify the sounds, i.e., clock ticking, snake crawling, etc.

Phase III—Exploratory Improvisation

Instructional Objective: To explore a variety of ways of producing and combining repeated patterns.

Procedure:
1. Pupils should select three sounds which they can play over and over again in the same manner with metal objects.
2. Allow an appropriate amount of time for selection of sound sources and sounds, and for rehearsals of the desired patterns.
3. As a class, or in small groups, listen to the repeated patterns performed by individual pupils.
4. Discussion can be centered on the following: Were any of the sound patterns difficult to repeat? Why?
   If some were difficult to repeat, can you suggest an easier way of playing them?
   Which two patterns do you think would sound well together (one after the other)?
5. Experiment with combinations of sound patterns as suggested by the pupils.
6. Tape combined performances of repeated patterns for immediate playback and discussions.
7. Play for the students some recording containing a repeated pattern of metallic sounds, such as the *Symphony of Machines—Steel Foundry* by Alexander Mosslov.
8. Discussion of the listening example can be focused with the following questions:
   What did you hear? Did you hear any repeated patterns?
   How could we build a sound machine?

Phase IV—Planned Improvisation

Instructional Objective: To arrange repeated patterns in ways which are expressive and meaningful.

Procedure:

1. Build a sound machine. A sound machine is a game in which a number of sound patterns, organized in various sequential combinations, aurally represent the moving parts of an imaginary machine. The patterns developed in the previous encounters may be used, or new patterns may be investigated.
2. Pupils may work in groups of three, four, or five, or the teacher or volunteer pupils may construct a sound machine by conducting members of the class in a sequential performance of their patterns. Students may wish to physically display the motions of the machine as well as their sounds.
3. Tape all the performances for listening and comparison of the differences and similarities.

   Were the sound machines different? If so, how were they different? If not, what could we do to make the sound machines sound different from one another?

   Were the sound machines the same in any way? If so, how were they the same?
4. When appropriate extend the discussion with the following:

   Were the conductors satisfied with their results? Did performers do what was expected of them?

   If not, discuss how better results might be achieved. Pupils should lead these discussions as much as possible.

   Note: In order to successfully control entrances and exits of groups of performers, pupil conductors may have to develop simple gestures for starting and stopping performers.
5. The following questions posed individually during follow-up encounters may stimulate further thought and experimentation:

   What would happen if:

   some patterns or sounds were played at the same time?

   all metal objects were silent some of the time?

   the sound machine slowly broke down rather than suddenly stopped?

   we had two sound machines—a big one and a little one?

MMCP Synthesis For students aged 9 and older, the Manhattanville Music Curriculum Program developed another publication, *MMCP Synthesis.* This consists of a spiral-type curriculum that considers the elements of music on gradually advanced levels called "cycles." As in *MMCP Interaction,* composing of music on the child's level is the major activity. The students compose, conduct, perform, and evaluate music. Sample strategies are suggested for teaching music at 16 levels (cycles). These begin with the same type of sound exploration described earlier, but move quickly into compositions that are taped in order that the composers and the class can hear them and evaluate them.

In cycle 1 the student begins with activities such as finding sounds made from objects in the classroom, performing different sounds from the same object, and experimenting with dynamics (degrees of loud and soft) and with combinations of sounds, adding a steady beat to ordered combinations of sounds. In each of the suggested activities, the book suggests questions to ask the students and recordings of music of all types and times that are intended to stimulate interest and furnish information needed by the student composers.

It is of importance that the college class experiment with some of the sample lessons provided in *MMCP Synthesis* in order that the prospective teacher understands this type of approach to learning music. It stresses children's understandings of the following aspects of music: timbre (tone quality), dynamics (degrees of loud-soft), duration (degrees of long-short and rhythmic elements), pitch (including melody, harmony, and polyphony), and form. Teachers are assigned the task of being guides, creators of problems to be solved by the children, and resource persons. They are to stimulate rather than dominate, and to encourage rather than to control. They are to question more than answer, and to be sensitive both to children and to the art of music. The classroom is to be a laboratory in which children act as musicians who have a world of sound to explore.

Examples from *MMCP Synthesis* follow:

SAMPLE STRATEGY I

Cycle 1. **The quality or color of sound, the timbre, is a major factor in the expressiveness of music.**

Each student selects an item or object in the room with which he can produce a sound. Preferably, the item or object will be something other than a musical instrument.

> After sufficient time has been allowed for students to experiment with sounds or selected objects, each student may perform his sound at the location of the item in the room.

Focus on "listening" to the distinctive qualities of sounds performed. Encourage students to explore other sound possibilities with the item of their choice.

> Discuss any points of interest raised by the students. Extend the discussion by including the following questions: How many different kinds of sounds were discovered?
> Could the sounds be put into categories of description, i.e. shrill, dull, bright, intense, etc.?
> After categories of sound have been established, experiment with combinations of sounds.

Is there any difference between sounds performed singly and sounds performed in combination?

> In listening to the recorded examples focus on the use of timbre.

How many different kinds of sounds were used?
Could we put any of the sounds in this composition into the categories we established earlier, i.e. bright, dull, shrill, etc?
Were there any new categories of sounds?
Could we duplicate these?

> ASSIGNMENT: Each student should bring one small object from home on which he can produce three distinctly different sounds. The object may be a brush, a bottle, a trinket or anything made of wood, metal, plastic, etc.

Suggested Listening Examples:
Steel Drums—Wond Steel Band; Folk 8367.
Prelude and Fugue for Percussion—Wuorinen, Charles; GC 4004.
Ballet Mécanique—Antheil, George; Urania (5) 134.

Cycle 1. **The pulse is the underlying beat that may help to create a feeling of motion in music.**

Allow 30 seconds for each class member to think of an unusual vocal sound. The sound can be made with the throat, voice, lips, breath or tongue.

Each student may perform his sound for the class. Focus "listening" on the distinctive qualities of the vocal sounds performed.

Discuss any points of interest raised by the students. Extend the discussion by including some of the following questions:
Did anyone perform his sound long enough to communicate a feeling of motion? How would you describe the motion?

Divide the class into groups consisting of 4 or 5 students. One person in each of the groups should be a conductor. Each group will concentrate on producing their individual sounds to the motion of an item of their choice or one which has been suggested to them, i.e., the steady motion of a carpenter hammering a nail, the steady motion of a worm crawling, the steady motion of a person jogging, the steady motion of a horse galloping, etc.

Allow approximately 10 minutes for groups to plan and practice their improvisations. At the end of the designated time each group will perform.

Tape each improvisation for immediate playback and analysis. Discuss any comments made by the students. Extend the discussion by including the following questions:
How would you describe the motion, slow, medium, fast?
Did it have a steady beat or pulse?

Summarize the discussion by introducing tempo as the characteristic which refers to the speed of music and pulse which is the underlying beat (sometimes not heard but only sensed).

In listening to the recorded examples focus attention on the use of tempo.
How would you describe the tempo—slow, medium, or fast?
Did the pulse or underlying beat change before the end of the composition? What was the effect?

Suggested Listening Examples:
Flight of the Bumblebee—Rimsky-Korsakov, Nicolai; Epic LC 3759.
String Quartets Op. 76, No. 5, No. 79—Haydn, Joseph; Turnabout TV 34012S.

Careful planning is the rule when teachers utilize improvisation and composition to achieve the forming of music concepts. This interesting way to learn has the potential of leading the learner to explore every aspect of musicianship in active ways. The January, 1980, issue of the *Music Educators Journal* features improvisation and contains helpful suggestions. Basic musical concepts can be developed by these creative activities from the outset of a pupil's musical experience if they are designed with thoughtful care.

Whether the activities to follow are to be accomplished by individual, small group, large group, or by the entire class is largely left to the teacher's judgment. The noise factor in the classroom can be upsetting at times; yet it has been found that children can concentrate despite surrounding noise when they are interested and if the volume is not too great. Some rooms have partitions that can be moved to make booths in which to work; others have several practice rooms attached; and still others have convenient side rooms or even hallways that can be pressed into service. In many situations all activities must take place within one room, with individuals and groups occupying corners and middle of that room.

The tasks are given time limits. Some of those listed here can be accomplished in two or three minutes, others in five or ten or fifteen minutes, while there are those that will require two or three class periods. Some assignments can be completed by individuals working at home or at school after regular hours or after other work has been done. There must be a predetermined signal, such a switching lights on or off, at which time the class reassembles to hear the results of the individual and group work and to analyze them.

Listening to recordings becomes listening *to find out* how other composers solved similar problems, thus there is an active, purposeful type of listening that should encompass all musical styles. It is obviously for a different purpose than simply trying to understand a composer or hearing certain music only because someone thinks you should. Improvisation and composition are personal matters, thus they can be of primary importance to students and can thereby become a major pathway to learning.*

Accompaniment. Provide an appropriate percussion accompaniment for selected poems and stories.

Beat and divisions of the beat. Have small groups create a piece by using rhythm patterns derived from names.

Repetition and contrast. Employing either vocal or instrumental sounds, plan a composition that begins and ends with the same sounds, but has different sounds in the middle. Invent a way to notate it. Tape the result; listen to it; and analyze the different ways in which contrast is achieved.

Beat, pitch, chant. Establish a steady drum beat over which individuals create a chant based upon *so mi,* using G and E on the bells to pitch the chant.

Word rhythms. Create new words to known songs. Example: "If You're Happy," page 250. Use words denoting action or motion with this song, and perform them.

Imitating. Listen to "Leap Frog," from *Children's Games* by Bizet, Adventures in Music 1 v 1. After acting out the music, compose a piece with similar sounds by experimenting with bells, piano, or Autoharp.

Muscular response. Improvise a dance to a recorded composition or song that suggests dancing.

* Some of the activities in this section are inspired by those in the *Comprehensive Musicianship* music series published by the Addison-Wesley Publishing Co. The reader is referred to the teachers' books of this series for a detailed, sequential treatment of the subject.

Dynamics, pitch. Improvise music with percussion instruments to demonstrate concepts such as crescendo, decrescendo, soft, loud, low pitch, high pitch. Following this, compose music, using f p, ———, and ———— to interpret the score.

Pentatonic melody, dynamics, duration. Improvise music on the black keys of the piano or bells in which dynamics and duration (long, short) are illustrated.

Repetition, contrast, duration, dynamics, notation. Improvise in small groups vocal pieces, using different mouth, tongue, and throat sounds, demonstrate long and short sounds in this music. Devise symbols and notate the sounds. Rehearse the compositions and tape them. Listen to the taped performances and have students evaluate them. After this, perform them again with the emphasizing of p, f, ———— and ———— to add interest to the scores.

Music can be improvised by a conductor. The teacher distributes from 4 to 6 percussion instruments having contrasting types of tone qualities. A student conductor will establish a steady beat, then will point to those children who are to play, cueing the players in and out, having them play alone or in combination. From this experiment should come interesting sound sequences and an attempt to organize a composition. This can be done with an entire class by assigning specific instruments to groups.

New or unusual sounds can be produced when tone qualities are combined. The teacher selects four sound producers, either invented ones, simple instruments, or a combination of these. Each sound producer will have a distinctively different tone quality. Assign groups of children to combine them in a musical score, experimenting with the sounds singly and in combination. It may be necessary to devise notation. Tape the results and evaluate them in class discussion.

Repetition, contrast, duration, notation. Compose in groups a composition using nonpitched percussion instruments, inventing a symbol for each instrument and ways to indicate the duration of the sounds.

Tone qualities, beat, rhythm patterns. Groups will improvise accompaniments to familiar songs with percussion instruments. Roles played by students include singer, instrument player, and conductor. Actors could be added for songs easily dramatized. Work songs are good for this.

Beat, tone quality, dynamics, articulation. Improvise an appropriate percussion accompaniment to a selected recording, demonstrating soft, loud, legato, staccato, and the beat.

Notation. Using line notation that suggests pitch levels and duration, each student will draw a score, explain his notation, and will interpret it vocally or conduct the class in a performance of it. The scores can be placed on transparencies for the class to view, analyze, and perform. See Figure 9.1 for examples.

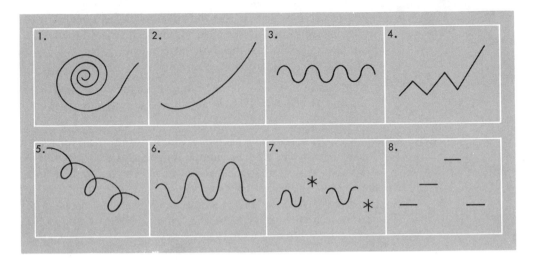

Figure 9.1. SAMPLE SCORES

Dynamics, pitch, duration, mood. Improvise vocal sounds for moods such as angry, sad, and happy. Analyze these in terms of dynamics, pitch, and duration.

Notation, pitch, tone quality, dynamics, duration. Pairs of students will compose sound frames such as those in Figure 9.2.

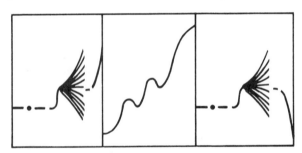

Figure 9.2. SOUND FRAMES

Perform these vocally, tape them, and discuss the relationship between eye and ear—how the visual describes the aural, and how the aural reflects the visual.

Ostinato. After hearing the recording *Ostinato Pianissimo* by Henry Cowell, Time Records S/8000, *Concert Percussion,* improvise a similar ostinato.

Rondo. Listen to *Sleeping Beauty Waltz,* by Tchaikovsky, Adventures in Music 4 volume 2, as an example of an A B A C A B A rondo. Compose and notate a simple percussion rondo.

Pitch, tempo. Make a recording of the expressive reading of a short poem at 3¾ per second. Make two copies: play back at other speeds, 7½ and 1⅞. Discuss the result. Use three tape recorders to hear the three speeds sounded at once, and tape this on a fourth recorder. Discuss the possibilities of this for composing music.

Tone qualities. Learn to make sounds of various pitches on a synthesizer. Select several of those you like and tape them. Then alter the taped sounds to produce an electronic composition.

The creative teacher

1. Will always keep foremost in mind that learning comes basically from the student's interest, curiosity, and self-motivation.
2. Will always remember that if the students believe an idea or musical effect is important, learning may take place.
3. Will not be satisfied with pat answers but will reply with "Why do you (or do you not) like the musical result?" "How did you know that?" "How can you be sure?" and other statements that lead students to deeper thought and analysis.
4. Will listen carefully to catch a child's comment that might lead to a personal learning opportunity.
5. Will not quickly decide issues between students by telling them the correct answer or his or her preference.
6. Will practice the art of divergent thinking so as to more readily communicate it to students.
7. Will try not to permit a school bell to stop important learning processes.
8. Will encourage, comfort, and make the learner feel secure.
9. Will not be committed to follow to the letter methods, course content, and the customary use of materials.
10. Will constantly evaluate and assess his or her behavior in terms of the above.

The Synthesizer and the Computer

The Synthesizer   There is increasing acceptance of the synthesizer as an important tool to help children learn music concepts. At the sixth grade level many students find the instrument to be of tremendous interest; accordingly, they are attracted to electronic laboratories where they can experiment with sound and compose music to their liking. The teacher should be sufficiently knowledgeable of the device so that it can be utilized with children from the age of six, and surely from the age of eight. Any strange or new sound is likely to attract children's interest, and since the synthesizer is rich in different types of sound, the instrument possesses a natural attraction when specific uses for it are planned. The oscilloscope should at times be a companion to the synthesizer because it gives a visual representation of the sound wave form of every sound producer. The device can be involved in experiments such as:

Tone quality	The effect of attack, decay, harmonies, vibrato, and tremulo on tone quality.
Melody	The relation of tempo, tonality, and tone quality to melody.
Harmony	Major, minor, harmonics, intervals, and experiences in ear training.
Transposition	Manipulation of transposition.

Synthesizers are available today in many degrees of complexity, from the sophisticated models suitable for a professional electronic laboratory to simplified models that are relatively inexpensive. The latter are easily portable, and are sometimes carried from school to school, permitting one to be shared by many children.

An electronic music studio may be housed in part of a room, in an unused office or practice room, or in an otherwise vacant room. When this equipment is of marked value, special security is necessary to prevent theft or damage. There must be electric outlets and a table on which to place equipment. A bulletin board is necessary not only to schedule use of the equipment but to place assignments and directions for individuals and small groups. No chalk should be used in the area because chalk dust can accumulate on sensitive equipment, particularly recording equipment. To eliminate chalk dust, pins are used to attach notices to bulletin boards, or dust-free plastic boards that employ wax crayons are obtained. Tape recorders with multitracks are part of most laboratories because they widen the possibilities for use of the synthesizer to include composition and further experimentation. Since most synthesizers include no speaker system, they must be attached to a portable public address system, a guitar amplifier, a small electric organ or electronic piano, or to a phonograph that contains its own speakers. Stereo equipment should be standard. A good quality four-channel stereo recorder is considered basic, although some teachers have done well with more limited equipment. Tape, a tape splicer, and a roll of leader tape will be with the tape recorder. The recorder's head must be able to monitor tracks already recorded while recording those tracks still open, that is, to synchronize the tracks so there will be no rhythmic disagreement among them. Teachers and students who use the laboratory need to know the techniques of editing tapes and the ways to manipulate them, such as playing and recording at various speeds to gain certain effects, creating tape loops, recording backwards, and time delay (possible on certain machines only).

The Computer Synthesizers have been built into some microcomputers. This allows one to compose and play back the piece. Synthesizers can be added to microcomputers. Some of these have keyboard attachments while others have the music come from a computer terminal. With a keyboard, music can be played and stored for later reproduction. The many different types of synthesizer add-ons vary in tone quality (some are discouragingly inferior), range, intonation, dynamics, and number of voices. In some instances, a not-so-pleasing computer tone quality is excused in light of the several functions performed by the device. A microcomputer usually has a terminal containing a keyboard resembling a typewriter, a televisionlike screen, and either a cassette tape player or a disk drive.

Computers can serve teachers in the following ways: record keeping (such as grades), drill and practice, testing, and teaching, usually individualized or in small groups. Once students have been introduced to a musical subject such as key signature, the computer can provide drill and exercises on that subject. If the topic is aural, such as hearing phrases, the computer can sound music to provide practice in phrase identification. Furthermore, the device can give immediate feedback and can store information regarding how well the learner did so that the teacher can inspect the results. Students can, by themselves, go through a module that teaches or presents information, provides drill and practice, and tests. Of course, this software must be available, which is sometimes one of the weak points in present-day usage. If none is available, then the teacher needs to master the skill of creating the program to satisfy specific needs. Because working with computers can be done at nearly all age levels—from nursery school through graduate school—the computer seems to have a very secure and significant future. It behooves every teacher to come to know and understand the machine and its functions. Think of it as a dependable teacher's aide.

When selecting a computer for purchase, keep in mind that the industry is not sufficiently standardized to permit the same software to be used on all machines. Select one that permits the desired software to be used.

Examples of computer software include Atarimusic I, which explains lines and spaces, sharps and flats, and whole steps and half steps. Both include games for drill. They can be obtained from Atari, P.O. Box 427, Sunnyvale, Calif. 94086. A free catalog of music software may be obtained from Musitronic, P.O. Box 441, Owatonna, Minn. 55060. The programs in this catalog include learning music theory, composition, and synthesis. The Silver Burdett Music Series, 1984 Centennial Edition, contains references to music fundamentals software for use on Apple II Computers or on Atari 800 and Atari 1200 XL.

The following is a list of sources for electronic and computer-related materials:

Computer Applications Tomorrow, P.O. Box 605, Birmingham, Mich. 48012

Control Data Corporation, 8100 34th Ave. South, Minneapolis, Minn. 55440

Educational Audio Visual, Inc., Pleasantville, N.Y. 10570

Electronic Courseware Systems, P.O. Box 2374, Station A, Champaign, Ill. 61820

MicroMusic and Temporal Acuity Products, 1535 121st Ave. S.E., Bellevue, Wash. 98005

Notable Software, P.O. Box 1556–ME, Philadelphia, Pa. 19105

Tutor Company, P.O. Box 41092, San Jose, Calif. 95160

Video Teaching Aids, P.O. Box 1104, Statesville, N.C. 28677

Organizations that publish newsletters concerning computer applications to music include:

Computer Music Association, 911 22nd Ave. South, No. 181, Minneapolis, Minn. 55404

National Consortium for Computer-Based Music Instruction, Music Education Division, School of Music, University of Illinois, Urbana, Ill. 61801

References and Materials

Books and Articles

COPE, DAVID, "The Mechanics of Listening to Electronic Music." *Music Educators Journal,* October 1977, pp. 47–51.

DENNIS, BRIAN, *Experimental Music in the Schools.* London: Oxford University Press, 1970. 76 pp. Introductory experiments; use of tape recorders.

Electronic Music issue. *Music Educators Journal,* November 1968.

FRIEND, DAVID, ALLAN R. PEARLMAN, and THOMAS D. PIGGOT, *Learning Music With Synthesizers.* New York: Hal Leonard Publishing Corp. Copyright 1974 by ARP Instruments, Inc., Newton, Mass. (ARP is a manufacturer of electronic instruments and equipment.)

MARSH, MARY VAL, et al. *The Spectrum of Music with Related Arts: Electronic Music, Sounds of Singing Voices, Sources of Musical Sounds.* New York: Macmillan Publishing Company, Inc., 1975. Booklets with recordings.

Music Educators Journal, technology issue (computers) January 1983; Synthesizer, uses of in class, November 1976, pp. 34–37.

PALMER, MARY, *Sound Exploration and Discovery.* New York: The Center for Applied Research in Education, Inc., 1974.

PAYNTER, JOHN, and PETER ASTON, *Sounds and Silences.* New York: Cambridge University Press, 1970. Thirty-six projects in creative music for intermediate grades through college.

SCHAFER, R. MURRAY, *Creative Music Education.* New York: Schirmer Books, 1976.

SELF, GEORGE, *New Sounds in Class.* London; Universal Edition, 1967. 41 pp. New music notation, scores included.

TAIT, MALCOM J., "Whispers, Growls, Screams, and Puffs . . . Lead to Composition," *Music Educators Journal,* February 1977, pp. 33–39.

WILLMAN, FRED, *Electronic Music for Young People.* New York: Center for Applied Research in Education, 1974.

CATALOG

Lyons Teachers Guide. Elkhart, Ind.: Lyons, 530 Riverview Ave. 46514. Contains components for classroom electronic music: square wave generators, triangle wave generator, sawtooth wave generator, white sound generator, theremin, filter, electronic switch, ring modulator, envelope control, amplifier, speaker with reverb unit, sequencer. Also includes audiovisual materials for exploring the new types of music.

INVESTIGATE

Materials from Keyboard Publications, 1346 Chapel St., New Haven, Conn. 06511: films, recordings, teacher guides for electronic music.

Films

Bing, Bang, Boom (National Film Board of Canada). Middle school; for teachers.

Pretty Lady and the Electronic Musicians (Xerox Films). For middle school and high school ages.

Discovering Electronic Music (Discovering Music Series: RSC-774).

New Sounds in Music (Churchill Films).

Filmstrips   *Creating Music Through Use of the Tape Recorder.* Keyboard Publications, 1346 Chapel St., New Haven, Conn. 06511. Two color sound filmstrips, one recording, eight study prints, one teacher guide.

Electronic Music. Keyboard Publications.

New Sounds of the Classics. Keyboard Publications.

Recordings   ELECTRONIC MUSIC

Badings: "Ragtime" from *Evolutions.* Epic BC 1118.

LeCaine: *Dripsody.* A drop of water makes music on a tape recorder. On *Electronic Music,* Folkways FM 3436.

Luening: *Gargoyles,* for violin and synthesizer. On *Columbia-Princeton Electronic Music Center,* Columbia MS 6566.

Luening and Ussachevsky: *Poem in Cycles and Bells for Tape Recorder and Orchestra.* Composers Recordings Inv. CRI 112.

Varèse: *Déserts,* Angel S-36786

UNCONVENTIONAL SOUND SOURCES

Cage: Second Movement, *Amores.* Wood sounds. Time 58,000.

Cage and Harrison: *Double Music.* Eight rice bowls. Time 58,000.

Harrison: *Canticle No. 1, on Concert Percussion.* Time 8,000.

Oliveres: *Sound Patterns.* Mouth sounds. Oddyssey 3216-0156.

Partch: *The World of Harry Partch.* Hand-made instruments; an invented tonal organization of 43 tones within the octave. Columbia MS 7207.

Sounds of New Music (Cage, Luening, Ussachevsky, Varèse). Reverberation, tape loops, music concrete. Folkways FX 6160.

PREPARED PIANO

Cage: *Amores No. 1.* Children can be inspired by this to try for new sounds on the Autoharp.

Cowell: *Banshee.* A banshee is a female ghost that warns of approaching death. Children can think in terms of Halloween and use the Autoharp to imitate the sounds made on the prepared piano. On *Sounds of New Music,* Folkways FX 6160.

MISCELLANEOUS

Country Moog: Switched on Nashville. Gilbert Trythall. Athena 6003.

Electronic Music: Vox Productions, Inc.

Silver Apples of the Moon: Morton Subotnick. Nonesuch Records H-71174.

Electronic Sound: George Harrison. Zapple Records ST 3358.

Music for Voices, Instruments and Electronics: Kenneth Gaburo. Nonesuch Records H 7199.

Also see Record Album for Book 6, *Exploring Music,* Holt, Rinehart and Winston, Inc., and other materials from the music textbooks.

chapter ten

Conventional Sound Sources

Now that we have explored experimental and new types of sounds, we turn next to conventional musical instruments with the hope that our explorations will help us to find expanded resources in the conventional. We begin with commonly used percussion instruments.

Percussion Instruments

Percussion instruments can be considered as extensions of the body. The body can produce sounds of rhythmic value. Hand clapping of various kinds (flat-palmed for loud, cup-palmed for lower pitches, and fingers only for soft) provide some possibilities. The sound made in pulling the tongue away from the roof of the mouth can be done in ways to produce high- and low-pitched clicks which imitate the ticking of a clock. Stamping feet, tapping toes, slapping thighs, and snapping fingers contribute their sounds too, and all of these can be done with a beat and with accents to form beat groups. Although making such sounds and using rhythmic speech help to build a feeling for rhythm, they are limited in tone quality, and children are happy to explore and use the sounds of the many percussion instruments, usually with great interest. The teacher can assist this exploration by asking: "How many ways can you play it?" and "How many different sounds can you make with it?"

The Early Years   As stated earlier, children in nursery school, kindergarten, and first grade need to experiment with the sounds made by miscellaneous objects of wood, paper, metal, glass, and stone when they are tapped, shaken, and struck. The teacher who is encouraging concept formation of high and low pitch will group the sound producers accordingly at either end of a table. Later the children will play the ear training game of sorting these according to different classifications such as high and low pitch. Others could be types of tone quality such as ringing, scratching, rattling, jingling, and booming. After handling, sounding, and naming all these sound producers and instruments, the children can face away from the table and piano while the teacher plays a game with them to test their ability to identify and describe the different sounds. They may also identify instruments that have short and long duration of sound.

A first-grade teacher made these comments concerning activities that culminated in the successful use of this equipment:

> The children are given many opportunities to initiate their own rhythmic activities. Duration, volume, accent, tempo, and moods are felt with hands, fingers, feet, and moving bodies. *Percussion instruments are but extensions of tapping feet and clapping hands.* Thus the children *gradually* use drums, bells, woodblocks and sticks to accompany or to create rhythm patterns. By careful listening children find one drum lower or higher in pitch than another. They discover differences in quality as well as in pitch by tapping different places on their instruments. They suggest that part of a song reminds them of a bell or a gong. Tambourines and other instruments can be used for spontaneous self-expression and interpretation during story time.

In this first grade the children had done "drum talk"—beating out the rhythm of words in drum language; they had walked, run, or tapped instruments as they spoke their names in rhythm; they had used scarves, streamers, and balloons to help them to feel and see other rhythms. Instruments were introduced slowly over several weeks, one at a time. Clapping generally preceded playing at first. Early playing was informal; each child played each instrument at one time or another. Songs such as "Little Miss Muffet" were used in which the light-sounding instruments played first, then the heavier-sounding wooden instruments took their turn as the climax of the song approached, and the two were combined in the concluding climax. Among the many other steps in learning to play the instruments was having those holding wooden instruments play on the primary accents and those holding metal instruments play on the other beats. After this, further discriminations between instruments were made, sometimes selecting those that seemed best to play with a piano piece, a song, or a recording. When the music changed, a need for a change in instrumentation developed. Some children made suggestions concerning the use of specific instruments.

Not until the second grade do most children perform either the metric beat *or* the melody-rhythm of a piece when asked. Prior to this, these phenomena are worked with separately, although many children can walk the beat while singing the melody.

Children are encouraged to explore percussion instruments that can be substituted for body movements such as walking, marching, and skipping. They sound them to feel the beat. They find that chopsticks can make a sound suggestive of rain falling on a roof, that sand blocks can imitate a train, that rattles and drums seem necessary to make some American Indian songs sound complete, and that words of songs sometimes suggest certain accompanying instruments or percussion sound effects. They find that instruments can be played to produce accents which will eventually outline the meter, and that instruments can reproduce the rhythm of the melody—usually the rhythm of the words. As they grow older, by keeping their toes on the floor they can make the *heel-clap* sound for two-beat meters, the heels sounding the downbeat and the hands clapping the upbeat. Dances are sometimes accompanied in this way. Transfer can be made to low drum-high drum for the same rhythm; other less heavy-sounding instruments can substitute for the high drum. Notation is brought in to explain what has taken place only after children have first heard and felt the rhythm pattern they are to see. After their experience with it, a picture of it (the notation) helps them visualize the concept.

In the early years the instruments are introduced slowly in connection with small or large group work, one or two at a time. This initial group work with the instruments is of necessity teacher-directed. Music books for these levels contain songs with which to introduce instruments. Since the emphasis today is upon children's growth in creative ability and in musical discrimination, fully written published scores for percussion instruments are rarely used. It should be made clear that there is nothing wrong with a teacher using such scores to introduce children to the potentialities of group instrumental performances; it is wrong only when this is continued to the exclusion of opportunities for children to grow in listening, discriminating, and in analyzing music in order to create their own scores. One logical approach to such scores is where, in place of standard notation, tiny drawings of the particular instrument tell the child when to play it.

The mass rhythm band activity for kindergarten and first grade, which was once popular, was never appropriate for that age group. Children at this age level are individualistic rather than fully cooperating members of a large group; the score had to be dictated by the teacher, which meant children's creativity and discrimination were practically absent; and there were sometimes aspects of exploiting little children for the entertainment of adults.

Later Years:
Ages 9–12 By the third grade children can create their own percussion scores for small and large ensemble use, based upon their growing understanding of rhythm, playing instruments, the tone qualities of instruments, notation, form, and general musical taste. To add instruments to recorded music, the children

first listen carefully, discuss what they have heard, theorize on what tone qualities and dynamics may be appropriate, experiment by performing with the instruments, and finally decide upon the completed score. Certain criteria should be used, such as:

Is the effect musical?

Can the recorded music be clearly heard when the instruments play?

Are there musical reasons for the selection of the instruments?

Is the form of the music reflected in the choice and use of the instruments—when they play and when they are silent?

Is the general effect of the music—heavy, light, thick, thin, high, low—reflected in the choice of the instruments?

There is opportunity in this activity to utilize rhythmic music of all types, from selected music by "name" composers and ethnic music to jazz and rock.

Using percussion instruments to contribute to the interpretation of songs continues through the elementary school into middle school. Sound effects heard on radio, television, and in the movies form a very real part of everyday living. Children at all levels enjoy the challenge of adding or creating descriptive sound effects to help communicate the message of certain songs. One or two drums can add immeasurably to an American Indian song; a tambourine or two can lend atmosphere to a Gypsy song; a combination of tambourine, drums, claves, and maracas can vitalize a Latin American song. A rhythm pattern drawn from the music at hand can be both experimental and creative for the children who are guided to discover it. This experience can relate to note-reading skill when the pattern is written on the chalkboard in notation to be analyzed—so that "we can see what we did" or so that "our work can be saved and remembered for tomorrow's lesson." This develops associations between playing instruments, feeling rhythm, and visualizing it. Percussion accompaniments may be constructed from part of the melody rhythm, from the meter, or from a combination of these. Two or three simple patterns may sound complex when combined. Contrasting rhythms can be played on two or more different instruments or groups of instruments, and the combinations of two or more patterns with the rhythm of the meter can be challenging, interesting, and tests of rhythmic growth. *Polyrhythms* may be either two contrasting rhythms within the same meter, or two different meters used at the same time, sometimes called "polymetric."

Percussion Instruments Described The successful use of percussion instruments demands knowledge of a variety of sounds. The teacher needs to know the tone qualities that can be produced by each instrument, and how to play each of them. In general, commercially made instruments are superior to those made by teachers and children, although some of the latter can be quite suitable for temporary use, and a few can be of permanent value.

Percussion Instrument Sound Chart

Wooden instruments that "click and have short duration

Rhythm sticks
Claves
Castanets
Coconut shells
Woodblocks
Tone block
Xylophone

Metal instruments that ring or jingle and have longer duration

Finger cymbals
Triangle
Jingle bells
Jingle clogs
Tambourine
Gong
Cymbals

Instruments that swish or rattle

Sandblocks
Strip rattles
Maracas and other rattles

Instruments that "scratch"

Rhythm sticks
Guiro (notched gourd)

Hawaiian Instruments

Pu'ili (slit bamboo sticks)
'Illi-ili (stones)
'I pu (large gourd)
Uli-uli (feathered gourds)

Instruments that "boom"

Drums

Wooden Instruments

Rhythm sticks can be made from dowel rods of from ⅜" to ⅝" in diameter, purchased from lumber yards. They are usually cut in 12" lengths. Hardwood produces the most resonant sounds and will not break as easily as softwood. Ends can be smoothed with sandpaper; they can be enameled any desired color. Children hold one in each hand and strike them together. They should explore differences in pitch and sound by tapping different places on the sticks, and by tapping the sticks on suitable objects such as the floor and desk.

Claves are paired resonant sticks about an inch in diameter. They can sometimes be satisfactorily made from six-inch lengths of a broom stick or from doweling that is an inch in diameter. The professional method of playing is to hold one clave loosely in the partly closed left hand, resting on the heel of the hand with the other end resting on the fingernails and on the thumb and index finger, and to strike this one with the other clave held stick-like in the right hand. This instrument is seldom used in primary grades. It has its major place in Cuban songs and Latin American dances of the intermediate grades. A favorite example of claves rhythm that can be learned through speaking the rhythm of words is:

Shave, hair— cut, six bits!
(or ten bucks!)

A more intricate claves rhythm is played in 4/4 meter on the underlined numbers representing eighth notes: 1 2 3 4 5 6 7 8 1 2 3 4 5 6 7 8.

Castanets used by children and by adult orchestra players are mounted on a handle. Of Spanish origin, the instrument is made of a pair of cupped pieces of resonant hardwood, usually chestnut, attached by a cord. The adult Spanish dancer holds a pair of unmounted castanets, one in each hand. The skilled dancer-player produces a variety of exciting effects from a sharp click to a sustained muffled rattle. Those played by children will produce only the sharp click. One castanet is sufficient, because of its penetrating sound. A recording of Chabrier's *España* rhapsody will illustrate its use in the adult orchestra.

Coconut shells are used to imitate hoofbeats of horses. Ripe coconuts can be purchased at food stores and the outside fibers can be removed, if desired, by a coarse kitchen "scratcher." They are then cut in half with a saw and the meat is scraped out. The two halves are then struck together to make a "clip-clop" sound. Children should explore the variety of sounds possible by striking them together in different ways including inside out, and striking them with sticks. Two paper cups can imitate coconut shells with a softer sound.

Woodblocks are best obtained from commercial sources, although imitations can be made from sections of old baseball bats. Woodblocks are sometimes held suspended by a cord to increase vibration. They are struck lightly with a hard rubber mallet at the hollow side near the edge over the slot. They can be played resting on a desk, preferably on a piece of felt, or held in the palm of the adult hand.

Children should experiment by striking them at other places, and with different beaters. They are useful to enhance songs about such subjects as ponies, cowboys, and clocks.

The *tone block* is produced commercially. The instrument is held in the left hand with the cut side toward the player. It is struck lightly on top with a stick, above the cut opening. Different sizes have different pitches, and this fact can be useful in song accompaniments.

The *xylophone,* a keyboard melody instrument, should be purchased for best results, although it has been made experimentally by teachers and students in upper grades from redwood strips or one-inch doweling resting on ropes. In early primary grades it is often used for a special *glissando* effect to describe such incidents in songs as "The mouse ran up the clock," in "Hickory Dickory Dock." Later on it is used as a melody instrument. The *marimba* is a xylophone of Latin American origin that has metal tube resonators.

Finger cymbals are tiny replicas of the larger cymbal, and are usually obtained commercially rather than made by teachers. One is usually held in each hand, and they are struck together lightly at the edge or flat together for different effects. They can also be played with one hand, with the two cymbals fastened to fingers that can strike the instruments together. This latter way enables a dancer to accompany his own dancing with delicate metallic punctuations. Finger cymbals are useful for subtle effects in Oriental songs and to portray elves or angels.

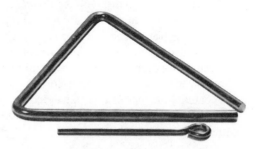

The *triangle* is struck lightly by a metal rod on the inside corner of the base of the instrument. A large nail or spike will sometimes make a satisfactory substitute. It is held suspended by a cord. The tone can be continued by moving the beater back and forth rapidly on the inside edges of the two sides. It can be silenced by touching it.

Jingle bells are purchased. They are played by shaking them vigorously. Some are mounted on sticks while others are worn around the wrist or ankle. A small tinkling sound can be produced by holding them toward the floor and moving them back and forth with a gentle motion of the wrist.

Jingle clogs are more easily purchased than made. Their major use is in primary grades. They are held in one hand and tapped against the palm of the other hand in a manner that leaves the jingles free to sound. When teachers make them from metal discs used in roofing, fastened loosely on a stick, they will gain added resonance if the discs are bent slightly. Sometimes the discs are alternated with bottle caps.

The commercially produced *tambourine* is best. It is held at the place on the instrument where there are no metal jingles. To play it, the head is struck against the heel of the hand, or it is shaken. The instrument strikes the hand; the hand does not strike the instrument. Experimental effects can be produced by tapping it on the knee, tapping it with fingers, and using a rubbing motion with the thumb followed by striking, tapping, or shaking. The head is coated with shellac and powdered rosin when professional drummers use the thumb roll. Tambourines lend atmosphere to Gypsy, Hebrew, Spanish, and Italian songs.

The true *gong* is relatively expensive. A large one could be borrowed from the high school band, perhaps. A gong can be made from German silver about one foot square. Cut a circle from this. Drill holes for the cord that will suspend it. Then hammer the edges, testing the sound from time to time, until the edges curve inward about two inches. A substitute can be found in the metal lid of the heavy barrel-like cardboard containers often used as waste baskets in schools. Ask the school custodian to save one of the containers (to use as a drum) and the lid to use as a gong. Drill a hole by which to suspend it. A suspended length of iron pipe can be another substitute. This instrument is used with songs about cathedral bells, huge clocks, and the Orient.

Cymbals of the best tone are commercially made, although some teachers have found good tones in aluminum pan lids. They are held one in each hand and struck together in a glancing blow with hands moving up and down in contrary directions. Other effects can be found by striking the cymbal on its edge, and with different beaters or sticks.

Instruments That Swish or Rattle

Sandblocks, used largely in primary grades, can be made from any soft wood from ¾″ to 1″ thick and about 3″ by 3″ square. Handles can be door or drawer pulls, spools, leather, or small pieces of wood. Fasten the handle with screws, and place No. 1–0 sandpaper or emery cloth (this lasts longer) on the rubbing side of the block with thumb tacks. Hold a block in each hand and rub the rough surfaces together. Some teachers believe that the motion of the arms required to play sandblocks is a superior means by which the five- and six-year-old can achieve rhythmic control in a very short time.

Maracas can be purchased or made from a pair of gourds by placing in them a suitable amount of dry seeds, pebbles, or bird shot. They are necessary for many Latin American dance songs. Maracas are held either by handles or by the neck of an elongated gourd, and are usually shaken in a steady eighth-note rhythm. The arms move back and forth; the wrists are stiff. For a soft effect they can be tapped by the fingers rather than shaken.

A single maraca on a long handle is used as an American Indian rattle. It can be decorated with feathers and furs. The *cabaca* or *cabaza* is a large enameled gourd that has small wooden beads strung loosely around it. This form of rattle is a Latin American instrument. *Strip rattles* can be made from walnut shells and bottle caps suspended alternately on 3″ to 4″ cords suspended from a band. They are worn on the wrist or ankle in American Indian dances. *Other rattles* can be made from spice cans, typewriter ribbon cans, pill boxes, ice cream and cottage cheese cartons, salt boxes, etc. The maraca-like rattle can be made from a large electric light bulb. Cover it with papier mâché: when dry, break glass.

Instruments That Scratch *Rhythm sticks* make a light scratching sound when they are stroked across notches. The notches appear in most commercially made sticks, and can be added to teacher-made ones by making a row of shallow saw cuts on one of each pair of sticks. These can be filed to the proper depth and smoothness, and the smooth stick is then stroked over the notched stick.

A *guiro* is a large gourd with ridges cut along its side. It is played with a small stick or a wire scratcher scraped back and forth across the ridges. It is a Latin American instrument. Besides the scratching sound it can be made to produce a tap-scrape-tap rhythm.

Hawaiian Instruments *Pu'ili* are slit bamboo sticks. They can be made from two 18″ bamboo sticks that are 1″ to 2″ in diameter. The lowest large joint is the handle. It can be drilled out and sanded. Holes ¼″ to ⅜″ in diameter are drilled above this joint to serve as guides for cutting out corresponding slices from the holes to the tip. The sticks are struck softly together and used in graceful motions as an extension of the arm. *'Illi-ili* are pairs of small rounded volcanic rocks to be held in the palm of the hand and clapped or rubbed together. Using many players gives an interesting effect. The *'I pu* is a drum made from a wide, jar-shaped gourd. The top of the stem end is cut off and the seeds and pulp are removed. It is played by slapping the side of the gourd with the palm of the hand. *Uli-uli* are feathered gourds.

Drums There are many kinds and sizes of drums, manufactured and teacher-made. Some have one head, others two. They come singly and by two's and even three's. For different effects they can be struck off-center or in the center, with the fingertips, the heel of the hand, or with various types of padded beaters. There should be at least two drums in every classroom; one of low pitch and one of high pitch. The many types of commercial drums include the tom-tom, tunable drums, bongo, and conga drums. Homemade drums of varying quality may be devised from chopping bowls, wooden kegs, lard cans, and wastebaskets with goatskin (soaked 24 hours), real calfskin, or heavy rubber thumbtacked, nailed, or laced on. Old drumheads can be used, salvaged from stores or from the high school bandroom. To paint skin drumheads, use watercolor paint applied on the *wet* head. Color is an important element in constructing any of the instruments because it makes them more attractive to children. Smaller drums can be devised from oatmeal boxes or other cardboard containers, used as they are or with ends covered with a rubber sheet or very heavy paper. Flowerpot "drums" can be made by stretching and taping wet heavy paper across the opening; the paper tightens as it dries. Ready-made drums of fair quality are found in the very heavy cardboard barrel-like cartons used to ship chinaware, seed, ice cream mix, and sweeping compound. These are stood open-end-down on two books (to raise them off the floor in order to increase resonance) and pounded. They can be useful as drums, and have added utility in that the metal cover can be used as a gong. These potential drums are often found as wastebaskets in school corridors.

Drum beaters can be purchased. They can be made from sticks of doweling of sufficient diameter cut to proper length, and soft rubber balls. The doweling is glued into a hole made in the ball. Instead of the rubber ball, a ball of cotton, covered with muslin and tied, can be used, or a ball can be made of aluminum foil covered with muslin and painted with two or three coats of the nitrate liquid used by airplane manufacturers.

The *conga drum* is a large long Cuban drum played with the palms of the hands, usually with the left hand with flat fingers striking the edge of the head and the right hand also with flat fingers striking the center of the head.

The *bongo drum,* another Latin American instrument, is a double drum; one is larger than the other. Held between the knees with the small drum on the right, it is played with the tips of the fingers and the thumbs. The bongo is used in Latin American music.

Summary Some of the many possible songs for introducing and expanding the use of percussion instruments are the familiar "Hickory, Dickory, Dock," "Jingle Bells," "Jingle at the Window," "Ten Little Indians," various songs about trains, "This Old Man," "Toodola," "When the Saints Go Marching In," "Mister Banjo," "Down the River," "Sandy Land," and "Tinga Layo."

Recordings of twentieth-century pieces that emphasize or are written solely for percussion instruments can be helpful in giving students ideas about how to compose their own percussion music. The following three pieces are pertinent:

Toccata for Percussion, Carlos Chavez, Columbia CMS 6447; HBR 21003, 2 discs.
Concerto for Percussion and Small Orchestra, Darius Milhaud, Capitol HBR 21003, 2 discs
Ionization, Edgar Varese, Columbia MS 6146, also on Folkways' *Sounds of New Music,* FX 6160

The Chavez *Toccata* is also helpful for learning to identify percussion instruments by sound.

Group improvisation can provide an enjoyable means for exploring rhythm patterns and contrast in dynamic levels. For example, a class of children may be asked to improvise a percussion accompaniment for a parade march like "Parade" from *Divertissement,* Adventures in Music 1, Volume 1. As an introduction, the teacher can discuss the drum and conventional and unconventional percussion, rhythm patterns, dynamic levels, and crescendo and decrescendo. After the improvisation, the class can be asked to notate some of the rhythm patterns used.

We have described some of the contributions that percussion instruments can make to children's explorations of tone qualities, dynamics, pitch, form, rhythm, and the interpretations of songs in which their use is appropriate. Concepts of the phrase, repetition, and contrast can be enhanced by creating percussion scores which reflect these aspects of form. Feelings for mood can be reflected in the choice of and the manner of playing the instruments. Notation can be learned and understood better when children find it useful to them in playing and composing percussion scores. Every concept of rhythm may be strengthened at times by the use of these instruments. The following is a list of addresses of companies that sell percussion instruments:

Kitching Educational, 1728 N. Damen Ave., Chicago, Ill., 60642

Lyons, 530 Riverview Ave., Elkhart, Ind. 46515

Magnamusic-Baton, Inc., 10370 Page Industrial Blvd., St. Louis, Mo. 63132

Music Education Group, 1415 Waukegan Rd., Northbrook, Ill., 60062

Nova Diversified, 1104 N.E. 28th Ave., Portland, Oregon 97232. Wooden drums and
   wood blocks with mallets.

Peripole, Inc., P.O. Box 146, Lewiston Rd., Browns Mills, N.J. 08015

Rhythm Band, Inc., P.O Box 126, Fort Worth, Tex. 76101

Scientific Music Industries, 525 N. Noble St., Chicago, Ill., 60622

West Music Company, 1212 5th St., Coralville, Iowa 52241

Pitched Instruments and Voices

Ages 9-12 When discussing tone qualities, the terms *tone color* and *timbre* (tám-br) are
often used. Tone color is a term borrowed from art; it implies that tone qualities are accomplished in music in the same general way the artist selects and
combines colors in painting. Timbre is synonymous with tone quality. Thus,
tone quality, tone color, and timbre mean the same thing: the difference in
sound between tones of the same pitch when produced by different instruments or voices. For example, the same pitch played on a violin, a trumpet,
or a flute varies greatly in tone quality.

In music education of the past there was emphasis on identification of
the sources of tone—the specific instrument or voice that produced it. Research has shown that very young children can learn to do such identification. The student's curiosity should be encouraged—what is there in the
construction of a given instrument that produces its particular tone quality;
how can the player of the instrument affect tone quality by his or her manner of playing; why are particular tone qualities selected by composers as the
most suitable to enhance melodies and harmonies; what is the effect of range
on tone quality; how does tone quality interrelate with melody, harmony,
texture, and form to make music more attractive? If the study of tone quality
can be based on the reasons for the employment of certain instruments in a
composition, the mechanical construction and the method of playing them,
then the identification of the instrument or combinations of instruments
should become part of a logical scheme of things rather than the memorizing
of isolated facts that may be soon forgotten.

When composers select certain instruments or voices to convey the
meaning of a composition, one of the reasons may be to imitate a sound of
nature. Children should decide why the clarinet, flute, and piccolo are often
chosen to imitate a bird, by comparing these tones with those of other instruments. It should be obvious why a composer would choose the tympani
rather than a tambourine to imitate a clap of thunder. There are interesting
psychological associations with listening experiences. When the French
horn plays a certain type of melody, hunting may be brought to mind; when
the oboe plays another type of melody, a pastoral scene, possibly with sheep

and shepherd, is suggested. However, there is a vast amount of music that has no such associative meanings. When dealing with this, the study becomes one of discovery—why great composers select certain instruments to perform certain melodies, why these instruments suit these melodies better than other instruments, and how poorly some would sound if assigned the same melodies. Of course teachers know that once in a while children may disagree with great composers, yet when the children have logical reasons for their point of view, their judgment is to be respected. The Leonard Bernstein film, *What Does Orchestration Mean?* (McGraw-Hill Films, 1 hour, grades 5-up) deals with choosing "the right instruments at the right time in the right combination." Sometimes the sound of certain instruments and combinations of instruments can unite with melodies, harmonies, and textures to produce music suggestive of particular nations and localities. One example is music used on television and in films to suggest the open spaces of the American West. This fascinating study requires an ability to analyze, and it is complex even for adults to manage. Therefore teachers must keep their expectations within the limits of the musical background of the class. However, every student should acquire some appreciation for the great contribution tone qualities supply to satisfying the need for contrast and variety in music.

In the primary grades there is an emphasis on the function of percussion instruments to produce sound effects, and the children are helped to explore the different types of tone qualities they can find by playing the instruments in experimental ways, as discussed earlier. Classification of percussion instruments according to their tone qualities is part of the process of learning concepts relating to why and how certain sounds are produced by instruments and objects. This inquiry might not take place unless the teacher plans questions such as, "Does the woodblock sound the same as the rhythm sticks?" "Why do you suppose the sound is different?" "Look at each to see how it is made." "Yes, the woodblock is hollow; what difference might that make?" The ways of producing several different tone qualities on each instrument stress the importance of the method used to play them. For example, if a player uses two rapidly alternating mallets on a resonator bar, the continuous effect will be different from striking it once with one mallet; if three players each use two mallets in this way to produce a continuous-sounding chord, there will be a shimmering effect. From such beginnings, other instruments are introduced in relation to their sound and function. Several different ways of playing the Autoharp are presented on page 397; children can find that playing on either side of the bridge yields a difference in tone quality. The enjoyment of beauty of tone is good in itself, and should be experienced often. Then there should come a time when attention is called to how this beauty is produced.

What Makes Sound? For sound to occur, something must vibrate. Young children can experiment with a rubber band stretched across an open-top box. When they pluck it, they can see it quiver at a fast rate, and they can hear that this vibration makes a sound. Every time the rubber band moves back and forth, a sound wave (cycle) is formed of molecules of air. The sound waves go through the air to reach our eardrums, causing them to vibrate. Nerves carry this sensation to the brain, and our stored experiences usually tell us what kind of a sound we are hearing. The learners will find that if the rubber band is pulled out far, then let go, the vibration is wide and the sound is louder; if the band is pulled a short distance, the vibration is less and the sound is soft. Through further experimentation it will be found that the lowest pitch will be sounded when the entire band vibrates, and that higher pitches will be sounded when a finger is placed on the band to shorten the vibrating portion. Thus, children may be able to generalize that the length of a vibrating object influences its pitch; the longer, the lower; the shorter, the higher. It should also be discovered that a shorter length vibrates more rapidly than a longer length.

In some woodwind instruments—the flute and piccolo—the sound is produced by a vibrating column of air, while in others—the clarinet, oboe, and bassoon—the sound is initiated by a vibrating reed. By taking a bottle and blowing across its open top, a sound can be made that comes from vibrating air. By pouring water into the bottle, children can discover that the longer the vibrating air column, the lower the pitch and the shorter the vibrating air column, the higher the pitch. To imitate the vibration of the double reed of the oboe and bassoon they can flatten one end of a soda straw, cut off the corners, and practice blowing into the straw through this flattened end. When brass instruments sound, the players' lips are the vibrating agent. Some children will be able to make a circular cup "mouthpiece" with their thumb and index finger, put their lips together on it and blow into it to produce a sound with their vibrating lips. They can watch large drumheads to see that striking them causes vibrations. They can examine a piano to discover that hammers strike the strings and cause them to vibrate. When string instruments are made to vibrate, the player either plucks the strings, as the children did the rubber band, or draws a bow across them. Perhaps the children can learn from a violinist that rosin is rubbed on the horse hair in the bow to increase the friction to make the strings vibrate. Perhaps they can answer the question, "Why is it that the player is never supposed to touch the horse hair of the bow?" (Because the oil in the skin transferred to the horse hair reduces the friction needed to make the string vibrate.) As this study continues with many different instruments, consideration should be given to the material the instrument is made of, the length of the instrument, the length of the vibrating section, and the existence of *resonating chambers,* such as those of the woodblock and the violin; all of these may affect tone quality. It might be noted that science tells us it should not matter what kind of material is used for instruments having vibrating air columns. However, many musicians continue to want recorders made of wood rather than of plastic, frequently arguing about the virtues of wood versus synthetic materials, while flute players now prefer metal instruments to the older wooden flute. Other topics of scientific or historical interest include the *vibrato* as it is used by instrumentalists and singers, the overtone series and its relation to tone quality, and the historical development of modern instruments; these can be investigated by older children. Some may be interested in the relation between the clavichord, harpsichord, and piano, in the relation of the viols and the modern string family, and in the evolution of the valve instruments.

There are teachers who plan experiences for children with such stress on qualities of sound and dynamics that they temporarily exclude melody. Children are encouraged to create new sounds with familiar instruments, such as placing materials of different types (pieces of metal, paper, felt pads) on piano and Autoharp wires, and combining these experimental tone qualities with percussion instruments like the gong and woodblock to create a background for a poem or choric reading. Some teachers challenge children to create new tone qualities by taking sounds from their environment, taping these, and arranging them in a suitable order. An example might be lunch-room sounds, in which a short piece would utilize the sound of feet, talking, trays being stacked, the bell, and so on. These could be varied by playing the tape at different speeds and retaping them. Another way might be to have children create a plan for using such sounds, then have the class imitate or reproduce them from an experimental score in the same general way that orchestra instruments imitate. Other ideas for children to work with could include sounds in the morning on the way to school, sounds of a shopping trip, sounds of the city, sounds of the country, and sounds of interesting tone qualities with no story.

Such an approach is used to involve children in the sounds of experimental composition. Electronic sounds are included, often using the assistance of a tape recorder; tone generators and mixers contribute to the many types of tone qualities composers use today.

Voices Earlier an activity was recommended in which young children learned to listen to the speaking and singing voices of their unseen classmates to identify them in a game situation. Children will notice that some voices are higher or lower pitched then others, and that some are clearer in tone quality than others. They can generalize that all persons have a different, and perhaps unique, quality in their voices. While the voices of older children are best identified in terms of high, medium, and low, the terms for adult voices—soprano, alto, tenor, baritone and bass—can be introduced as degrees of high and low in the instance of women and men, respectively. Suitable recordings may be used to compare the qualities of each. If possible, the children should hear a soprano and an alto sing the same song in the same range, then discuss the difference in tone quality that will be revealed. The same can be done with a tenor and a bass. They will be interested when a man and a woman sing the same song an octave apart, and they should try to describe the tone quality in each of the above experiences. For eleven-year-olds these adult classifications may be subdivided further. For example, there are subdivisions of the soprano voice: *coloratura* (the highest), lyric, and dramatic. The *contralto* is a low alto, the lowest female voice. The male voice falls into three major classifications, tenor, baritone, and bass. The baritone is the middle range male voice. There are subdivisions of the male voices, but there is little need to enlarge upon this. Perhaps the essential knowledge consists of knowing the five major classifications and that each of these can be further subdivided. Each voice type has a characteristic tone quality.

The tone qualities of combinations of voices are studied by ten- and eleven-year-olds. They should know the duet, trio, quartet, and quintet (and possibly the sextette, octette, and nonette), as well as the different types of choral groups—men's, women's, and mixed—and be able to recognize the sound of choral music, choruses singing sacred music, and choruses singing secular music. These small and large ensembles should be compared to instrumental groups; for example, children should be aware of similarities and differences between a vocal quartet of soprano, alto, tenor, and bass, and the string quartet of first violin, second violin, viola, and cello.

Recordings to illustrate voices are usually not found in the educational collections. Examples of arias from operas are a possibility. Middle school students may enjoy classifying the voices of popular singers, carefully selected, of course, and the comparison of operatic and popular styles can be of interest. They should verbalize about the tone qualities, and in the process expand their descriptive vocabularies. The teacher's role is to make possible the students' exploration, discovery, identification, comparison, evaluation, and description of tone qualities, telling them only what is necessary to help them learn for themselves.

Strings   The string family of the orchestra is made up of the violin, viola, 'cello, and double bass (string bass, bass viol). They are approximately the same shape except that the violin is the smallest, the viola somewhat larger, the 'cello so large that the player must sit in a chair and rest the instrument on the floor, and the double bass so very large that the player ordinarily stands up to play it. These instruments are called "the first family of the orchestra." Study of the seating plan of an orchestra will show one reason why. Listening carefully to symphonic music will reveal that the strings are truly the backbone of the orchestra, with the brass, woodwinds, and percussion sections assisting by adding many contrasting tone qualities.

The string instruments produce a variety of tone qualities within their family. The violin, viola, and 'cello use *vibrato,* a slight varying of pitch produced by rapid movement of the left hand and forearm while pressing down on a string. The term *con sordino* means with a mute; when the mute is attached to the bridge, the device that supports the strings, the tone becomes smaller and more nasal. These instruments produce *harmonics,* higher pitches of reduced resonance with flute-like tones that occur when the player touches, but does not press down on a string, and bows very lightly on that string. When these instruments are played by plucking strings, this is called *pizzicato;* it produces still another tone quality. A short, fast stroke played in the middle of the bow with a slight bounce from the string is *spiccato* bowing. Double stops, the playing and bowing of two strings at once, gives another effect. The *tremulo* produces a rather tense impression; it is done by moving the bow back and forth a short distance at an extremely fast rate. A flute-like effect is made by *sur la touche,* a slight bowing over the finger board, and a glassy effect, *sul ponticello,* is made by bowing very close to the bridge. An unusual effect is the *col legno,* which means using the wood of the bow rather than the hair. The *glissando* is produced by playing scale passages with many tiny movements of the left hand to change the pitch in almost a sliding effect. The normal tone qualities of these instruments can be described in various ways. A beginning can be made with these:

violin   The string instrument that most resembles the qualities of the human voice; great versatility in range of expression; extremely sensitive tone qualities.

viola   a veiled and nasal quality; darker in color than the violin.

'cello   the bass violin; a deep masculine voice of soulful quality.

double bass   very low, heavy tone quality; it sounds one octave lower than the cello.

Children, older students, and adults should be asked to demonstrate these instruments. While films and recordings are helpful, nothing takes the place of a good, well-qualified, live performer.

The harp is another string instrument; the player is seated with the string section of the orchestra. It can be compared to the piano in some ways; it has a range of six octaves and a fifth. There are seven foot pedals, each of which can be pressed down two notches, each notch representing one halfstep. The harp makes splashing, cascading effects. The *glissando* is used frequently to produce these. Harmonics are sounded by placing the palm of the hand in the middle of the strings; this places the pitch one octave higher than normal, making possible a quality of mystery. A different effect is made by plucking strings close to the sounding board.

The keyboard instruments include the piano, harpsichord, and celesta. The tone qualities of the piano should be thoroughly explored; special experimental effects can be made. In the piano, felt hammers strike the strings; the harpsichord strings are made to vibrate by means of a plucking mechanism. The celesta is basically a percussion instrument. Its keyboard causes hammers to strike the steel bars of what approximates a type of glockenspiel (bell set). The tone is of unusual light quality; a famed celesta piece is "Dance of the Sugar Plum Fairy" from the *Nutcracker* Suite of Tchaikovsky. The harpsichord—older than the piano—was the favorite keyboard instrument at the time of Haydn and Mozart. Its tone quality is considerably lighter than the piano, and it has less expressive capability. The Young People's Record 411, *Said the Piano to the Harpsichord,* is informative, and it communicates to children.

String instruments not part of the symphony orchestra include the guitar, banjo, ukulele, mandolin, lyre, zither, Autoharp, and others. These should be explored to identify the tone qualities they produce. There is excellent guitar literature, much of it from Spanish sources; children should know of Segovia and others who play the classical guitar. Bowmar 84 includes a guitar selection.

Examples of recordings portraying tone qualities of the symphony strings include:

violin cadenzas	*Scheherazade* Suite, Rimsy-Korsakov
violin	*Flight of the Bumblebee,* Rimsky-Korsakov, Bowmar 53
strings	*Eine kleine Nachtmusik,* Mozart, Adventures in Music 4 v.1
violin	*The Wonderful Violin,* Moore, Young People's Record 311
viola plays second theme	*Danse Macabre,* Saint-Saëns, Bowmar 59
'cello	"The Swan," *Carnival of the Animals,* Saint-Saëns, Bowmar 59, Adventures in Music 3 v. 2
double bass	"Elephants," *Carnival of the Animals,* Saint-Saëns, Bowmar 51
double bass	"Jimbo's Lullaby," Debussy, Bowman 51

Suggested films include:

Listening to Good Music: The String Quartet, Encyclopaedia Britannica Films
String Sounds, Churchill Films
The String Choir, Encyclopaedia Britannica Films
The String Trio, Coronet Instructional Films
The Trio, World Artists, Inc.

Woodwinds   The woodwind instruments not only blend well with the strings of the orchestra, but they add other interesting tone qualities which can be used in the performance of melodies or subsidiary parts that contribute to the effect the composer plans to achieve. It is of interest that the woodwinds in the concert band seem to substitute for the strings in the orchestra; for example in examining a concert band, one finds many clarinets instead of many violins.

The modern flute is a descendant of the recorder. It is a *transverse* flute, which means that one holds it at right angles to the mouth and blows across a hole in the side of it. The recorder is an end-blown flute. While it is said that the best recorders are made of wood, the modern flute is generally made of silver. Its tone quality varies with the range. Low pitches are relatively big and somewhat breathy, while higher tones become increasingly bright and penetrating with ascending pitches. An impressive flute solo at the beginning of a composition that emphasizes tone qualities can be found in Debussy's *Afternoon of a Faun,* followed by colorful effects on a harp. (Remember that a *faun* is a creature from rural Roman mythology, a man principally human, but with a goat's tail, pointed ears, short horns, and sometimes cloven feet.) Another favorite composition featuring flutes is Tchaikovsky's "Dance of the Toy Flutes," from the *Nutcracker* Suite, Bowmar 58. The piccolo is a small flute, half as long, and pitched one octave higher. It plays the highest pitches of any instrument in the woodwind family, and its tone quality is exceedingly brilliant and penetrating. A favorite piccolo solo is in Sousa's *Stars and Stripes Forever,* Bowmar 54. Others are found in the "Chinese Dance" from Tchaikovsky's *Nutcracker* Suite, Bowmar 59, and "Entrance of the Little Fauns" by Pierné, Bowmar 54.

The most commonly found clarinet is the B♭ instrument; some of the children who are studying this single reed instrument can demonstrate it. There is a family of clarinets, with the E♭ being smaller and higher in pitch, and the alto and bass being lower, as would be expected. There are other less common clarinets, including the clarinet in A and the double bass in B♭, the latter being an octave lower than the bass clarinet. The B♭ clarinet has three registers, each with a different tone quality. The lowest is rich and full-bodied, the middle is sometimes breathy and is the most difficult to make sound well; the highest is brilliant and versatile. This variety of tone qualities gives the clarinet a good deal of breadth of expression. Examples include Prokofiev's *Peter and the Wolf*, Saint-Saëns' "Cuckoo in the Deep Woods," from *Carnival of the Animals,* Bowmar 51, and the second movement of Rimsky-Korsakov's *Scheherazade* Suite. Clarinets are made of wood, ebonite, and occasionally of metal.

The saxophone is seldom used in orchestras, but it is widely used in bands and dance bands. There is a family of saxophones, including soprano, alto, tenor, baritone, and bass. The most commonly seen are in the following order: alto, tenor, and baritone. These are in most school bands and in many dance bands. Although they have cane reeds like clarinets, they are made of metal. The tone quality of the instruments is such that it blends with woodwinds or brass instruments. This tone quality can be changed markedly by the player, thus can be sweet, raucous, or brusque as desired in certain types of jazz, rock, and dance music.

The oboe family includes all of the double reed instruments. The oboe is about the same size as the B♭ clarinet. The English horn is an alto oboe and the bassoon is the bass instrument of the family. The contra-bassoon is an octave lower than the ordinary bassoon. The oboe tone quality is often described as nasal, pastoral, oriental, and plaintive. *Peter and the Wolf* demonstrates the oboe tone quality, as does the second movement of Tchaikovsky's Symphony No. 4 and his "Puss in Boots and the White Cat," from the *Sleeping Beauty,* Adventures in Music 3 v. 1. The English horn has a pear-shaped bell which is one source of its melancholy tone quality. Examples of its sound appear in the "Largo" of Dvořák's *New World* Symphony, Sibelius' *Swan of Tuonela,* and "Puss in Boots and the White Cat," mentioned above. Children should discover how the bassoon is built, since the design permits it to have a great length of tube. (The contra-bassoon has over sixteen feet.) Besides serving as a bass instrument, its tone blends well with the French horn and enables it to play solo passages of distinction. While its tone quality is rather even except at extreme high and low ranges, it has a versatility which enables it to project plaintive, gruff, and humorous impressions. It can play over a wide range with both legato and staccato articulation. Examples are found in "In the Hall of the Mountain King," from *Peer Gynt* Suite, by Grieg, Adventures in Music 3 v. 2, and Bowmar 59; "Berceuse" from Stravinsky's *Firebird* Suite; the second movement of Tchaikovsky's Symphony No. 4; and in *Rondo for Bassoon and Orchestra,*

Children's Record Guild 1009. The grandfather theme in *Peter and the Wolf* is played by a contra-bassoon.

Additional variety in the performance of woodwind instruments is attained by legato and staccato tonguing, as well as double, triple, and flutter tonguing. Double tonguing can be explained by letting out the breath with a series of repeated "t-t" tonguings; triple tonguing is a repeated "t-k-t." These are of particular importance in flute playing.

The film *Introducing the Woodwinds,* Indiana University, introduces the instruments of the woodwind quintet to children. These are flute (and piccolo), clarinet, oboe, bassoon, and French horn—the brass instrument that possesses a tone quality which blends with both the woodwinds and the brasses. *Wind Sounds,* Churchill Films, deals with woodwinds and brasses.

Brasses Children can quickly find a major difference between a bugle and a trumpet, or cornet, in that the bugle lacks valves. They can then discern why the bugle can play only bugle calls whereas the other instruments can play both bugle calls and melodies. They should study the valve and its length of tubing to find what valves do to the length of the air column, and how much each valve lowers a pitch. They will see that the cornet is shorter than the trumpet, and they will hear that its tone quality is less brilliant. The player has a great deal to do with the sound of these instruments, producing tones of both coarse and pleasing qualities at will. The baritone is a larger instrument found in bands; the mellophone is an instrument about the size of a French horn but which lacks the golden quality of the French horn tone; it is used for marching bands and for students who may later progress to the more difficult French horn. The tubing of the French horn should be examined to try to determine how long the instrument would be if it were a straight horn like the alphorn, a folk instrument from the Alps. Both tone quality and pitch are influenced by a practice called *stopping,* which is the insertion of the hand into the bell. Mutes made of metal, wood, or fiberboard change the tone qualities of the cornet, trumpet, French horn, and trombone. Both school band and dance band players of trumpet and trombone can demonstrate their several types of mutes in the classroom. While the cornet and trumpet have the most commanding tones, the French horn has the tone that blends with other instruments the best, although it can be bold and brassy when this is desired. The tones of these instruments can be varied by legato and staccato tonguing, double and triple tonguing, flutter tonguing, and the use of mutes. Four sizes of trombones are used in the symphony orchestra, the most common being the tenor. This instrument and an occasional bass trombone will be seen in school bands. The trombone and baritone have larger mouthpieces than those of the cornet, trumpet, and French horn; this results in a tone quality of less brilliance, but of more dignity and solemnity. Children will be interested in how the trombone's slide shortens or lengthens the air column in place of the valve mechanism. Because of the slide, trombones can produce a *portamento,* which is a gliding from one tone to another through all degrees of pitches. The lowest pitched instruments of the brass family are the tubas and sousaphones. The sousaphone is the instrument carried on the shoulder of its players in marching bands; its huge shiny bell makes an impressive appearance. New plastic materials are being used today in place of metal in order to reduce the weight the player must carry. The tuba player is seated in the orchestra and appears occasionally in the band. As expected, these bass instruments have the largest mouthpieces. As told in the children's recording, *Tubby the Tuba,* Decca Records, the tuba seldom plays melodies. Instead, it normally supports the band as the primary low bass instrument, and it assists the double basses of the orchestra. Its tone is deep and its execution somewhat ponderous.

Examples of brass instrument tone qualities include:

Trumpet	"Finale," *William Tell* Overture, Rossini, Adventures in Music 3, v. 1; Bowmar 76
	"Changing of the Guard," *Carmen* Suite, Bizet, Adventures in Music 3 v. 2
	The King's Trumpet, Children's Record Guild 5040
French horn	*Peter and the Wolf,* Prokofiev
	"Nocturne," *Midsummer Night's Dream,* Mendelssohn
	"Third Movement," Symphony No. 3, Brahms
Trombone	"Prelude to Act 3," *Lohengrin,* Wagner
	Stars and Stripes Forever, Sousa, Adventures in Music 4 v. 2; Bowmar 54
Tuba	"Bydlo," *Pictures at an Exhibition,* Mussorgsky, Adventures in Music 2; Bowmar 82
	"Departure," *Winter Holiday,* Prokofiev, Adventures in Music 2

Percussion Examples of percussion instrument tone qualities include:

Cymbals, Drums	*Danse Macabre,* Saint-Saëns
	"Dagger Dance," *Natoma,* Herbert, Adventures in Music 3 v. 1
	Sempter Fidelis, Sousa, Adventures in Music 3 v. 2
Drums, Timpani	"In the Hall of the Mountain King," *Peer Gynt Suite,* Grieg, Adventures in Music 3 v. 2; Bowmar 59
Tambourine	"Tarantella," *Fantastic Toy Shop,* Rossini, Adventures in Music 3 v. 2; Bowmar 56
Xylophone	*The Alligator and the Coon,* Thomson, Adventures in Music 3 v. 2
Piano, Harpsichord	*Said the Piano to the Harpsichord,* Young People's Record 411

The following selected current popular recordings feature percussion:

Concert Percussion for Orchestra, Cage, Cowell, *et al.,* Time 58000
Music of Bali, Period SPL 1613

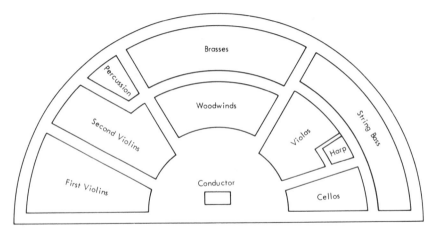

Figure 10.1. THE ORCHESTRA

Films can also be useful in teaching percussion:

Percussion Group, Encyclopaedia Britannica Films
Percussion, Pulse of Music, Indiana University
Percussion Sounds, Churchill Films

Figure 10.1 shows the seating position of the various instruments in the orchestra.

Band and Orchestra in the Elementary School

Clarinets, trombones, cornets, saxophones, and other large instruments can be played by children in the intermediate grades. However, their tones are too powerful to blend with the light voices of children; thus they are ill-suited for inclusion in a classroom orchestra that is associated with the singing program. The authors of some music textbooks have nonetheless included some interesting uses for these instruments. These include instrumental solos, duets, descants, and true orchestrations of some of the songs. It appears that the best use for these orchestrations is in the playing of instrumental introductions and/or accompaniments for songs on special programs or for large vocal groups.

Lessons given on these instruments by the teacher of instrumental music should be scheduled in the special interest period when possible. The temporary withdrawal of some children from the room may be a disruption unless the classroom teacher can make plans in accordance with it. Much of the irritation that sometimes comes when children leave the classroom for these lessons can be avoided if all teachers concerned have an opportunity to plan the instrumental music schedule cooperatively.

Teachers of general music in grades four and up can encourage membership in band and orchestra classes. Preliminary steps towards this end can include bulletin board displays of instruments and instrumentalists; presenting recordings, films, and film strips that illustrate instruments and families of instruments in ways that attract the interest of the age group; displaying attractive catalogues obtained from instrument manufacturers; displaying commercially produced charts of orchestra instruments; and making available to the children books that include pictures of children playing instruments. The general music teacher and the specialists in instrumental music should plan together times when the specialist can speak to the class and when he or she and children can demonstrate instruments. The sending of notices to parents and the planning for parent-teacher conferences about the selection, rental, or purchase of instruments should also be done by joint consideration of the general teacher and the specialist. A time should be decided upon when the specialist will bring instruments to the class and permit children to try them. (This will necessitate use of a germicide.) The specialist should explain to the class why certain children are suited to the playing of certain instruments but not others and should demonstrate the importance of finger size, length, and flexibility in playing the clarinet, for example, and the importance of being able to "buzz" the lips in playing the trumpet. Teeth formation should be revealed as important. For instance, a small overbite is preferable for small brass instruments while a large overbite is acceptable for bass and baritone. The instrumental teacher should avoid teaching fingering in a way that confuses "finger numbers" with scale-tone numbers. To say that A is played with the first and second fingers is correct, but to say that "A is two" is confusing to the child who is learning numeral names of scale tones. Both the general music teacher and the specialist can utilize instrumental scores in textbooks, and they can plan some of these correlated activities together. Singing in the instrumental class can assist in pitch accuracy on the instruments and in the growth of balanced musicianship. To sing, then play rote melodies demands and teaches musical skills. The instrumental score can at times be sung.

The child most likely to succeed in band and orchestra will be one who is sufficiently mature physically to play the instrument, who is generally musical, and who possesses reliability and perseverance.

Activities for More Advanced Students

Tone qualities and note reading. Examine an orchestra score. While the composition is played on a record player, follow a specific instrument part with the finger.

Music history. Listen to a recording of instrumental music. Then design a record jacket that will include information about the history of the composition and facts about its composer.

Evaluation. Listen to several recordings of the same composition and compare the conductors' interpretations and the performers' skills and the quality of the recording.

General Suggestions

1. Students can identify and compare the recorded tone qualities of the orchestra and band.
2. Have students study the many folk instruments and their tone qualities. One

reference is Album L 24, *Folk Instruments of the World,* Follett Publishing Company, with an explanatory folder that includes drawings of the instruments.

3. Have students identify and compare the tone qualities and the make-up of various vocal and instrumental ensembles: duets, trios, quartets, quintets, sextets, etc.

4. Students can investigate the seating arrangement of a band: draw it, and compare this plan with that of the orchestra.

5. Students can research the organ as a class of instruments: listen to masterworks for the organ; describe the tone qualities of organs and compare them with other instruments.

6. When students examine a band or orchestra score they will find that instrument parts are written in different keys. They may find that some instruments are built in different keys. By experimenting with playing written notes on instruments and comparing the resulting pitch with the piano or bells, they can discover that when B♭ instruments play written C, the pitch is that of B♭, and when E♭ instruments play C, the pitch sounded is E♭. The teacher could plan a discrepant event by asking children who play instruments to all play the same song from a music book. This would be one way to discover which instruments are "transposing" instruments and which are not.

7. Plan for advanced older children to explore acoustics. Help them study resonance, harmonics, the overtone series, partials, and vibrato. Relate music and science.

8. Arrange to have children hear some electronic music. Have them discuss the tone qualities they hear and try to determine the function of this music.

9. Students can compare the tone qualities and the instrumentation of the military band, the symphonic band, and the dance band.

10. Arrange for a group of children to create a dance based upon the various instruments heard in a colorful symphonic recording.

11. If possible, let students work with an *oscilloscope,* an electric machine which pictures the sound waves produced by tone qualities. Let them compare the wave forms of the flute, violin, and trumpet when they sound the same pitch.

12. Listen to a recording of a gamelan orchestra from Indonesia. Then create an imitation which will require a conductor to bring in different sections and to have other sections stop playing at times. Groups of students select, or are assigned percussion instruments of contrasting tone qualities. Each group will repeat a very short rhythm pattern as long as the conductor desires. For example, long-short-long could be one such pattern. A bell set or other melody instrument could be used to improvise a tune to sound along with various combinations of the groups. Have the group evaluate the experiment.

References and Materials

Books   COPLAND, AARON, *What to Listen for in Music* (rev. ed.). New York: Mentor Books, 1964, Chapter 7.

GARY, CHARLES L., ed., *The Study of Music in the Elementary School—A Conceptual Approach.* Reston, Va.: Music Educators National Conference, Washington, D.C., 1967. pp. 136–56.

WALTON, CHARLES, *Teaching Guide.* Camden, N.J.: RCA-Victor, (for Instruments of the Orchestra Recordings).

Pictures and Charts

Construction of the Grand Piano; Evolution of the Grand Piano, Baldwin Piano Company, Cincinnati, Ohio. Also pamphlet, Story of the Baldwin Piano.

Instruments of the Band and Orchestra, F. A. Owen Publishing Co. (publishers of *Instructor Magazine*). Pictures of children playing instruments.

Instruments of the Orchestra Charts, J. W. Pepper and Son, 1423 Vine Street, Philadelphia, Pa. 22 charts for use with RCA recordings.

Meet the Instruments, Bowmar Records, Belwin Mills, Melville, N.Y. 11747. 25 laminated posters.

Musical Instrument Pictures, C. G. Conn, Ltd., 2520 Industrial Parkway, Elkhart, Ind. 46516.

Musical Instruments, York Band Instrument Company, Grand Rapids, Michigan.

Range Chart for Band and Orchestra Instruments, C. G. Conn, Ltd., 2520 Industrial Parkway, Elkhart, Ind. 46516.

Recordings

BOWMAR ORCHESTRAL LIRARY

Ensembles, Large and Small, Album 83. Includes Britten's *Young Person's Guide to the Orchestra,* a string quartet, percussion ensemble, brass ensemble, and chorale.

COLUMBIA RECORDS, 799 Seventh Ave., New York, N.Y.

Carnival of the Animals, Saint-Saëns, and *Young Person's Guide to the Orchestra,* Britten. ML 5768.

First Chair, ML 4629. Features bassoon, cello, clarinet, flute, French horn, oboe, trumpet, and violin. For middle school.

The Military Band, Col. 1056

Peter and the Wolf, Tubby the Tuba, and *Pan the Piper,* all on CL 671.

FRANSON CORPORATION, 225 Park Avenue South, New York, N.Y. 10003. Children's Record Guild and Young People's Records.

Drummer Boy
Hunter's Horn, The
King's Trumpet, The
Licorice Stick (clarinet)
Little Brass Band
Mr. Grump and *The Dingle School Band*
Neighbors' Band
On Lemmer Lemmer Street (violin)
Rondo for Bassoon and Orchestra
Runaway Sheep (wind instruments)
Said the Piano to the Harpsichord
Strike up the Band
Wonderful Violin

MERCURY RECORD CORPORATION

The Composer and His Orchestra, Vol. 1. Howard Hanson tells how he uses instruments.

Guitar Music from the Courts of Spain, Caledonia Romera plays.

MUSIC EDUCATION RECORD CORPORATION, Box 445, Englewood Cliffs, N.J. *The Complete Orchestra.* 5 records, 33 instruments featured. Ages 10–adult.

RCA VICTOR
Popular Classics for Spanish Guitar. Julian Bream plays.

IDENTIFYING CLASSES OF INSTRUMENTS
Third Movement of Symphony No. 4, Tchaikovsky, BOL # 71 (Bowmar Orchestral Library)

SPECIFIC INSTRUMENTS
The King's Trumpet, Franson Corporation, 225 Park Avenue South, New York, N.Y. 10003, Children's Record Guild (CRG) 5040 (ages 5–8)

Licorice Stick: Story of the Clarinet, Franson, Young People's Record (YPR) 420 (ages 6–10)

Guitar Music from the Courts of Spain (Romera) Mercury

Pan the Piper, on Columbia CL 671

Peter and the Wolf (Prokofiev), on Columbia CL 671

Popular Classics for the Guitar (Bream), RCA Victor

Rusty in Orchestraville, Capitol Records

Said the Piano to the Harpsichord, Franson YPR 411

Tubby the Tuba, Decca (ages 6–7)

The Wonderful Violin, Franson YPR 311 (ages 6–10)

Do You Know? by Virginia Kreuger. Individualized programed instruction for ages 5–10 via cassette and hard cover workbook with color photographs of child players and 10 wipe-off work pages. 12 instruments are identified. MuGin Publications, Box 36528, Los Angeles, Ca. 90036.

INSTRUMENTS OF THE ORCHESTRA
Many manufacturers have albums under the title *Instruments of the Orchestra:* Capitol, Columbia, Decca, Vanguard, Victor, Bowmar, Wonderland, Keyboard.

Child's Introduction to the Orchestra, Golden Records

The Orchestra and Its Instruments, Folkways

The Symphony Orchestra, Decca

Films and Filmstrips
Churchill Films, 622 N. Robertson Blvd., Los Angeles, Ca. 90069: *What is Music? Wind Sounds, String Sounds, Percussion Sounds, New Sounds in Music*

Instruments of the Symphony Orchestra (recordings with six filmstrips) Jam Handy, Prentice-Hall, Media, 150 White Plains Rd., Tarrytown, N.Y. 10591

Meet the Instruments (recordings with two filmstrips) Bowmar Records, Belwin Mills, Melville, N.Y. 11747

Music for Young People Series, NET Films Service, Indiana University, Bloomington, Ind. 47401; *Introducing the Woodwinds, Percussion, Pulse of Music,* and more

Musical Books for Young People, a series of six filmstrips, Society for Visual Education, 1345 Diversey Pkway., Chicago, Ill., 60614. Strings, brass, woodwinds, percussion, keyboard, and folk instruments. (ages 9–13)

Symphony Orchestra, The, Encyclopaedia Britannica Films, 1150 Wilmette Ave., Wilmette, Ill. Traces growth of the symphony orchestra from string quartet to the modern orchestra. (ages 9–11)

We Make Music, Film Associates, 11559 Santa Monica Blvd., Los Angeles, Ca., 90025. *The Violin, The Bassoon,* and more.

chapter eleven

Movement, Rhythm, and Dance

Émile Jaques-Dalcroze — In any discussion of rhythm, the name Émile Jaques-Dalcroze (1865–1951) appears as a pioneer of musical learning by means of body movements. Dalcroze was a Swiss musician-educator who established the Dalcroze Institute in Geneva, where it continues to function today. His theories are contained in his two books, *Rhythm, Music and Education* (1921) and *Eurhythmics, Art and Education* (1930). Dalcroze found that unless the learner experiences aspects of music by body movement, the music that individual later performs will be mechanical, without feeling, and the expressive responsiveness essential to genuine musicianship may never develop. Today, every teacher of early childhood education knows that children learn first by using their muscles. His followers claimed that Dalcroze Eurhythmics developed the whole child, meaning good physical development and muscular control, mental awareness, social consciousness, and emotional health as well as understanding and appreciating music. The body and mind are to respond to what the individual hears and feels. The method stresses 1) rhythmic movement (eurhythmics), 2) ear training, and 3) improvisation. Rhythmic responses to music are commonly performed in today's schools, but usually in an insufficient amount that lacks much organization.

The familiar body responses to quarter notes (walking) and eighth notes (running) form part of the Dalcroze approach. Students are to respond to the teacher's playing of drum or piano patterns by movement of feet, arms, and body. A rhythmic game results when the teacher alters the patterns, perhaps by reversing them. Simple tunes such as "Hot Cross Buns" can be acted out, with walk, walk, step-bend for quarter, quarter, and half note. "Silent Night" can be felt rhythmically with:

$$\text{♩.} \qquad \text{♪ ♩} \qquad \text{♩.}$$

step-spring,   run walk   step-bend-bend

or, in today's classrooms, with motions devised by the children. Simple movements, well learned, become units for performing more complex responses. Children who perform music with their muscles and bodies are believed to become more musical than those who sit quietly and are thought to be learning music. Rhythm and dynamics are logical concepts to be learned through physical responses.

Children with Dalcroze training will refine their movements into those that express dynamics, pitch, phrasing, form, and style. For example, clapping can become a graceful, shapely gesture that expresses a particular piece of music. Emotion and feeling are translated into movement.

Learners are asked to improvise rhythm patterns on a pitch or pitches, on percussion instruments, and to improvise melodies, rondos, and moods. The teacher is expected to be able to improvise music on the piano that places the learners on a developmental course in rhythmic-musical growth. A simple example would be improvisations on "Hot Cross Buns" designed to expand the creative experience and demand intense concentration. There are extensions of the Dalcroze method into dance, physical education, and therapy. *Solfège,* the singing with syllables, is assumed to sharpen the sense of pitch and relationship of tones. Through this training, the students learn to hear harmonies and to read music and improvise vocally.

Children in kindergarten and first grade are often enrolled in preparatory classes in the comparatively few authentic Dalcroze schools in the United States, most of which are in large cities. The primary aim of the method is to develop good musicianship. Dalcroze believed that musicality can be encouraged by consciously using one's body movement in association with keen hearing. Furthermore, he planned his procedures to assist young and old, the gifted and the handicapped, as well as the average person.

A list of references concerning the Dalcroze method is included at the end of this chapter (p. 215).

Carl Orff   *Carl Orff* (1895–1982), a German composer-educator, agreed with Dalcroze's insistence upon rhythm as a foundation for musical growth, and he developed an educational approach that begins with the speech rhythms present in children's names and in familiar words and old sayings to begin a creative, improvisatory learning process. He grouped the children in low and high speaking voices to produce better dramatic effects. Orff believed, as did Dalcroze, that the study of standard musical instruments should begin only after the learner acquires the skills of hearing, moving to music, discerning and playing basic rhythms, and discerning and singing basic tonal patterns and intervals. Dalcroze used the piano extensively; Orff considered it not well suited for true children's music. Speaking, moving, and singing are regarded as a composite act, illustrative of how young children engage in music when left to their own resources. While Dalcroze prescribed creativity in the form of improvisations, Orff organized improvisation in ways to make it easy for children to create their own speech-movement-singing-instrumental music. The common pentatonic (5-tone) mode, tones 1, 2, 3, 5, 6 of the major scale, is used in the beginning, and ostinato patterns (repeated rhythmic or melodic fragments) and borduns (the open-fifth interval and variations constructed from it) are to be created and played on simple instruments by children to accompany pentatonic melodies. It is assumed that within these limitations children can create music that is truly children's music rather than music that is basically too adult and too harmonically complex for children to fully comprehend. When children have learned to make music within the pentatonic framework, they move on to major, minor, and modal tonalities.

Orff advocated, as did Zoltán Kodály (see pp. 288–293 for a more complete discussion of the Kodály method), the use of folksongs and children's traditional rhymes and melodies from the heritage of the particular nation or people. Children were encouraged to use rhythmic and melodic ideas from songs to make introductions, codas, interludes, and accompaniments. He designed percussion instruments of high quality to create an instrumental ensemble that included glockenspiels (soprano and alto), metallophones (soprano, alto, bass), and xylophones (soprano, alto, bass), with removable tone bars, and played with mallets. This ensemble, with other instruments of Orff's design and some from centuries past, produces a sound related to that of the Indonesian gamelan (see Figure 11.1 for a display of these instruments). The following example gives some idea of the use of well-known verse to create a pentatonic song with borduns and ostinati to accompany it.

Accompanying borduns and ostinati possible with the above melody:

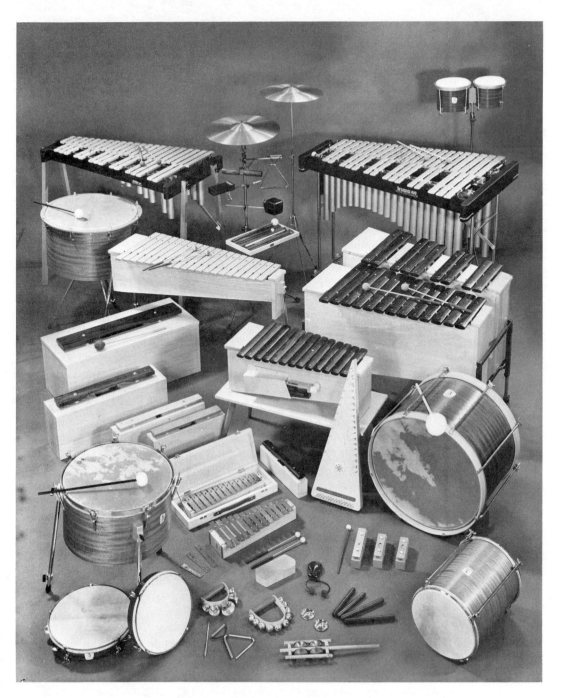

Figure 11.1. ORFF-DESIGNED INSTRUMENTS. Courtesy of Magnamusic Baton, Inc. St. Louis, Missouri 63132

soprano glockenspiel	sounds two octaves higher than written
alto glockenspiel	sounds one octave higher than written
soprano metallophone	sounds one octave higher than written
soprano xylophone	sounds one octave higher than written
alto metallophone	sounds as written
alto xylophone	sounds as written
bass metallophone	sounds one octave lower when written in the treble clef
bass xylophone	sounds one octave lower when written in the treble clef

The ostinato can be heard in pieces such as:

Grieg: "Anitra's Dance" from *Peer Gynt Suite*
Guarieri: *Brazilian Dance*
Bizet: "Carillon" from *L'Arlesienne Suite*
Herbert: "Dagger Dance" from *Natoma*
Pierné: *Entrance of the Little Fauns*
Herbert: "March of the Toys" from *Babes in Toyland*

The increasing popularity of the Orff approach and of these fine quality instruments has led to their manufacture both in Europe and in the United States, to imitations of them, and currently to their availability from nearly all the suppliers of percussion instruments and Autoharps. Sonar and Studio 49 are respected European manufacturers.

Both Orff and Kodály used the "children's chant," the descending minor third, as a tonal beginning that young children naturally understand and perform. The tones of the chant form part of the pentatonic scale. The pentatonic mode is employed because it requires no harmonization (chord changes) and because pentatonic melodies can be played or sung in canon fashion and in combination, making satisfying musical experimentation and performance within the reach of children.

Basic to the process is the progression from rhythmic speech to accompanying movements—clapping, finger snapping, stamping, and patschen (slapping knees or thighs) and substituting percussion instruments for these. Nursery rhymes, chants, old proverbs, names of children, animals, geographical places, plants, gems, and any speech designation of interest can grow into musical activities, with improvised dance as another possibility, perhaps a culminating one. Through a creative approach to speech, concepts of phrasing, dynamics, repetition, contrast, and simple form can be learned and then applied to musical pitch in logical sequence.

Orff and Gunild Keetman, an associate, wrote a series of books, *Music for Children,* containing examples of the activities comprising the Orff approach. The books, written in German, were adapted by Canadians Doreen Hall and Arnold Walter for use in English-speaking countries. The Orff-Keetman books are valuable references, but much of the material is not arranged in sequential fashion. Orff intended his examples to be germinal rather than prescriptive because he wanted children and teachers to create their own speech-rhythmic movement-tonal productions. This slowed, for a time, acceptance of the Orff ideas in the United States. However, American music educators have developed three levels of skills using sequenced American materials, and have succeeded in communicating these concepts to an ever larger number of teachers. The American Orff-Schulwerk Association has led in organizing teacher training programs on three levels, with certificates granted upon completion of the work on each level. *The Orff Echo* is the association's official magazine and the address of both is Cleveland State University, Department of Music, Cleveland, Ohio 44115.

Orff did not intend that children be confined to the pentatonic mode for long periods of time, particularly since their experimentation and environmental influences lead them to other tonal arrangements. However, there is no doubt that he intended the developmental framework he laid down, beginning with the common pentatonic, to be utilized in a creative program. Orff and Kodály concepts of music education agree in part and are complementary to some degree, thus many teachers use "Orff-Kodály" in their teaching. Both use the syllables. Kodály places great emphasis on singing and note reading, and this will be discussed in a later chapter. The Orff procedure is one of guided exploration of sound, space, and form within a given structure.

Education Through Music (ETM)

Mary Helen Richards is a pioneer adapter of Kodály concepts to the English-speaking world who organized the Richards Institute of Music Education and Research, which concentrates upon how children learn. Certain principles gleaned from research are being applied and continuously studied. Kodály advised Mrs. Richards personally to utilize the language and songs native to the people living in the United States. Consequently, American folk songs and games were selected that reflect the rhythm, accents, and inflections of English as spoken in the United States. Kinesthetic (movement) experience is stressed in the many singing games or games with songs, and through body motions the child is led to discover repeated words, rhythm patterns, phrases, and tonal patterns. Important patterns, both rhythmic and vocal, are learned in ways to produce their recognition in notation, thus encouraging the learning of sightsinging, a Kodály objective. The Curwen hand signs and the corresponding syllables are employed. (See Zoltán Kodály, pp. 288–293)

ETM is mentioned here because of its emphasis on a game approach that involves the learner physically. The singing games have clearly defined educational purposes; they are not selected randomly, thus ETM has added emphasis to the claim that children learn by physical activity, an idea with which Dalcroze, Orff, and Kodály would agree. ETM's music learning stimulates thought processes by means of games, purposeful movement and simple dramatization. Discrimination, sequencing, evaluation, comparing, and contrasting are all important cognitive skills that can be acquired by means of this approach. Relationships to language arts, mathematics, and social growth are claimed. The publications of Education Through Music are available from The Institute, 149 Corte Madera Road, Portola Valley, Calif. 94025.

For further exploration of the methods of these theorists, see the reference section at the end of the chapter (p. 215).

Movement to Music

Expressing rhythm through movement is an activity that music shares with physical education and creative dramatics. Music assists physical education by helping movement be more rhythmic; it assists creative dramatics by heightening the dramatic expression. When physical education gives children more control over their bodies, and when creative dramatics helps to free them to interpret what they hear in music, these areas can in turn contribute to understanding music. By moving to music, children can learn to hear music with perception, to respond to it with imagination, and to explore the expressive ideas it contains.

Of primary concern is listening to the rhythm in music and responding to it with physical movement. When children aged five, six, and seven begin their school year, many of them will not be able to sing in tune. Therefore there is logic in first listening to music, then responding by physical movement to what is heard, and in the process becoming oriented to rhythm, pitch, and mood. This builds a background of experience for better singing a little later.

There are important values in rhythmic responses other than the building of a background for successful singing. Among these are the development of body control, imagination, willingness to experiment, rhythmic responsiveness, and concepts of fast and slow, heavy and light, loud and soft, and long and short, in terms of body movement. Furthermore, rhythmic activity is a necessity in carrying out a balanced daily program of education for children. It is *unnatural* for boys and girls to sit quietly for long periods of time. There is evidence to show that teachers who guide their pupils in appropriate rhythmic responses, and who know the proper times to do this, can reduce pupil tension and fatigue to a marked degree, which makes learning much more likely.

Fundamental Movements
"Fundamental movement" is a term used in physical education. It describes simple, basic movements such as walking, running, skipping, and galloping. Teachers' books for kindergarten and first grade contain helpful song and piano material as well as suggestions for teaching such movements. Also, teachers can quickly learn to use percussion instruments or the Autoharp to improvise rhythms for the simple fundamental movements to which children learn to respond. In these grades the teacher should not expect every child to respond in the same way; some children need time to experiment before being able to do what the others do. Children need time in which to explore *their own* tempo. Thus, at first the teacher observes and uses the

child's natural tempo before asking conformance to one predetermined by the teacher.

Music is not always required to initiate rhythmic response. For example, words for walking can be chanted, then patschen, then walked, before appropriate music is added in the tempo and rhythm of the children's walking. Other fundamental movements can be introduced by the teacher's drum beat or by word rhythms and learned by patschen and clapping before the children move to them with their whole bodies. The music can then be brought in after the rhythm is learned. The words of songs can be learned first in rhythmic speech, and the melody added later.

Further understanding of fundamental movements can be gained by using songs that suggest impersonation (imitative play). Children who are five and six years of age tend strongly to *be* what they impersonate, such as the horses that gallop and the rabbits that hop. The teaching of fundamental rhythms can continue also from the point of view of free rhythmic play. The teacher may tap a drum, play the piano, or use a recording, and ask the children what it "makes them feel like doing." From their prior experience should come such movements as clapping, walking, running, skipping, galloping, sliding, hopping, and jumping. Through freedom to respond to the rhythms of music they can discover other body movements which may include swinging, pushing, bouncing, pulling, bending, stretching, and striking. During all of this the teacher controls and guides learning by helping the children relate familiar physical responses to the music they are hearing. The teacher should do this in such a manner that each child feels she or he has made a personal contribution.

In kindergarten and first grade the terms "walking note" and "running note" make sense to children because they represent body movements they know. Since children in these grades have limited knowledge about fractions, terms like "quarter" and "eighth" are without much meaning. However, learning the adult terminology should follow learning the "movement" terms *as soon as this seems practical.*

It takes time to develop skill in these activities; beginning teachers are likely to try too many things at first. They should "make haste slowly," striving for a simple and thorough approach. By the end of the first grade most children will have learned to walk, skip, run, and hop in time to music. During the second grade most children will have learned to slide, jump rope, and bounce a ball in rhythm. In third grade the ability to leap and step-hop is generally acquired.

Teachers may take a rhythm from something a child is doing, or from nature or machines outside the classroom, and repeat this on a percussion instrument or on a piano. The children are then asked to identify the rhythm and move to the playing of the teacher. Percussion instruments may be selected to accompany or to represent the rhythm. There are some simple guidelines to follow as children move, such as not to touch other children or get in anyone's way, and for all to move in the same direction. In a small classroom perhaps only four or five children will do the moving, after which the teacher can select others to take their places. The children not moving may create unobtrusive motions at their seats to interpret what the small group does.

The Piano The piano can assist in promoting fundamental movements and other rhythmic responses. The recording, useful as it is, will never be a complete substitute for a teacher's flexible use of the piano. Even though a classroom teacher may have little or no piano training, the instrument can be used in improvisatory ways.

The black keys provide a ready-made pentatonic scale that has the wonderful quality of always sounding acceptable, no matter what one does with the various notes either singly or in chords or clusters. (With the entire forearm, for example, try pressing down on a large cluster of black keys.) With the right hand, find a combination of black keys that sounds satisfactory and play steady quarter notes for marching or walking; play the long-short 6/8 pattern ♩ ♪♩ ♪ :|| quickly for skipping and galloping or slowly for swinging and swaying. Sound eighth notes for running. With the left hand, try adding single tones or open fifths $\begin{smallmatrix} o \\ o \end{smallmatrix}$ in the bass below the patterns you have learned to play with the right hand. You will soon be experimenting with other sounds.

Another approach is to play a major scale for walking. Selected chords in the bass can portray characters or animals for rhythmic dramatizations, such as an elephant walking and a leopard stalking. When chords are played in time with jumping, an accompaniment to that movement results. Playing small parts of the scale up and down in rapid succession can do the same for running. Chords alternating between treble and bass (using both hands) can inspire swinging or the idea of a seesaw. Music textbooks for early childhood often contain helpful suggestions that assist nonpianists as well as formally trained ones. No recording can adapt tempo to a child's movements.

Free Rhythmic *Children should not be asked to respond to rhythm until they have had the op-*
Play *portunity to listen carefully.* Teachers often ask them to close their eyes while they listen. After this comes the question, "What did the music tell you to do?" There may follow a discussion, then the music will be repeated and the children will begin to contribute ideas to the group. The teacher will often help free rhythmic responses to develop by asking such questions as, "Does the music make you feel like walking or running or skipping?" "Is it happy, sad, fast, slow?" "How many different motions are good to use with this music?"

Free rhythmic responses are so numerous that it is doubtful that any listing of them can ever be complete, particularly since each of them can be varied almost endlessly. Some, in addition to those already mentioned, are:

trotting	tapping	stroking	swaying
dipping	reaching	patting	rolling
tripping	grasping	creeping	hammering
stamping	banging	rocking	whirling
tossing	circling	crawling	tumbling
skating	beating	turning	sliding

Others are rising and falling in terms of crescendo (gradually louder) and decrescendo (gradually softer) and in terms of rising and falling pitch. For example, one way in which crescendo and decrescendo can be acted out is by a circle of children coming together at the height of the crescendo, and being at the farthest point apart at the lowest level of the decrescendo.

Space is needed for freedom of movement, and it must be admitted that it is at a premium in some classrooms. However, good work can be done despite admitted handicaps, by keeping the following suggestions in mind. First, rhythmic activities need never be boisterous or unruly. Second, activities requiring space may be arranged in some larger room. The room should seldom be the size of a gymnasium because this can destroy the intimate feeling desirable for this type of music work. Third, many substitute responses can be made. Children can "walk" with their hands in the air above their heads, and they can "march" with their heels while their toes remain on the floor. When clapping is required, it can be done in quiet ways such as striking the tips of the fingers of both hands together rather than using the palms, or striking the fingertips of one hand on the palm of the other hand. Fourth, part of a class can do the rhythmic activity while others sing, chant, clap, evaluate, or perform a quiet substitute.

To sustain interest, variety is essential. Since no child enjoys skipping to the same music over a long period of time, a variety of accompaniments is recommended. The teacher may use recordings, the piano, various percussion instruments, and the chanting of the voice. Still more variety may be attained by changing the tempo of the music. Jumping ropes, bouncing balls, scarves, flags, and balloons may be used to make appropriate activities more colorful and impressive. These often aid the self-conscious child by focusing attention on the object, and assist the development of big, free movements. Scarves for this purpose are made of silk or lightweight nylon, longer than the child. Such length permits many uses, including dramatization.

It is important that teachers know the physical limitations of the age groups they guide in activities that require physical exertion. For example, if teachers are unaware that to "waddle like a duck" during a song about a duck is a strenuous exercise for children in the first grade (or any grade), they might easily continue this activity for too long and see children fall down from exhaustion. Any teacher who intends to ask children to do such activities should try them personally in advance.

Action songs and singing games are enjoyed in the primary grades, and more complex games and dances are emphasized in the intermediate grades because children aged nine to eleven have gained the physical control and coordination that enables them to perform them.

Although many action songs can be done without first acquiring a background of fundamental movements, this is not true of most singing games and dances. *Action songs* are those to which children can add appropriate motions. *Singing games* are those that involve elements of game, chance, and sometimes dance. *Dances* are more formalized. Teachers and children with imagination will find that they can transform some "ordinary" songs into action songs, singing games, and dances of their own invention.

Most folk dances are easily taught in the intermediate grades. Some of them are taught to primary grade children in simplified versions. The easiest "dance" would be the American Indian type in which six-year-olds do a thumping walk or hop. Occasionally a simplified waltz is introduced in those grades also. However, most basic dance steps are taught in grades four and five, and they are embellished in grade six. Children in these grades can easily learn the polka, schottische, minuet, polonaise, and mazurka.

When children sing and at the same time do extensive body movement, the result is usually detrimental to either good singing or good rhythmic action or both. Consequently it is best to divide the class into two groups that alternate in singing and in doing the game or dance. The group that does the singing frequently adds hand clapping and percussion instruments to its accompaniment.

Many singing games and dances contribute to organized play on the playground. The song provides the accompaniment. When these activities take place indoors, the piano and recordings contribute variety.

One of the values of singing games and folk dances is the contribution they can make to social studies, for through them children can form a better understanding of the peoples of the world and their customs.

When dances are used in music class, they serve musical objectives; when they are used in physical education classes, teachers use them to realize the objectives of physical education. Sometimes these objectives are related; sometimes they are not. Dances can be useful in the study of beat, meter, pattern, notation, instruments, syncopation, and in relation to dance rhythms utilized by composers: for example, the waltz and Johann Strauss, the mazurka and Chopin, the bolero and Ravel, the polka and Dvořák, Weinberger, and Shostakovich.

Most of the formal dances are taught in the intermediate grades, although the simple waltz and minuet are sometimes introduced in the third grade. The waltz is first presented as a type of walk in which a large step then two smaller steps are made as dancers move in a circle. The teacher can learn how to teach dances from readily available sources—the music text books, physical education books, record jackets, and from courses of study.

In situations where students are reluctant to have only one partner throughout a dance, mixer-types are useful. Examples of these found in many of the books are "The Old Brass Wagon," "Red River Valley" (both in *Singing With Children*, Wadsworth Publishing Company), and "The Caller's Song" in *Music for Young Americans*, Book 6.

Examples of familiar dance songs are "Holla Hi, Holla Ho," "Stodola Pumpa," "Du Du Liegst Mir im Herzen," and the American songs "Buffalo Gals," "Four in a Boat," "Goin' to Boston," "Sourwood Mountain," and "Turkey in the Straw." Recordings include the RCA Victor Series *The World of Folk Dances*, Bowmar Records' *Singing Games, Singing Games and Folk Dances, Folk Dances, Singing Square Dances,* and *Play Party Games,* and many more from other sources. See the reference section at the end of this chapter (pp. 266–267).

Teaching Folk Dances There are folk dances from all over the world. The four American types are (1) play-party games, (2) round dances, (3) long-ways and circular formation dances, and (4) square dances. The origin of the *play-party game* is interesting; at a time in American history when dancing was sometimes frowned upon, people sang dance accompaniments instead of playing them, and called the dance a game, thus getting around the restrictions of those days. *Round dances* are performed with partners. They are "round" because to move easily about a crowded hall, the partners dance in the same circular direction. Examples of this type include the waltz, polka, schottische, rye waltz, and the varsovienne ("Put Your Little Foot . . ."). *Long-ways* and *circular* formation dances include the Virginia Reel. The *square dance* is one in which eight dancers (four couples) salute, curtsy, and change partners in a square formation while performing many interesting figures. Possible steps in teaching a folk dance follow:

1. In preparation, study the directions of the selected dance. It should be one of which the children already know the basic movements required, but if they do not, be sure to teach these as separate rhythms as a preparatory step to their learning the dance.
2. As you study the dance, practice the steps without the music. Then listen to the music or learn the music, and do the steps in rhythm to it.
3. If necessary, write any difficult part of the directions on a small pad or card that can be carried inconspicuously in the hand.
4. Teach the song (if it is a dance song) so that the children know the melody and words well before attempting to learn the dance.
5. Direct the children into the proper dance formation.
6. Have the children practice the first set of steps with no music. Then have them do these steps while speaking the rhythm of the words of the song, and guide them to associate the word-rhythm with the steps. Repeat until the steps are learned. Counting the steps can be helpful.
7. Do this much of the dance with the music.
8. Repeat Steps 6 and 7 with the next set of steps. Continue this process until the entire dance is learned.
9. Do the entire dance with the music.

There are rhythms and dances characteristic of peoples of the world, often related to their historical origins. The current interest in the rhythms of Africa and Asia will inevitably produce new materials of instruction.

Latin-American Patterns

Basic Rhythms (combine the three)

Timbales (paired single-head drums)

Maracas

Claves

Traditional Dances†

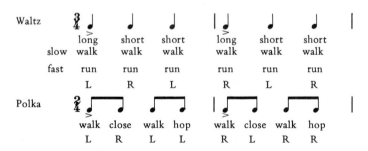

---

* Recorded examples include "Habañera" from *Carmen* (Bizet) and *Jamaican Rumba* (Benjamin), both in Bowmar 56, and *Grand Walkaround* (Gottschalk) in Adventures in Music, V. 5–1.

† These dance patterns are strummed and related to songs in *Teaching Music with the Autoharp* (Northbrook, Ill. 60062: Music Education Group), pp. 23–30.

Scottische

run run run hop   run run run hop
L   R   L   L   R   L   R   R

Mazurka

walk walk hop   walk walk hop
L   R   R   L   R   R

References and Materials

Orff and ETM

BIRKENSHAW, LOIS, *Music for Fun, Music for Learning.* Toronto: Holt, Rinehart and Winston of Canada, Ltd. Obtainable from Magnamusic-Baton, 10370 Page Industrial Blvd., St. Louis, Mo. 63132. Magnamusic-Baton is a good source of materials concerning Orff Schulwerk.

BURNETT, MILLIE, *Melody, Movement and Language.* San Francisco: R and E Research Associates, 1973. Games with the four basic elements of Schulwerk.

CARLEY, ISABEL, ed., *Orff Re-Echoes.* Cleveland: American Orff-Schulwerk Association, 1977. A collection of excerpts from the *Orff Echo,* the Association's magazine.

GILL, RICHARD, et al., *Singing, Saying, Dancing, Playing.* St. Louis: Magnamusic-Baton, Inc. Six cassette tapes and teacher's guide.

KEETMAN, GUNILD, *Elementaria,* translated by Margaret Murray. London: Schott and Co. Ltd., 1974. An introduction to Orff techniques.

LANDIS, BETH, and POLLY CARDER, *The Eclectic Curriculum in American Music Education: Contributions of Dalcroze, Kodály, and Orff.* Reston, Va.: Music Educators National Conference, 1972.

Music for Children (record album), Angel Records. English children perform.

Music for Children (film), National Film Board of Canada, 1251 Avenue of the Americas, New York, N.Y. 10020. A 1968 treatment.

NASH, GRACE C. ET AL., *The Child's Way of Learning, Do It My Way.* Sherman Oaks, Calif. 91403: Alfred Publishing Co., Inc., 1977. Levels K–6.

RICHARDS, MARY HELEN, *Aesthetic Foundations for Thinking.* Portola Valley, Calif.: Richards Institute of Music Education and Research, 1977. Education Through Music. *Part Two,* 1978; *Part Three,* 1979.

RICHARDS, MARY HELEN and ANNA P. LANGNESS, *The Music Language:* Section One. Portola Valley, Calif.: Richards Institute of Music Education and Research, 1982.

STRINGHAM, MARY, *Orff-Schulwerk, Background and Commentary.* St. Louis, Mo.: Magnamusic-Baton, 1976. A selection of articles from European sources.

Dalcroze Method

Dalcroze School of Music, Hilda M. Schuster, Director, 161 E. 73 Street, New York, N.Y. 10021.

FINDLAY, ELSA, *Rhythm and Movement: Applications of Dalcroze Eurhythmics.* Evanston, Ill.: Sumy-Birchard Company, 1971.

LANDIS, BETH, and POLLY CARDER, *The Eclectic Curriculum in Music Education: Contributions of Dalcroze, Kodály, and Orff.* Reston, Va.: Music Educators National Conference, 1972.

WILLOUR, JUDITH, "Beginning with Delight, Leading to Wisdom: Dalcroze," *Music Educators Journal,* September 1969.

Recordings   FREE RHYTHMIC RESPONSE

My Playful Scarf, Franson Corporation CRG 1019 (ages 2–4)

Ravel: "Laideronette, Empress of the Pagodas" from *Mother Goose* Suite, BOL 57 (Bowmar Orchestral Library Album 57)

Mussorgsky: "Bydlo" from *Pictures at an Exhibition,* AM 2 v 1 (Adventures in Music, Grade 2)

Donaldson: *Under the Big Top,* BOL 51

Mussorgsky: "Ballet of the Unhatched Chicks" from *Pictures at an Exhibition,* AM 1 v 1

Animals and Circus, BOL 51

Pierné: *Entrance of the Little Fauns,* BOL 54; AM 2 v 2

Pierné: *March of the Little Lead Soldiers,* BOL 54

Prokofiev: "March" from *The Love for Three Oranges,* BOL 54

Pictures and Patterns, BOL 53

WALKING

Children may develop different types of walking by pretending they are different characters or animals. Marching is an outgrowth of walking. Walking is normally relaxed and swinging.

Thomson: "Walking Song" from *Acadian Songs and Dances,* AM 1 v 1

Kabalevsky: "Pantomime" from *The Comedians* (big steps), AM 1 v 1

Mussorgsky: "Bydlo" from *Pictures at an Exhibition* (lumbering steps), AM 1

Prokofiev: 'Departure" from *Winter Holiday* (fast steps), AM 2

Herbert: "Dagger Dance" from *Natoma,* AM 3 v 1

Grieg: "In the Hall of the Mountain King" from *Peer Gynt* Suite, AM 3 v 2

MARCHING

While the interest of young children in marches focuses on body responses, the older children may be interested in comparing and analyzing different march styles. Military band marches can be compared with the favorite marches of the young children—those having to do with toys, dwarfs, and such. Older children could add to these the march movements of Beethoven's Third Symphony and Tchaikovsky's Sixth Symphony as well as the "March and Cortege" from Gounod's opera, *The Queen of Sheba.*

Rossini-Britten: "March" from *Soirees Musicales,* AM 1 v 1

Herbert: "March of the Toys" from *Babes in Toyland,* AM 2 v 1

Vaughan-Williams: "March Past of the Kitchen Utensils" from *The Wasps,* AM 3 v 1

Lully: "March" from *Ballet Suite,* AM 3 v 2

Sousa: *Semper Fidelis,* AM 3 v 2

Grieg: "Norwegian Rustic March" from *Lyric* Suite, AM 4 v 1

Gould: *American Salute,* AM 5 v 1

Coates: "Knightsbridge March" from *London* Suite, AM 5 v 2

RUNNING

Running on tiptoe is commonly stressed; the movement should be kept light.

Gluck: "Air Gai" from *Iphigenie in Aulis,* AM 1 v 1

Bizet: "The Ball" from *Children's Games,* AM 1 v 1

HOPPING

Hopping is done on one foot.

Mussorgsky: "Ballet of the Unhatched Chicks;" from *Pictures at an Exhibition,* AM 1 v 1

Bach: "Gigue" from Suite No. 3, AM 1 v 1

Gretry: "Tambourin" from *Cephale et Procris,* AM 2 v 1

Jumping is done with both feet together. Overly heavy movements are to be avoided.

Massenet: "Argonaise" from *Le Cid,* AM 1 v 1

Bizet: "Leap Frog" from *Children's Games,* AM 1 v 1

Meyerbeer: "Waltz" from *Les Pateneuers,* AM 2 v 1

SKIPPING OR GALLOPING

Skipping is a step, hop, first on one foot and then on the other. Children enjoy a large fast skip that gives them the feeling of moving high in the air. When galloping, one foot is kept ahead of the other throughout, and the back foot is brought up to meet it. Heels never touch the floor

Bach: "Gigue" from Suite No. 3, AM 1

Gretry: "Gigue" from *Cephale et Procris,* AM 1

WHIRLING

Massenet: "Argonaise" from *Le Cid,* AM 1

Rossini-Respighi: "Tarantella" from *The Fantastic Toy Shop,* AM 3 v 2

SWAYING, ROCKING

These movements can relax children after the stimulation of the more active movements. Swaying trees, branches or flowers are often imitated, as are swings, the pendulum of a clock, rocking a baby to sleep, and rowing a boat.

Bizet: "Cradle Song" from *Children's Games,* AM 1 v 1

Fauré: "Berceuse" from *Dolly,* AM 2 v 1

Shostakovich: "Petite Ballerina" from *Ballet Suite* No. 1, AM 2 v 1

Offenbach: "Barcarolle" from *Tales of Hoffman,* AM 3 v 1

Chabrier: *España* (for a spirited swinging), AM 4 v 1

SLIDING, GLIDING, WALTZING

Prokofiev: "Waltz on Ice" from *Children's Suite,* AM 3 v 2

Tchaikovsky: "Waltz" from *The Sleeping Beauty,* AM 4 v 2

Khachaturian: "Waltz" from *Masquerade* Suite, AM 4 v 2

For specific suggestions, study the Teachers Guides for the *Adventures in Music* albums. Older children can study the waltz with the purpose of expanding that concept. The *Adventures in Music* albums provide many different types to study. Contrast the Viennese and American concepts of waltz.

REVIEW OF FUNDAMENTAL MOVEMENTS

When working with recordings that illustrate several different movements, small groups of children can be asked to respond appropriately whenever their assigned movement is heard.

A Visit to My Little Friend, Franson CRG 1017 (ages 2–4)

Animals and Circus, BOL 51

Marches, BOL 54

Nature and Make Believe, BOL 52

RHYTHMIC DRAMATIZATION

Rhythmic dramatization implies that children are able to respond physically to rhythm, melody, mood, tempo, dynamics, and instrumentation. First they listen to the music to ascertain how an action or a story is suggested. Then they associate the action or story with related aspects of the musical elements. In the instance of a story, some call these "cues." Finally, they create a dramatization. The Teacher's Guide for *Adventures in Music* recordings is helpful.

Bartók: "Bear Dance" from *Hungarian Sketches,* AM 3 v 2

Ibert: *The Little White Donkey,* AM 2 v 1

Kabalevsky: "March and Comedian's Gallop" from *The Comedians,* AM 3 v 1

Debussy: "Golliwog's Cakewalk" from *Children's Corner* Suite, BOL 63

Grieg: "Ase's Death" from *Peer Gynt* Suite No. 1, BOL 59

ANIMALS

Imitating animals seems to be a natural interest of young children, thus recordings such as those that follow have possibilities for listening-moving-dramatizing activities. Older children should be asked, *"How* does the music describe the animal?" Their answers should be in terms of the elements of music—rhythm, melody, tempo, dynamics, harmony, and instrumentation. The question encourages analysis of the music.

Rimsky-Korsakoff: *Flight of the Bumble-Bee,* BOL 52

Respighi: *The Birds,* Mercury 90153; "Prelude" from, BOL 85

Liadov: *Dance of the Mosquito,* BOL 52

Griffes: *The White Peacock,* AM 5 v 1

Saint-Saëns: "The Swan" from *Carnival of the Animals,* AM 3 v 2

MACHINES

Villa-Lobos: "Little Train of the Caipira" from *Bachianas Brasileiras* No. 2, AM 6 v 2

Honneger: *Pacific 231* (a railroad locomotive of World War I)

Mossolov: *Iron Foundry,* on *Sounds of New Music,* Folkways FX 6160

NATURE

Debussy: "Reflections in the Water" (piano music and an example of impressionist style)

Debussy: "Nuage" (Clouds), BOL 70

Thomson: *The River,* Vanguard 2095

Debussy: *La Mer* (The Sea), section from, BOL 70; AM 6 v 2

Ives: *Three Outdoor Scenes,* Composers Recordings CRI 163

Grofé: *Death Valley* Suite, Capital T-272

Grofé: *Grand Canyon* Suite, BOL 61

Vivaldi: *The Four Seasons*

chapter twelve

Teaching Rhythm-Related Concepts

To help children learn music concepts, the teacher can choose among a number of different approaches from which a teaching strategy will be developed. Based upon the level of attainment of the student, they are: *movement,* in which the muscles and nerves of the body are the medium, *improvisation and composition,* in which the learner performs various musicianly roles, *singing and playing instruments,* and *analysis* of music, a skill learned both concurrently with the other approaches and as a result of them. Listening is recognized as an essential part of all musical activities.

At the beginning of music instruction for young children, teachers have certain basic concepts in mind. Children can develop these by means of movement. They are:

Duration	*Dynamics*
Beat	Loud, soft
Divisions of the beat	Accent
Meter	Crescendo
Rhythm pattern	Decrescendo
Rest	
Word-rhythm	*Tempo*
Articulation	Fast, slow
staccato (detached)	Accelerando
legato (connected)	Ritard

Pitch	Form
High, low, same	Same (repetition)
Up, down	Different (contrast)
Contour	Phrase
	Harmonic changes

Tempo and Dynamics

Tempo and dynamics can be clearly associated with rhythm and melody. Fast-slow and loud-soft are among the first music-related concepts young children learn at the beginning of their music instruction.

The teacher can help children discover their own natural tempo by playing a drum or the piano to their steps as they walk across the room, perhaps on some errand or as part of a game. After the relation between their steps and the sound the teacher makes has been learned, the children will be able to govern their steps in accordance with the tempo the teacher plays, and can walk slower or faster. This can be a challenging game. The character of slow and fast music can be examined by comparing two songs, one of them slow and the other fast. Children can be guided to discover that much fast music is "light" and much slow music is smooth, calm, or perhaps "heavy." These descriptions of slow and fast music should be discovered through and reinforced by physical responses to music, and these responses may include aspects of impersonation and dramatization, often of animal movements. Body movement, percussion instruments, and hand clapping are used to develop the concepts *accelerando* (gradually faster) and *rallentando, ritardando,* and *ritard* (gradually slower). These can be felt and seen when two children throw and catch a large ball as the music changes tempo. They come closer together for a more rapid bouncing for fast tempos and farther apart for slower tempos.

Loud and soft are easily understood concepts, and from them are gradually learned the gradations of relative degrees of loud and soft. Percussion instruments and hand clapping can assist in learning about *crescendo* ———— (gradually louder) and *decrescendo* or *diminuendo* ———— (gradually softer). Some teachers have children imitate them as they clap hands or sound an instrument softly when held low, near the floor, then gradually increase the volume as the hands move higher. This becomes *crescendo* and its reverse becomes *decrescendo.* These aspects of musical expression should be related to, or discovered and identified in, songs and recordings at once, and reviewed and identified repeatedly. *Accent* is a quality of dynamics easily taught in relation to loud-soft and to meter. *Adventures in Music* recordings which can help teach this concept include "Petite Ballerina," Shostakovich; "Can Can," Rossini; "Departure," Prokofiev (all from II), "Dagger Dance," Herbert; and "Tarantella," Rossini (from III).

From the third grade up, recordings such as "Pacific 321," Honegger, (concerning a railway locomotive of World War I vintage), and "Fêtes," Debussy (concerning a festival) can be useful in studying tempo and dynamics on a large scale. Attention should always be given to their function in the music being studied. Songs should be selected which exemplify their use. Indexes of music textbooks will be helpful. The teacher can draw the attention of the children to tempo and dynamics by well-planned questions: "Would this song be better if it were sung (slower, faster, softer, louder)?" "Let's try it that way." "Was it better, or not as good?" "Why do you think so?" "Can you think of other ways we might try it (perhaps utilizing accent, crescendo, decrescendo)?" "Let's try to find the very best ways to sing the song expressively."

As for terminology, English terms are ordinarily learned in the primary grades and their Italian counterparts introduced in the intermediate grades. Some of the terms in more common use are listed in the Structure of Music Outline, Chapter Six. Such a vocabulary should be a *useful* one—not one to be learned because a book lists terms. They are terms that need to be employed by teacher and children to describe the tempo and dynamics of any given piece of music, the explain *how* fast or slow, loud or soft the children's own compositions should be performed, and to be able to discuss music intelligently. Memorization of this terminology is usually boring and self-defeating, but practical use of it makes good sense. In the intermediate grades a glossary of musical terms should be made available to the children to help them solve their musical problems and to enable them to answer their own questions. Some music books have such glossaries. Other terms related to the character of performance are:

cantabile	in a singing style	*maestoso*	majestic
dolce	sweetly	*molto*	very much
grandioso	grand, pompous, majestic	*poco*	a little

Some teachers and children have made imaginative posters illustrating terminology. For example, *adagio* might be illustrated by the turtle, *allegro* by a swift-flying bird, *accelerando* by a rocket taking off, and *grandioso* by a regal king.

As work on tempo and dynamics continues through the years, relationships between these and the other elements of music should be discovered, and appreciation of them should grow. There are relationships between tempo and dynamics, and between them and melody, harmony, form, and texture. These are waiting to be explored through experiences planned by teachers.

The Beat and Its Subdivisions Adults are apt to overlook or underestimate the need children have for a great deal of experience with the regular and continuous beat that is characteristic of most music. To the adult, this regular beat seems to be too simple for much consideration and some teachers tend to give it little attention. The result of this becomes obvious later when children have difficulty understanding division of the beat and meter, and when a large number of adults cannot march, keep in step or walk in a natural, rhythmic manner. All children need extensive rhythmic experience, and they need teachers who realize how important it is to musical growth, as well as to physical and personality development.

Beat and pulse are terms most people use interchangeably. The authors will use the term beat in this book, in the sense that in moderate tempo the 4/4 meter has four beats.

The ear, the eye, and the body are employed in building the concept of the beat. Children *listen* to the teacher's playing on a drum, the piano, or clapping hands. They also listen to selected recordings which stress the beat. They *see* the teacher play on a drum or clap hands and try to imitate those motions, and by so doing, learn little by little to be "in time" with the motions. Children explore and analyze the beat for themselves through their body responses and by experimenting with various percussion instruments. They also see the beat pictured in simple notation:

(Notice that these simple 4/4 measures are written in a manner corresponding in miniature to the printed page of a reader.)

The body is employed in a number of ways. The children *feel* the beat with their whole body by walking, marching, swaying, hopping, or by clapping, slapping thighs, and making other hand-arm movements. They can also respond with words that reflect the beat and its subdivisions which are repeated over and over, such as:

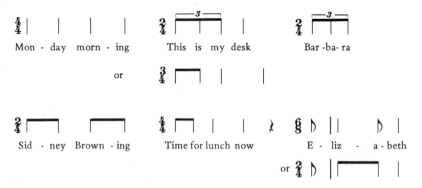

Percussion instruments or hand clapping are often employed when a rest falls on the last beat of the measure (see the 4/4 example above).

An aim of the teacher is to have all children feel the beat together. It is a *good* feeling, enjoyed by people all over the world.

From street calls and jingles most children have experienced the beat and many of its divisions. For example:

One potato, two potato, three potato, four;
Five potato, six potato, seven potato, more.

Teachers should bring such playground rhymes into the classroom and make use of them. (See Table 12.1 for examples of jingles to be used in this way.)

The quarter rest can be introduced by challenging the children to invent motions to do when the beats are like this:

Mrs. Richards, in her *Threshold to Music* materials, Fearon-Pittman Publishers, tells of Hungarian children throwing their hands up and away and

Table 12.1. Word Patterns*

Chant	*Play Instruments*
Chant in a deliberate manner, emphasizing the last word in each line of the following:	*Six children, each with a different instrument, play in turn the underlying beat, while the class chants.*

Bonefish, bluebird, black sheep, CROW	Triangle
Chickadee, doodlebug, robins in a ROW	Tambourine
Banty rooster, peep squirrel, caterpillar, FLEA	Sticks
Muley on the mountain and a BIG BUMBLE BEE	Drum
Fly in the cream jar, frog in the POOL	Finger cymbals
Clap for all the children here at SCHOOL	Maracas

* From *This Is Music,* Book One, by Adeline McCall. Copyright © 1965 by Allyn and Bacon, Inc. Used by permission.

saying "Sw-sh." Children will think of many ways to express or act out the quarter rest. After involving the children this way, and deciding on a motion, the symbol for the rest ( ) is written in. Another approach is with pictures. Mrs. Richards' Chart 4 of the First Year Charts, with the empty dog houses as rests, has become a favorite.

Music series books for the kindergarten and first grade provide easy piano pieces which encourage responses to the beat, and their publishers provide recordings of marches, march-like songs and dance songs which do the same for all grade levels. Other commonly used recordings include the RCA Basic Record Library for Elementary Schools, the Adventures in Music albums (also RCA), and the Bowmar Orchestral Library, particularly Album 54, Marches. The teacher should seek out these collections, study the suggestions provided for teachers, and select the music appropriate for the class.

Word-Rhythms The use of word-rhythms is a natural way to introduce rhythmic response. There is rhythm to be discovered in the spoken word, and children use and enjoy this rhythm in their play. The *sound* of words attracts children in the early primary grades, and people of all ages react to them, as testified by the rhythmic cheers at athletic events. Also, the rhythms of both simple and complex note values can be assimilated with ease when teachers relate these to familiar words.

Examples:

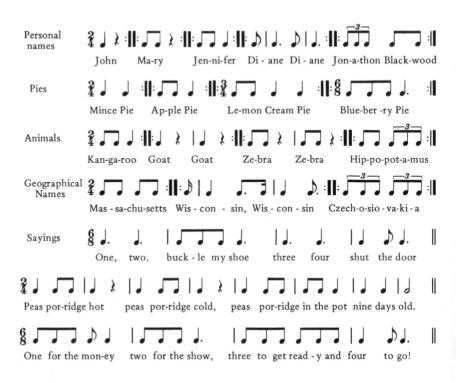

Let's go to grand-ma's Let's go to day!

Percussion instruments, clapping, and the use of feet can be added to enhance the rhythm and add to the interest—for names can be "said" with feet and instruments. The teacher should be alert to the fact that most of these word-rhythms can be altered according to different ways of accenting words. For example, "Lemon cream pie" might be:

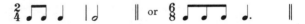

Several rhythms may be correct for one word. Rhythms of some radio and television commercials are interesting to work with and they have the advantage of being well-known by children.

Echo-Clapping Echo-clapping, a favorite Orff activity, is one appropriate introduction to rhythmic instruction because normal children of school age have the physical coordination to do it with ease (although a few six-year-olds need to be taught how). If children can imitate the teacher's clapping perfectly, the teacher knows that they are comprehending the rhythms and that they possess the physical coordination to respond. Children of all ages are interested when the teacher suddenly says, "Listen to what I clap; then you clap it." First, establish the beat, then:

Soon children will be able to clap improvised patterns to be echoed by the class.

Another interesting type of echo-clapping is the question-and-answer, in which the teacher or a child claps a rhythmic question to be answered creatively, such as:

This activity leads to discovering and creating questions and answers in melody, and to increasing comprehension of the phrase.

Later on, echo-clapping in canon form can develop rhythmic memory. In this activity the class echoes perhaps one measure behind the leader and in so doing must (1) remember what was clapped and repeat it later *while at the same time* (2) hearing and remembering what the leader is doing at the moment. For example:

Children can take the part of the leader, and percussion instruments can be used instead of the clapping.

Children may also be taught to associate the different note values with specific hand movements, speaking sounds, or foot movements. Table 12.2

Table 12.2. Some Possible Responses Relating to Note Values

Note	Clapping	Speaking	Stepping
Whole	clap-squeeze-squeeze-squeeze	who-o-ole note ta-a-a-a du-u-u-u	step-point-point-point
Dotted Half	clap-squeeze-squeeze	half-note-dot ta-a-a du-u-u	step-point-point
Half	clap-squeeze	half-note ta-a du-u	step-bend
Quarter	clap	quart-er ta du	walk
Eighth ♫	clap-clap	eighth-eighth ti-ti du-de	run-run
♩ ♪	clap-clap	skip-ty ta-ti du-di	skip-ping
♫♩	clap-clap-clap	tri-o-la tri-ple-ti du-da-di	ŕun-run-run
♫♫	clap-clap-clap-clap	ti-ri-ti-ri du-ta-de-ta	ŕun-run-run-run

gives examples of such systems of association. After children have learned to respond to note values in these ways, they can analyze the notation of simple songs by clapping, speaking, and stepping. Songs such as "Hot Cross Buns" can be studied in this way by young children.

Notation is often associated with specific body measurements, and certain rhythm syllables have been invented or adapted by many teachers to be used with the different note values. Table 12.3 shows body movements, systems of notation, and the rhythm syllables of Kodály and Gordon as they are associated with movement and notation.

Table 12.3. Body Movements, Rhythm Syllables, and Notation

Movement	Line Notation	Rhythm Syllables	Music Notation	Meter
walking thigh slapping hopping clapping	— — — —	ta ta ta ta du du du du	| | | |	$\frac{2}{4}$ or $\frac{4}{4}$
running clapping tapping	- - - - - - - -	ti-ti ti-ti ti-ti ti-ti du-de du-de du-de du-de	⊓ ⊓ ⊓ ⊓	$\frac{2}{4}$ or $\frac{4}{4}$
skipping, galloping	— - — - — - —	ta-ti ta-ti ta-ti ta-ti du-di du-di du-di du-di ti-iri ti-iri ti-iri ti-iri du-ta du-ta du-ta du-ta	♩♪♩ ♪♩ ♪♩ ♪ ♩.⌐♩♩.⌐♩♩.⌐♩♩.⌐♩	$\frac{6}{8}$ $\frac{2}{4}$ or $\frac{4}{4}$
swaying sliding skating rocking swinging	———	ta-a-a du-u-u	𝅗𝅥.	$\frac{3}{4}$
step-bend jumping	—— ——	ta-a ta-a du-u du-u	𝅗𝅥 𝅗𝅥	$\frac{2}{4}$ or $\frac{4}{4}$

Some teachers make charts such as the following for children to study.

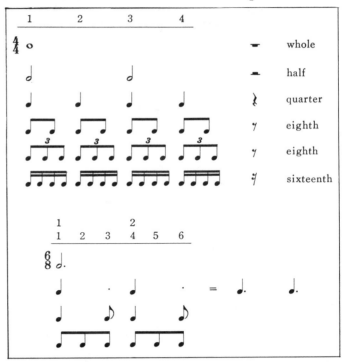

BINGO

American Folksong

There was a farm-er had a dog, And Bin-go was his name-O,

B - I - N-G-O, B - I - N-G-O,

B - I - N-G-O, and Bin-go was his name - O.

Teaching the Concept "Rest" At the time the song "Bingo" is learned, the beat and the rhythm of the melody can be experienced by marching to the song and clapping. Point out the repeated pattern long long short-short long and sing it: tah tah tee-tee tah

(♩ ♩ ♫ ♩). Clapping softly with the fingers, not the palms, the class sings the song as written, then on its repeat, omits singing "B" and squeezes fists instead of clapping on that beat. On the next repeat, the letters "B" and "i" are not sung, the fists clenched on those beats. This is continued until silently clenched fists are squeezing the complete pattern. The name "rest" can be attached to the short and long silences the children have felt with their muscles. A dance can be created for the song.

Divisions of the Beat

The necessity for divisions of the beat appears very soon after learning the concept of the steady beat. Although the beat may be fast or slow, the impressive aspect of divisions of the beat comes from relative length. Words such as "Rain, rain, go a-way" demand | | ⊓ | and provide learners with obvious instances where the short-short sound is equal to one long sound. Another way of picturing this is in short and long lines: — — – – —· The Hungarian methods "speak" the quarter note beat *ta* (tah) and the eighth note is *ti* (tee). Thus, the above rhythm pattern would be *ta ta ti-ti ta.* The Gordon syllables would be *du du du-de du.* Young children can easily read and write this introductory form of notation. Later on they can add a slanted line to form the note head ♩ . The triplet ♪♪♪ was once regarded as a complexity to be taught in intermediate grades, but today young children can easily identify it as *tri-o-la, tri-pl-et,* or *du-da-di* and begin to comprehend that in this division of the beat there are three notes to one beat. The Gordon rhythm syllables have the advantage of *du* being always on the beat point. (Some older children don't like the *ti-ti's.*)

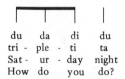

du   da   di   du
tri - ple - ti   ta
Sat - ur - day   night
How do   you   do?

From this beginning the seven-year-old can eventually use and understand the concept of four-to-one:

du   ta   de   ta   du
ti   ri   ti   ri   ta
huc - kle - ber - ry   pie

and its variants:

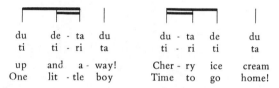

du   de - ta   du   du - ta   de   du
ti   ti - ri   ta   ti - ri   ti   ta

up   and   a - way!   Cher - ry   ice   cream
One   lit - tle   boy   Time to   go   home!

Any division of the beat should be studied in relation to words, body movement, songs (melody-rhythms), and children's improvised percussion patterns. For example, let us say that children are guided to sense and observe the melody of "Hey, Betty Martin," which begins with a fast *long short-short long* or, in this instance, a *ti ti-ri ti ti* or *du de-ta du de* pattern.

Later they can find that "Ten Little Indians" is constructed from the same rhythm pattern used in a different way, with the first part of it repeated many times.

Dotted Notes   While the rhythm of the dotted quarter note may have been felt for some time and practiced by imitation, emphasis on this concept is usually in third and fourth grades. A familiar song like "America" is useful. By writing it in notation, the fact of the dot being worth half again the value of the note it follows is pictured. Also, the class should be guided to discover where the second beat-point falls (on the dot). A teacher-made chart can then be studied. It could be:

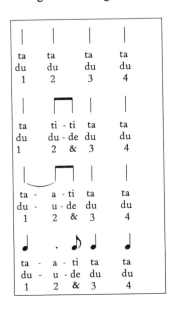

All uses for the dot should be explored in the notation of songs, and the fact that the dot adds half again the original value of the note it follows should be reviewed as frequently as it is needed to understand the music being performed or composed by the children.

When this relationship of dots and beats has been established, it is not difficult to apply it to the dotted-eighth-and-sixteenth note pattern. This is identical to the dotted-quarter-and-eighth pattern except that it is ordinarily (but not always) twice as fast. "Battle Hymn of the Republic" is a song often used in this study. The children should have numerous experiences with the rhythm of this melody, singing it, clapping it, listening to recorded versions, and listening to performances of it by members of the class. They might conduct experiments with changing the rhythm, such as singing it in even eighth notes, then discussing if this would be preferred to the uneven rhythm of the written song. They should examine the notation carefully. After comparing the even eighth notes with the dotted-eighth-sixteenth notes, the following teacher-made chart should be studied:

By means of the chart the children should be able to analyze the divisions of the beat by dividing it into halves (eighth notes) and then into quarters (sixteenth notes) to understand mathematically and visually the dotted note rhythm they already "know" from previous listening, clapping, and singing.

By means of the type of activities mentioned above, children can be discovering and identifying beat units and divisions of the beat. They can find them in words, with clapping, by playing on percussion instruments, and in the melodies of songs. By looking at notation of music they have worked with and know, they will find that beat units can be written in different note values:

They will discover equal division of the beat:

and unequal divisions:

They will also find that three notes of equal value can occupy a beat unit normally divided in two's:

Competent teachers know that it is much more fun for learners to find these for themselves than to be lectured about them.

Articulation   *Staccato* and *legato* can be included in the study of the duration of sounds. These are expressive aspects of music having relationships with note values. They are ways of *articulation,* staccato being detached or disconnected sounds and legato being smooth and connected, with no silence between the sounds. The German folk song "My Hat"* can be sung in either staccato or legato style; the children can "think over" and evaluate the effect of each of these kinds of articulation in this and other songs and instrumental pieces.

MY HAT

German Folksong

My   hat   it   has   three   cor - ners;____   Three   cor - ners
Mein Hut   der   hat   drei   Eck - en;____   drei   Eck - en

* This becomes an action song by touching the chest for "my," the head for "hat," holding three fingers high for "three," and drawing the three corners in the air for "corners." After this, the actions are continued, but one of the four action words, probably "hat," is omitted, leaving only silence in its place. The next time another word is omitted until all four words are indicated only by the action.

		C							

has | my | hat; | | | And | had | it | not | three
hat | mein | Hut; | | | Und | hät' | er | nicht | drei

cor - ners, | | It | would | not | be | my | hat.
Eck - en, | | denn | ist | dass | nicht | mein | Hut.

Among the many recordings that illustrate articulation are:

LEGATO

Stravinsky: "Berceuse" from *Firebird* Suite, AM 1 v 1

Fauré: "Berceuse" from *Dolly*, AM 2 v 1

Bizet: "Cradle Song" from *Children's Games*, AM 1 v 1

Offenbach: "Barcarolle" from *Tales of Hoffman*, AM 3 v 1

STACCATO

Mussorgsky: "Ballet of the Unhatched Chicks" from *Pictures at an Exhibition*, AM 1 v 1

Anderson: *The Syncopated Clock*, Keyboard Junior Recordings

Stravinsky: "Dance Infernale" from *Firebird Suite*, BOL 69; Keyboard Junior Recordings

Vaughan-Williams: "March Past of the Kitchen Utensils" from *The Wasps*, AM 3 v 1

von Suppé: *Light Cavalry* Overture

Another aspect of duration of sound is the *fermata,* or hold (⌒). This is found in some familiar songs such as "Erie Canal" and "We Three Kings of Orient Are." It can be identified in recorded compositions when the regular beat stops for a time and one tone or chord is sustained before the beat and the melody continue.

Rhythm and Pitch

Rhythm is an integral part of melody. As soon as pitch is added to a rhythm pattern some kind of melodic fragment or tune results. Because of the ease in singing the descending minor third interval, this descending pitch pattern has become an important beginning point in relating rhythm and pitch.

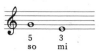

These two notes represent *high* and *low* pitch concepts, thus the beat, divisions of the beat, and high-low pitch concepts can be taught or involved simultaneously.

When the descending minor third is introduced, it can be related in game form to clapping and thigh-slapping (patschen), *so* (scale tone 5) to clapping, and *mi* (3) for slapping. After establishing the pitches and relating them to the motions, the teacher can make the motions while the class, group, or individual listens and watches, after which the learner responds with both making the motions and singing the pitches. Also, the teacher can sing those pitches using a neutral syllable (la, loo) and the students can respond by singing the syllables or numerals, imitating the rhythm sung by the teacher. Eventually students can take the part of the teacher. This activity leads directly into steps in learning the Curwen hand signs, as will be discussed in Chapter Fourteen. Many simple words can be sung in quarter-and-eighth note patterns:

Young children need singing conversations like this, and enjoy having teachers sing instructions to them rather than always speaking them. They also enjoy the creative possibilities in singing answers to the teachers' statements; they need not always reply with the same pitches the teacher sings. The experience with 5-5-3 is quickly expanded to include other pitches; the next one is usually scale tone 6 or *la*. In the classroom, working on problems of rhythm and pitch are often integrally related. For example, speak the following words to decide upon their natural rhythm:

Star-light, star bright,
First star I see to-night;
Wish I may, wish I might,
Have the wish I wish to-night.

Then ask a few classmates to sing the words in this rhythm, using only C scale tones 5 and 3 (G and E). When the class agrees that a version so improvised is logical and pleasing, notate it. Next, have some other students improvise tunes using scale tones 5, 3 and 6. Notate a pleasing one of these. Finally, ask others to improvise tunes with scale tones 5, 3, 6, 2, and 1, and notate the best tune. Remember that what the college class can do in a few minutes may take weeks at elementary school levels. Try combining the tunes, evaluating the result, adding Orff instruments and creating borduns and ostinati.

Accent, Meter, and Rhythm Patterns

Rhythmic
Exercises
Beginning with very easy movements, teachers help children to feel basic rhythm by having them perform thigh-slapping, finger-snapping, desk-tapping, and heel-stamping sounds, first as exercises, then in connection with

verse, songs, and recordings. A major purpose is to build concepts of metrical rhythm. The long-term objective has three stages, beginning with the concept of symmetrical meters—those divisible by two or three—because they are easiest and therefore the logical starting point. These include the familiar 2/4, 3/4, 4/4, and 6/8. Next the children meet the interesting stage of discovering, exploring, and devising alternations and combinations of these meters. The third stage is learning asymmetrical meters such as 5/4, 7/8, and others not divisible by two or three, which have irregular accents. Ten- and eleven-year olds will discern that these are formed from the familiar two- and three-beat groups they know from their study of the more conventional meters, but now arranged in a different, less regular order. Movement, spoken words, or phrases can be found or invented to help the children learn to feel these meters just as appropriate movement and words helped them with the common ones. Such meters are commonly used in the musics of Africa and Asia, and they comprise an important element in Western music being written today. Thus, school music has been freed from the metrical straightjacket of earlier years and is ready to undergo an exciting expansion in rhythm. Some example of Orff-type rhythmic exercises follow.

March rhythms such as "This Old Man," "The Caisson Song," "Pop! Goes the Weasel," "Clap Your Hands," "Four in a Boat," and "Shoo Fly" can be felt by:

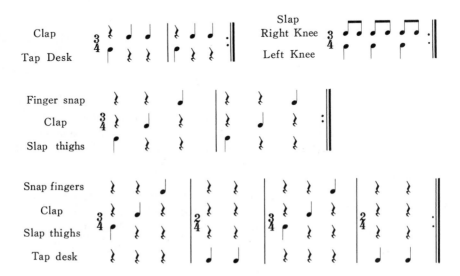

Waltz rhythms such as "Ach du lieber Augustin" ("The More We Get Together") can be moved to by:

The above pattern could be written as two measures in 5/4 meter. Other rhythmic exercises:

Clap
Tap Desk

Finger Snap
Clap Hands

Clap
Stamp

Percussion instruments can be used instead of body movements to produce the sound in such exercises. Even tone bars or bell sets can be employed. While the class does one pattern softly in unison, one child can improvise rhythmically by clapping or by playing a percussion instrument. If the basic beat is felt and understood, children should be able to place many of their patterns in notation. They should be guided to discover that the natural accent produces the measure by dictating where the bar lines are placed.

Rhythmic Development of "Hickory Dickory Dock"

The approach of Carl Orff includes body percussive sounds such as stamping feet, slapping thighs (patschen), clapping hands, and snapping fingers. (Notice that the sounds have four levels of pitches from low to high: stamp, patsch, clap, and snap.) These motions not only help children feel the beat and rhythm patterns, but the physical action adds to their pleasure.

Speak clearly and convincingly:

thighs   clap   thighs snap-snap   thighs   clap   thighs snap-snap
Hickory dickory dock (tick-tock); the mouse ran up the clock (tick-tock).

        thighs   clap   thighs   clap   thighs   clap   thighs snap-snap
The clock struck one, the mouse ran down; hickory dickory dock (tick-tock).

After this has been mastered, some of the class can add the percussion instruments suggested with the song.

A new melody for the song can be improvised on a small keyboard instrument on the pitches of the C pentatonic scale: C–D–E–G–A. In this learning sequence one progresses creatively from speech sounds and word rhythms to adding body percussion, then percussion instruments, and finally a melody. Find other rhythmic speech patterns and experiment similarly with those of your choice.

For generations this Mother Goose song has been accompanied by children playing rhythm sticks slowly, two beats to the measure, in imitation of the clock which is a big old grandfather's clock that really ticks and tocks. In addition, one child is privileged to be the mouse and will play *glissandos*

HICKORY, DICKORY, DOCK

on the bells—going up in pitch when the mouse runs up, and down in pitch when the mouse runs down. The tick tock indicated during the rests can be performed by a child playing on two tone blocks, one higher than the other in pitch. Which tone block will play the "tick" and which one the "tock"? Tick is a higher vocal sound and tock is a lower one, so the tone blocks should imitate these different pitches. Try to have the children discover this. Also have them decide what to do on the accent; perhaps a different instrument should play at that point.

Conducting Conductors' beat patterns are another rhythmic response to the meter, usually in intermediate grades, and after they have been learned they can be used by the children to identify meters they hear from recordings. The primary (heavy) accent of each measure is indicated by a downbeat, as illustrated, (see Figure 12.1). A drum played on this beat (marked *1*) will help the children to hear and feel the accent. A secondary accent occurs in 4/4 and slow 6/8 meters on beats 3 and 4, respectively.

Left-handed children will conduct all left and right motions as right and left—the reverse of the drawings. Such an exercise by children while singing a song will assist them in giving each measure the correct number of beats. One of the Dalcroze exercises consists of children's conducting meters while marching.

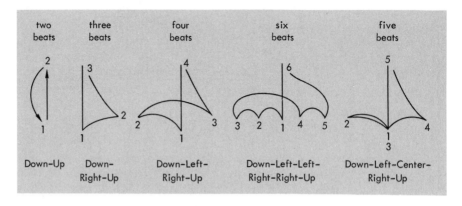

Figure 12.1. CONDUCTING PATTERNS

Exploring Common Meters

When short word rhythms are repeated and when longer groups of rhythmic words are spoken, there is a natural tendency to group the beats by accenting some of them. In their most common usage these accents are spaced regularly, at intervals of two or three beats. If children lower their hands on the accents and raise them on beats between the accents they can find whether the beats are grouped in two's or three's. This can be done with songs or recordings but the teacher may find it appropriate to introduce the search for meter with a drum. From these groupings, formed by accents, they can theorize on what the meter may be.

Songs and recorded music useful for exploring common meters are very easily found because most of the music for elementary school exemplifies such meters.

Number of Beats	Duple Meter	Triple Meter
1		3/8 3/4 (tempo di valse)
2	2/4, 2/2	6/8 6/4
3		3/8 3/4 9/8
4	4/8 4/4 4/2	12/8

What do meter signatures mean? They tell us only how many of a certain kind of note or its equivalent can be found in one measure. If the signature is 3/4, there are three quarter notes or their equivalent value in the measure. Whether each receives one beat or not is usually not revealed by the meter sign alone. Most of the time they will receive one beat, but when the tempo is very rapid the entire measure would receive only one beat. If the meter is 6/8, we know that there are six eighth notes or their equivalent in each measure, but we do not know from the meter signature whether there are two or six beats in those measures—whether each eighth note receives one beat or one third of a beat. Thus, the upper figure does *not* always tell us the number of beats in a measure, and the lower figure does *not* always tell us the kind of note that receives one beat. Meter signatures tell us only the number of a certain kind of note or its equivalent that can be written into one measure.

There is a possibility that in stressing meter accent teachers limit the capacity of children to think beyond its regularity. One way to begin to overcome this is to have them listen for accent in a rendition of "America" from a recording or played on the piano by the teacher. The correct performance will reveal little or no meter accent. To add a definite accent to the first beat of each measure would destroy the solemnity and dignity of this melody. Hearing recordings of Gregorian chant will reveal no regular recurring beat or accent. Aspects of music which tend to make rhythm more free—less bound to the rigidity of regular beats and accents—include *rallentando* and *ritardando* (gradually slower) and *accelerando* (gradually faster). *Rubato* is a term which implies that the performer treats the tempo and note values very flexibly, employing many slight accelerandos and ritardandos. This may be done in two ways, either by applying this freedom to the melody while the beat remains stable, or by applying it to the music as a whole. Many jazz players illustrate the former; Liszt and Chopin, among many other nineteenth-century composers, employed the latter. There is Oriental, Indian, and Hungarian music which has no metrical beat. Syncopation upsets the normal meter and accent by deviating from the regular recurrent accent; it shifts accents to normally weak beats. The familiar "Hokey-Pokey," "Dry Bones," and "Rock Island Line" are among the many songs from which older children can learn about syncopation. Again, the teacher should examine the indexes of music books for the heading "syncopation." Recorded selections such as Gershwin's "I Got Rhythm" and "Anything Goes" and many selected tunes of the day can be useful, as are standard selections such as Gottschalk's "Grand Walkaround" (Adventures in Music 5 vol. 1). When possible, the rhythmic notation should be written on the chalkboard to help children analyze syncopation. The *beat points*—the place or note in the measure where the metric beat falls—should be indicated, and the accents clearly marked.

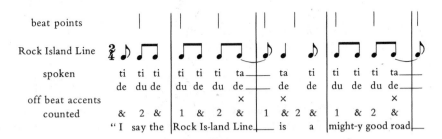

Latin American music is a useful source in studying syncopation, and some Negro spirituals are excellent for this function. An important matter concerning the performance of syncopated music is that performers should relax and permit themselves to be natural mediums for transmitting the rhythm. The more they tense themselves and "try very hard," the less success they are apt to have.

Music of our day reflects a desire for some contrasts to the more commonplace meters and rhythms. Thus there is new emphasis on exploring less familiar meters once the common ones have been mastered. Some examples are:

Meter	Title	Source
5/4 (3+2)	2nd Movement	Sixth Symphony, Tchaikovsky
7/8 (3+2+2)	"Donkey Cart"	*Music Around the World*, Silver Burdett
7/8 (3+2+2)	"The Shepherd Boy"	*The Spectrum of Music, Junior High School Book*, Macmillan
5/4, 7/8	4th Movement	*Trio*, Ravel
5/4, 6/4	"Promenade"	*Pictures at an Exhibition*, Mussorgsky
5/4, 3/4	"One May Morning"	Book Six, *Birchard Series*
5/4	*Take Five*	Desmond. The Dave Brubeck Quartet, Columbia CS 8192
5/4, 6/4	"How Far to Bethlehem?"	*The Music Book 5*, Holt, Rinehart & Winston

Look for others in the current music textbooks.

Experiments in Music Creativity, Contemporary Music Project, MENC, 1966, lists rhythmic recordings recommended for classroom study on page 23. Some record jackets of Asiatic Indian music explain the metrical organization of that music, and the indexes of the music textbooks guide the reader to songs and recordings having composite meters. For further study of polyrhythms and polymetric concepts see *The Study of Music in the Elementary School: A Conceptual Approach,* MENC, 1967, pp. 47–50.

Older students enjoy experimenting with less common meters, composing percussion pieces and songs having such beat groupings. Composite meters are normally combinations of 2 and 3 beat groups. The meter 5/4 is either 3+2 or 2+3; 7/8 either 2+2+3, 2+3+2, or 3+2+2. An interesting challenge for a class is to devise a logical conductor's beat for 7-beat and other less standard beat groups. An assignment for individuals and small groups could be structured as shown in the blank score to be filled in (Figure 12.2). The first experience with this should be very simple, using only two or three instruments for four measures. By means of an opaque projector the entire class can study, read, perform, and evaluate such scores.

Alla breve meter (¢) is really 2/2 meter. It could also be considered as 2/4 written in 4/4 so as to be more easily read, the notation being "less black" in that it has fewer eighths and sixteenth notes to decipher. 3/2 is not uncommon; songs such as "Kum Ba Ya" are written in that meter, and 9/8 is the meter for "Down in the Valley." Familiar songs can and do change meter, as testified by "Goodbye, My Lover, Goodbye," and "We Three Kings of Orient Are."

The most commonly found meters are 2/4, 3/3, 4/4, and 6/8. Techni-

	1	*2*	*3*	*4*	*5*	*1*	*2*	*3*	*4*	*5*	*1*	*2*	*3*	*4*	*5*	*etc.*
Triangle																
Tambourine																
Wood block																
Bongo drums (or small drum)																
Conga drum (or large drum)																

Figure 12.2. PERCUSSION SCORE IN 5/4 METER

ONE MAY MORNING — English Folksong

Flowing (♩=152)

As I went out___ one May morn-ing, One May morn-ing___ be-
time, I met a maid,___ from___ home had stray'd,___ Just
as the sun___ did shine.

cally, the 9- and 12-note compound meters can be changed to become composite by alternating normal accents. In composite meters one finds two or more meters in some form of alternation (see Figure 12.3).

Figure 12.3. CHART OF METERS

	Simple				Compound				Composite		
	♩	♪	♬		♩	♪	♬		♩	♪	♬
2	$\frac{2}{2}$	$\frac{2}{4}$	$\frac{2}{8}$	6	$\frac{6}{4}$	$\frac{6}{8}$	$\frac{6}{16}$	5	$\frac{5}{4}$	$\frac{5}{8}$	$\frac{5}{16}$
3	$\frac{3}{2}$	$\frac{3}{4}$	$\frac{3}{8}$	9	$\frac{9}{4}$	$\frac{9}{8}$	$\frac{9}{16}$	7	$\frac{7}{4}$	$\frac{7}{8}$	$\frac{7}{16}$
4	$\frac{4}{2}$	$\frac{4}{4}$	$\frac{4}{8}$	12	$\frac{12}{4}$	$\frac{12}{8}$	$\frac{12}{16}$	11	$\frac{11}{4}$	$\frac{11}{8}$	$\frac{11}{16}$

Words adapted by H. V. N.

1. Ger - a - ki - na, one fine day,____ Took a walk just to dis -
2. Ger - a - ki - na did not look,____ Took a step and fell ker -

play her brace - lets fine, Jing - jang - ling on her way,____
floop! down in the well, Jing - jang - ling on her way,____

Then, as she went a - long, she gai - ly sang a song to brigh - ten the
And, as she fell down in the well, she sang a song to brigh - ten her

day, gai - ly sang a song to brigh - ten the day.____
stay, gai - ly sang a song to brigh - ten her stay.____

From *Toward World Understanding With Song.* Reproduced by permission. Copyright 1967 by Vernice T. Nye, Robert E. Nye, and H. Virginia Nye.

3. Gerakina gave a shout, Soon a young lad pulled her out for all to greet,
   Jing-jangling on her way.
   Then, as she thanked the lad, she gaily sang a song to brighten his day, gaily
   sang a song to brighten his day.
4. Gerakina took a look, Looked and felt her heart go floop! then very soon,
   Jing-jangling, they were wed,
   So, all through life, they say, they gaily sang a song to brighten each day, gaily
   sang a song to brighten each day.

The original Greek song ends less happily. Gerakina (pronounced "Yehr-ah-kee-nah") went to the well to bring fresh water, with her bracelets resounding. When she fell, shouting, into the open well, young and old ran to the rescue, and the singer, who felt miserable because he was in love with her and she had ignored him, ran with them to help her but never succeeded in attracting her attention.

What instruments would you choose to depict Gerakina's jingling bracelets?

The tempo is rather fast; it will be found that counts 1, 4, and 6 mark the beat points:

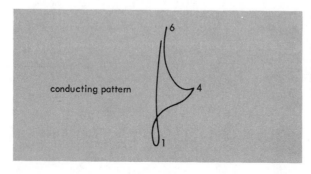

conducting pattern

From *Toward World Understanding With Song.* Reproduced by permission. Copyright 1967 by Vernice T. Nye, Robert E. Nye, and H. Virginia Nye.

Rhythm Patterns in Songs

One of the ways students become conscious of definite rhythm patterns is by means of such activities as echo-clapping, described earlier. Teachers help children to recognize the patterns found in selected songs. For example, they can discover the patterns in "Jingle at the Window" from which the entire rhythmic structure of the song is derived:

JINGLE AT THE WINDOWS

"Au Clair de la Lune" consists of a four-measure phrase rhythm pattern which is used four times; it is the rhythmic unifying element for the entire song.

 - four times

All of "Ten Little Indians" except the concluding two measures consists of the pattern:

 - three times

With the exception of the final three measures, "I Love the Mountains" (page 388) is constructed upon two rhythm patterns:

- two times

- four times

Younger children can identify patterns, and teachers can write them on the chalkboard if the children are unable to notate the rhythm of what they hear. Older children can look for these repeated patterns in notation, as well as identifying them when listening to songs and recordings.

All songs do not contain such distinct patterns. Teachers must seek songs and recorded music which are best suited to build specific musical concepts. Words of songs can assist in performing rhythm patterns. A simple example is the song "Sally Go Round," in which seven-year-olds decide they want to use the rhythm of the first four notes as an ostinato played by sticks throughout the song.

English Singing Game

Sal-ly go round the sun._____ Sal-ly go round the moon,_____

Sal-ly go round the chim-ney pot on a Sun-day af-ter-noon._____

The children can remember the rhythm of the pattern by repeating silently the words: "Sally go round" ( ). They might decide to have a wood block play the rhythm of the last two measures over and over along with the one the sticks play. It could be remembered by the rhythm of the words "Sunday afternoon" ( ). A rhythm pattern has been defined as a specific grouping of sounds related to an underlying beat.

Some of the many songs usable for the identification and study of rhythm patterns are "When Johnny Comes Marching Home," "Jingle Bells," "Over the River and Through the Woods," "Hanukkah," "The Old Brass Wagon," and "Skip to My Lou." Examples of the many recordings which serve the same purpose are "Country Gardens," arranged by Grainger, RCA Rhythm Album 6, "The Little White Donkey," Ibert, Adventures in Music 2, "Habañera," from *Carmen,* Bizet, Dowmar Orchestra Album #56, and "Golliwog's Cakewalk," Debussy, Bowmar #63.

An Expanding Concept of Rhythm

Besides expanding their concept of rhythm in music, children should be helped to find rhythm in other areas of living. There is rhythm all about us—in the waves of the ocean, day and night, life cycles of plants and animals, the heart beat, moving oars, the grain of wood, in machinery, poetry, speech, dance, and when we walk. How does Debussy compose music that reflects the rhythm of the ocean? Hear his *La Mer.* How do composers of art songs manage the rhythm of the poems they set to music? Might there be a relation between the beat, its divisions, and certain architecture? Are there evidences of unity, balance, and variety in man's many experiences with rhythm? There is a world of rhythm to be explored.

Rhythm-Related Compositional Devices

As children compose, they have an interest in and a need for some of the devices used by the adult composer. The terminology may seem complex at first, but it is rather simple when once explained. Consider the terms *augmentation* and *diminution.* To augment something, one makes it larger; to diminish something, one makes it smaller. This is what happens in rhythm. If young composers are writing a score for percussion instuments based on the pattern ♩ ♫♩ ♩, they find that they can, if they choose, apply diminution by making the pattern one half its original value and repeating it. Writing this down, it looks like this:

original pattern   *diminution*

The extension of the original pattern by repetition adds considerably to a feeling of tension the children want to achieve. They might follow this with an application of augmentation by making the original twice its duration, and thus construct a four-measure composition which builds up to a climax followed by a feeling of release. Next they could utilize a canonic treatment of the pattern, and assign this to the woodblock player. They might decide that a continuous eighth-note pattern played by maracas would add some stability and help to unify the piece. They could choose to experiment with polymetrics by adding a hand drum playing quarter note beats in 3/4 meter. Now the composition is complete. The children have done what many adult composers may do—used diminution, augmentation, canon, and polymetrics. All they need is a group of classmates to read, perform, and evaluate their composition. Learning music can be exciting, creative, experimental, and intellectual—all at once.

The above 3/4 part is written in 4/4 meter by using the bar lines of the other parts. The accent dicates the true meter.

chapter thirteen

Activities for Teaching Rhythm

Individual Since children are different in makeup, teachers can expect that what is an
Differences easy rhythmic response for one child may be a difficult one for another. To
assist children who find rhythm difficult, teachers seek to guide them to success either in the same rhythm at a slower tempo, or with a different and
more simple action to which they can respond at their own natural tempos.
When they succeed, they should then be helped to synchronize their movements with gradually slower and faster tempos. It helps some children to
produce the sound of the rhythm by clapping, singing, speaking, chanting,
or making up sounds; their sounds and actions are then more easily
synchronized and a habit of doing an action with a sound begins to develop.

Sometimes six-year-olds do not understand that there is supposed to be
a definite relation between the sound they hear and what their muscles are
to do. Therefore, they cannot march in time with music until they are guided
to discover this relation, possibly by the example of other children. Teachers
should remember that when children are asked to move in time with music,
they are expected to (1) control a specific movement, (2) listen to the music,
and (3) synchronize the two. It is natural that some children find the
teacher's request confusing, and the teacher must help children by permitting them to learn the movement well before asking them to add the other
two aspects. Sometimes the use of a paper streamer or a scarf will help chil-

dren to comprehend a motion that they cannot understand by use of the arm alone.

When some children cannot clap their hands in time with music, they can sometimes succeed by striking both hands on the thighs. Some teachers slow the speed of recordings for action-responses of subnormal children. When this is done with songs, it also lowers the pitch. Thus, the pitch cannot be lowered out of the natural vocal range if the recording is to be used for singing with the action. For children who are above average in physical control, the teacher encourages responses of a creative nature of which they are physically capable. Body movements and playing percussion instruments can provide means for successful participation other than singing, for children who need to experience success.

Normal Expectations

Rhythmic activities for young children are free and informal; they emphasize use of the big muscles in large, free motions. The children do imaginative and creative play in imitation of people, animals, and things. They become able to respond to simple patterns played on the drum, piano, tone block, or record player with actions such as walking, marching, running, jumping, hopping, skipping, galloping, and tiptoeing. Concepts of high-low, heavy-light, long-short, and soft-loud can be acquired. Simple directed action songs and singing games are played, such as "The Elephants," "Eensy Weensy Spider," and "Hey Diddle Diddle." Such songs are found in quantity in nursery and kindergarten series books. Dramatizations, finger plays, and hand movements are done. Children learn to use some percussion instruments to tap in time with music and for sound effects that add interest and variety to musical experiences.

Levels One and Two

Ability to respond to fundamental movements with large free motions: walking, running, jumping, hopping, skipping, and combinations of these.

Performance and enjoyment of action songs (such as "If You're Happy") and singing game songs (such as "Wee Little Man," "My Pretty Little Miss," "Looby Lou," "Clapping Land," and "Pony Land").

Ability to respond to rhythm with movements such as swinging, bending, twisting, swaying, stretching, pushing, pulling.

Creative response to rhythm (rhythmic dramatization).

Ability to do simple dance steps, skills, and formations including galloping, sliding, skipping, bowing, circling, singing games, circling with partner on the right.

Understanding of the relation of rhythmic movement to quarter, eighth, and half notes (walking, running, and step-bending or bowing), and ability to use these rhythms by playing them on percussion instruments.

Growth in ability to suggest suitable percussion accompaniments for piano pieces and for recorded music.

Comprehension of whether the music "swings" in two's or three's (duple or triple meter).

Ability to combine movement and some percussion instruments with greater skill and for more specific purposes in level two.

Awareness of repeated rhythm patterns and repeated and contrasting phrases or sections of music in level two.

Levels Three and Four
Mastery of rhythmic concepts and skills taught in kindergarten through levels one and two.

Knowledge of many action songs, singing games, and simple play-party games and dances.

Ability to create and notate simple percussion scores.

The transfer of rhythmic understanding gained from body responses to note and rest values, including the dotted note. (4)

Continued development in understanding beat, patterns, accent, meter, and form through body responses.

Development of increased awareness of the differences between descriptive music and pure ("pattern") music through creative rhythmic dramatization.

Knowledge of conductor's patterns for 2-, 3-, and 4-beat meters.

Ability to perform combined movements of walk-step, step-hop, skip-hop, step-slide, slide-hop, and to use these movements in dances and dramatizations. (4)

Ability to march to duple and quadruple measures, accenting the first beat of each measure.

Recognition and identification of 2-, 3-, and 4-beat meters in recordings or in the singing and playing of the teacher.

Ability to step the melody rhythm of selected familiar songs.

Ability to clap, step, and write in notation simple rhythm patterns played by the teacher.

Recognition of the musical phrase through body movement.

Ability to create and notate percussion scores to songs and recordings.

Ability to interpret songs and recordings with rhythmic movement.

Ability to use percussion instruments to play both metric and melody rhythms.

Ability to use percussion instruments with discrimination.

Levels Five and Six

Mastery of rhythmic concepts and skills of the earlier levels.

Ability to dramatize work songs and ballads.

Ability to notate more complex rhythm patterns.

Knowledge of meter, notation, and melody rhythm in relation to the beat.

Creative interpretation of music's emotion and structure through movement.

Ability to use conductor's beat patterns in all common meters.

Ability to create more complex and tasteful percussion scores and to use percussion instruments with discrimination for sound effects with music.

Understanding the concept of syncopation through movement and the use of percussion instruments.

Increased skill in moving to and in reading the notation of more complex patterns.

Growth in comprehension and use of asymmetrical meters.

A repertoire of many American play-party games and dances and folk dances of the world; an understanding of the place of these in the world of music.

Ability to play and enjoy Latin American percussion instruments.

Selected Songs for Experimentation

IF YOU'RE HAPPY

2. . . . tap your toe, *(tap, tap)*
3. . . . nod your head, *(nod, nod)*
4. . . . do all three, *(together)*

SOME SUGGESTED RHYTHMIC ACTIVITIES

Children

Suggest action words for more verses.

With one student playing a set of bells, have him or her listen carefully to the melody with the bars F G A B♭ to play on. Beginning on F, play the first note of each measure as the class sings the song.

Teacher

Have students conduct verses of the song.

Ask students to propose motions to make for the rests (three places).

DOWN BY THE STATION

Traditional School Song
For ages 5—7

Down by the sta - tion ear - ly in the morn - ing.
See the lit - tle puf - fer - bil - lies all in a row.
See the en - gine driv - er pull the lit - tle han - dle.
Choo! Choo! Toot! Toot! Off they go!

SOME SUGGESTED RHYTHMIC ACTIVITIES

Children

Clap the meter, four beats to the measure, as in measure 7; say "Chug, chug, puff, puff."

Clap the word-rhythm as you say the words.

Combine 1 and 2 by selecting appropriate percussion instruments for these rhythms.

Teacher

Select a rhythm pattern such as the note values in the first two measures and have this played on a percussion instrument throughout the song. Children can learn it by repeating the words "Down by the station" in the rhythm of these measures.

Older children may sing this song as a round.

Nine-year-olds can step the note values, first of selected measures, then in two-measure parts until the entire song can be stepped.

Older children can identify each rhythm pattern, step it, and notate it.

SAILING

Italian Melody
for Grades Two and Three

Leisurely

Come, sail - ing with me; Let's float on the sea. O - ver the waves with the spray fly - ing high, Come sail - ing with me.

SOME SUGGESTED RHYTHMIC ACTIVITIES

Children

Sway in time with the music.

Clap hands or use percussion instruments on the first beat of each measure and in the rhythm of the meter in three beats to the measure.

Teacher

Encourage the children to invent with movement or percussion instruments an appropriate way to mark the end of each of the four phrases, thus teaching phrase awareness.

Have the class conduct 3/4 meter.

Teach a simple waltz run or step. Example:

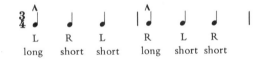

L R L R L R
long short short long short short

OLD MACDONALD

American Song

1. Old Mac - Don - ald had a farm, Ee - i - ee - i -
2. Old Mac - Don - ald had a farm, Ee - i - ee - i -
3. Old Mac - Don - ald had a farm, Ee - i - ee - i -

o, And on that farm he had some chicks,
o, And on that farm he had some ducks,
o, And on that farm he had some pigs,

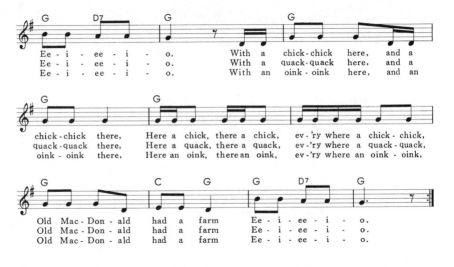

Ee - i - ee - i - o. With a chick-chick here, and a
Ee - i - ee - i - o. With a quack-quack here, and a
Ee - i - ee - i - o. With an oink-oink here, and an

chick-chick there, Here a chick, there a chick, ev-'ry where a chick-chick,
quack-quack there, Here a quack, there a quack, ev-'ry where a quack-quack,
oink - oink there, Here an oink, there an oink, ev-'ry where an oink - oink,

Old Mac-Don - ald had a farm Ee - i - ee - i - o.
Old Mac-Don - ald had a farm Ee - i - ee - i - o.
Old Mac-Don - ald had a farm Ee - i - ee - i - o.

SOME SUGGESTED RHYTHMIC ACTIVITIES

Children

Sing the song, discuss aspects of it that may influence a percussion accompaniment, then create a percussion score and notate it.

Invent actions each time "Ee-i-ee-i-o" is sung. Dramatize the song.

Teacher

Review the basic beat by having the class conduct the meter.

Ignore chord designations and treat the song as pentatonic. Add bordums and ostinati. Have children improvise a simple dance to the result.

THE PAW-PAW PATCH

Kentucky Singing Game for Grades Three through Five

Where,O where is pret-ty lit-tle El - lie?Where,O where is pret-ty lit-tle El - lie?

Where O where is pret-ty lit-tle El - lie? Way down yon-der in the paw-paw patch.

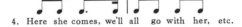

2. Come on, boys, let's find El - lie, etc.

3. Pickin' up paw-paws, put'n'em in a bas-ket, etc.

4. Here she comes, we'll all go with her, etc.

SOME SUGGESTED RHYTHMIC ACTIVITIES

Children

Create a dance-dramatization of the song.

Teacher

Use the song to teach the relation of word-rhythms to note values; use the different word-rhythms of the verses in a percussion score.

RIG - A - JIG - JIG

SOME SUGGESTED RHYTHMIC ACTIVITIES

Children

Create a dance; learn and compare 2/4 and fast 6/8 meters in the process.

With percussion instruments, enhance the leisurely walking effect of the verse and the excited skipping effect of the refrain.

TO PUERTO RICO

R.E.N.

With languor

Song for Grades Five and Six

soft breeze will blow from off the sea; ____ I'll bask in the warm sweet sun.

SOME SUGGESTED RHYTHMIC ACTIVITIES

Children

Devise a Latin American percussion score and notate it. Possibilities include:

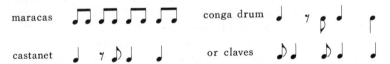

maracas   conga drum

castanet   or claves

Teacher

Teach for the concept of syncopation.

(For part-singing, improvise a new part a third higher than the melody.)

THE COUNT

Brazilian Song for Grades Five and Six

1. He wrote me a let-ter, ca-ram-ba! It asked for my
2. This he told my fa-ther, ca-ram-ba! Fa-ther shook with

hand.   I wrote him my an-swer, ca-ram-ba!
wrath.   He broke ev-'ry pot in the kich-en;

Said, "No wed-ding band."   I ran down the path!

SOME SUGGESTED RHYTHMIC ACTIVITIES

Children

Devise a Latin American percussion score.

Teacher

Teach the ♪ ♩♩ ♩ rhythm pattern through use of the word "caramba," which children enjoy emphasizing in the song.

Teach ♫ ♫ ♩ by comparing it with ♪♩ ♪♩ ♩ in "To Puerto Rico"; it is the same rhythm twice as fast. The generalization is that the same pattern can occur in lesser or greater note values (in diminution or augmentation).

Additional Activities and Suggestions for Lesson Plans

Learners may imitate, explore, discover, recognize, identify, inquire, contrast, differentiate, classify, verbalize, recall, and evaluate. They may utilize one or more of the following activities to do these things: singing, playing instruments, moving, creating, reading, dramatizing, impersonating, improvising, composing, and discussing. Utilize all the appropriate senses in a lesson plan: hearing, seeing, feeling with body muscles. Plan so that children listen before they attempt to respond with movement or with voices. Avoid presenting too much in one lesson.

Help children sense the beat by sounding some type of clearly stated rhythmic introduction to performance-type activities. This can be done with hand clapping, with stroking the Autoharp, with percussion instruments, with counting, and with the teacher's singing or playing.

Readers should not feel responsible for knowing how to work with each of the activities listed in the following pages; the activities are presented as a list from which to choose. Some of them will require teaching experience to do well. Therefore, those activities and suggestions can be dealt with in part in the college class, in part during student teaching, and in part during later years of professional teaching. They combine both American and European teaching strategies and are listed in order of increasing difficulty.

Tempo A DEVELOPMENTAL PLAN

The children discover their natural tempo.	The teacher adapts drum or piano accompaniment to the natural tempo of the individual learner.
The children recognize relative fast and slow in songs, drum beats, and in recorded music.	The teacher provides the opportunity for the children to compare two songs, one fast and one slow; and two recordings, one fast and one slow.
The children discover the concept of tempos appropriate for imitating animals or describing activities. The eye aids the ear.	The teacher uses songs and recordings that suggest appropriate rhythms for the movements of animals and man. The teacher draws chart-pictures of tempo vocabulary: a marching soldier—Di Marcia; a turtle—Adagio; a sleeping baby—Largo; a jet liner—Presto; a spinning top slowing down—Rallentando; a rocket taking off—Accelerando, and so on.
The children see and identify tempo designations in the musical score and understand them.	The teacher selects music that encourages such identification.
The children are able to provide appropriate tempo names for music sung and heard.	"What would happen if the tempo of this song is slowed down?" "Let's try it." "Is the result better, or worse?" "Why do you think so?" "Can you think of ways to vary the tempo that might improve this song?" "What terminology can you use to describe the changes in tempo?"

BEHAVIORAL OBJECTIVE:

The children reveal their understanding of concepts of degrees of fast and slow by..... (what specific performance, under what conditions, and to what extent.)

Dynamics A DEVELOPMENTAL PLAN

The children begin to understand the difference between soft and loud and degrees of softer and louder by hearing and by acting this out in body movements. The comprehension of variations in dynamics increase; the children are able to express these in creative ways such as in body movement and in drawings.

piano (p)—soft
forte (f)—loud
The teacher plans experiences in which the children find these terms useful. Songs and recorded music offer experiences to build increasing comprehension of the variations in dynamics.

Vocabulary additions become useful to the learners in their own compositions.

Accent, crescendo (cresc.), decrescendo (decresc.), mezzo piano (mp), pianissimo (pp), mezzo forte (mf), fortissimo (ff).

Increasing ability to enter into a deeper analysis of music with respect to dynamics.

The children will suggest dynamics for their musical interpretations, and they will experiment with dynamic levels for the purpose of communicating ideas by means of music. They will listen analytically to several selected recordings and compare the use of dynamics heard in them.

Crescendo, decrescendo are identified.

Listen to recorded music that clearly portrays these dynamics, such as "Bydlo" from *Pictures at an Exhibition,* Mussorgsky, Adventures in Music 2, vol. 1. Have the students decide how to act them out with body movements of their choice.

BEHAVIORAL OBJECTIVE:

The children reveal their understanding of concepts of loud and soft by ... (what specific performance, under what conditions, and to what extent.)

Rhythm *Beat (pulse).* The teacher adapts patschen, clapping, a drum beat, or piano improvisation to the natural rhythm of the learner's walk.

Tempo. After children have learned to respond physically to a steady beat, they are asked to dramatize an activity that is done to a steady beat, such as chopping wood, shoveling snow, hammering, sawing, and rowing. They will do different dramatizations in appropriately different tempos, adding to their concepts of fast and slow.

Heart beat. Find, feel, and imitate the heart beat. Have children find out when the heart beats slow or fast.

Beat. Dramatize the beat by walking, "How many different ways can you walk?" (tired, slow, lightly, fast, heavily, like a toy soldier, like a rag doll.)

Notating the beat. After young children have learned to walk in time with the beat, ask them to draw their original pictures or notations of the beat.

Beat. Use rhythmic speech with rhymes such as "Hickory Dickory Dock," and "Sing a Song of Sixpence," speaking the words and clapping and/or walking the beat on the word syllable accents.

Eighth notes. Dramatizing running. "How many ways can you run?" (as if in a race—fast, as if you are tired—slow, jogging, quietly so no one will hear you, etc.)

2-to-1 relationship. Select children's names that have one and two syllables. Have children speak the names while drumming or clapping on the first syllable:

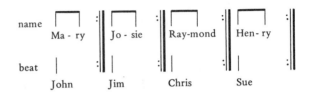

Beat, word-rhythms, rest. Chant, step, and/or contrive motions for rhythmic verse such as "Ding Dong Bell," (invent a motion at the end of appropriate phrases for the rest); "The Bear Went Over the Mountain"; "Pease Porridge Hot" (rest concept also); and "Wee Willy Winkle"(| ⊓   and 𝄽).

Drum talk. Children play their names on a drum as they speak them. Other children answer, speaking and playing their names. The experience is heightened by using two drums, one of high pitch and the other of low pitch available to each child as he speaks and plays. Example:

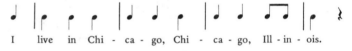

After this experience has been absorbed, the child can begin to use drum talk to say things such as:

♩ | ♪ ♪ ♪ | ♩ ♩ ♪ | ♩ ♩ ♫ | ♪ 𝄽

I   live   in   Chi - ca - go,   Chi - ca - go,   Ill - in - ois.

Two such statements can be combined as an experiment in sound.

Fundamental movements. The teacher improvises with drum or piano; the children respond with the appropriate motion: walking, running, skipping, galloping, hopping, swaying, rowing, as they are able. When the piano is used, the black keys provide an easy way for the non-piano player to improvise acceptably. Galloping is done with one foot kept ahead of the other, the back foot being brought up to meet it. Children pretend they are ponies or horses.

Notation. The teacher writes a simple quarter note or quarter-and-eighth note pattern. Children first act it out in their own original ways. Then they write it on paper either with $\mid$ $\sqcap$ notation or with invented symbols such as large and small circles:

| | | | ⊓ | | | ○ | ○ | ○ | ○ | ○ |

ta   ta   ti - ti ta
du   du   du-de du

Beat and divisions of the beat. A beat is established by everyone clapping, and the tempo is held steady. The teacher says, in time with the beat, "My ńame is Ďan-iel Éck-hart," and the students will echo, "His ńame is Ďan-iel Éck-hart." Each student does this in turn, stating his or her name in accord with the beat, and the class restating it in echo fashion. Later on, names can be written in abbreviated notation, and still later, in traditional notation without the staff. Relate the rhythm of names to movement and eventually to notation.

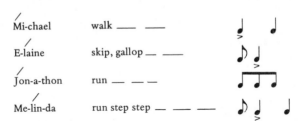

Mi-chael   walk ___ ___

E-laine   skip, gallop __ ___

Jon-a-thon   run __ __ __

Me-lin-da   run step step ___ ___ ___

Divisions of the beat (*eighth notes*). Teacher and children can make up patterns for the class to read with rhythm syllables and with percussion instruments. Example:

Triplet (*tri-ple-it, tri-o-la, tri-ple-ti,* or *du-da-di*).

Find many interesting words to write in this simple notation.

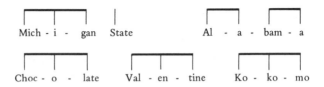

Rest. Young children can be helped to understand *rest* by the use of sheets of colored paper.

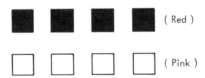

Learn about rests by removing a sheet or sheets of paper.

Accent. Learn about accent by the use of two shades of any one color.

Then go into any meter the teacher wishes.

Divisions of the beat. Use paper cutouts for note values.

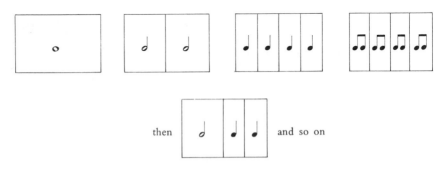

Children play games by arranging these note values and performing them. However, the note groupings cannot be larger than the whole sheet as illustrated by the whole note.

Beat. The class beats a slow, steady beat with clapping, pounding lightly on desks, or with percussion instruments while each child says his name twice in time with the beat. Next, the class translates the rhythm of some of the names into rhythm syllables. The teacher selects some of these to be written in quarter and eighth note abbreviated notation (without note heads). This last step requires that names be screened by the teacher because some demand a complexity beyond the present ability of the children to notate them. In such cases a nickname might be substituted, or only a first or a last name would be used. The class could chant the complex names but not notate them at this time.

Percussion score. Young children can invent percussion scores through use of word rhythms such as:

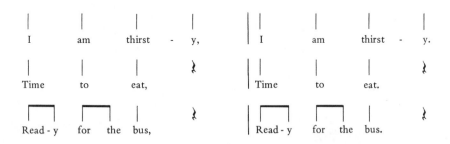

I	am	thirst - y,		I	am	thirst - y.
Time	to	eat,		Time	to	eat.
Read - y	for	the bus,		Read - y	for	the bus.

Rhythm pattern. Such patterns can be transferred to percussion instruments, hand clapping, thigh slapping, etc. One child creates a rhythm pattern within limits set by the teacher, such as using only *ta* and *ti-ti*. A second child creates a different one that "fits with" the first one. The two patterns may be written on the chalkboard; the students and/or the class plays or claps them in sequence, then in combination. Percussion instruments of contrasting tone qualities may be selected to play them.

Improvising patterns. Game: Establish a steady beat in a specific meter. Give each child in turn an opportunity to clap a pattern to "fit with" the beat. Each pattern must be different from what anyone else has clapped. The meter 4/4 would probably be an easy one to start with. Each child continues clapping his or her pattern until the result equals the amount of complexity the class can absorb, then the game begins again. The teacher may wish some of the improvised patterns notated. They can be transferred to percussion instruments for further exploration of pattern, combinations of patterns, and their instrumentation.

Rhythm pattern. Utilize words whenever they can assist children's comprehension of the pattern. Examples:

violet, daffodil, peppermint, bumblebee ♫♪

marigold ♫ ♩

water-lily ♫ ♫

"Sit in a circle and clap your hands" ♫♩ ♫♩ | ♩ ♪♩. |

wisteria ♪ | ♩. ♩ ♪

Rhythm pattern, improvisation. Several students will take percussion instruments. One will establish a basic pattern to be performed throughout an original percussion composition while others will enter and depart at different times to add interest and variety to the piece.

Divisions of the beat. Let students manipulate colored sticks or colored sheets of paper cut in sizes to represent the relative values of whole, half, quarter, and eighth notes. Students are to arrange sticks or paper into various combinations with the stipulation that no combination can be of larger size than the largest stick or sheet. Students can place these on the floor and walk or step them as they count the beats of the measure. More advanced students can chart short songs in this manner.

Divisions of the beat. Use *Threshold to Music* Experience Charts, First Year, charts I–XI. These assist the understanding of the beat, and quarter note, eighth note, and quarter rest values. The teacher plays a series of measures by beating a drum. The children respond by translating these into rhythm syllables.

"Which one did I clap?" The teacher asks children to identify the measure he claps:

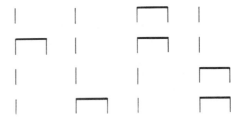

Note values and note reading. "Which one did I play?" The children select the correct rhythmic grouping or pattern from six different small cards or small charts at their desks or from six large charts on the wall. This can be done in traditional notation.

Rhythm pattern and note memory. Use flashcards with simple rhythm patterns. The teacher shows a card, then conceals it. The class then claps it, thus promoting note memory.

Divisions of the beat. Experiment with clapping one note value while stepping another note value with the feet.

Rhythm patterns. Experiment with clapping a simple rhythm pattern while doing another one with the feet.

Accent and Meter

Accent. Use selected words to discover accent. Examples:

mu-sic   a-rith-me-tic   ge-og-raphy

Regular accents result in meters. Try acccenting beats grouped in two's and three's:

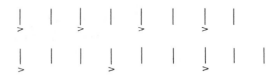

(this can be related at once to familiar songs):

Words can help too:

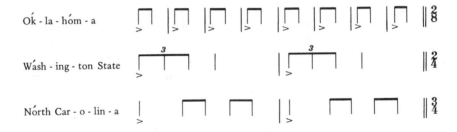

Such examples can introduce children to the concept that in normally accented music, the bar line is placed *before* the heavily accented beat, and that variety in rhythm can be accomplished in any meter by changing the accents to accommodate a different meter for a time. For older students:

There are many meters. Invent a number of meters by placing regular accents at different intervals by clapping, stamping, or using percussion instruments.

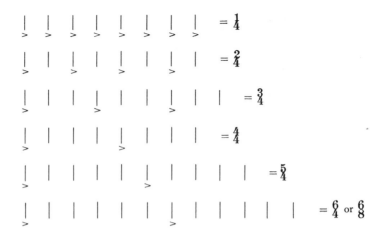

Inventing responses to meter. Ask children to invent ways to respond to the beats and accents in various meters. Possibilities:

2/4 touch knees, then head

3/4 touch knees, hip, forehead

4/4 clap above head for the first beat, clap normally (opposite chest) for the second beat, slap thighs for the third beat, and touch knees for the fourth beat.

For all meters: push both hands high into the air for the first beat and pull back for the other beats

Changing meters. Assign children the task of composing a percussion score with an unusual meter pattern such as one measure each of 3/4 and 4/4 in succession throughout. Try other "different" meter combinations.

Syncopation. Syncopation can be introduced and explained by using a song the children know, such as "Li'l 'Liza Jane."

The students should be able to deduce with the aid of the teacher's questioning that while the clapping is regular because it is on the beat, the accents are not. They may be able to discover that syncopation takes place when the accent falls on a part of the measure not usually accented. Some people call this a *displaced* accent. After this, the students may wish to employ syncopation in their percussion compositions. They can experiment with syncopation in several ways:

Writing accent marks on beats not normally accented (beginning a measure with an eighth note followed by a quarter note).

Using a tie to connect a weak beat with a strong one:

Placing a rest at the beginning of the measure as in "Li'l 'Liza Jane."
Ordinarily, the longer the note value, the more stress it receives (the louder it is in relation to the other shorter note values).

Polymetrics. Polymetrics result from unlike meters sounding at the same time. They can be introduced by word rhythms.

Students can write simple polymetric scores to play, tape record, and evaluate in class.

Accent, meter, patterns, form. Utilize dance. Students can create dances based upon specific accents, meters, rhythm patterns, and forms.

Some dance improvisations based on these elements can be done by couples with hands on each other's shoulders. Traditional dances can be learned, and their notated rhythm patterns can be observed and related to body movement.

Rhythm, analysis of. Listen to two contrasting recordings and compare the rhythmic aspects heard.

Form   *Phrase.* The students listen to a phrase of music, and select a place in the room to move. The manner of movement to the music is decided upon. As the phrase is sounded again, the students move to their selected place so that they arrive there at the time the phrase ends.

Phrase and cadence. The students decide upon a movement or body position to reflect whether the phase ending (cadence) rests on the tonic (I or home) chord, thus giving a feeling of repose (a *perfect* cadence), or whether it rests on some other chord, usually the dominant (V, V$_7$—an *authentic* cadence) or the subdominant (IV—a *plagal* cadence), giving feelings of being incomplete or not being final. The phrases can be "acted out" and the different cadences described by movement and/or body position. When a new phrase begins, change direction.

Rondo. The class or group agrees upon a rhythmic pattern to be used as a basis for a rondo. This pattern is "A." After A is performed, a previously selected child creates in body percussion sounds a new part called "B." Then A is performed again, after which part "C" is created in body percussion by another child. Thus the composition develops into A B A C A D A E and so on until each child selected has had opportunity to create and perform his or her part. Next, the body percussion patterns can be transferred to percussion instruments appropriate to the pattern. Variations: One or two rhythm patterns can be combined with A. Crescendo could be incorporated into A. Parts B, C, D, and E could include melody instrument improvisations. The resulting piece could be tape-recorded, listened to, and discussed. A dance could be created to reflect the patterns and their sounds. Recordings of rondos could be studied as sources of more ideas to incorporate into future rondos.

References and Materials

General   ANDRESS, BARBARA, *Musical Experiences in Early Childhood.* New York: Holt, Rinehart and Winston, 1980.

FAULMAN, JO, "Montessori and Music in Early Childhood," *Music Educators Journal,* May 1980, 41–43.

Music Educators Journal, March 1974. Early childhood issue.

POND, DONALD, "The Young Child's Playful World of Sound," *Music Educators Journal,* March 1980, 39–41.

REGELSKI, THOMAS A., *Teaching General Music: Action Learning for Middle and Secondary School.* New York: Schirmer Books, 1981. Based on the Manhattanville approach.

RICHARDS, MARY HELEN, *Aesthetic Foundations for Thinking.* Richards Institute for Music Education and Research, 1977.

TAIT, MALCOM J., "Whispers, Growls, Screams, and Puffs . . . Lead to Composition," *Music Educators Journal,* February 1977, 33–34.

Movement, Games, and Dance   ATHNEY, MARGARET, and GWEN HOTCHKISS, *A Galaxy of Games for the Music Class.* West Nyack, N.Y.: Parker Publishing Company, 1975.

CARLSON, DEBORAH LYNN, "Movement as a Channel to Understanding Music," *Music Educators Journal,* September 1980, 52–56. Includes bibliography.

CHASE, RICHARD, *Singing Games and Play Party Games.* New York: Dover Publishers, 1967.

CHERRY, CLAIRE, *Creative Movement for the Developing Child.* Belmont, Calif.: Fearon Publishers, 1971.

DOLL, EDNA, and MARY J. NELSON, *Rhythms Today.* Morristown, N.J.: Silver Burdett Co., 1965.

Handy Play Party Book. Order from World Around Songs, Route 5, Burnsville, N.C. 28714

HSUS, GRACE, "Movement and Dance are Children's Play," *Music Educators Journal,* May 1981, 42–43.

JONES, BESSIE, and BESS LOMAX HAWES, *Step-it-Down.* New York: Harper & Row, 1972. Games, plays, songs, and stories from the Afro-American heritage.

KENNEY, MAUREEN, *Circle Around the Zero* (1974). Play chants and singing games of city children. Order from 63 E. Clinton St., New Bedford, Mass. 02740.

METHODIST CHURCH PUBLISHING HOUSE, *World of Fun Folk Dances* and *New World of Fun.* Nashville, Tenn., 407 Church Street.

PALMER, HAP, *Hap Palmer Favorites.* Sherman Oaks, Calif.: Alfred Publishing Company. Songs for early children learning through music and movement.

STECHER, MIRIAM B., HUGH MCEKHENY, and MARION GREENWOOD, *Music and Movement Improvisations,* Threshold Early Learning Library, vol. 4. New York: The Macmillan Co., 1972.

WUYTACK, JOS, and TOSSI AARON, *Play Sing Dance,* American play parties for voices, recorders, Orff instruments, with dance instructions. Paris: Alphonse Leduc, 1972.

For Hawaiian dances, refer to *Comprehensive Musicianship* textbook Zone 111-A.

Helpful recordings include RCA's *Festival of Folk Dance* and *The World of Folk Dance,* Bowmar's *Folk Dances* and *Singing Square Dances,* and Folkways Records' *American Square Dance Music.* Good marches include "March from *King David,*" Vanguard VR 6-1090; "Stars and Stripes Forever," BOL 54, AM IV-2; "March from *Aida,*" BOL 61; and "March from *The Love for Three Oranges,*" BOL 54.

Reading Music CURATILO, JOSEPH S, RICHARD C. BERG, and MARJORIE FARMER, *The Sight and Sound of Music.* Delaware Water Gap, Penn.: Shawnee Press. A program to develop sight-reading skills beginning in grades 2–4. Includes books, cassette tapes, transparencies and spirit masters.

DANIEL, KATINKA, *The Kodály Approach: Book 3.* Belmont, Calif.: Fearon-Pitman Pub.

ELLIOTT, CHARLES A. "The Music-Reading Dilemma," *Music Educators Journal,* February 1982, 33–34, 59.

Music Educators Journal, "Sound Before Sight: Strategies for Teaching Music Reading." April 1980, 53–55, 65–67.

RICHARDS, MARY HELEN, *Threshold to Music:* Experience charts for the first year. Teachers text/manual *The First Three Years.* Belmont, Calif.: Fearon Publishers, 1964. Also see revised edition by Eleanor Kidd (1974).

TEMPORAL ACUITY PRODUCTS, Inc., Belleview, Wash. *TapMaster Rhythmic Sight Reading System.* Elementary Series K–4; Intermediate Series 4 through college. Cassette tapes and book.

Sources of Materials Bowmar Records, Belwin Mills Corp., Melville, N.Y. 11747. See catalog for recordings for rhythmic responses, singing games, folk and ethnic dances. Also march and dance music in the *Bowmar Orchestral Library.*

Capitol Records, 1750 N. Vine St., Hollywood, Calif. 90028. See the Capitol and Angel Records Educational Catalog.

Children's Book & Music Center, 2500 Santa Monica Blvd., Santa Monica, Calif. 90404. See the helpful catalog of tested materials.

Children's Record Guild and Young People's Records, Franson Corporation, Distributors, 225 Park Ave. South, New York, N.Y. 10003. Recordings for children ages 2–10.

Educational Activities, Inc., 1937 Grand Ave., Baldwin, N.Y. 11510. Catalog available.

Folkways Records, 43 W. 61st St., New York, N.Y. 10023. Rhythmic recordings including those of Ella Jenkins. Also a source of ethnic recordings; see catalog.

Lyons, 530 Riverview Ave., Industrial Park, Elkhart, Ind. 46514. A comprehensive catalog. Distributor of *Listen, Move, Dance,* Vols. 1, 2, for movement and electronic sounds.

Methodist Church Publishing House, 407 Church St., Nashville, Tenn. Source of *World of Fun Folk Dances* and *New World of Fun.*

RCA Victor *Dance-A-Story* Records (storybook-record), Ginn and Company, Boston, Mass. 02117; Ginn and Company, 35 Mobile Drive, Toronto, Canada

RCA Music Service, Education Dept. A., 1133 Ave. of the Americas, New York, N.Y. 10036.

Temporal Acuity Products, Inc., 1535 121st Ave. S.E., Belleview, Wash. 98005. *Tap-Master Rhythmic Sight Reading System* with integrated hardware and software. Elementary through professional levels.

Films, Filmstrips, Cassette Tapes

Creative Audio-Visuals, 12000 Edgewater Drive, Cleveland, Ohio 44107. Filmstrips, cassette tapes, self-correcting sheets, and books.

Dance Your Own Way, UCLA Educational Film Sales Department; also from Dance Films, Inc.

Discovering Rhythm, United World Films, Universal Education and Visual Arts, 221 Park Ave. South, New York, N.Y. 10003. Concepts in rhythm for children from preschool to seven years.

Hello, I'm Music: EMC Corporation, 180 E. 6th St., St. Paul, Minn. 55101. Six color filmstrips, six records or three cassettes, 240 worksheets and a teacher's guide. Melody, rhythm, harmony, form, and tone color are presented to children.

Let's Begin With the Beat, EMC Corporation, St. Paul, Minn. 55106. A sound-filmstrip.

Pantomimes, Brandon Films, New York, N.Y. 10019. How the body communicates ideas.

Reading Music: No. 2 Finding the Rhythm, Coronet Films, 65 E. S. Water Street, Chicago, Ill. 60601.

What is Rhythm? and *Discovering Dynamics in Music,* BFA Educational Media, 2211 Michigan Avenue, Santa Monica, Calif. 90404.

The American Music Conference, 1000 Skokie Blvd., Wilmette, Ill. 60091, publishes a list of recommended films.

Recordings for Specific Concepts

TEMPO, FAST
Corelli: "Badinerie" from *Suite for Strings,* BOL 63
Kabalevsky: "Intermezzo" from *The Comedians,* BOL 53
Rossini-Respighi: "Tarantella" from *The Fantastic Toy Shop,* AM 3 v 2

TEMPO, SLOW
Ravel: "Pavanne of the Sleeping Beauty" from *Mother Goose* Suite, BOL 57
Corelli: "Sarabande" from *Suite for Strings,* BOL 63

FAST AND SLOW
Slow Joe, Franson YPR 9003 (ages 6–10)

ACCELERANDO
Grieg: "In the Hall of the Mountain King" from *Peer Gynt* Suite, AM 3 v 2; BOL 59

ACCENT
Prokofiev: "Departure" from *Winter Holiday,* AM 2

Rossini-Respighi: "Can Can" from *The Fantastic Toyshop,* AM 2 v 1

Herbert: "Dagger Dance" from *Natoma,* AM 3

PERCUSSION
Strike Up the Band, Franson CRG 5027 (ages 5–8) Children can play a game to identify percussion instruments. The order on the recording is drum, cymbal, wood block, jingle bells, sticks, triangle, tambourine

BEAT (PULSE)
Gounod: "Waltz" from *Faust Ballet* Suite, AM 3 v 1

Herbert: "Dagger Dance" from *Natoma,* AM 3 v 1

Dvořák: Slavonic Dance No. 7, AM 4 v 2

   and various marches

FERMATA, RITARD, ACCELERANDO
These interrupt the regular beat.

Brahms: Hungarian Dance No. 5, BOL 55

Shostakovich: "Petite Ballerina" from *Ballet Suite No. 1,* AM 2 v 1

METER
Game: Select recordings that are clear examples of specific meters. Play these, asking the children to identify the meter they hear. One way to help them solve the problem is to tell them to make the hand and arm go *down* on the strong accent of the first beat of the measure, then raise the arm slightly for each of the intervening beats until the next strong downbeat comes. They should count the downbeat as "one," and continue to count the intervening beats. The last number before the next downbeat tells the listeners the number of beats in the measure. From this they may be able to determine the meter (time signature).

Sousa: *Stars and Stripes Forever,* AM 4 v 2 (2/4 meter)

Bach: "Gigue" from Suite No. 4 AM 1 v 1 (two beats, 6/8 meter)

Delibes: "Waltz of the Doll" from *Copelia,* AM 1 v 1 (3/4 meter)

Ippolitov-Ivanov: "Cortege of the Sardar" from *Caucasian Sketches,* BOL 54 (four beats, 4/4 meter)

Offenbach: "Barcarolle" from *Tales of Hoffman,* AM 3 v 2 (6/8 meter)

CHANGES IN METER
Cailliet: *Pop Goes the Weasel* (variations) AM 4 v 2 (6/8, 3/4, 4/8, 3/4, 2/4)

Copland: "Street in a Frontier Town" from *Billy the Kid,* AM 6 v 1

Piston: "Tango of the Merchant's Daughter" from *The Incredible Flutist* (5/8), Mercury 90423

LESS COMMON METERS
Ginastera: "Wheat Dance" from *Estancia,* AM 4 v 2

Copland: "Hoe-Down" from *Rodeo,* AM 5 v 2

Guarnieri: *Brazilian Dance,* AM 6 v 2

Brubeck: *Time Out,* Columbia CL 1397

Brubeck: *Time Farther Out,* Columbia CL 1690 (7/8)

POLYRHYTHMS

Copland: "Street in a Frontier Town" from *Billy the Kid,* AM 6 v 1

See *The Study of Music in the Elementary School: A Conceptual Approach,* Charles L. Gary, ed. (Music Educators National Conference, Washington, D.C., 1967), pp. 47–50

See *Source Book of African and Afro-American Materials for Music Educators* (Music Educators National Conference, Washington, D.C., 1972) for two beats against three, p. 34.

RHYTHM PATTERNS

Bartók: "Bear Dance" from *Hungarian Sketches,* AM 3 v 2

Cui: *Orientale*

Tchaikovsky: "Fourth Movement" from Symphony No. 4

Beethoven: "Second Movement" from Symphony No. 8

Ibert: "The Little White Donkey" from *Histories No. 2,* AM 2

Bizet: "Habañera" from *Carmen,* BOL 56

Milhaud: "Copacabana" from *Saudades do Brazil,* AM 4 v 2 (ask children to find and identify the four major patterns used by the composer)

BOLERO PATTERN

Ravel: *Bolero*

BEGUINE PATTERN

Porter: *Begin the Beguine*

HABAÑERA PATTERN

Bizet: "Habañera" from *Carmen*

Gottschalk: "Grand Walkaround" from *Cakewalk,* AM 5 v 1

Benjamin: *Jamaican Rhumba,* BOL 56

SYNCOPATION

Gottschalk: "Grand Walkaround" from *Cakewalk,* AM 5 v 1

Debussy: "Golliwog's Cakewalk" from *Children's Corner* Suite, BOL 63

Copland: "Hoe-Down" from *Rodeo,* AM 5 v 2; BOL 55

Chabrier: *España,* AM 5 v 1 (also for study of the beat)

3

Singing, Harmonizing, and Playing Pitched Instruments

chapter fourteen

Singing and Melody

In the preceding pages it was stated that there are relationships between body movement in response to music and learning concepts of pitch and melody. By means of movement the learner can improve his or her ability to listen to music and to grasp tonal and other relationships. From this foundation the teacher assists children to hear pitch accurately and to reproduce vocally what they hear, to sing with understanding, and to use their singing voices for self-expression in daily living.

Research Studies on children who have difficulty in singing pitch accurately have led to the following conclusions:

Many more boys than girls experience this difficulty.

Singing the "oo" vowel is useful in learning to sing.

About 18 percent of the students may be uncertain singers.

Intervals larger than adjacent scale tones, at least that of a minor third, are easier for children to sing.

At least part of the difficulty comes from poor vocal control.

Out-of-tune singing may be a symptom of more inclusive learning problems.

An opinion survey included as part of a research project by A. Oren Gould estimates children who teachers classify as "nonsingers" to be 50 percent in first grade with a steady reduction to 5 percent in the sixth grade. The percentage of children that teachers classified as "problem singers" was 36.6 percent in the first grade with a gradual reduction to 11 percent in the sixth grade. This study claims to have established two basic principles of learning to sing: (1) the child must *learn to hear his or her own voice* in speaking and singing and to control high and low pitch levels with it, and (2) the child must experience unison with another voice or instrument and *learn the sound and feeling of his or her voice as it matches the pitches heard*. Both visual and tonal associations are needed to develop concepts of high and low in speaking and singing. Recommended activities include speech-to-song activities; repeated patterns in play or game songs such as found in echo songs, songs about animals, and roll call songs, use of humming and neutral syllables, body movements of many types which dramatize pitch and tonal direction, and mechanical devices such as bells and piano keyboard to hear and visualize pitch changes. The survey revealed "a certain amount of consensus" in the following:

1. All children can be helped to participate to some extent in singing activities with enjoyment and success.
2. Inability to sing a prescribed pitch does not prove that the child cannot hear pitch differences; it may mean only that he or she has not yet learned "what it feels like" to use his or her voice in unison with another.
3. The most common vocal problem is that of the low speaking voice coupled with the child's inability to sing comfortably at the higher pitch the teacher prescribes for the class.
4. Many of the children's psychological inhibitions toward singing can be traced to attitudes and remarks of parents and teachers.
5. Remedial measures in the group are more easily employed during kindergarten through grade three; in later grade levels more individual attention is necessary.

A study by Dr. Robert B. Smith at the University of Illinois, *The Effect of Group Nursery School Music Training on Later Achievement and Interest in Music: A Ten Year Progress Report,* found that in general the children sang lower pitches more easily than high pitches—"low" meaning the range from middle C up to A, and "high" meaning the range from G above middle C to D, a fifth higher. Furthermore, girls were more advanced than boys, as a group, at all grade levels. However, the experimental group boys appeared to close the gap at the fifth grade level. Tentative conclusions in the ninth year of the study included:

1. Lower tones should be used in those songs selected for younger children. (The control group boys found relatively good pitch accuracy only in the range of low B♭ to first space F.)
2. It is possible that songs emphasizing the upper range pitches should not be a major part of the song repertoire until the intermediate grades. (All boys were improving at the fifth-grade level.)
3. Teachers should be conscious of sex differences as they plan singing programs for young children. Boys are usually slow beginners and make less progress than girls in the early years. It was indicated that boys can "catch up" to the

girls in pitch accuracy at about the fifth grade level if vocal ranges appropriate for them are used.

The Child Voice

The child voice is often described as light in quality as well as in volume. It is also an extremely flexible mechanism, as illustrated by the strident cries of the playground. The teacher, then, is confronted by a voice that is capable of expressing many moods in song. Since there are many moods to express, this child voice can be sweetly soft and ethereal as it sings "Lullaby and goodnight" and can be momentarily harsh as it sings "David *killed* Goliath!" A logical way of deciding upon the voice quality desired in any song is for the teacher and children to discuss what manner of voice should be used to express the meaning of the words properly and to evaluate this continually when they sing. Although the child voice is light in quality, it should not sound weak or overly soft.

Many of the problems related to singing are soon solved when one adds to the above idea the following:

1. To make a generally pleasing sound (simple, natural, and clear).
2. To sing in a manner that avoids strain and tenseness.
3. To take breaths where one does when speaking the words (usually as the punctuation indicates); do not interrupt the phrase by breathing in unnatural places.
4. To enunciate clearly, but pronounce r's as some Southerners do [ah(r)], and sound final consonants distinctly and in unison.

Voice Range and Production

Classroom teachers insisted for years that songs in the older books demanded too high a range for many voices. As the years passed, these teachers observed a gradual lowering of the ranges in later books. However, individual voices vary greatly in range, particularly in the ability to sing high pitches. A minority of children can sing well above the top line of the staff, but in *group* singing this line is the upper limit for most classrooms. Three-year-olds generally sing in a range of three to five notes; four-year-olds sing in a range of five to six notes; five-year-olds can expand this to an octave. Because most preschool children sing within the following range, it follows that it will be useful *at the beginning* of the first grade for group singing.

The range within which most songs in series books are written is the following:

This range seems to be a basic one; it suits most adult voices well, and is also the playing range of many of the small wind instruments. The one that most children are able to sing by the sixth grade follows. However, some of the boys cannot sing as high if their voices are in the first stage of change.

Ranges children can sing successfully and which include those of many "problem singers" are:

There should be no hesitancy on the part of teachers to use these ranges for all of the children *some* of the time. It is obvious that there are different ranges for different age groups and for boys and girls at some levels. However, all children, even in kindergarten and first grade, should be encouraged to use all of their comfortable range, especially that of middle C to fourth line D.

Teachers often search for songs of limited range with which to initiate easy singing experiences. Examples follow:

3-note range:	Hot Cross Buns	Trampin' (refrain)
	Merrily We Roll Along	Fais do do (Go To Sleep)
	Good News (refrain)	(first part)
4-note range:	Sally Go Round the Sun	A-Hunting We Will Go (one
	Hokey Pokey	version)
5-note range:	Go Tell Aunt Rhody	Whistle, Daughter, Whistle
	Cradle Song (Rousseau)	Grandma Grunts
	Lightly Row	Old Woman (some versions)
	Sleep, Baby, Sleep	When the Saints Go
	Mary Had a Little Lamb	Marching In
	Oats, Peas, Beans, and Barley	Jingle Bells (refrain)
	Flowing River	Hey, Lidee
	Green Gravel	Love Somebody
6-note range:	This Old Man	Caisson Song
	Baa Baa Black Sheep	Jolly Old St. Nicholas
	Old MacDonald	Up On the Housetop
	London Bridge	Au Clair de la Lune
	Lovely Evening	Susy, Little Susy
	Hey, Betty Martin	The Mocking Bird
	Skip To My Lou	Tom Dooley
	Goodbye, My Lover, Good-	Twinkle, Twinkle, Little Star
	bye	Old Paint
	O Susanna	Michael, Row the Boat
	Old Brass Wagon	Ashore

Pop! Goes the Weasel	Cindy
Hickory Dickory Dock	Kum Bah Yah
Looby Lou	Bluebird

When a textbook presents a song in a particular key, the writers have selected that key with the vocal range in mind. While it is indicative of a proper range for children's voices, there are considerations that lead teachers to change this range. Most of the songs in recent books are pitched in an easy, fairly low range. Therefore, after a song has been learned, the teacher should pitch it and other songs gradually higher, by half-steps, until teacher and children have extended their range into that considered normal for voices that have had help in developing the range to its natural span. Other songs will be printed in keys that demand a high range. Should a class be as yet unable to reach this range, the teacher will pitch these songs somewhat lower—usually not more than two whole steps at the most—then gradually pitch them higher as the singing range of the children improves. In today's music fundamentals classes for classroom teachers, simple transposition of the key by building the tonic chord (1-3-5) on the new keynote on bells or piano or singing it from a note sounded on a pitchpipe is commonly taught. Teachers need to be able to change the key of a song when the stage of development of the children's voice range makes this advisable.

The matter of correct pitching of songs becomes more complex in the sixth grade, where some of the boys may be in the first stage of voice change. The full range of these voices will normally fall approximately a fourth; thus a well-developed range of B♭ below middle C up to top line F will drop to a range of from F on the bass staff extending up to an octave above middle C.

Since the highest and lowest pitches of any range are somewhat more difficult to sing than the middle pitches, teachers select music that does not stress these extremes. The implications of this are two: first, that many of the melodies in sixth-grade song books cannot be sung by boys in the range in which they are written, and second, that part-singing thus becomes a necessity. To sustain interest in singing, the teacher plans vocal parts boys can sing easily in their range and takes special care to provide for this type of individual difference. Low harmony parts and chord root parts are helpful in this instance.

A successful music specialist declares that the natural range of the voice—both the children's and the classroom teacher's—is fairly high when properly developed, and that normal voices should be able to sing the F on the top line of the staff with ease. She states that vocal range is largely a matter of correct breathing, breath support, and voice production. In her intermediate grade classes, the children enjoy standing, then bending deeply with arms hanging limply, taking breaths—inhaling and exhaling—while noting the fact that the diaphragm, not the chest, is primarily involved in breathing. Then, remembering to breathe with the diaphragm, they stand erect, closed fists held near the shoulders with arm muscles taut, inhale, then pretend to "chew" the air while slowly exhaling at the teacher's signal. At other times, instead of "chewing" air, they place the index finger of the right hand on the lips and slowly and steadily exhale against the finger. These and other exercises, such as holding a piece of thin paper against a wall with the breath for gradually longer periods of time, are done to develop breath control. The teacher's approach appeals to the boys, for she emphasizes that they should take part in sports and in physical development to acquire the muscles they need in order to sing! There is truth in this, and the trained vocalist will not use the word "relax" that is employed in this chapter, but substitute "flexibility" instead, a word having somewhat different connotations.

To extend the range further, this teacher has the students vocalize up and down the first five tones of the major scale with vowels such as "ah," "oh," and "oo," one half step higher each time, as one hears adult vocalists practice. When the higher range is reached, the children are instructed to relax their faces to look as if they "had no sense at all," with the jaw held naturally and loose. The teacher takes special care not to injure voices by vocalizing them too high or too low, and can tell by the facial expression when the children attempt pitches beyond their range at a given stage in vocal development. In this way, the teacher extends the vocal range of her students to one believed suitable by the vocally trained.

A problem of some classroom teachers is that they have not learned to use their singing voices properly, and therefore hesitate to sing pitches they consider high. Many have used only a chest voice which they try to force upward in an attempt to sing high pitches. They need to learn how to sing in their high voice. Usually when these teachers try singing high pitches softly in what can be termed a "half-voice" (i.e., it feels as though one is using only half the usual voice; it is the head voice without the chest voice), they find that they can soon sing in a high voice that is very comparable to the child voice, and that eventually they will sing the high pitches with ease.

The teacher needs a clear, natural voice. Children are attracted by singing that sounds natural and normal. The male teacher's voice is no longer as rare as it once was in elementary school music. Most children are well-oriented to listening to and singing with this octave-lower voice on recordings, television, and radio as well as at home with their fathers. Once in a while a child will be confused by it and try to match its pitch. When this occurs, the male teacher should explain that his voice changed, and that he cannot sing as high as the children. He should play the song on an instrument that gives proper pitch, have a child who knows the song sing it, or sing falsetto. In instances where teachers believe they cannot sing well enough to use their singing voices in teaching music, they can employ substitutions such as recordings, musical instruments, and children who sing well.

The following are physical requirements for good singing:

1. *Posture.* Place feet on the floor with the weight of the body somewhat forward, not on the back of the chair. Sit up straight, but not in a stiff or tense way. If standing, place the weight of the body toward the toes, not on the heels.
2. *Breathing.* Fill the abdominal region with air first (i.e., breathe "low," not high in the chest). This is the kind of breathing we do when lying flat on the floor or flat in bed. The goal in breathing is a controlled, continuous flow of breath. A husky or breathy sound indicates wasted breath.
3. *Open Throat.* Use the open, relaxed throat one has when about to yawn. Sing with the mouth open wide, but not so wide that it causes tension. Use "oo" and "ah" to relax the throat.
4. *Good Enunciation.* Open the mouth and use lips *generously* in pronouncing words. Be sure to pronounce final consonants distinctly.

Poor results often come from singing too loudly, singing too softly, not opening the mouth sufficiently, a slouching posture, a stiff and tense posture, a lack of interest, an unhealthy room temperature, and failure of the teacher to let the children comprehend the pitch and harmonic background of a song before asking them to sing it. The above physical requirements for good singing presume that children are seated on chairs most of the time, rather than on a rug, because of the effect of posture on the proper use of lungs and diaphragm. Standing is also good.

Pitch Discrimination and Learning to Sing

To adults who learned about high and low long ago, these concepts which are vital to listening and singing appear to be extremely simple. Yet, some seven-year-olds will confuse them. Young children often confuse *high* with *loud* and *fast* and *low* with *soft* and *slow.* When adults analyze this they find that high and low in pitch are abstractions; the association of high and low pitch with high and low physical levels is artificial, however necessary for understanding. To make these experiences concrete for children it is essential that they be made "real" in terms of high and low physical position both with the body and with objects, in pictures, and by relating to things in the child's world such as airplanes, trees, and stars (high), floor, rug, and grass (low). Step bells and ordinary bells held on end with the large bars down can relate high in pitch with the high bars and low in pitch with the low bars; this is effective because bells serve as audiovisual aids. Teachers employ songs in the kindergarten which children dramatize and later relate by discussion to high and low. One of them is "Red Birds Flying."

RED BIRDS FLYING

Red birds fly - ing,   red birds fly - ing,   Now they stop   on the ground.

Children are taught to play little action games in first grade such as:

The above example relates high and low to widely spaced pitches illustrating these words and dramatizing them in terms of physical movement. The following example is relatively more complex:

Many simple examples of song material useful in teaching these basic concepts are to be found in books on the kindergarten and first-grade levels. However, teachers can improvise their own songs for this purpose.

Acting out the melody line of songs in terms of pitch levels is a device that aids people of all ages to be more conscious of differences in pitch. The hand is used with a generous motion to move up, down, or to stay the same according to differences in pitch. When children are guided to respond in this manner their concepts of pitch relationships often improve to a remarkable degree. In the above example the hand would move vertically as follows to reflect the melodic contour:

Clouds are up high   *Raindrops fall down.*

The fact that at a certain stage of development a child does not sing in tune in no way proves lack of being musical. Instances can be cited to illustrate that it is possible for an out-of-tune singer to be an excellent musician. Among examples known to the authors are the concert master of a symphony orchestra and an eight-year-old pianist who played Bach with understanding, composed music of some quality, and who was an opera enthusiast. There is also the story of the secondary school music specialist who assumed that the superintendent could not hear how his music groups sounded because the man could not match tones. The specialist was wrong; the superintendent listened to them with critical judgment. Apparently these people never learned to relate their vocal mechanisms to what their ears heard; they did not know how this felt. Other reasons for people being unable to match tones with their singing voices are said to be general immaturity, a deprived musical environment, psychological blocks imposed by adults who tell them they cannot sing, lack of interest, failure to try as a result of fear, boredom, or of deprived background, and physical abnormalities which require attention of physicians. At another stage of musical development the child is something of a borderline case. If the teacher establishes a favorable environment, the child can sing in tune. However, if the teacher does not establish the pitch, if there is an accompaniment that confuses, or if the psychological situation is one in which muscles become tense, the child will probably fail to match tones.

In theory, inability to sing in tune should disappear during the elementary school years if children are given consistent help. There are skilled music specialists who insist that there should be no out-of-tune singers by the end of the second grade. However, in today's schools there are often a few students in each of the upper grades who cannot match tones well. Teachers should be ready to assist these students toward pleasurable and accurate singing at whatever level they find them. A few may not find their singing voices, or cannot control pitches accurately, until they are in high school. Teachers sustain the musical interest of such students through a program of varied activities—rhythmic responses, playing instruments, creating music, reading about music and musicians, and continuing to try to sing. There should be three major points of emphasis in helping them: they should participate in music activities that are happy, interesting, challenging, and successful; they should have many experiences in which they listen carefully to pitches and to pitch differences; and because they learn by singing, they should be encouraged to try.

During some stages of development, children do not sense the pitch of their own voices and often sing loudly (and happily) off key. There arise the following problems: (1) how to help them to listen, (2) how to keep these voices from hindering other children who are trying to keep on pitch, (3) how to help them to make as real a contribution to the group as the children who sing well, and (4) in the upper grades, how to help them with their errors in such a way that they are encouraged to try and remain confident of eventual success.

For young children who have not yet learned how to sing, the chanting of old rhymes such as "Humpty Dumpty," "Mary, Mary Quite Contrary" and "Rub-a-Dub-Dub, Three Men in a Tub" can be helpful. Children like the *feel* of rhythmic or repetitious words; they enjoy saying them together. If the teacher will establish the pitch of a low note such as middle C and help them *chant* the words on that pitch, a beginning can be made in singing one-pitch songs.

Many of the children who cannot match tones try to sing with the same voice they use when they speak. Therefore, it is the task of the teacher to help such children find their "high" or singing voices. This may be done in a game situation. A favorite device is to have children pretend to be the wind, a bird, or a siren. Children often sense pitch differences more keenly through actions such as the teacher's lifting a child's hand up high, or the children's starting from a squatting position (low) and moving to a standing position (high). Another popular device is to have a child pretend to call someone who is far away. When this is done, a sustained speech results—and when speech is thus sustained (vowel held) singing takes place.

When a child sings, but sings low and does not match the anticipated pitch, the teacher and class should *match the child's pitch* and sing the song in that key. This will often begin a procedure that brings success with the gradual raising of the pitch by singing the song in successively higher keys over a period of time.

The term "tone-matching" is not intended to convey emphasis upon an isolated drill technique. It is the authors' intention that it be thought of as "songs and games" for helping uncertain singers. Such a song or game may be sung by a class and a child may be selected to sing a part at the correct time. The part will sound at the right time because the teacher will sing with the child in case of faltering. Little or no attempt is made to correct faulty pitch while the song is being sung. It takes patience and faith on the part of a teacher to wait weeks and months for some children to sing correctly.

A commonly used device for listening and tone-matching is the calling of the roll in song and having each child answer on the same pitches. If someone is absent, the entire class responds by singing "absent," thus adding variety to this game. The teacher varies the pitch of these conversations-in-song, singing to each child in the range in which success will be most likely. Later, the purpose of the teacher will vary according to the progress of each child, and for some will be working to extend the range of already successful singers. Some successful singers may begin to improvise answers on pitches other than those the teacher sings; little question-and-answer tunes are created in this manner.

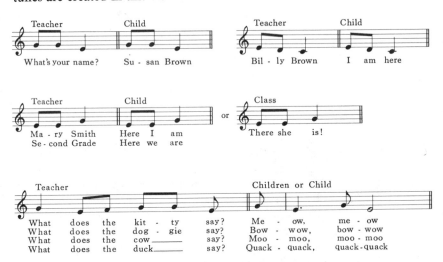

Another well-known tone-matching game is one in which the teacher places various objects in the hands of the children, who may be told to put their heads down on their desks and close their eyes. The game is played by the teacher singing, "Who has the _____?" and the child who possesses the object sitting up and singing, "I have the _____." An additional listening experience is to ask the class to identify an unseen child by the sound of the singing voice.

Teacher					Child				
Who	has	the	pen	- cil?	I	have	the	pen	- cil
Who	has	the	pen	- ny?	I	have	the	pen	- ny
Who	has	the	thim	- ble?	I	have	the	thim	- ble

After learning to play this type of game, the teacher can sing questions such as, "What did you do last Sunday?" and "What did you have for breakfast?" and the child can create an answer with rhythmic and melodic variety. When a child has difficulty in matching tones with the teacher in any of these tone games, matching tones to another child's singing may do the trick. It is not wise to remain working with any one child too long in any of these procedures. To do so would make the other children restless because the progress of the game would be stopped, and it would unduly draw the child's attention to a relative lack of success. This refers to primary grades. A further aid to listening is the suggestion that the children "tune in" their voices just as they tune in radio stations. This is a concept children can understand because they know that the dial must be in exactly the right place for the station to "come in" properly. Another suggestion is to sing a familiar grouping of tones (or even a single pitch) for the children while they listen. Then ask them to listen with their "inner ears" while this is repeated for them. Next, ask the children to sing it. Finally, ask them if they sang exactly what they heard. Some of the children who cannot yet match tones will know that they have not sung what they heard. This process when repeated over weeks and months has notably improved the ability to listen and to match tones, especially when the teacher plans so that part of the class listens to and evaluates the singing of groups within the class, thus involving every child in the room with either singing or listening. Spontaneous tone games such as creating a "song" from children's words—i.e., "Johnny has a hair cut,"—and having children sing these words or additional words of their own in turn can sometimes help.

Picking out melodies or parts of melodies on the bells, xylophone, or piano can be a listening experience of value. These instruments can be used with songs that contain tones or tone patterns which are both played and sung. Listening for the proper time to play the instrument, and being sure the correct piches have been sounded constitute a good listening experience in a situation of challenge and interest, and it helps build the background that leads to eventual singing on pitch.

There are certain tonal groups that are particularly easy for children to sing. It follows that if the teacher selects songs that contain these tonal groups, especially if they are repeated in the songs, and if these songs are pitched in easy singing range, there should result more than average success in group singing:

Among these are:

1. Minor third   2. Children's play song   3. 3-2-1   4. Fourth

so   mi   so   mi la so   mi   mi   re   do   mi   la

5. Songs based on pentatonic scale tones (1-2-3-5-6 of the major scale)

so   mi   la   so   mi   re   do   mi

Number 1 is the easiest interval for children to sing; it is the descending minor third (5–3 or 1–6₁). Number 2 is an extension of number 1; it is sung by children all over the world in their natural, undirected play. Number 3, a descending series of three tones in whole-step arrangement, and Number 4, the ascending fourth, are easy to sing. Number 4 is often found in 5–8 position in major scales. Number 5, a pentatonic mode, is an important aspect of music children create spontaneously; songs based on it are easy to sing because no half-steps are involved. "This Old Man" and "The Caisson Song" emphasize the minor third. "Three Blind Mice" and "Mary Had a Little Lamb" stress the 3–2–1 note group, with the ascending fourth also stressed in "Three Blind Mice." The popularity of many songs can be traced to their utilization of these easily sung tonal groups. It follows that if easy-to-sing songs are pitched in easy-to-sing keys, they can speed the progress of children in becoming more skilled in tone-matching, which is hearing what is sounded, and reproducing this with the voice.

At times it is impossible to prevent the voices of out-of-tuners from hindering to some extent the progress of those children who are farther advanced in singing skills. A decision that is only of temporary value is to select out-of-tuners to make such contributions as the "zz" of a bee, the "tick tock" of a clock, the "ding dong" and other sound effects instead of singing. Since faulty singers learn to sing by singing, this device is no solution to their problem. Furthermore it would be unwise to make any obvious division of a class into singers and those who do something else. Careful listening is essential, but listening and never singing will not produce singers. Out-of-tuners should have many opportunities to listen to good examples of singing. These include the use of small groups or solo singers as examples to be listened to and constructively evaluated, and the inclusion of some good singers with the out-of-tuners when such temporary groupings are made. When out-of-tuners respond rhythmically to music, when they play the Autoharp, bells, and percussion instruments, and when they offer ideas for interpretation, dramatization and experimentation, they are making real contributions to group music even though they do not yet sing well. Teachers should give them full credit for what they contribute so that they feel they are first-class members of the group.

The traditional seating arrangement for music classes was dictated by concern for the out-of-tuners. They were seated in a group in front of the room, with the good singing voices of other children behind them and with the good singing voice of the teacher in front of them. It was supposed that this seating arrangement, which gave them correct pitches from both behind and in front, was of aid to them. Its disadvantage seems to have been that the obvious segregation of the out-of-tuners was a greater psychological block than the seating was an aid. It has been largely abandoned today. If children are seated in this manner, such seating is done in a way that presumably makes them unaware of its purpose. Actually, the increasing informality of seating in today's classrooms tends to make any rigid seating plans for music unlikely. The arrangement should permit the teacher to move freely among the class so as to listen to each singer.

In the intermediate grades a problem may be how to continue to help the out-of-tuners without discouraging them. One teacher begins each year with "making a joyful noise." The entire emphasis is upon the joyous participation of every child with no regard as to singing on pitch, although the teacher is learning and studying the capabilities and problems of each child during this time. As soon as the first objective is achieved, work begins in assisting every child to sing on pitch. The teacher walks among the children as they sing, giving help to those who need it. While the singing is in progress, Jimmy is told that he is singing lower than the song is sounding, to listen with more concentration, and perhaps to sit with his friend Billy and tell Billy to help him. All of this is done in good spirit, without setting anyone apart and always emphasizing to Jimmy that he is going to sing in tune soon—to keep on trying. Usually this teacher has eliminated out-of-tune singers by January.

Older children who cannot sing in tune know very well that they cannot, and they appreciate any help adults can give them as long as they are not embarrassed before their peers. Therefore, small group work apart from the class is desirable. A plan that has proved helpful is for the teacher to work with out-of-tuners in groups of two or four, with each child paired with another of like voice quality and range. With four, the teacher will place each child at a far corner of the room. The activity may begin with a story of children who have become separated in the woods or in the hills, and who are trying to find (call to) each other. One child is then asked to call in sustained speech (which is singing) to a partner across the room as though the partner were a city block distant. The call will ordinarily be sung in two pitches—the descending minor third pattern. The partner is to answer on the same pitches; this is the game. When this contact through tone matching has been established, they next begin singing other information back and forth, such as "Where are you?" "I'm over here," "Are you hungry?" and so on. The two children in the other corners of the room first listen to the pitches sung by the first two, then take their turn. Most of these children will find that they can hear the pitch given them in this way, and that they can answer it with surprising accuracy. After this introduction comes the repetition and extension of the singing back and forth, then eventually the singing of easy songs pitched in a range comfortable to the voices, and soon four more accurate singers have been added to classroom music.

Individual work with bells, including step bells, trying to match tones with the pitch of different metal bars in experimental fashion, can help. Time and relative privacy should be provided for such individual learning.

Time in which to practice hearing only one voice seems necessary as a prerequisite for group singing. That this has not already occurred may indicate a lack of singing in the home. The singing of a mother to her baby and to her young children is highly important in musical development. Music education begins at home, in the cradle.

When a problem singer can experiment over a period of time with singing into a tape recorder and playing back what was taped, the interest generated can result in ultimately singing on pitch. "The excitement from hearing one's voice on tape may lead the problem singer or reluctant singer to work diligently toward improvement of that sound, especially if the recording is made when alone or in a corner of the room, or even at home, with no one else to criticize or laugh. The child who never sings in person may proudly present the teacher with a recording revealing success." (*Meske, 1975*)

Some boys have psychological difficulty that stems from attempting to imitate their father's low voices and wanting to sound like men, not like their mothers, their female teachers, or girls. This can be overcome by explaining to the boys that their voices ordinarily change in grades seven through nine, and that shortly before the change begins, they will have better high voices than the girls, a soprano voice that signals the change to come. In fifth and sixth grades this is important to boys, and their understanding of this may determine whether they will use their still unchanged voices naturally or whether they will attempt to sing "down in their shoes." It is best to avoid using the adult terms "soprano" and "alto" and use instead "high" and "low." In three-part singing the parts are "high, middle, and low" rather than the terms descriptive of adult voices.

The Changing Voice

While soprano voices remain in the majority at ages eleven and twelve, the voices of some students become somewhat heavier in quality, reflecting the beginning of the changing voice. Some boys' voices will be breathy, with the upper range faltering while the lower range drops approximately the interval of a fourth, although there are many variations of this. The range in which most of these voices can sing is usually from F below middle C to G above. A few boys in the late thirteenth and fourteenth year will have baritone voices with a range of approximately the B♭ octave below middle C. Some will have wider ranges than these.

The teacher should take great care that music be provided that accommodates the range of every voice. Straining to reach high pitches must be avoided to prevent permanent voice damage, thus the teacher will write special parts for changing voices when printed music cannot supply the required ranges. Simple ostinato parts can help here.

There are few true alto voices among the girls, and most music for this age group is of a range that permits every girl experience in singing both parts. The quality of the speaking voice provides one clue to voice classification. (The alto part presents the best challenge for note reading in most music.) The boys' voices need to be classified into soprano, cambiata (changing), and baritone. Voice testing is best done quickly in the large group because individual testing can cause tension, embarrassment, and takes valuable time. The teacher listens for both range and quality to determine assignment of parts. Cooper and Kuersteiner (1972) present class voice testing in detail. Part of their suggested method is to have the boys sing "Jingle Bells" in D major in the range most comfortable for them. Those who choose to sing in the lower register are baritones. The remaining boys sing the song in A♭ major while the teacher listens to detect soprano voices. Those remaining are the cambiate (changing voices).

A publisher that specializes in music for the changing voice is Cambiata Press, P.O. Box 1151, Conway, Ark. 72032.

Establishing Pitch for Singing

One of the most common failings of teachers is that of not giving the children sufficient time in which to hear the beginning pitch of songs a class is reviewing. This is because the teacher will "hear with the inner ear" the song in its proper harmonic setting, but will forget that the children, or many of them, are not hearing this. Too often these teachers sound a pitch and start the singing long before children have had time to orient themselves to this pitch, its relation to the scale in which the song is to be sung, and the harmonic setting of the first tones of the melody. This failure to help the children sense the pitch fully places some of them at such a disadvantage that they are out-of-tune singers when they need not be. When reviewing a song with a class, the following procedure is recommended:

1. Sound the 1–3–5 (tonic) chord built from the keynote* of the song by means of the piano, the bells, or by singing it. Sound 1–3–5–3–1. This is to establish a feeling for the key, that is, a feeling for the home tone in relation to the scale. The playing of the chord sequence I–V$_7$–I on the piano or Autoharp does this excellently.
2. Sound at some length the keynote of the song. This should be sounded on an instrument such as the piano, bells, or pitch pipe.
3. Sing the keynote with the neutral syllable "loo."
4. Ask the children to sing this pitch, helping those who have difficulty. They can also sing 1–3–5–3–1 (and 1–5$_1$–1 if the range permits).
5. Sing or otherwise sound the first note of the song if it is a note other than the keynote.
6. Ask the children to sing it and help them to match it.
7. Set the tempo by counting, directing, or clapping the rhythm of the meter and saying "Sing!" or, in rhythm, "Ready, sing!" after which the singing begins on the beat following the instruction "sing." Another way is for the teacher to sing the first two or four measures of the song as an introduction and direct or say "Sing!" as stated above. Doing this establishes the tempo and spirit of the song.

Selecting Songs for Tone-Matching

The teacher must analyze the melodies of songs to determine whether or not they may be useful in "listen-then-sing" activities. There are songs with easily sung repeated-note patterns and phrases, songs with parts that can be echoed, songs with a limited range, songs with final measures that can be repeated to create aesthetically satisfying codas, question-and-answer songs,

* See pages 298–299 for how to find the keynote.

and dialogue songs. These permit the children to take turns in singing and in constructive critical listening to the singing of others.

Three song examples follow, the first two for primary level and the third for intermediate level. The third example, "When the Saints Go Marching In," has a tone pattern repeated twice in the original melody, and can be used in this form. However, it is printed here in a specially arranged form to repeat the pattern four times, and to add another repeated pattern near the end. It is an example of how teachers arrange songs to adapt them to tone matching. The song has a small range, and rhythm and spirit that children enjoy. The second group must listen carefully to the first group, and is challenged to echo the tone pattern perfectly. Other examples include "Old Texas," page 353, which is an echo-type song when sung as a canon, and "The Keeper," page 351. These and others are in many of the textbooks.

I HAVE A LITTLE BIRD

Peggy Burgess

Elementary Education Class
University of Oregon
Arr. R. E. N.

I have a lit - tle bird, who is well-known to you. He lives with - in a clock, and each hour he sings cuck - oo.

CODA
Class or Group — Teacher — Group — Child

Each hour he sings cuck - oo. Cuck - oo cuck - oo cuck - oo.

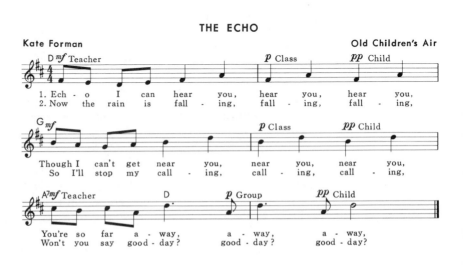

THE ECHO

Kate Forman

Old Children's Air

1. Ech - o I can hear you, hear you, hear you,
2. Now the rain is fall - ing, fall - ing, fall - ing,

Though I can't get near you, near you, near you,
So I'll stop my call - ing, call - ing, call - ing,

You're so far a - way, a - way, a - way,
Won't you say good - day? good - day? good - day?

WHEN THE SAINTS GO MARCHING IN

New Orleans Song
Arr. R. E. N.

Examples of other echo-type songs are:

"Are You Sleeping?
"By'm Bye"
"Barnyard Song"
"Sipping Cider Through a Straw"
"Three Blind Mice"
"Today is Monday"
"Who Did?"
"Bill Grogan's Goat"
"Every Night When the Sun Goes In"

(in *Singing With Children*)
"How Do You Do?"
"If I Ask You"
"Getting Acquainted"
"What Did You Do Last Summer?"
"John the Rabbit"
"The Sparrow's School" (Chichipapa)
"Follow On"
"Old Texas"

Examples of other repetitious songs are:

"Good-bye, Old Paint"
"Hot Cross Buns"
"Rain, Rain, Go Away"
"Old Woman's Courtship"
"Polly Wolly Doodle"
"Tideo"

(in *Singing With Children*)

"Angel Band"
"Clickety-Clack"
"Grandma Grunts"
"Hole in the Bucket"

"Tisket, a Tasket"	"Hush Little Baby"
"Trampin'"	"Whistle, Daughter, Whistle"

Tonal Memory   Tonal memory is necessary for the singer. Teachers can assist the development of tonal memory by such activities as:

1. Humming a familiar tune and asking the children to identify it; then asking children to hum it back to the teacher.
2. Arranging a signal whereby children stop singing during the performance of a familiar song, but continue to *think* the tune for a phrase or two. Then the teacher signals them to change from thinking the tune to singing it, and so on.
3. Playing a game in which children hum a tune for the class to identify.
4. Having the class sing songs with neutral syllables (*la, loo*) rather than the words so that the singers can concentrate on the melody.
5. Challenging the class to sing songs with numbers and/or syllables.
6. Challenging individual children to explore the black keys of the piano—to work alone to find the melodies of pentatonic tunes they know such as "Old MacDonald," "All Night, All Day," "Get On Board," "Auld Lang Syne," "Land of the Silver Birch," "The Campbells Are Coming," and "Swing Low, Sweet Chariot." They can also create and try to remember tunes of their own.
7. Asking children to notate parts of well-known tunes from memory when they are sufficiently advanced for this activity.

Zoltán Kodály (1882–1967)

Kodály, the distinguished Hungarian composer-educator, created a method for teaching music that is based upon the Hungarian language and authentic verse and folk music of that nation. It has become the national music education program of Hungary. The method includes a carefully sequenced curriculum with specific materials of instruction and activities. Stress is put on good singing and music literacy—the ability to read music fluently. When adapted for use in other countries, the language and authentic folk songs of each particular nation provides the foundations of the method.

Techniques from the method became known in the United States before the method as a whole, in part due to the adaptation made by Mary Helen Richards in her *Threshold to Music* charts (Fearon-Pittman Publishers). Teachers were attracted to the prenotation symbols, such as drawings of objects and note stems without heads, then to the transition to notation in a setting that made learning music more of a game. The apparently successful use of Latin syllables and Curwen hand signs led to a renewed interest in those devices in many American schools. Kodály's manner of compiling his method is a good example for music teachers. He first established his objectives, then felt free to borrow, seek, and create the means to gain them. In this sense he was eclectic in his approach.

The following description is of the Kodály program for music in early childhood and first grade. Rhymes and children's game songs are selected for specific purposes; body movement is an important means for learning music, including aspects of form; conforming to the regular beat is emphasized; songs are selected with the pitch configuration to be learned, such as *so-mi, mi-re-do, so-la-mi, so-mi-re-do, do-la-so, mi-re-do-la;* inner hearing (thinking pitches silently) is stressed; game songs merge into simple dance; learning is based on games and songs; the sequence is held to quite rigidly in order for the proper foundation of musical knowledge to be built; generally, no instrumental accompaniments are used in singing; live musical performance is preferred to listening to recordings; daily singing is recommended; teachers may add songs and listening experiences to the established curriculum; and songs within a range of a sixth are standard fare.

The program through the elementary and middle school years has a balance of singing, listening, playing, moving, thinking, and creating. The method has been called "The Kodály Choral Method." When applied to the children's chorus, there have been exceedingly successful results in choral performance in this country that equal those in Europe. Kodály composed excellent music and exercises for children to sing. The current music textbooks contain applications of the Kodály method, as they do Orff-Schulwerke. (See textbook indexes.) American adaptations differ from the Hungarian in song material, rhythm patterns (from English speech), rhymes and folklore, and technical aspects such as learning of compound meters and the seventh degree of the major scale. A leading writer of Kodály music education is Lois Choksy. The following is a list of references for further study of the Kodály method:

BACON, DENISE, *50 Easy Two-Part Exercises.* Clifton, N.J.: European American Music Distributors Corp. Primary-college.

———, "Kodály and Orff: Report from Europe," *Music Educators Journal,* April 1969, 53–56.

———, *Let's Sing Together: Songs for 3, 4, and 5 year olds.* Oceanside, N.Y.: Boosey and Hawkes, Inc.

CHOKSY, LOIS, *The Kodály Context.* Englewood Cliffs, N.J.: Prentice-Hall, Inc., 1981. Includes teaching older students and curriculum construction.

———, *The Kodály Method: Comprehensive Music Education from Infant to Adult.* Englewood Cliffs, N.J.: Prentice-Hall, Inc., 1974. Describes the method, adapts it for American schools, and includes 153 songs to use.

DANIEL, KATINKA S., *The Kodály Approach,* vols 1, 2, 3. Sequentially written workbooks for the primary grades. Belmont, Calif.: Fearon Publishers, 1973.

ERDEI, PETER, and KATALIN KOMLES, *150 American Folk Songs to Sing, Read, and Play.* Oceanside, N.J.: Boosey and Hawkes, 1974.

The Kodály Envoy, official journal of the Organization of Kodály Music Educators, edited by Betsy Moll and Christine Kunko. School of Music, Duquesne University, Pittsburgh, Pa. 15219.

The Kodály Center of America. Denise Bacon, Director, 1326 Washington St., West Newton, Mass. 02165.

The Kodály Musical Training Institute. Jerry L. Jaccard, Director, University of Hartford, Hart School of Music, West Hartford, Conn. 06117.

LANDIS, BETH, and POLLY CARDER, *The Eclectic Curriculum in Music Education: Contributions of Dalcroze, Kodály, and Orff.* Reston, Va.: Music Educators National Conference, 1972.

PERINCHIEF, ROBERT, with LORNA ZEMKE, *Kodály Transparencies.* Whitewater, Wis.: Perry Publications. An eight-level program of supplementary teaching aids.

Silver Burdett Music, *Kodály Curriculum Guide* for Grades One through Six. Morristown, N.J.: Silver Burdett, 1983.

Hand Signs   In the Kodály method, pitch discrimination and the concepts of high and low are explored by beginning with the descending minor third interval, 5–3 (*so-mi*). First, many names, nursery rhymes and other poems or words are sung on the two pitches. Next, hand signs may be performed by the children in response to them (see Figure 14.1). The teacher sings *so* or *mi* and the children learn to identify both as high or low and with the hand signs. After children have learned the hand signs individual children can "think" the pitches and give signs to the class to be translated into pitch. Next, *la* (6) is added, and the three pitches are used in many ways in improvising short songs, setting poems to them, learning the hand signs, devising ear training games with them as described for *so* and *mi* above, and seeing the relation of the piches in notation. Notice that the eye, ear, and body are all involved in learning pitch discrimination. Eventually *re* and *do* are added, and there are the hand signs, notation, improvisation of little melodies, playing of the pitches and the tunes on bells and xylophones, and using the five pitches of the common pentatonic scale. Rhythm patterns performed with body and percussion sounds can be utilized all the way through this process; the learning of notation and its description of the *duration* of pitch (note values)

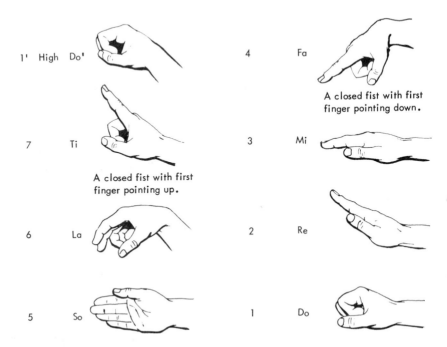

1' High Do'

7   Ti
A closed fist with first finger pointing up.

6   La

5   So

4   Fa
A closed fist with first finger pointing down.

3   Mi

2   Re

1   Do

Figure 14.1.   KODÁLY HAND SIGNS

can be applied throughout this developmental experience with pitch. Children can discover that rhythm and melody are integrally related; that one cannot have a melody unless the pitches are assigned duration, which is basic to rhythm.

The low *do* is formed at waist level. The signs move upwards step by step. *So* is made approximately even with the mouth. High *do* is made even with the forehead.

To illustrate how rhythm syllables, Latin syllables, and hand signs are used by many teachers, the following excerpts are reproduced from *Twenty-Two Music Lessons,* published by the Nova Scotia Department of Education, part of a Kodály-inspired sequence.

LESSON 15

Using Roll-Call to Reinforce So-Mi and Hand Signs

1. Teacher says, "I will clap the Rhythm Pattern of someone's name. I would like that person to (stand and) answer by saying and clapping it." (There may be several people whose names have the same Rhythm Pattern—let them all respond at once.) Then the whole class responds by clapping and saying the rhythm syllables (ta & ti-ti).

Examples:

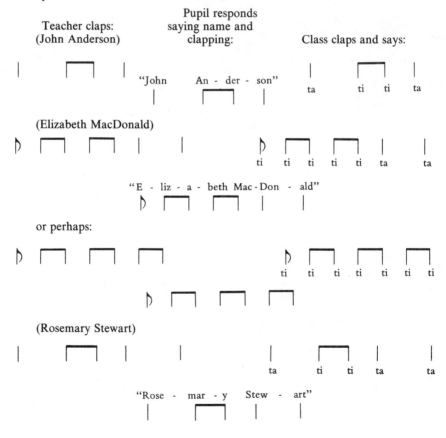

or it might be considered:

2. Using *so* and *mi*, the teacher calls each child by name (full name preferably), and each child echoes, as in the examples below:

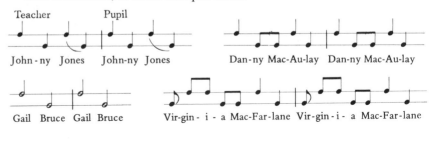

3. Teacher sings   Pupil responds   Class responds—
   and uses   with his name—   singing tone
   hand signs   singing and   syllables and
                   using hand signs   using hand signs

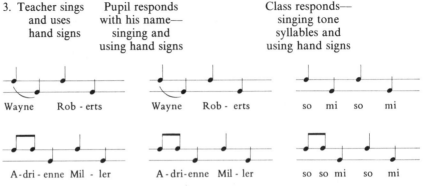

4. Teacher sings as before, but now instead of the echo, the child responds to the teacher's question, singing and using hand signs. The class responds, as in (3):

PART OF LESSON 19

Added suggestions: using recorder, melody bells, piano, or "loo":

1. Give a four-beat rhythmic pattern using *so* and *la*. The asterisk (*) indicates *so*.

so la so la   so so so so la so   so la la so la

2. Now try the roll-call patterns, employing *mi, so,* and *la,* as outlined in Lesson 15. Here are some examples:

Teacher: Pupil: Class:

Ka - ren Mur - phy   Ka - ren Mur - phy   so la so mi

Sing your name   Don - ald Wat - er - man   so la so so mi

Teacher: You will find that the children will usually echo your tonal pattern. You will have to do the hand signals with them, at least at the beginning.

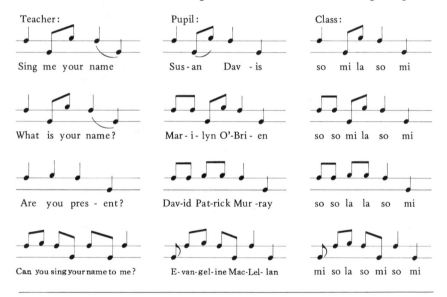

Teacher: Pupil: Class:

Sing me your name   Sus - an Dav - is   so mi la so mi

What is your name?   Mar - i - lyn O'-Bri - en   so so mi la so mi

Are you pres - ent?   Dav-id Pat-rick Mur -ray   so so la la so mi

Can you sing your name to me?   E-van-gel-ine Mac-Lel- lan   mi so la so mi so mi

Teaching Rote Songs

Selecting Songs for Rote Teaching   When one tries to describe the teaching of rote songs it will be found that there are almost as many approaches as there are songs. Many short songs can be taught as complete songs rather than in sections. However, one of the easiest types to begin with is the song which calls for an answer. "John the Rabbit" is one in which children reply, singing the words "Yes, ma'am." "Old MacDonald" is another. Children want to sing "Ee-i-ee-i-o" while the teacher sings the rest of it.

293   SINGING AND MELODY

OLD MACDONALD

American Song

1. Old Mac - Don - ald had a farm, Ee - i - ee - i -
2. Old Mac - Don - ald had a farm, Ee - i - ee - i -
3. Old Mac - Don - ald had a farm, Ee - i - ee - i -

o, And on that farm he had some chicks,
o, And on that farm he had some ducks,
o, And on that farm he had some pigs,

Ee - i - ee - i - o. With a chick - chick here, and a
Ee - i - ee - i - o. With a quack - quack here, and a
Ee - i - ee - i - o With an oink - oink here and an

chick-chick there, Here a chick, there a chick, ev -'ry - where a chick - chick,
quack-quack there, Here a quack, there a quack, ev -'ry - where a quack - quack,
oink - oink there, Here an oink, there an oink, ev -'ry - where an oink - oink,

Old Mac - Don - ald had a farm, Ee - i - ee - i - o.
Old Mac - Don - ald had a farm, Ee - i - ee - i - o.
Old Mac - Don - ald had a farm, Ee - i - ee - i - o.

Try giving "Old MacDonald" a pentatonic treatment with ostinato and bordun. What permits this? What is ignored when you do it?

After the children have learned to sing the three-pitch "Ee-i-ee-i-o" part, the teacher may suggest that they learn the one-pitch "Here a chick, there a chick, ev'rywhere a chick-chick" section. Soon part of the class can sing the first two measures, "Old MacDonald had a farm," and another part can sing "Ee-i-ee-i-o"—and everyone will sing "Here a chick, etc." As the learning progresses, the teacher will ask questions which assist the children in reviewing or learning the words. "What did Old MacDonald have?" (A farm) "Sing it: Old MacDonald had a farm." (They sing.) "What did he have on his farm?" (He had some chicks.) "Sing that part." (They sing.) "Where were those chicks?" (A chick-chick here and a chick-chick there.) "Sing it." Soon the entire song can be sung by the class. It is always fun— and it adds variety—to have different groups sing different parts. "Girls, you sing the parts about Old MacDonald and what he had on his farm. Boys, you sing 'Ee-i-ee-i-o.' All of you sing the 'chick-chick' parts." Sometimes all the girls with red dresses can sing a part, or all children with brown eyes or white shoes; this adds to the game atmosphere.

Young children will react in individual ways. Some may want to begin singing too soon, before they have listened to what they are to sing; there must be an understanding that they are to listen carefully "before their turn comes." Some may not sing; they need to listen longer, or their interest needs to be further stirred. Most of them will want to contribute actively as soon as possible; this is why songs with easy answering parts or parts suggesting simple physical responses are enjoyed and usually learned rather quickly. The logical procedure is to always work from the easiest parts first.

The echo-type song is one in which children sing parts which repeat pitch for pitch what the teacher has sung. "Are You Sleeping?" is one of this type. Every measure of this song is followed by an exact repetition. Thus the teacher presents it as a complete song first, then eventually asks the class to sing each part in imitation. Signals are developed that indicate the teacher's turn to sing and the children's turn. "Old Texas" can be sung in the same general way; six-year-olds who can sing on pitch will perform it well. "Follow On" is an echo song for older children. When they have learned the song, some of the children will sing with the teacher, and ultimately the class can be divided into two groups, one of which will sing the teacher's part.

FOLLOW ON!

Old Song

Repetitious songs are easily taught by rote. "A-Tisket, A-Tasket" is a young children's song centered about the 5–3–6–5 tone pattern. Its sing-song repetitiveness makes it easy for children to learn. Other songs of this type include "Tideo," "Rig-A-Jig-Jig," "Pick a Bale of Cotton," "Hole in the Bucket," and "Standin' in the Need of Prayer." "Trampin'" is also an example.

After the teacher introduces "Trampin'" by singing it all the way through, the children may begin entering on the chorus part, "Tryin' to make heaven my home." In reviewing the words and meaning of the song the teacher may ask, "What is the singer doing?" (trampin') "What does that mean?" "What is he trying to do?" "Has he ever been to heaven?" "What has he been told about it?" Later on, a child or group of children will sing the teacher's solo part, with everyone singing the chorus. "Trampin'" is a call-and-response song; "Swing Low, Sweet Chariot" is another of this type for older children. "Trampin'" can be treated as a pentatonic song if desired. Try "Swing Low" also.

TRAMPIN'

Songs such as "O Tannenbaum" and "Lightly Row," which have a phrase organization of *a a b a,* and other songs of longer length than these, are commonly taught by phrase-echoing. The teacher sings the song or plays a recording of it, discusses its meaning with the children, and then sings the first phrase; the children echo this. The teacher sings the second phrase; the children imitate this also. Then the children are asked to sing both phrases, and they do.

The teacher next sings the *b* phrase, which seems more difficult because it is different; the children echo this. The process continues, phrase by phrase until the song is learned. More complex songs may require a combination of these different approaches. Teachers need to study each song, analyze each thoroughly, then plan the best strategy for learning the particular melody.

Music Concepts and Rote Teaching

While rote singing is a necessary step in musical growth—and it is an honored procedure from an historical viewpoint—if teachers go no farther than this type of teaching, the result can be only a form of music illiteracy. Phyllis E. Dorman writes, "There is a certain dignity and logic in the simplest song. A song, any song, makes use of the same tools present in the most complicated of the musical classics. Every element is there: rhythm, melody, form, tonality, texture, dynamics, color, and aesthetics. Songs should be used to teach musical concepts."* She recommends that *music* be taught instead of only songs.

Although singing of rote songs may take place at any level and at any age, more of this type of learning is necessarily used with very young children who can do little or no reading of notation. However, every song contains elements of music the teacher can use in some way to prepare for or begin work with understanding music and learning about notation. The following can be considered steps in teaching young children rote songs, keeping music concepts in mind while doing so.

Establishing the Pitch. Because the range of any song is a crucial matter, the teacher *must* establish the key and the beginning pitch accurately.

Motivating Interest. There are many ways to motivate interest in songs. Sometimes the teacher announces the title and tells briefly with what it is concerned. Sometimes it is all a surprise—the children listen to the song to find out what it is about. It is wise to take a little time for this. Pictures may help. After the teacher sings the song the children may be asked what its story or message is. A series of questions illustrated earlier may then follow.

Beat and Meter. The teacher might walk quietly in place to the beat while singing the song again as the children do likewise or imitate walking with creative adaptations, such as with the hands in the air, fingers on desks, or silently clapping hands. Accents may call attention to the meter, whether or not children at the earliest levels understand what meter is.

Phrase. As the teacher sings the song again, the phrase order can be stressed. For young children, the teacher may ask them to stand and imitate—move arms to depict a phrase, step the beat while turning the body, reverse directions for a contrasting phrase, hold up a finger for phrase one, add a finger for each subsequent phrase, and so on. Some of this can be done with older students; however, those with good music backgrounds can sense the phrase order by listening, using their better-developed tonal memory. Logical

* Phyllis E. Dorman, "A Protest Against Musical Illiteracy," *Music Educators Journal,* November 1967, p. 99.

questions to ask include, "How many phrases did you hear?" "Are there any that are the same?" "Similar?" "Different?" "Which ones?"

Melodic Direction: Contour. The teacher can ask the children to show by their hand positions what they think is the up and down direction of the melody. In a later lesson their analysis can give them answers to questions regarding steps and skips in the melody line and if certain phrases conclude up or down in pitch.

Independent Singing. After the children have heard a song several times with this kind of analytical guidance, they should sing it without the teacher's voice. The teacher can assist by high and low hand positions, but will join in singing only if absolutely necessary. A goal is to assure the children's independence of both the teacher's voice and the piano. Also, teachers cannot listen to children's singing if they too are singing.

Texture. The next time the children sing the song, the teacher may use accompanying instruments to provide different textures. If the piano sounds exactly the same as the melody the children sing, it is sounding only the melody in unison with their voices. It is an example of *monophony.* If the Autoharp or guitar sounds a chordal accompaniment which supports the melody, there is *homophony,* a quite different texture. "Did it sound the same or different this time?" "What made it sound different?" comprise a way to begin a discussion of texture even though the children may not know the adult terminology. Different types of accompaniments can be discussed, described, analyzed, and evaluated for their suitability for the melody. Two or more melodic lines sounding at once constitute *polyphony.*

Tone Quality. Tone qualities of voices and of accompanying instruments can be evaluated in terms of their suitability to express the meaning of the song or in terms of beauty.

Dynamics. The children can be encouraged to sing the song at different dynamic levels—loud, soft, crescendo, decrescendo, with accents, and so on. They should determine the dynamics most suited to the song, thus learning about interpretation and aesthetic discrimination.

Thus the teaching of rote songs becomes "rote-note" teaching because it can expand children's music concepts to the place when what they already have sensed and worked with is described in notation which, after all, is only a kind of picture-description of the melody.

General Directions   **Finding the Keynote in Major Tonalities.** This is necessary to enable the teacher and students to establish the pitch and key feeling (tonality) of a song. The ways to find the keynote (home tone) from key signatures are:

1. The sharp farthest to the right is scale tone 7 or *ti.* Count up to 8 or *do,* or down to 1 or *do.* The letter name of 8 or 1 is the name of the key.
2. The flat farthest to the right is scale tone 4 or *fa.* Count down to 1 or up to 8; the letter name of 8 or 1 is the name of the key. A quicker way for key signatures

containing two or more flats is: the next-to-the last flat on the right *is* the key-note.

Songs in major tonalities ordinarily end on 1, 3, or 5.

Finding the Key in Minor Tonalities.

1. Find the major tonality indicated by the key signature.
2. Find the sixth degree of the major scale (6 or *la*). This note is the keynote of the relative minor tonality.

Songs in minor usually end on *la,* and rarely on *do* or *mi.*

Suggestions   Learn the song thoroughly before attempting to teach it. Have the children participate actively in some way as soon as possible. Don't plan too much to do with the same song on the same day; this can become boring. Possible activities for children to do while they listen to a teacher introduce a new rote song by singing it to them include:

Clapping hands (tips of fingers) soundlessly to the beat;

Clapping hands soundlessly to the rhythm of the words or melody;

Standing in place and trying to discern phrases by making heart-shaped movements with the hands and arms;

Conducting the meter or determining the meter by trying to conduct it;

Determining whether the music swings in two's or three's;

Acting out pitch levels and/or melodic contour with hands and arms;

Analyzing what is heard in terms of scalewise and skipwise patterns;

Listening for prominent rhythm patterns;

Listening for prominent tone patterns.

Take breaths generally at the end of phrases. People do not "break a phrase" by taking a breath during it when speaking; neither should this be done when singing. Periods, commas, and semicolons often point out the proper places to breathe.

Encourage children to suggest ways for better interpretation of the song.

Seeing What   The above discussion has considered the teaching of songs by means of
We Hear   guided repetitions. The teacher's plans lead from purely rote singing to understanding music concepts that help children toward reading notation. Some activities that build notational concepts include having children:

1. Compare the notation of two familiar songs of the same tempo, one which uses many eighth and sixteenth notes and another which has whole notes, half notes, and quarter notes. Guide them to discover that the "whiteness" of notation relates to long note duration and the "blackness" of notation relates to short note duration.
2. Look for familiar rhythm patterns and note patterns in the notation of selected songs.

3. Look at the notation of phrases of known songs to find out that when phrases sound the same they look the same, and when they sound different, they look different.
4. Watch the notated melody line and follow it on the page with an index finger, all the while relating high and low in pitch with high and low on the staff.
5. Relate the keyboard to notation by providing easy songs to play on the bells by number, by the note names stamped on the bars, and eventually by notation.

Using Recordings of Songs

Recordings can be substituted for teachers' voices in teaching songs. Children learn some songs from recordings they play at home, and from radio and television programs. Singing commercials are frequently learned also. However, when recordings are used, many of the flexible techniques suggested above cannot be employed.

The children must sing softly in order to hear the recording. The volume of the record player can be gradually turned down as the children learn a song so that they will become increasingly independent of the recording. A test to determine how well the children have learned a song is to have them begin singing with the recording, then lift up the needle and have them continue without its help.

It is well to emphasize teaching the words when songs are learned by rote from recordings; they are frequently written on the chalkboard. Another technique, useful as a later step in the learning process, is to have small groups of children, no more than six, stand by the record player and sing with it while the remainder of the class listens to evaluate their efforts constructively and awaits their turn at doing the same thing.

The recordings that accompany the textbooks and some other song books can be of genuine value in teaching songs. They usually provide worthy examples for children to hear and imitate: they often bring to the classroom fascinating instrumental accompaniments that could be provided in no other way. They aid the teacher who studies them even though not using them in the classroom, because with their assistance songs are learned correctly, both rhythmically and melodically. Beginning teachers should study the recordings that accompany the books they are to use in their classrooms. Before the fall terms begins, if they hear these over a period of days they will have absorbed a repertoire of songs they need to know, and will have saved time by not having to pick out each song on a keyboard instrument and learn it without a model to follow. When a child tends the record player the teacher is free to move about the room to listen to individual voices and to direct class activities. The teacher can stop singing and listen to the children—something every teacher of music needs to do. No matter how well qualified a music specialist may be, there are times when a recording will provide an effective way to teach some songs. However, recordings cannot completely take the place of the teacher's voice; younger children sometimes find it difficult to understand the diction of voices strange to them. In all of the grades, a machine is no substitute for the personality of a teacher who sings.

The piano or bells may be substituted for the voice or recording by teachers who lack confidence in their singing voices and do not have recordings of songs they need to teach. Words for such songs may be learned by rote or written on the chalkboard. The teacher will then play the melody of the song. This may be repeated while the children do several of the activities of the rote singing process already described in this chapter, the instrument thus taking the place of the voice or recording. For a song of some length the phrase method may be desirable. After the playing of the entire song, the melody of the first phrase will be played; the children will mouth the words silently as it is played again. Then the children may sing this phrase with the piano; and next, sing without its support. This can be continued throughout the remaining phrase, combining some of them along the way. As the song is learned, the support of the instrument is gradually withdrawn to gain independence from it. A child in the class may be a teacher's assistant by singing to the class phrases or entire songs learned from the teacher's playing the piano, bells, or recorder.

Although it is highly desirable to have a piano available, the instrument is not essential to teach or to accompany songs. In a normal situation where the teacher sings, the piano has its greatest use at the end of the learning process. A song may be introduced by playing it on the piano in a simple manner. Since younger children find it difficult to hear a melody when an elaborate accompaniment is played, a simple accompaniment that permits the melody to predominate distinctly is the most effective style of playing. Most of the time the piano has little use, for two reasons: (1) when the teacher is playing the piano the children cannot be heard well enough to determine if each child is singing correctly, and (2) the teacher is in a stationary position and is unable to move through the class to hear and to help children with their problems. Another reason for not using the piano much of the time is that if it is used constantly the children cannot sing independently of it, and may become semihelpless in its absence. However, after a song has been learned, the addition of a piano accompaniment can be a thrilling and satisfying experience, adding greatly to the musical effect of the performance.

The piano is an important means of enrichment and a tool for developing many music concepts. Thus, it has its rightful place in the well-equipped classroom, but not as a dominating instrument.

Creating Songs

Teachers at all elementary levels are alert to children's spontaneous creating of songs and calls. They notate or tape-record those believed to be of value to the child or to the class so they can be saved for later use.

Jumping-rope verses and nursery rhymes can be set to music; original songs from the playground can be taken indoors.

One sunny morning a little girl in the first grade was holding her teacher's hand as she left the building to go to directed play. Deeply affected by the beauty of the day, she sang:

A BEAUTIFUL DAY

First Grade, Washington School
Eugene, Oregon

The teacher asked the child to repeat her song and they sang it together so that they could remember it when they returned to the classroom and share it with the others. Another teacher of a first-grade group had just concluded a reading lesson in which children had learned new words. It was shortly before lunch, and the children suddenly related the new words to their interest in food:

The above examples illustrate the point that creating simple songs is an ability children possess and one that grows under the guidance of capable teachers. It is only a short step from spontaneous creative activity to the point where a teacher says of a well-known poem, "Let's sing it today instead of speaking it," and the setting of poetry to music becomes a classroom activity.

The classroom teacher is in the most strategic position to establish an environment in which children can create music. This teacher knows the interests of the children and has most to do with encouraging creative responses as normal aspects of the entire school day. Children are *normally* creative, and when they find they have the ability and skill to compose simple songs or instrumental pieces, they will frequently do this at home as a play activity, bringing their compositions to school.

Short verse that has a clearly defined rhythm should be selected. As a background for this activity children should have sung many short poems and simple word rhythms. The words are spoken by the children in a regular beat pattern set by the teacher. A pentatonic treatment of the poem can be made, or a diatonic treatment by older students in which the teacher establishes key feeling by chording the familiar I–V₇–I sequence in a selected key, and may sing the first word of the poem, thus suggesting to the children the beginning note of the song-to-be. While the teacher beats time (it is basic to the method that the rhythm never be interrupted) individual children are asked to sing the poem. The older children may be urged to continue to speak the words softly while they listen to the song being born. The rhythm is stressed, the assumption being that if the rhythm is maintained, a melody will appear from each child which can be as spontaneous and uninhibited as speech. It is further assumed that it is as natural for children to have many musical ideas as it is for them to have many ideas expressed in language. This approach to song creation can be effective on any level and is believed by some to possess virtues that are superior, from the standpoint of creativeness, to the phrase approach, which will be described later. If children experience this type of creative expression, which keeps the rhythmic flow proceeding without interruption, there might be fewer adult musicians who lack a feeling for rhythmic consistency.

Instruments such as the bells and piano are sometimes of aid in stimulating the creative process. A teacher used four tone bars from a set of resonator bells with a first-grade class. The children were interested in new shoes, which several of them wore that day, and with the aid of the four tones they created a song on the subject called "New Shoes," which they also learned to play on the bells. Its repetitious words are typical of first-grade children. This song was sung throughout the term whenever one of the children came to school with new shoes.

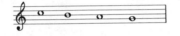

NEW SHOES

Laboratory School
University of Wisconsin
Milwaukee

Melodies without words are created by children who have opportunities to experiment with tuned water bottles, xylophones, bells, piano, recorder-type instruments, and instruments of the band and orchestra.

Teachers save worthy compositions by writing them down in music notation. If a teacher has had ear training, he or she can "take dictation" when the children create a song—that is, associate at once the tones with degrees of the scale. For instance, several song examples in this chapter are based on the same note pattern—the familiar 1–3–5 chord or the *tonic* chord. The recognition of this fact makes notating such songs a simple matter. Since few classroom teachers have had much of this kind of training, most of them rely on other means. For example, the teacher who heard Ann sing "A Beautiful Day" sang it with her so that when she returned to the classroom she could find the song on the bells or piano. To help remember the melody of a child's song, the less experienced teacher can invent pictorial ways to record melodies by such means as drawing a continuous or a broken line showing the directions of the pitches and by drawing short and long dashes to represent comparative note values. Some teachers write melodies with numerals or syllables and determine the notation later. Some use tape recorders and "take it off" the tape later. Others have the children help them remember the song until a special music teacher or another classroom teacher has time to help notate it. Some students in the intermediate grades can be of help. There is always a way to notate these songs, and any teacher who tries will improve in skill with practice.

An activity that deserves respect is adding original verses to songs, When children do this, they must feel the fundamental rhythm and accommodate new words to this rhythm. It is good preparation for later activities in which poems are set to music. Words must be set to music so that accents we use naturally in speech fall on musically accented beats. For example, "the" and "a" are normally unimportant words; they will be sung on parts of the measure of little rhythmic importance—almost never on accented parts of the measure or notes of long duration, since this would give them emphasis to which they are not entitled.

As soon as children understand and can use notation, the song-creating process in the classroom should include the notating of the song on the chalkboard or a transparency where everyone can participate to some degree in seeing that it is written in a manner that correctly pictures what was created. Also, when good songs are notated in or transposed to keys that children find easy to use when playing recorder-type instruments, such songs may be duplicated and given to the children. When children take such songs home to play on these instruments or on the piano, they are learning about music notation as a by-product of their creative activity and sharing this with their parents.

A SUNSHINY DAY

Second Grade
Eliot School
Portland, Oregon

I want to go out to play._____ I want to jump

up to say, "I'm hap - py I'm hap -

py be - cause it's a sun - shin - y day!"_____

When children can compose poetry and songs, the writing of simple operettas is not beyond the possibilities of the intermediate grades. Another opportunity is more teaching about musical form. Since the form of most of the songs children compose is simple in structure, often being a question-and-answer type with repeated phrases, teachers can guide children to discover elements of form in music by having them examine their own compositions. To analyze song form is interesting to children when it concerns a song they have written.

The procedure many teachers follow when they guide students in group song writing in grades three and above is as follows:

1. Choose words that are simple, have steady rhythmic flow, and are understood by children.
2. Write the words on the chalkboard under the staff. Discuss the meaning of the words, seeking ideas that will influence the song writing. Such ideas will include mood and anything that may reflect descending or ascending pitch.
3. Have the class read the words in unison so that a definite rhythm is established. Use clapping or stepping if necessary. The most heavily accented words or word syllables can be underlined. Measure bars can be drawn before (to the left of) these words or word syllables.
4. If this activity is comparatively new to the children, sound the tonic chord by singing 1–3–5–3–1 (do-mi-sol-mi-do), or by playing it on Autoharp or piano. If these instruments are used, it is better to play the chord sequence I–V_7–I to establish a definite key feeling. If the children are experienced in song writing, this step is not necessary because they "hear with their inner ears" what they create, and the arbitrary setting of a key may interfere with the creative process.
5. Ask for suggestions to start the song. There are several approaches. In the earliest stages of learning to compose, a teacher may have all or part of the first phrase written and ask the class to finish that section of the song. This can be done by the class *thinking* what the rest of the song might be (after singing the first part several times) and finally singing it, the teacher accepting the majority opinion. Soon individuals will have melodic suggestions to offer, and the process becomes one of both group and individual contribution. The group is the controlling force, however, and exercises discrimination in choosing between versions of parts of the song that are volunteered by individuals. The composition generally proceeds phrase by phrase with the group singing frequently from the beginning of the song. The teacher notates the song as it grows in length. Those teachers who can take musical dictation will write stemless notes on the staff. Since it is necessary to proceed with rapidity to avoid lagging interest, these are usually little lines (/) instead of filled out notes (•). Some teachers will prefer to use numerals or syllables and "figure" from these. Others will use the keyboard directly, and still others will employ lines on the chalkboard or on a transparency that indicate high and low in pitch and tonal duration. Some may tape the song and complete the notation later.
6. Have the class decide what the meter signature is. If the bar lines have not already been placed, they can be written before the heavily accented notes. Sometimes the song will need to be transposed to a more suitable key for the voices. The key signature will be determined, as will note values. Stems, flags, beams, and dots will be added wherever necessary.
7. Autoharp or piano chords can be added as desired.
8. The children can now evaluate their song. Does it reflect the meaning of the words suitably? Does it communicate the mood desired? Can the song be improved? Is it notated correctly?
9. If the song is of good quality, it should be saved by placing it in a class book. If it is in a key in which children can play recorder-type instruments, reproduce it on a duplicating machine so that the children may use notation at home in playing the song for their parents.

The goal of this group work is to develop the ability of individuals to compose music—for each child to write songs with the same ease with which children paint pictures.

When children write their own music, they are personally concerned with melody, form, tempo, dynamics, and correct notation. They are further concerned with tension and release, repetition and contrast, range, and how the tones move. Creating songs is a superior means of acquiring music concepts. It is a genuine musical experience.

What Do Melodies Communicate?

Songs are the union of poetry and melody; their words describe rather clearly the thought being communicated. Students should be encouraged to form judgments about how well the melody reflects the message of the words. "This song is said to be a lullaby." "How does the melody suggest that it is a lullaby?" "How well does it succeed in communicating this idea?" A song such as "Sleep, Baby, Sleep" could be used as an example. When such questions are stated, the teacher is relating people and music in recognition that most of the music of the world is functionally used rather than set apart as an art for the connoisseur. How does the melody of a work song, a street vendor's song, a dance song, suggest the message of the words? How well does it do it? The first question stimulates analysis and the second a value judgement. Analyze "Sleep, Baby, Sleep" to find how the relative instance or absence of fast, slow, note values, range, dynamics, form, repetition, contrast, climax, release, and other aspects affect the communication of the song's message.

SLEEP, BABY, SLEEP

2. *Sleep, baby, sleep! The large stars are the sheep.*
   The little ones, the lambs, I guess,
   The gentle moon, the shepherdess,
   Sleep, baby, sleep! Sleep, baby, sleep!

Melodic Movement and Scales—Some Technical Aspects

How Do Melody Tones Move? Young children can discover that the tones of melodies move in three ways: they can repeat, they can move in steps (scalewise or conjunct), and they can move in skips or leaps (often chordwise or disjunct). When these concepts are being developed, the teacher selects songs and recorded music that most clearly reveal these tonal movements. Prior to this the children's first discovery may be that melodies move in single lines, horizontally. While the contour of a melody may move up and down or stay the same for a while, there is a steady linear progression. In songs such as "That's the Way Tunes Go" and "Space Ship" the concepts of both repeated tones and stepwise progression can be studied by the children in response to the teacher's question, "In what different ways do you think this melody moves?"

THAT'S THE WAY TUNES GO

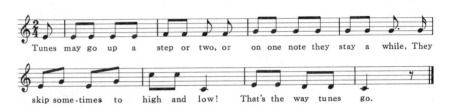

SPACE SHIP

Wilma Wittemeyer
Arr. R. E. N.

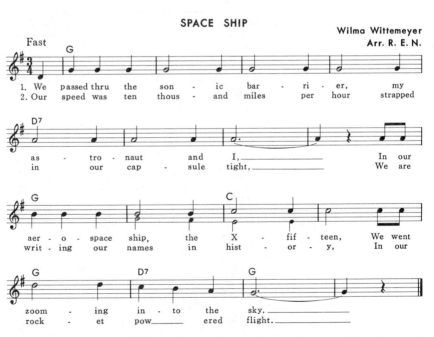

From *Exploring Music with Children* by Robert E. Nye and Vernice T. Nye. © 1966 by Wadsworth Publishing Company, Inc. Reprinted by permission of Wadsworth Publishing Company, Belmont, Calif. 94002.

"Taffy" is another scale-line song with repeated notes; it is also useful for experience with the octave leap.

From *Singing With Children* (2nd ed.) by Robert and Vernice Nye, Neva Aubin, and George Kyme. © 1970 by Wadsworth Publishing Company, Inc. Reprinted by permission of Wadsworth Publishing Company, Belmont, Calif. 94002.

Suggestions for use: "Taffy" can be used to introduce children to the C scale. Children find the C scale easy to play on the piano because of the consecutive white keys.

After the song is learned, one child can sing the first measure, another the second measure, another the third and fourth measures, and so on. Children enjoy this method, which also serves to strengthen tonal memory.

"Sandy Land" exemplifies a chord-line song; it contains skips and leaps besides repeated notes. By experimenting, older children can find that F, A, and C and G, E, and C are notes that can be played together on bells or piano to accompany the song, and thus begin to relate chord-line melodies with accompanying chords.

Make my liv-ing in sand-y land, La-dies, fare you well.

2. *Raise potatoes in sandy land, etc.*
3. *Dig potatoes in sandy land, etc.*

What Is a Scale? The term *scale* means "ladder." It refers to an arrangement of rising pitches. Children soon become familiar with the major scale through experiences with scale songs and playing the C scale on bells and xylophone. They quickly find that one can sing or play down the scale as well as up. The bells and piano keyboard are effective audiovisual devices for children to use in determining a definition or description of the C major scale as consisting of both whole steps and half steps, and for the eventual discovery of their precise arrangement. Following this could be "trying out" the major scale pattern, beginning on notes other than C to find if it sounds the same. Although F and G are often the notes tried next, there are eleven black and white keys other than C with which to experiment. The fact that the major scale can be played from any black or white key is an important discovery. (See Figure 14.2.) The children may find that the major scale consists of one repeated

Major scale of	B♭	F		C	G
	B♭	F	do	C	G
	A	E	ti	B	F♯
	G	D	la	A	E
	F	C	so	G	D
	E♭	B♭	fa	F	C
	D	A	mi	E	B
	C	G	re	D	A
	B♭	F	do	C	G

How are syllables and letter names related?
Play these on the bells. Find the same scale
starting on a note not written here; play it.

Figure 14.2

pattern: whole step, whole step, half step, (whole step) whole step, whole step, half step. (See Figure 14.3.) There should be provision in the classroom for individualized study of this diatonic scale pattern. Some teachers use hand signs to explore the scale and its intervals. The advantage is said to be that signs have somewhat the same function as fingering on an instrument, and it is assumed that they make scale tones less abstract to the learner; a disadvantage is that pitch movements expressed in hand signs must be done rather slowly to be seen and understood.

The major scale should be compared with a pentatonic scale in which there are no half steps. (See Figure 14.4.) Both the keyboard and charts are needed to explore and explain these scale patterns. (See, for example, Figure 14.5.) A large chart of the keyboard, placed in a commanding position in the classroom, is considered an essential piece of equipment by a great many teachers to explain tonal relationships visually.

In any study of scales there should be an immediate association with song materials to explore how a scale is used in music. Because so many American songs are in major keys, this association is fairly obvious. The less commonly used tonalities need to be sensed in like fashion through songs that employ their scale structures. In working with a song built on a scale which is strange, the children might first determine on which note the tonal center (keynote) seems to be, then try to construct the scale from that note, utilizing notes from the melody to complete it. Minor keys are not "strange" to the children; they have heard them many times from their environment. Eight-year-olds can begin to learn their precise structures through experiences with songs which are built on them. There are two ways to conceptualize the relationship of minor scales to major scales. (Since adults argue

Figure 14.3

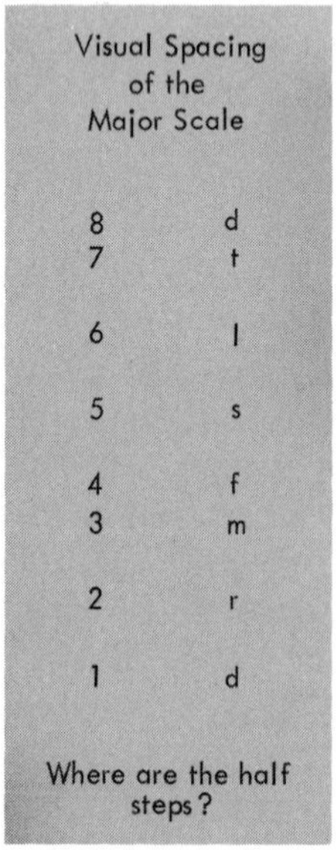

Visual Spacing of the Major Scale	
8	d
7	t
6	l
5	s
4	f
3	m
2	r
1	d
Where are the half steps?	

Figure 14.4

	1	2	3	4	5	6	7	8
Major Scale	d	r	m	f	s	l	t	d
Pentatonic Scale	1	2	3		5	6		8
	d	r	m		s	l		d

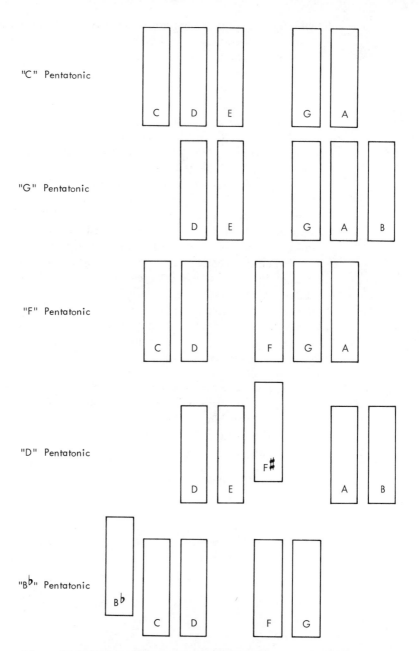

Figure 14.5. PENTATONIC SCALES ON KEYBOARD INSTRUMENTS

about them, it should be interesting for the teacher to watch how the children's thinking about them evolves.) One way is to consider every minor scale a relative of a major scale, that is, every minor scale can be thought of as beginning on the sixth step (*la*) of a major scale. Thus, it would be sung from *la* to *la* or from 6 to 6. This way of thinking has adherents because the syllables and numbers remain stable—attached to the major scale concept. Another way is to think only of the minor scale, call the home tone 1 or *do,* and sing it as though it began on the same scale step as a major scale does. This is of advantage when it comes to piano chording becase the I-chord corresponds by number to scale tone one. Either way can be used. Most adults believe that the "best" way is the one they have been taught. The first way is generally preferred.

With selected song material (see the indexes of books), the three kinds of minor scales in common use can be worked with, and the children should use them to write their own compositions. (See Figure 14.6.) Sometimes recordings will initiate an exciting exploration of a minor scale; Cui's *Orientale* is one example.* A problem for students to solve is "What feelings are communicated by use of minor tonalities in music?" They should find that there are at least as many communicated by minor keys as by major keys, and that minor is not necessarily associated with "sad."

When the teacher creates an environment in which students are stimulated to discover and explore these scales for themselves, subject matter that under other conditions can be a rather puzzling, teacher-pressured memorization of three kinds of minor scales (natural or pure, harmonic and melodic) can be part of a thrilling adventure in expanding the concept of "scale." Learners can discover for themselves the truly fascinating ways in which many different kinds of scales express and communicate feelings.

Passive and Active Scale Tones

A typical scale involves a specific tonality. Students learn easily to identify the home tone as the most important pitch to which all the other scale members are related. Through expanding musical experiences, children will rate scale tone 5 as the next most influential, and scale tone 4 would be third in general importance. However, when persons sense the tonality of scales thoroughly, they come to feel that certain of the pitches tend to give them a sense of satisfaction and stability, while certain other pitches give them the

What scale is this? Find it on the bells.							
2 whole steps, 1 half step, 3 whole steps, 1 half step							

1	2	3	4	5	6	7	8
1	2	3	4	5 6	7		8
1	2	3	4	5 6		7	8
1	2	3	4	5	6	7	8

Try to play these on the bells. What are the names of these scales? How would you sing them with the syllables?

Figure 14.6. MINOR SCALE STUDY

* *Orientale* also has a rhythmic ostinato.

feeling that they should move on to an adjacent pitch above or below. Using the major scale as an example, the *passive* tones are those of the tonic (I) chord, 1, 3, 5, and 8. The active tones are 2, which tends to move down to 1 or up to 3; 4, which tends to move down to 3 or up to 5; 6, which tends to move down to 5 or up to 7; and 7, which pulls strongly to 8, and is called the *leading tone* because of this. These qualities of scale members can be discerned by children. Older students feel them more strongly than young children because their harmonic sense is more developed. To explore the passive and active qualities of scale members, ask the children to sing slowly up and down the scale, directing them to stop at different scale tones. Then ask them which way they feel the pitch should move—up, down, or stay the same. The movement of melodies with regard to active and passive scale tones relates to beauty, ease of singing, note reading, use of tones in their own compositions, and to expanding concepts of scale and tonality. (See Figures 14.6 and 14.7.) Notice that "Scarborough Fair" contains a contrasting phrase in major tonality and although a song in minor, it contains some major chords. The key selected here makes possible the playing of the melody by the recorder.

MAJOR			do	re	mi	fa		so		la	ti	do
PENTATONIC			do	re	mi			so		la		do
MINOR natural	la	ti	do	re	mi	fa		so		la		
MINOR harmonic	la	ti	do	re	mi	fa			si	la		
MINOR melodic	la	ti	do	re	mi		fi		si	la		

Figure 14.7. COMPARISON OF SCALES

SCARBOROUGH FAIR

Pentatonic Melodies. The term "pentatonic melody" is sometimes puzzling because they may be classified into four types. The first is the tune which is clearly pentatonic in both melody and any accompanying pitches and in which no harmonization (chord change) is desired. Second is the melody which has been harmonized; tunes in this classification can be treated successfully as either those in which no chord change takes place or as those in which harmonization can be applied. Third is a melody which contains a few nonpentatonic tones—such as major scale steps 4 and/or 7; these appear in unimportant places in the melody (not on the beat) so that no harmonization need take place. Fourth is the type which has a melody within the common pentatonic scale but in which harmonization seems essential. Each type is useful in one or more ways in teaching. Pentatonic songs will be found listed in classified indexes of books. Examples not mentioned earlier include "Goodbye, Old Paint," "Grandma Grunts," "The Riddle Song," "Nobody Knows the Trouble I've Seen," and "Night Herding Song." As stated earlier, they can be played on the black keys of the piano, an activity which assists the development of tonal memory.

PENTATONIC SCALES

Tonal center ↑

Key Signatures. Students who have explored the scales and understand their organization will have no difficulty in determining why key signatures are necessary. When they fit the major scale pattern to different places on the keyboard, they find black keys essential. From these, key signatures can be derived. Unless students find use for scales and key signatures, they will soon forget them. One logical use is in their own compositions. Another is in the performance of instrumental music; one must use the key signature in order to know what note to play and what fingering to use. Vocal music does not demand the same analysis of key signatures that instrumental music does; all the singer needs to know is the beginning pitch and *where that pitch is in the scale.* However, in order to know where the pitch of a new song is in the scale, one needs to know the key signature. If the teacher knows this, the students hardly need to, for the teacher can then give them the pitch and tell them where it is in the scale by having them sing first 1–3–5–3–1, then up or down the scale to the beginning note. Thus, in a purely vocal approach the teacher must invent situations in which the signature is of use to the learner. One is to select a student to be the teacher of a new song and ask the class to help the teacher plan what to do. Usually the need to know where the beginning note is in relation to the scale will appear early in the process. It is best to use two or more songs, each beginning on a different scale tone. For how to identify the key from the key signature, see p. 298, this chapter.

The Less Common Modes Some scales were used more frequently in earlier centuries than recently. Today both contemporary composers and folk singers have brought them to a more prominent position in the music that surrounds us. They can be utilized to compose songs and instrumental pieces with a "different" flavor and to reflect older periods. For example, a troubadour song could be written with both words and melody that communicate feelings from that time in world history. Indexes in books guide teachers to modal songs. The Ionian mode is the major scale pattern; the Aeolian is the pure minor scale pattern. The less common modes are shown in Figure 14.8.

Another way to explore modal scales and melodies is to measure them against a major scale. The major scale begins and ends on *do,* the minor scale on *la,* the Dorian mode on *re,* the Phrygian mode on *mi,* and the Mixolydian on *so.* Find and play these scales on a keyboard instrument or recorder.

Some examples of songs written in less common modes are the folk songs "I Wonder as I Wander," "Every Night When the Sun Goes In," "The Shanty Boys in the Pine," "Old Joe Clark," "The Days of '49," and "Ground Hog." Plainchants from church sources which exemplify the older use of the modes are in some of the books.

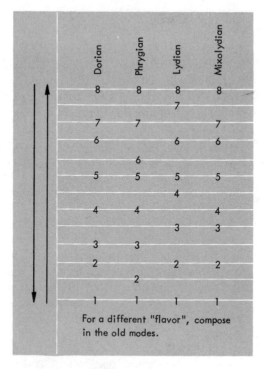

For a different "flavor", compose in the old modes.

Figure 14.8. LESS COMMON MODES

Accidentals (sharps, flats, or cancel signs not stipulated by the key signature) are to be found in two of the minor scales, in songs written both in these minor keys, and in major keys as well. A song such as "I Heard the Bells on Christmas Day," contains some half steps with accidentals. This can lead to exploring the *chromatic* scale, which consists entirely of half steps. Another approach to this scale can be through a recording of "Flight of the Bumble-bee" by Rimsky-Korsakov (BOL #52).

CHROMATIC SCALE

WHOLE - TONE SCALE

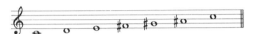

The chromatic and whole-tone scales can be used as "discrepant events" following the study of active and passive scale tones. These scales lack the feeling of tonality characteristic of major and minor scales. When students analyze why songs based on major and minor scales have home tones, they will find that the half steps have something to do with this feeling of tonality. When they analyze the chromatic scale, they will find nothing but half steps; neither the whole-tone scale nor the pentatonic scale has half steps. Interesting generalizations may come from this. When would a composer not desire a feeling of tonality? What kinds of feelings would he be trying to communicate? *Mists,* by Howard Hanson, is a composition which utilizes the whole-tone scale.* The whole-tone scale can be compared to the common pentatonic, and students can determine which has the larger degree of key feeling. (The authors always assume that when they write of scales or any other of the "music fundamentals," the teacher will be utilizing related songs and recordings which bring the study of the concept to musical life, and that the students will be using these in their own compositions for specific reasons. The good teacher knows that unless these aspects of music are truly interesting or useful to the learner, little will be gained from studying them.)

* From *For the First Time,* Mercury Recording. A song constructed on whole-tone scale is "The Cage" by Charles Ives. It appears in several of the music textbook series of recent date.

Ethnic Scales   The concept of *scale* is further expanded when ethnic scales are discovered or introduced. There are many of these scales; music education is only at the threshold of beginning to recognize them. They relate very well to some aspects of social studies. For example, in the study of Japan, children can listen to music and compose music based upon ethnic scales of that country. One is the common pentatonic scale. Another type of pentatonic scale is that used in the song "Sakura" (BOL #66). Beautiful "Japanese" songs can be composed by those who use this scale:

Much of the popular music of Japan is based on this pentatonic scale:

A gypsy scale:

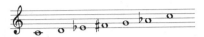

A scale of Afro-American origin:

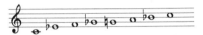

A source of some selected ethnic scales is Gertrude Wollner's *Improvisation in Music,* Doubleday & Company, Inc., Garden City, New York, 1963, Chapter Five, "Adventures in Unusual Scales." Pentatonic, whole-tone, four-tone, chromatic, Hungarian, Arabian, Hindu, Asiatic Indian, Egyptian, Irish, and modal scales are notated. The explanations on some of the record jackets of Asiatic Indian music explain the scale structures utilized in this music. To invent an *original* scale upon which to base songs and instrumental compositions, the learners plan to have either an irregular arrangement of whole steps, half steps, and other intervals as in the above examples, or a regular arrangement such as a consistent alternating of whole and half steps or a consistent use of an interval such as the minor or major third.

The Tone Row   This scale is an invented one, often based on the 12 steps of the chromatic scale. The elementary school learner can use resonator bells. Place the bars in an order that when sounded will not remind the listener of any tonality; this will require moving the bars about until the new scale sounds "atonal"—that is, without any definite tonal center. The row will include all 12 tones, but not in the original consecutive order. Experiment with this arrangement of scale tones by playing familiar melody rhythms such as

"Three Blind Mice" to discover new melodic sounds. Then attempt composition with your new scale, using the succession of pitches over and over again in different ways. (Your scale can also be constructed with fewer than 12 tones.) When one listens to this type of music from recordings, it will be found that certain compositional techniques of long standing are employed to manipulate melodies. Manipulation of traditional melodies will be discussed later; the same techniques apply to tone row music. Composers have used some of them for centuries. With the tone row, traditional harmony is absent; a new concept of harmonization is constructed, often being built from the vertical "happenings" of multiple melodic lines instead of the chords of old.

Tone Patterns and Intervals

Understanding and being able to use tone patterns and intervals relate to learning to read music effectively. When children can comprehend tonal and rhythmic groups as they comprehend words of English, they are learning to read music. Rhythm patterns were discussed in the previous chapter. Tonal patterns found in songs can be taught as parts of those songs. Tone patterns common to many songs include the following:

1.	the minor third	"So Long" "Brahms' Lullaby" "The Blacksmith"
2.	the children's chant	"The Caisson Song" "A-Tisket, A-Tasket" "Camptown Races"
3.		"Hot Cross Buns" "Are You Sleeping" "Polly Wolly Doodle" "Golden Slippers" "Shortnin' Bread"
4.		"Star Spangled Banner" "Blue Danube" "Dixie" "Goin' to Boston" "Bow, Belinda"
5.		"There Was a Little Woman" "Dixie" "The First Noël"

When children have identified these and other tone patterns and can find them in songs and hear them from recordings, the next step is to identify variant uses of the patterns. For example, with reference to pattern number 5 above, the teacher may ask, "Find out how this scale-line pattern is used differently in 'Twinkle, Twinkle, Little Star,'" and "Look for it in 'Joshua Fought the Battle of Jericho'; how is it different in that minor song?"

Intervals In order of using and learning melodic intervals, the young learner usually begins with the descending minor third. The second is part of any scale line pattern; the octave, the fourth, and the fifth are commonly used in children's songs. The sixth, then the seventh, would probably come next in order of usage. They are learned through associations with their use in familiar songs, followed by games of interval identification. To be certain they have identified the interval correctly, students can test their decision by beginning with 1 or *do* and "singing up to it."

The minor third is exemplified in "Brahms' Lullaby," "The Caisson Song," and "Lightly Row"; the major third in "Mary and Martha," "Little David," and "Swing Low, Sweet Chariot"; the fourth in "Taps," "I've Been Working on the Railroad, "Auld Lang Syne," and "Hark! the Herald Angels Sing"; the fifth in "Twinkle, Twinkle, Little Star," and "Baa, Baa, Black Sheep"; the sixth in "My Bonnie," "Bendemeer's Stream," and "It Came Upon the Midnight Clear"; and the octave with "Annie Laurie," and "Wait for the Wagon." The minor sixth is often identified by thinking the major sixth first, then comparing it with the half-step smaller interval. The minor and major sevenths are often identified by comparing them with the octave.

Ability to read music through knowledge of intervals becomes essential in the instance of contemporary melodies that do not move in the scalewise and chordwise manner of traditional melodies.* If syllables are used with this music, the teacher should consider using the *fixed do* system in which C is always *do*.

The usefulness of tone patterns and intervals in reading music can be understood when songs are analyzed with these aspects in mind. For example, "Love Somebody" contains several tone patterns and the interval of a perfect fourth numerous times. Anyone knowing these and the rhythm patterns discussed earlier can sight-sing the song. How many times do each of the tone patterns occur? How many times is the interval of the fourth used?

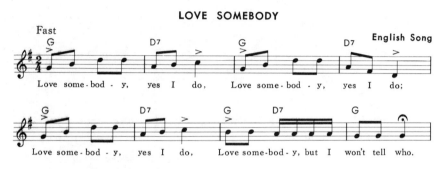

LOVE SOMEBODY

English Song

Love some-bod-y, yes I do, Love some-bod-y, yes I do;

Love some-bod-y, yes I do, Love some-bod-y, but I won't tell who.

* That is, music with no tonal center.

Chord-line melody patterns are another helpful factor in note reading; this will be referred to in the next chapter. "Love Somebody" contains G and D chord lines and an inversion of the G chord appears in the last two phrases. Analyze "Alouette" in terms of tone patterns and intervals. (See Piano Chording in Chapter Seventeen for an explanation of chords.)

ALOUETTE (Skylark)

Analyzing Melodies When students analyze melodies, they should seek answers to such questions as:

How do tones move? (scalewise, stepwise, repeated tones)
What is the phrase arrangement?

What is the type of tonal organization? (major, minor, modal, pentatonic, tone row, ethnic scale, etc.)

What is the range?

Is there evidence of tension and release? If so, how is this achieved?

Is there evidence of a climax? If so, how is this achieved?

Are there other significant aspects? (such as rhythm patterns, tone patterns, dynamics, sequence)

Some Activities With Songs   There are numerous activities possible with songs. Among them are:

1. Move in time with the beat by motions such as clapping, swinging, tapping, rocking, skipping, and jumping.
2. Walk on the beat while standing in place or moving in a circle formation.
3. Walk to the beat anywhere in the room, but with directions given such as "Do not touch or bump anyone" and "Walk in the same general direction."
4. While walking to the beat of the song, do things such as slowing down, speeding up, and dramatizing loud and soft.
5. Clap the rhythm of the melody.
6. Clap the rhythm of the melody while walking the beat.
7. Clap the beat while stepping the melody. (The song should be very slow and simple.)
8. Think the melody and clap it while stepping the beat.
9. Sing the first phrase; do "inner hearing" with phrase two; sing phrase three; do "inner hearing" with phrase four, except for singing the last pitch of the song. Try this while walking the beat.
10. Establish the pitch and tempo. Clap the beat, think the song with "inner hearing," then sing only the final word.
11. The teacher or student leaders turn the singing on and off; the children try to keep the rhythm steady so that they can come in at the same place in the song.
12. The children stand in a circle. As they sing an object is passed from hand to hand on the beat. Next, it is passed on the first word of each phrase. (Maybe two objects can be used, one for the beat and one for the phrase.)
13. A one-measure rhythm pattern can be selected from the song, or created, to be sounded throughout the song as an ostinato while the children sing that song.
14. If the song is pentatonic, select a phrase from the song which a group can sing repeatedly while the rest of the class sings the song.
15. If the song is pentatonic, try it as a round.
16. If any two pentatonic songs are in the same meter and have the same number of measures, they can be sung at one time as "partner songs."
17. Have the students conduct the song by using the appropriate metrical beat pattern.
18. Act out pitch levels and/or the melodic contour with hands and arms
19. Have the class identify significant rhythm and tonal patterns.
20. Determine whether the music swings in two's or three's.

Additional Suggestions for Lesson Plans

Rhythm-Related Experiences   *Rhythm pattern.* Select words or word-groups which occur in the text of a song or which reflect ideas associated with the song. By speaking them, discern their rhythm patterns. Select an appropriate percussion instrument and play one or more of the patterns throughout the song as an accompaniment.

Tonal memory. To develop tonal memory in the "inner ear," the teacher or a child claps hands or plays a percussion instrument in the melody rhythm of a song that is familiar to the class. The game is to identify the song from hearing its rhythm. With very young children, ask them to choose between two or three known songs. Older children can vary the game by having each child in turn perform a different melody rhythm for the class to identify.

Combining melody rhythms. Experiment with combining the melody rhythms of two songs. Example: "Are You Sleeping?" and "Row Your Boat," even though they are in different meters, 2/4 and 6/8. Clap or play the rhythm of one melody at the same time as that of the other. At first teachers select well-known melodies having the same meters or combinable ones such as the above. Songs of different meters having the same tempo for experimentation with polymetrics are selected later.

Tonal memory; Rhythmic notation. Game: The children tap a steady beat while the teacher plays or sings a short tune to the beat. The tune can be one the children know, or it can be improvised by the teacher. The game is for the children to remember the tune and write it in rhythmic notation. A third grader wrote this teacher-improvised melody rhythm correctly:

Rhythm pattern; Ostinato. Ask students to devise a notated rhythm pattern to use as an ostinato throughout a familiar song. Let them evaluate its degree of success as they listen to a few perform it with appropriate percussion instruments. Then ask them to clap it while they sing the song. (They will be performing two rhythms at one time.) Two or three suggested ostinati might be combined and the result evaluated by the class. The teacher should use a tape recorder whenever this assists the evaluation.

Changing meter. Experiment with well-known songs to find answers to questions such as "What would it sound like if 4/4 became ¢ in this song?" "If slow 6/8 became fast 6/8?" "If 3/4 became 3/8?" "Can we change this song from 4/4 meter to 3/4?" "How?"

Changing meter. Experiment with writing a familiar song in a number of different meters, including some less common ones such as 5/4 and 7/8.

Changing note values and meters, note reading. Ask students to alter familiar songs of their choice by changing note values and meters. Write them on a transparency and have the class sing them as a fun experience in note reading.

ABA form; Improvising a dance. This experience with form is for the primary level. The song "Shoo Fly," commonly found in music textbooks, is a good one to improvise a dance for, and in doing so to enact A B A form. It might go like this:

Shoo, fly, don't bother me, (Walk in a circle to the
Shoo, fly, don't bother me, right as the class sings.)
Shoo, fly, don't bother me,
For I belong to nobody.

I feel, I feel, I feel, (Walk to the center of the
I feel like a morning star, circle.)
I feel, I feel, I feel, (Walk backwards from the center
I feel like a morning star. to form the circle again.)

Shoo, fly, don't bother me, (Walk in a circle to the right
Shoo, fly, don't bother me, as the singing continues.)
Shoo, fly, don't bother me,
For I belong to nobody.

The above dance is perhaps one of the most simple possible for the song. The teacher will ask questions that lead to the children's generalization, "When the music sounds the same again, we make the same motion," and the observations, "The song is different in the middle," and "If the song were drawn on the chalkboard, it might look like this."

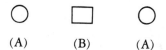

There are many other ways to emphasize A B A form. For example, children could slap thighs for A and clap for B; they might draw something to represent A, and something different to represent B. The "game" is to show the difference between A and B in some interesting way. (There are many similar songs.)

Traditional dances. Songs for specific dances can be useful when teaching those dances. Examples: "Weggis Song" for the schottische; "Buffalo Gals" for the polka, "Sweet Nightingale" (in *Singing With Children*) for the mazurka. The indexes of the music text books, books concerning dance, and some song collections will guide the teacher to song-dance relationships and the dance directions. These dances are generally for older students. Refer to pp. 212–213.

Ethnic dances. Many songs and dances are closely related as they are taught and performed in conjunction with each other. Here is an example from the Maori people of New Zealand, "Me He Manu Rere." Figure 14.9 illustrates the dance steps that accompany this song.

ME HE MANU RERE

Contributed by Cheryl Lau Oi

Me he ma - nu re - re a - hau e,
Kei te mo - e to ti - na - na,

Ku - a re - re ki to mo - e - nga,
Kei te o - ho te wai - ru - a,

Ki te a - whi to ti - na - na,
Kei te ho - tu te ma - na - wa,

E te tau ta - hu - ri mai.
E te tau ta - hu - ri mai.

Me he manu rere ahau e,
Kua rere ki to moenga,
Ki te awhi to tinana,
E te tau tahuri mai.

Kei te moe to tinana,
Kei te oho te wairua
Kei te hotu te manawa,
E te tau tahuri mai.

Had I the wings of a bird,
To your side I would fly,
To hold you there and see you,
Please turn to me.

Though you are enchained,
Yet my spirit is free to roam,
My heart yearns for you,
Please turn to me.

Action songs or chanted songs accompanied by simple steps and gestures are developed from the Maori term *waiata kori,* or dance song. The actions, which are completely complementary to the words and music, mirror and often intensify the meaning conveyed by the song. The song merits serious study, for it is a reflection of the modern Maori culture. It typifies the harmonious blending of the old and new; it embodies the music and poetry which is the soul of the race, and it expresses pride and hope for the Maori future.

Pitch Discrimination

Pitch. Game: Children turn their backs to the teacher, identify the sound producer, and tell which pitch of two sounded is high or low. Later, ask them to match the pitch with their voices *if the pitch is in their normal singing range.*

Vocal imitation. Ask children to imitate vocally by singing, whistling, or other mouth sounds, the sounds of birds, animals, musical instruments, train whistles, auto horns, and other environmental sounds.

VERSE 1

4 times

Me he manu rere ahau e, 1-4

3 Times

Kua rere ki to moenga, 5-8

Turn a full clockwise circle in 6 steps

Ki te awhi to tinana, 9-12

E te tau tahuri mai. 13-16

VERSE 2

Kei te moe to tinana, 1-4

Fists move back and forth 6 times in time to music

right left
right left
right left

Kei te oho te wairua, 5-8

Kei te hotu te manawa, 9-12

E te tau tahuri mai. 13-16

Figure 14.9. DANCE STEPS FOR "ME HE MANU RERE"

High, low. Game: The teacher of young children groups simple instruments or other pitch producers according to high and low in pitch. The children (one, two, or three at a time) experiment with them and compare their high and low sounds. Later the teacher mixes the sound producers and the children are asked to group them into those that produce high pitches and those that produce low pitches.

High, low. Have children relate high and low in pitch to relative high-low positions of the body and of objects. Reach high and low in relation to obvious high and low pitches. Use body movements, marks on a chalkboard, a glockenturm (a German bell-type instrument that is played vertically and shows visually the relationship of keyboard and staff), step bells, standard bell sets placed in vertical position with large bars down. Find or discover high-low in speaking voices, bars on resonator bells, and different sized drums. Work toward such generalizations as "the larger the sound producer, the lower the pitch."

High, low. Game: Use three pitches, middle C, the octave above, and the G in between. When the children hear the highest pitch, they place their hands over their heads; when they hear the middle pitch, they place their hands in front of them; when they hear middle C, they place their hands on their thighs (or hips, if standing). Having eyes closed at times will permit the teacher to find out if some are imitating others or if they are hearing the pitches. Another approach is to let the children freely dramatize the pitches to reflect high and low physically.

High, low. The teacher produces a pitched sound (on anything) in medium range, and repeats it at intervals so the children can remember it. They then explore the room to find objects that will produce (1) a lower sound, then (2) a higher sound. After this, "What can you do to change the kind of sound you made?"

Inner hearing. Prepare for inner hearing by singing loud and soft phrases of a known song, the soft phrases to eventually be silent, but heard in the mind.

Rhythm of words related to the minor third interval, high, low. Establish the rhythm of selected words. Then relate these to the minor third in a vocal range comfortable for the child.

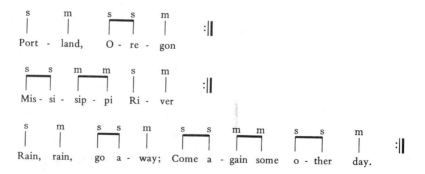

```
 m    s   s   m  m      s    s    m
 ♪  | ♩   ♩  ♪  ♩.  | ♩   ♩   ♩.  :‖
The bus is com-ing,  let's  go  home.
```

Melodic contour. Use parts of exemplary songs to discover that pitches can move in three general ways, up, down, or stay the same. Relate melodic contour to tension, climax, and release in melodies of songs. "I Love the Mountains" is an example, as are "Riddle Song" and "Jacob's Ladder" in *Singing With Children.* Some songs are obviously more clear in this than others, and the teacher is to select the best examples.

Improvised question-and-answer. Use tonal conversations in which the teacher sings questions, comments, or directions to which the children improvise singing replies. They may use any pitch they like. Examples:

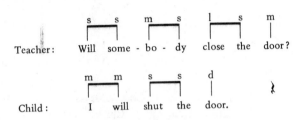

```
           s    s    m    s    l    s    m
Teacher:  Will some-bo-dy  close the door?

           m    m    s    s    d
Child:     I   will  shut the door.
```

Hand signs for so, mi. Have children first clap hands on hearing *so* (5), and slap thighs upon hearing *mi* (3). The teacher sings various combinations of the two pitches; the children listen, then respond by singing and the above body responses. Later, have them hold palms together for *so* and hold palms down for *mi* (no clapping or slapping). Later, relate the tonal patterns sung to rhythm syllables and to the abbreviated notation:

```
  s        m        s   s     m
  |        |        |   |     |
```

"Children's chant" 5-3-6-5-3. Use this tone pattern in many creative combinations. Show it on the staff as a picture of what is sung. Expand the activities used with *so-mi* to include *la* (6).

```
 s        l         s    s    m
Port   -  land,      O  - re - gon

 s    s   s    l      s    m
Mis - si - sip - pi   Ri - ver

 s    l    s    s    m    s    s    l    l    s    s    m
Rain, rain, go   a - way, come a - gain some o - ther day.

 m    s    l    s    m    l    s    m
The  bus  is  com - ing, let's go  home.

 s    s    l    s    s    m    s    s    l    s
Moth - er  is  wait - ing, and she's all   a - lone.
```

Hand sign for la. Teach the hand sign for *la* and ask the children to sing with the three signs they now know (*so, mi,* and *la*). Game: The teacher makes hand signs for some sequence of the three pitches. The children watch, think silently what the pitches will sound like, then at the teacher's signal, sing what signs they observed, first in syllables, then with rhythm syllables.

Name songs. Using bars C D E G A from a set of resonator bells, have each child play a tune representing the rhythm of his name.

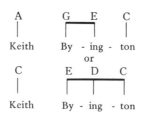

Then sing the name with the words, syllables, letter names, and rhythm syllables.

Home tone. The teacher sounds the chord sequence that centers the children's hearing on the home tone: I–V$_7$–I, using Autoharp, guitar, or piano. The class may also sing the scale demanded by these chords, and the teacher will again center attention on the home tone (*do* or 1). Next the teacher plays on piano, bells, small wind instrument, or sings well-known melodies such as "Mary Had a Little Lamb," omitting *do* each time it appears. The class is to sing every *do* omitted by the teacher. Next, the teacher will sound the tune in a different key so that the class will have the experience of identifying and singing the home tone in other keys.

Ear training. The teacher sings the child's name in pitches of the common pentatonic scale. The child answers by singing the same pitches in syllables or numbers.

Improvisation. The teacher plays a repeated drone interval of a perfect fifth on the piano or low-pitched xylophone, metalophone, or cello. After listening to the drone, a child or small group experiments vocally, relating their improvised pitches to the drone. The mood may vary from an Indian dance to a lullaby.

Tonal memory, Inner Hearing. Words, syllables, or numbers can be used. The teacher or a child hums a familiar melody, or sings it with a neutral syllable such as "la" or "loo." The children then try to identify the melody. When it is identified, the entire class may sing it with the leader.

Hand signs for re and do. Teach these signs; then use scale tones 1, 2, 3, 5, 6 for song-like drills and for the creation of tunes and songs by the children. Eventually show the pitches on the staff to explain, "This is what it looks like when it sounds that way."

Tonal memory. After giving the pitch of 1 or *do* the teacher makes hand signs in silence. The children remember the signs and sing the signaled pitches. At first the teacher repeats the signs as the children sing, but later does not. (They are to develop memory of pitches without this repetition of signs.)

Improvising endings. The teacher provides the first two measures of a four-measure phrase. Individual children improvise vocally the final two measures to complete it. Example:

So, mi, do. Game: The teacher sings at random the pitches of scale tones 5 3 1 (*so, mi, do*). Children use hand signs to identify which of the three pitches is sung.

Fa. The hand sign for scale tone 4 (*fa*) is taught. The teacher sings in syllables or numbers the pitches 1, 2, 3, 4, 5, 6 in song-like drills. Children make hand signs to match the pitches sung. Later the teacher sings these pitches with *loo or la* (neutral syllables) and the children continue to identify the pitches by hand signs.

Tone patterns. Game-drill: Children sing selected common tone patterns from chalkboard, transparency, magnetic board, or flash card, responding with numbers, syllables, or note names as the teacher requires.

Tone matching. Game: The class is divided into two teams. Each has an interesting name the children invent. Corners of the room are the four bases of a baseball diamond. A score-keeper is appointed. At first the teacher uses scale tones 1–2–3–4–5 and later increases these to the complete major scale. Short tone patterns that always begin on 1 are played on an instrument. At first there are no skips, only scale lines and repeated tones. After careful listening, the one "at bat" reproduces what was played by singing each pitch accurately. If he or she does this successfully, this person advances to the next base. After three players strike out, the other team goes to bat. Score is kept on the chalkboard. The difficulty is increased as the players' skill grows. A variant of the game adds a flannel or magnetic board on which what was played is notated. Another variant asks that the children respond with syllables or numerals. Still another asks them to respond with hand signs.

Pitches. Employ the following scale patterns in improvised drills, using a pointer, or hand signs, or notation. The children are to sing in response to the teacher's directions. The major objective is to become familiar with common scale patterns.

$$
\begin{array}{l}
5\ 4\ 3\ 2\ 1 \\
\quad\ \ 3\ 2\ 1\ 7|\ 6| \\
6\ 5\ 4\ 3\ 2\ 1\ 7|\ 6| \\
1|\ 7\ 6\ 5\ 4\ 3\ 2\ 1
\end{array}
$$

Pentatonic scale. Create song-like drills with scale tones 5₁–6₁–1–2–3–5–6. The children can respond with syllables, hand signs, numbers, and the rhythm syllables.

Notation of Pitch

Tonality. Examine known songs and analyze the melodies to find and notate pitches which form the scales upon which these songs are constructed. They may be major, minor, pentatonic, or modal scales. Assist the students to discover that the final pitch of a song is a fairly reliable clue to the first step of the scale. Example: "Wayfaring Stranger," p. 405. Some students may decide that the scale is D minor while others may find a pentatonic scale with D as the tonic (tonal center).

Note values and composing. Select a simple poem of four phrases to be set to music. Give the children the first phrase with the pitches written in even note values. The words are placed under the staff. The class changes note values to add rhythmic interest to this first phrase. Then the teacher assigns groups to compose the melody for the other three phrases. The class evaluates the results and suggests changes if these seem necessary.

Modulating melodies. Challenge the class to learn to read examples of modulating melodies with syllables, numbers, and hand signs. Example:

d r m f   s l s   d t l t   d d   s f m r   d r d

Atonal melodies. The teacher writes an example of an atonal melody on chalkboard or transparency. The class is challenged to sing it, using the *fixed do* system in which middle C is always *do.*

Scales and the Tonal Center

Scale. Write the major scale vertically on the chalkboard in numbers or syllables. Game: The class or child sings the pitches to which the teacher points. Make it very easy at first, then increase the difficulty as the children master the relation of the pitches to their position within the scale.

Home tone. In emphasizing the tonal center or home tone, the teacher sings or plays a melody, but stops before it is complete. The children are to sing the home tone or make up an ending that concludes with the home tone, depending upon what point in the melody the teacher ceases singing or playing.

Major and minor. Plan so that children experience major and minor tonalities through familiar songs. For example, first sing "Merrily We Roll Along" in a major key, with a chorded accompaniment. Then sing it in minor, again with a chorded accompaniment. Ask the class to describe the differences, and ask them which suits the spirit of the song best. Do the same with "Old Aunt Rhody" (" The Old Grey Goose").

Relative minor. Analyze "The Erie Canal" to find out why there can be major and minor sections in a song with the key signature unchanged. What kind of minor scale is used? (relative) What are the two relative keys? (F major and D minor) Notate, compare, sing and play these scales. Use the keyboard to see how the two keys are related and can use the same key signature. Try playing the following major and relative minor scales on the bells or piano by ear: C major and A minor; G major and E minor.

Key signatures. Explore the reasons for key signatures. Play familiar songs with arbitrarily changed key signatures. What is the result? Why are key signatures used by composers? This study can relate to scales.

Pentatonic scale. Relate the common pentatonic scale to the black keys of keyboard instruments. Then transpose this scale pattern of whole steps and minor thirds to keys that we think of as C, F, and G. Compare the pentatonic scale pattern to the major scale pattern in those keys. After this, find the form of pentatonic scale that reminds us of the natural minor: major scale steps 6–1–2–3–5–6. Use these scales to compose pentatonic songs and tunes. Listen to a recording of pentatonic music such as Bartók's *An Evening in the Village* (Adventures in Music 5, v 2).

Relative minor. Write major scales in a two-octave range. Find the relative minor scale in each of these and enclose them with bar lines.

Parallel minor. Parallel scales have the same first pitch (tonic). Write and compare C major and C minor; G major and G minor; F major and F minor. Help the students conclude that these scales, unlike the relative scales, need different key signatures. Ask the students to form their own definitions of relative and parallel scales.

Minor chords. Relate major and minor scales to major and minor chords by singing and playing the first, third, and fifth steps of each scale. Find parallel and relative chords on the Autoharp. The 15-chord instrument can sound D major and D minor; G major and G minor; F major and D minor; C major and A minor; B♭ major and G minor.

Relative minor. Examine "We Three Kings of Orient Are." Decide whether relative keys or parallel keys are present, and justify your decison.

Parallel minor. Listen to Bizet's *Farandole* from L'Arlesienne Suite No. 2, AM 6 v 1. Try to determine whether there are relative or parallel keys present.

Parallel minor. Sing "Streets of Laredo," p. 372, in major as written except the last verse; sing that in minor. Determine whether you have sung in parallel or relative keys; notate the scales.

Natural minor. Find the natural minor scale pattern by beginning the scale on *la* or 6 of the major scale in any given key signature. Draw its pattern to show where the whole and half steps are. Relate the scale to songs in this tonality—the Aeolian mode. Compare the natural minor scale pattern with the major scale pattern. Have children play the two scales on the bells or small wind instruments. Have them compose melodies in this minor tonality.

Whole-tone scale. Notate "Lovely Evening" in a whole-tone scale and sing it from notation.

Invented scales. Have the students invent their own original scales. These might have as few as four steps or as many as twelve. Ask them to write melodies based on these scales. Use them with familiar songs to discover what happens when a song is played in a new scale setting.

EXPLORATORY ACTIVITIES

1. Make a collection of songs that can be taught in ways that give the out-of-tune singers pleasurable participation and experiences that lead to their eventual singing in tune.

2. The black keys of the piano form a pentatonic scale. Compose a song or tune on the black keys. Add a bagpipe (open-fifth) bass for an accompaniment.

3. Investigate ways other than numerals, syllables, and note names to help identify scale tones. The American shapenote system is one. Another is an idea of the late W. Otto Miessner which he stated in an article, "The Art of Tonal Thinking," *Music Educators Journal,* January 1962.

4. Learn to identify songs that are in minor keys from the notation of the song. If the song's final note can be identified as scale tone six in the *major* scale derived from the key signature, then the song is in minor, and this note is the name of the minor key in which it is written.

5. A fifth-grade boy asks, "Why are there two flats in the key of B♭ major?" Ask him to answer his own question by using the bells. Clues: remember the half steps between scale tones 3 and 4, and 7 and 8; build the scale beginning on B♭.

6. Listen to Mary Helen Richards' *Threshold to Music* Teacher Training Recording and identify more activities teachers use to attain their objectives.

References for singing will be found at the end of Chapter Sixteen.

chapter fifteen

Understanding Musical Form

Forms of Melodies The answers to the questions, "Is the tune the same or is it different now?" and "How is it different?" guide children into learning concepts of the different ways melodies are put together. Very young children can answer these questions. The mind seeks a sense of order, and music is one of the better ways to foster the concept of form. Students can listen for form, hear it, analyze it, and apply it in their own compositions. The concepts of same, different, repetition, contrast, and variety can grow through finding the phrases of songs and comparing them. This is done first through the ear; later it can seen in notation. In Part Two body movement was shown to be a means of demonstrating these similarities and differences, and percussion instruments were used to emphasize them.

It is important to remember that one-part (unary), two-part (binary), and three-part (ternary) song forms have many variants. Teacher and class should expect to find songs with phrase orders which are modifications of these model forms, and songs with different forms. For a simple example, "Whistle, Daughter, Whistle," has a unary form in which the same phrase is repeated note for note; it could be described as *a a.* "Hole in the Bucket" is also unary, but the phrase ends differently, hence it could be described as *a a'.* (Try adding a bordun and ostinato.)

HOLE IN THE BUCKET

American Folksong

Quickly

1. There's a hole in the buck - et, dear 'Li - za, dear 'Li - za,
2. Then mend it, dear Wil - lie, dear Wil - lie, dear Wil - lie,

There's a hole in the buck - et, dear 'Li - za, a hole.
Then mend it, dear Wil - lie, dear Wil - lie, mend it.

"Go Tell Aunt Rhody" is an example of binary form in which there are two unlike phrases, thus *a b.* "Li'l 'Liza Jane" is a variant of this, with four phrases, *a a' b b'.*

GO TELL AUNT RHODY

American Song

Sadly

1. Go tell Aunt Rho - dy, Go tell Aunt Rho - dy,
2. The one she's been sav - ing, The one she's been sav - ing, The

Go tell Aunt Rho - dy, the old gray goose is dead,
one she's been sav - ing to make a feath - er bed.

There are many examples of ternary (three-part) form, of which "O Tannenbaum" is one, *a a b a.* The important aspect is a melodic statement, contrast, then a return to the beginning. Theorists ignore the first repetition of *a,* consider the form to be *a b a,* and compare it to an arch in architecture. "O Tannenbaum" includes another aspect of melody structure, the *sequence,* part of the melody repeated at a higher or lower pitch level. This is a device children can use in their compositions. "I Love the Mountains" is a song which is sequential in character (see page 388).

O TANNENBAUM (O Christmas Tree)

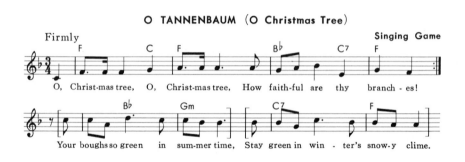

Singing Game

Firmly

O, Christ-mas tree, O, Christ-mas tree, How faith-ful are thy branch - es!

Your boughs so green in sum-mer time, Stay green in win - ter's snow-y clime.

O, Christ-mas tree, O, Christ-mas tree   How faith-ful are   thy   branch-es!

O, Tannenbaum, O, Tannenbaum,
Wie treu sind deine Blätter!
O, Tannenbaum, O, Tannenbaum,
Wie treu sind deine Blätter!
Du grünst nicht nur zur Sommerzeit
Nein auch im Winter, wenn es schneit.
O, Tannenbaum, O, Tannenbaum,
Wie treu sind deine Blätter!

Phrases are often thought of as being four measures in length, and while most songs seem to demonstrate this, phrases can be found that vary from two to eight measures and even longer. The important concept is not their length as much as it is that melodies can be divided into logical parts called phrases. This, of course, is the generalization teachers want students to make. Sometimes two phrases relate to each other in a special way; these two phrases are called a *period*. They can be improvised in the classroom by the teacher singing the first phrase and students taking turns improvising the second phrase; the teacher sings a "question," and the student sings an "answering" phrase.

Sometimes an entire phrase or a part of the melody within a phrase is found to be repeated on a different degree of the scale, either higher or lower than the first appearance of the phrase or note pattern. This was identified as the *sequence.* *

Identifying *same* or *different* is the key to understanding form. Young children's experience with this is at first more physical than it is intellectual. The teacher suggests that they move their bodies in relation to what they hear in the music and "act out" the music to show when it is the same and when it is different. In learning to recognize different phrases or larger contrasting sections of music, children may change movements or steps, reverse directions, and play different kinds of percussion instruments. Phrase repetition and difference are found in the songs children sing and in recorded music to which they listen. As in all aspects of teaching music, teachers select *very clear examples* of the phrase or larger sections of music when their objective is to help children distinguish "same" and "different." Very young children can compare Bartók's *Bear Dance*, which consists of repeated A sections separated by interludes, with Prokofiev's *Waltz on Ice* (both in Adventures in Music 3 v 2) which has three different sections in simple rondo form— A B A C A. Their discoveries may include that music is made of different tunes or parts; sometimes these are the same, sometimes they are different, and some music has more parts than other music. Teachers can use visual aids, such as hats, costumes, streamers, masks, dancers, and colors, to

* A recorded example of sequence in orchestral music is "The Hurdy-Gurdy" from Carpenter's *Adventures in a Perambulator,* Adventures in Music 5 v 2.

dramatize same and different parts of music. To emphasize this in phrases, one group of children can be asked to sing phrases that are alike and another group those that contrast—boys and girls, those with black hair and those with brown hair, those with rubber-soled shoes and those with leather-soled shoes, and so on. Children can sound finger cymbals to mark the ends of phrases; this gives them a purpose for listening carefully. Older students can classify phrases as being alike, different, and almost alike; they can study the notation of recorded music or familiar songs to form the generalization that when phrases look alike, they sound alike. Suggestions in the booklets that accompany the *Adventures in Music* Albums are helpful.

Children are sometimes guided to "act out" phrases in ways such as the arm movements suggested in Figure 15.1.

Students do not always agree in their physical responses to a phrase, some feeling the phrase to be half the length that others may feel it to be. In certain songs it is interesting to note that adults are more apt to feel long phrases than are children, who often feel twice the number of phrases that adults do. When this occurs, children usually divide each long phrase into two shorter ones. In the opinion of the authors, this is not of particular importance, the real point being that children learn to sense that *music is divided into logical sections or parts.* In view of individual differences in musical background, unanimity of response to phrase length cannot be expected. However, the simplicity of most of the songs makes for fairly obvious phrase lengths.

In many songs, recordings, and piano selections there are obviously contrasting, larger sections of the music, each of which may be comprised of a number of phrases.

Teachers have learned that some older students are not greatly interested in phrases and some other structural aspects of music. While from an artistic point of view form is highly important because all works of art have form, and while scholars have written that understanding form is the most fundamental aspect of music learning, children do not always find themselves in agreement with the scholars. These students are practical people, and they are not impressed unless they can understand the *function* of phenomena like form. The function of form seems to be to provide for two

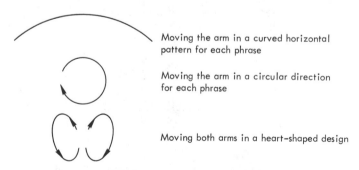

Moving the arm in a curved horizontal pattern for each phrase

Moving the arm in a circular direction for each phrase

Moving both arms in a heart-shaped design

Figure 15.1. "ACTING OUT" PHRASES

opposing concepts, *unity* and *contrast* (variety). Students who have acquired concepts of unity and contrast may find meaning in form. For example, when they are confronted with a phrase order such as *a a b a,* or *a b a c a,* and the teacher asks, "What is there in this tune that gives us a feeling of variety or contrast?" and "What is there that gives us a feeling of unity?" the function of form is made clear. Phrases *b* and *c* provide variety, and phrase *a* provides unity with its repetitions. Understanding this brings added meaning to the form of their own compositions. There are a number of interesting discoveries when they apply the principles of unity and contrast. Perhaps they will decide that the sequence serves both; it offers unity because it is a repetition, but it offers variety because the pitch is different.

Another discovery which concerns form is that melodies can be extended and altered by composers in various ways. By listening to music, making music, and creating music, students discover and use introductions, codas, and interludes. Introductions and codas are usually derived from melodies, but an interlude is often a contrasting section. Repetition is an obvious way to extend melodies. *Thematic development* is a term that describes what composers do with themes (tunes) they use in their larger compositions. When themes are developed they are extended or altered in many ways, including augmentation, diminution, canon, inversion, retrograde, and octave displacement. These are only a sampling of what composers do with the two themes in the middle (development) section of sonata-allegro form.

Before we leave forms *in* music, we should again refer to unity and variety. Aspects of form should be tested and analyzed in these terms. The various forms of melodic alteration sometimes contain both elements. For example, an inverted melody has a natural relation with the original melody; because of this there should be some degree of unity found in it. The students can discover that the rhythm remains the same, providing rhythmic unity. The inverted melody sounds different, however, so variety is also achieved by the inversion. Eventually students will discover that they must analyze unity and variety in terms of the elements of music. Unity may be attained by *repetition* of rhythm, melody, harmony, texture, tempo, dynamics, and tone quality. Variety may be attained by *changes* in rhythm, melody, harmony, texture, tempo, dynamics, and tone quality. When the form *of* music is understood, form can be added to the above list of musical elements. This infers that teachers' questions can be quite to the point. "How is unity achieved in this composition?" "Was there repetition of (any of the above elements of music)?" "How was contrast achieved?" "Was there a change in (any of the above elements of music)?" "How did it change?" In this way analytical listening is guided, and the function of these aspects of form is made clear to the learner. Form becomes a logical scheme of things.

Forms of Music   The songs in music textbooks have been identified as being made of phrases, some repeated note-for-note, some repeated with changes, and some contrasting and different. These are placed in an order that makes musical sense. Songs such as "At Pierrot's Door " ("Au Claire de la Lune"), "The

Blue Bell of Scotland," "The Marines' Hymn," "O Susanna," and "Long, Long Ago," have clearly defined phrases, both repeated and contrasting. Most of the songs are printed with one phrase on each line of a page. When songs are not printed that way, commas, semicolons, and periods in the texts, or rests in the melody offer semireliable clues as to the length of phrases. Song forms presented earlier were one-part (unary) with a phrase arrangement of *a a;* two part (binary) with a phrase arrangement of *a b* or *a a b b;* and three-part (ternary) with a phrase arrangement of *a b a* or *a a b a.* It was stated that there are many variants of these forms.

Examples of one-part songs are Bach's "Cradle Hymn," and the folk song "Whistle, Daughter, Whistle." Other commonly used examples include:

Two-Part Song Form	*Three-Part Song Form*
"Du, Du, Liegst Mir im Herzen"	"Cradle Song" (French folksong)
"Go Tell Aunt Rhody"	"Lightly Row" (includes sequence)
"Li'l 'Liza Jane"	"Rosa, Come and Go Dancing"
"Shortnin' Bread"	(includes sequence)
	"Shoo Fly" (includes sequence)
	"Twinkle, Twinkle, Little Star"
	"Drink To Me Only With Thine Eyes"

From the child's point of view, identifying phrases and larger sections in terms of letters of the alphabet is not very appealing or even as logical as some other ways. To dramatize phrase differences, some teachers find that freeing the children to draw the form in their own creative ways can attract interest and induce far more learning. For example, phrases *a b a* might be:

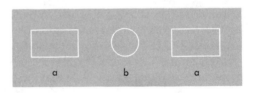

The sections of a rondo could be:

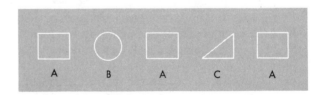

Another form might be drawn as:

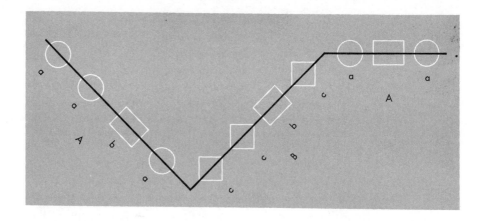

Using colors adds more interest because color highlights the contrasts. Some students will draw objects rather than the geometric designs illustrated here. The evaluative criterion is, "Does this drawing tell us clearly what the form is?" or "Does it show us all the parts in their true order?"

The A B A sectional form is common to many larger compositions. It is the same principle as the *a b a* phrase arrangement except that the concept is expanded into large sections instead of only several phrases.

Larger
Instrumental
Forms

Thematic development. Thematic development as a means of extending melodic-rhythmic ideas can be studied by having older students explore the beginning of Beethoven's Fifth Symphony. "What different things did the composer do with his short idea?" "List them." (The first thing Beethoven did was to write a sequence.) "Listen for an inversion."

Two-part (Binary) Form.

Ginastera: "Wheat Dance" from *Estancia,* AM 4 v 1
Handel: "Bourrée" and "Menuetto" from *Royal Fireworks* Music, AM 3 v 2; BOL 62
Milhaud: "Copacabana" from *Saudades do Brazil,* AM 4 v 2
Respighi: "Danza" from *Brazilian Impressions,* AM 5 v 2
Bach: "Badinerie" from Suite No. 2 in B Minor, AM 3 v 1

Three-Part (Ternary) Form.

Brahms: *Hungarian Dance No.1 in C Minor,* AM 5 v 2
Debussy: *En Bateau,* BOL 53
Offenbach: "Barcarolle" from *Tales of Hoffman,* AM 3 v 1
Schumann: "Traumerei" from *Scenes of Childhood,* AM 4 v 2; BOL 63

Stravinsky: "Berceuse" from *Firebird Suite,* AM 1
Tchaikovsky: "Trepak" from *Nutcracker* Suite, BOL 58
Vaughan Williams: *Fantasia on Greensleeves,* AM 6 v 2
Walton: "Waltz" from *Facade* Suite, AM 6 v 2

Compound Ternary Form. The compound ternary form is one in which each of the A B A sections may be a binary or ternary form within itself. It is found in classical minuets of Haydn and Mozart.

Bizet: "Minuetto" from *L'Arlésienne* Suite No. 1, AM 4 v 2
Haydn: "Menuetto" from Symphony No. 6 in G Major, BOL 63
Mozart: "Menuetto" from Divertimento No. 17 in D Major, AM 5 v 2
Mozart: "Minuet" from Symphony No. 40 in G Minor, BOL 62
Sousa: *Stars and Stripes Forever,* AM 4 v 2 BOL 60

Rondo. The principle of the rondo is a basic theme or section, A, which is alternated with two or more contrasting themes. Children sometimes compare its scheme with a sandwich. The shortest rondo is A B A C A. If one compares A to a slice of bread and B and C to different sandwich fillings, the result is a special kind of double-decker sandwich. Longer rondos may be A B A C A B A or A B A C A D A. (The rondeau is similar; it is an extension of the latter example using a different contrasting section each time; only A repeats.) A beginning concept of the rondo is acquired by young children in simple ways. This might begin with establishing a beat, then asking the class to say the name of the school ("Oak Ridge School") followed by the name of a child, then the name of the school followed by the name of another child, and so on. The teacher's questions will help the class to realize the scheme of what they are doing—what is the same and what is different. Next, the same rondo principle is done with percussion instruments and even with rows of objects in the room. From here the children apply the scheme to short melodies and soon they are composing rondos. To help them compose, the teacher may write the recurring section of a rondo on the chalkboard and assign groups of children (or individual children) to extend the composition according to the plan.

Rondo for Bassoon and Orchestra, Franson, YPR 1009 (ages 6–10)
Beethoven: "Scherzo" from Symphony No. 7, BOL 62
Dvořák: Slavonic Dance in C Minor, AM 4 v 2
Haydn: "Gypsy Rondo" from Trio in G Major, BOL 64 (A B A C A Coda)
Khachaturian: "Waltz" form *Masquerade* Suite, AM 4 v 2 (A B A Interlude C A B A)
Mozart: "Romanze" from *Eine kleine Nachtmusik,* AM 4 v 1 (A B A C A Coda)
Prokofiev: "Waltz on Ice" from *Winter Holiday,* AM 3 v 2
Smetana: "Dance of the Comedians" from *Bartered Bride,* AM 6 v 2; BOL 56
Tchaikovsky: "Waltz" from *Sleeping Beauty,* AM 4 v 1
Kodály: "Viennese Music Clock" from *Háry János* Suite, AM 2 v 1; BOL 81

Variation Form. This form is an extension of the concept of altering melodies. However, as learners' concepts of variation grow, they find that the music can be varied in terms of its melody, rhythm, harmony, texture, tempo, dynamics, form, tone quality, and its general style. This can make listening to variations somewhat like a mystery that gradually resolves itself as the listener detects which musical elements the composer changes in order to create the variation. Generally there is a theme (melody), followed by the different treatments of it. Unity is provided by the theme, which is always present in some form; variety is provided by the changing of any of the musical elements. There are variations in which a melody or chord progression is repeated over and over, with variety coming from changes in the other elements.

Hot Cross Buns, Franson CRG 5005 (ages 5–8)
Guarnieri: *Brazilian Dance,* AM 6 v 2; BOL 55
Anderson: *The Girl I Left Behind Me,* AM 5 v 2
Copland: "Simple Gifts" from *Appalachian Spring,* BOL 65
Cailliet: *Variations on Pop! Goes the Weasel,* AM 4 v 1; BOL 65
Ives: *Variations on "America,"* Louisville Records*
Kraft: *Variations for Percussion Instruments,* BOL 83
Gould: *American Salute,* AM 5 v 1: BOL 65

Variation Form: Teaching. The Cailliet *Variations on Pop! Goes the Weasel* cn be useful as an example of how to help children learn the principles of the form. Its sections are as follows:

Introduction and theme:	Can the students sense the meter? Can they tell if a full orchestra is playing? Can they hear whether or not one section of the orchestra predominates?
1. Fugue	In a fugue, the same melody is played at different times by different instruments at different pitch levels, but it gives the impression of a round because of the entries of these parts. Does it sound that way here? What is the order of the entering instruments? (Six instruments are featured before the entire orchestra plays the tune.)
2. Minuet	What is the meter in this formal dance, the minuet? Hear two melodies played at once. Which instrument plays the melody and which plays another tune? Can *augmentation* (playing the melody in longer note values) be identified?
3. Adagio	What elements of the music produce the mood here, and what do you think this mood is? A new tune is introduced, a Jewish wedding song.

* An analysis of Ives' *Variations on America* appears in the October, 1974, *Music Educators Journal,* pp. 66–67. The recording referred to in the article is Columbia MS-6161, *The Organ in America.*

4. Music box	What is a music box? What instruments are used to sound like a music box? What did the composer do to make the "oomp-pa-pa" effect?
5. Jazz	What meter does the composer choose here? Listen to the trumpet with the "Wa-Wa" mute. What do you think the player does with the mute to make this sound? How does the composer make the music sound like jazz? What happens to the melody this time? Now ask the class to define "variation form" in their own words. Ask them in how many ways they think a melody can be varied in a variation form.

Listening to recorded variations such as *Laideronnette, Empress of the Pagodas,* by Ravel, AM 4 v 2, and *Pop! Goes the Weasel,* by Cailliet, AM 4 v 1, will assist young composers in their search for techniques to employ in their efforts to write variations of simple tunes such as "Hot Cross Buns." The teacher may ask questions of the listeners concerning what they hear in terms of texture (monophonic, homophonic, and polyphonic), melody, ostinato, countermelody, major, minor, tempo, and meter.

Fugue. The fugue is a rather complex polyphonic form. A theme (subject) is introduced by two or more voices in turn, developed in what can be considered another section, then restated in the final part of the form. If students should describe a fugue after listening to it carefully, they might say that when one voice or instrument states a theme and then continues playing another melody while a second voice states the theme a fourth lower or a fifth higher, the beginning of a fugue has been created. The melody the first voice plays or sings when the second voice sounds the theme is called the *countersubject.* This process may continue with the entrance of other voices, each beginning with the subject. This first section is called an *exposition.* It is followed by a free section consisting of statements of the subject, often in altered forms, and *episodes,* something akin to interludes, based on tone patterns or rhythm patterns found in the subject and countersubject. Sometimes there is a *stretto* near the end, when the voices sound the subject in a way in which there is overlapping of the entrances. The subject is restated at the end to establish unity. Contemporary composers do not always plan their fugues in the traditional scheme described here.

The fugue may appear complicated by its description, and the teacher must use good judgment in knowing how far to expect a class of eleven-year-olds to proceed with it. Depending on the group, going into fine detail will be something only advanced students will find interesting. However, the entire class can detect the unique beginning and the texture of the fugue; even young children can do this.

McBride: *Pumpkineater's Little Fugue,* BOL 65
Thomson: *Fugue and Chorale on Yankee Doodle,* BOL 65
Scarlatti: *Cat's Fugue,* Keyboard Junior Recordings

Bach: Little Fugue in G Minor, BOL 86, AM 6 v 1
Bizet: "Farandole" from *L'Arlésienne* Suite No. 2, AM 6 v 1

Sonata-Allegro From. The sonata-allegro form is an expanded A B A form. Its plan is a statement of two different themes followed by a development of those themes as a contrasting section, then a restatement of the themes to provide unity. Sometimes one of the themes will be in a familiar song-form. The first theme is apt to be masculine and vigorous while the second theme may be feminine and lyrical, thus providing contrast. Often there are transitional passages between this first part of the form, the *exposition,* and the second part, the *development.* In the development section the themes and parts of themes are treated in many different ways, and the listener may identify inversion, rhythmic alteration, sequence, change of key, and many other techniques composers use in creating variety. The final section is the *recapitulation,* in which there is a restatement of the themes, often followed by a coda. This form is used as the first movement of a symphony, sonata, concerto, quartet, and quintet, as well as appearing in some overtures and other forms.

Schubert: First Movement from Symphony No. 5, AM 5 v 1
Mozart: First Movement from Symphony No. 40, BOL 71
Prokofiev: *Classical* Symphony, BOL 73

The Suite. The suite has an interesting history which some advanced students may want to research. The suites we hear today are often dance suites in which a series of related dances constitute the composition, the ballet suite, the opera suite, and suites based on dramatic (stage) works. The dance suites are usually made up of dances of the sixteenth and seventeenth centuries, the allemand, courante, saraband, gigue, and a number of others. The suites based on stage works such as opera, ballet, and drama, are selections taken from music written for these works and arranged for concert performance. Still other suites are written on ideas such as philosophy, psychology, and geography.

DANCE SUITES
Bach: *English* Suites
Handel: *Harpsichord* Suites

BALLET SUITES
Tchaikovsky: *Nutcracker* Suite, BOL 58
Stravinsky: *Petrouchka* Suite
Ravel: *Daphnis and Chloe* Suite No. 2, BOL 86
Rimsky-Korsakov: *Scheherazade* Suite, BOL 77

BASED ON STAGE WORKS
Grieg: *Peer Gynt* Suite, BOL 59
Walton: *Facade* Suite

OPERA SUITES
Bizet: *Carmen* Suite
Menotti: Suite from *Amahl and the Night Visitors,* BOL 58

GEOGRAPHICAL SUITES
Grofé: *Grand Canyon* Suite, BOL 61
Grofé: *Mississippi River* Suite, BOL 61

Tone Poem. The symphonic poem or tone poem is a work for symphony orchestra in which the form is dictated by a story, a description, or a character.

Strauss: *Til Eulenspiegel and His Merry Pranks* (a lengthy work for older children)
Mussorgsky: *Night on Bald Mountain,* BOL 81. This short tone poem is a favorite at Halloween time.
Saint-Saëns: *Danse Macabre,* BOL 81. (Another Halloween favorite)

Opera, Oratorio, Cantata. These are large vocal works. The opera is a stage play in which the words are sung and in which the singers are accompanied by an orchestra. There may be duets, trios, quartets, sextets, and other ensembles, a chorus, and even a ballet. The *recitative* is a rather declamatory vocal style that attempts to imitate speech; an *aria* is a solo; an *arioso* is a style midway between the recitative and aria.

Menotti: *Amahl and the Night Visitors* (can be used in its entirety at Christmas)
Humperdinck: *Hansel and Gretel* (use selections from, and relate to the story)
Bizet: *Carmen* (use selections from, and the story)
Rossini: *William Tell Overture* (an opera overture to hear, and the story) BOL 76; AM 3 v 1
Verdi: *Aida* (use selections from, and the story)
Britten: *The Little Sweep* (can be used in entirety)
Mozart: *The Magic Flute* (selections from, with simplified story)
Child's Introduction to Opera, Childcraft Records, Album 38. (includes *Barber of Seville, Amahl and the Night Visitors,* and *Hansel and Gretel*)

Multiple Concepts. A recording that contains examples of various forms is Jurey's *Design in Music* (Bowmar Records). It contains the following pieces: a waltz (A B A form); rondo (A B A C A); theme and five variations; symphony in miniature:

> First Movement: Sonata-Allegro form with the songs "Erie Canal" and "Red River Valley"
> Second Movement: Song form with "All Through the Night" and "All the Pretty Little Horses"
> Third Movement: Scherzo form with "Merrily We Roll Along" and "Good Night Ladies"
> Fourth Movement: Rondo form with more children's game songs
> (transparencies for overhead projector containing themes of all compositions are available)

See also at the end of this chapter (p. 348) the list of films useful for teaching about form.

Exploring the Manipulation of Melodies

In a preceding chapter certain aspects of music composition were explored with percussion instruments in a nonmelodic situation. These were augmentation, diminution, and canonic treatment. (See p. 245, "Rhythm-Related Compositional Devices.") These can be applied to melodies in the same way, and older learners can experiment with them in their compositions. Other composer's techniques that children can learn to employ include *transposition,* placing the melody in another key, *inversion,* writing it upside down, *retrograde,* writing it backwards, giving it a *variations* treatment by altering it rhythmically, melodically, or harmonically, and using *octave displacement,* which is distorting the melody with octave leaps. Octave displacement, inversion, and retrograde are illustrated below with "London Bridge." Stravinsky's "Greeting Prelude" exemplifies octave displacement

LONDON BRIDGE

Singing Game

Lon - don Bridge is fall - ing down, fall - ing down, fall - ing down.

Lon - don Bridge is fall - ing down, My fair la - dy. ____

Inverted

(complete it)

Retrograde

(complete it)

Octave Displacement

(complete it)

Table 15.1. Song Melodies in Symphonic Music

Composer	Title	Song
ANDERSON	Irish Suite	"Irish Washerwoman," "Minstrel Boy," "Wearing of the Green," "The Girl I Left Behind Me"
BARLOW	The Winter's Passed	"Wayfaring Stranger," "Black Is the Color of My True Love's Hair"
BEETHOVEN	String Quartet Op. 59, No. 2; Symphony 8, Second Movement, Third Theme; Symphony 9, Fourth Movement; Wellington's Victory	Russian hymn "Praise to God" (*This Is Music Book 4*); "The Metronome" (Adventures in Music 6 v 1); United Nations Hymn" ("World Anthem") (*This Is Music Book 6*); "For He's a Jolly Good Fellow"
BLOCH	America	"Yankee Doodle," "Old Folks at Home," "Hail Columbia"
BRAHMS	Academic Festival Overture	"Guadeamus Igitur" (student song often found in series books for grades 7–8) (Bowmar #76)
CAILLIET	Variations on Pop! Goes the Weasel	"Pop! Goes the Weasel" (Bowmar #65) (Adventures in Music 4 v 1)
CHOPIN	Fantasy Impromptu	"I'm Always Chasing Rainbows"
COPLAND	Appalachian Spring; Billy the Kid, Fourth Theme; Lincoln Portrait; Rodeo	"Simple Gifts" (Bowmar #75); "Goodbye, Old Paint"; "Camptown Races," "Springfield Mountain"; "Hoe-Down" (Adventures in Music 5 v 2) (Bowmar #55)
DOHNÁNY	Variations on a Nursery Tune (for older children)	"Twinkle, Twinkle, Little Star" (piano and orchestra)
DVOŘÁK	Symphony 5	"Swing Low, Sweet Chariot" (First Movement, Third Theme) "Going Home" (Second Movement, First Theme)
GOULD	American Salute; Cowboy Rhapsody; Variations on When Johnny Comes Marching Home	"When Johnny Comes Marching Home" (Adventures in Music 5 v 1) (Bowmar #65); "Goodbye, Old Paint," "Home on the Range"; "When Johnny Comes Marching Home"
GRAINGER	Londonderry Air	"Londonderry Air" (Adventures in Music 4 v 2)
GROFÉ	Death Valley Suite	"O Susanna" (Adventures in Music 4 v 1), "Old Folks at Home," "Old Black Joe"
GUION	Turkey in the Straw	"Old Zip Coon" (same tune)
HARRIS	Folk Song Symphony	"Irish Washerwoman," "Bury Me Not on the Lone Prairie," "Streets of Laredo," "Turkey in the Straw," "When Johnny Comes Marching Home"
HAYDN	"Emperor" Quartet in C Major	"Glorious Things of Thee Are Spoken" (Austrian National Hymn) Appears in several of the music series

Composer	Work	Related Songs
HINDEMITH	Trauermusic (Funeral Music)	"Old Hundred" Both melody and harmony are manipulated
HUMPERDINCK	Hansel and Gretel, Prelude to Act 1	"Prayer," "Song of the Gingerbread Children," "Partner, Come and Dance With Me"
IVES	Fifth Movement, Symphony No. 2	"Camptown Races," "Long, Long Ago," "Reveille"
KAY	Western Symphony	"Red River Valley," "The Girl I Left Behind Me," "Golden Slippers," "Jim Along Josie" (Vox Recording)
McBRIDE	Mexican Rhapsody Pumpkineater's Little Fugue	"Hat Dance," "Rancho Grande," "La Cucaracha" "Peter, Peter, Pumpkin Eater" (Bowmar #65)
McDONALD	Children's Symphony	"Farmer in the Dell," "Jingle Bells" (Adventures in Music 3 v 2), "London Bridge," "Baa, Baa, Black Sheep," "Oh, Dear, What Can the Matter Be?" "Little Bo Peep"
MAHLER	First Symphony, Third Movement	"Are You Sleeping?"
MUSSORGSKY	Boris Godunov, Coronation Scene	"Praise to God" (This is Music Book 4)
NELSON	Kentucky Mountain Portraits	"Cindy," "Skip to My Lou," "Paw Paw Patch"
QUILTER	A Children's Overture	"Girls and Boys Come Out to Play," "St. Paul's Steeple," "Dame Get Up and Bake Your Pies," "Over the Hills and Far Away," "The Frog and the Crow," "The Frog He Would A-Wooing Go," "Oranges and Lemons," "Baa, Baa, Black Sheep"
ROSSINI	William Tell Overture	"Lone Ranger Theme" (Bowmar #76) (Adventures in Music 3 v 1)
SIBELIUS	Finlandia	"Song of Peace" and other titles
SOWERBY	Irish Washerwoman	"Lane County Bachelor" and other titles
STRAVINSKY	Greeting Prelude	"Happy Birthday to You" (Columbia Record Instrumental Miniatures)
R. STRAUSS	Aus Italien	"Funiculi, Funicula"
THOMSON	"Cattle," from The Plow That Broke the Plains	"My Home's in Montana," "I Ride an Old Paint," "The Streets of Laredo" (Bowmar #76)
THOMSON	Fugue and Chorale on a Yankee Doodle Theme	"Yankee Doodle" (Bowman #65)
TCHAIKOVSKY	1812 Overture Symphony 4, Fourth Movement	"Russian National Hymn" and other titles "The Birch Tree" (Adventures in Music 6 v 2)
VARDELL	Joe Clark Steps Out	"Old Joe Clark" (Mercury Recording)
VAUGHAN-WILLIAMS	Fantasia on Greensleeves	"What Child Is This?" ("Greensleeves") (Adventures in Music 6 v 2)

347

with the familiar tune, "Happy Birthday to You," and it is useful at every elementary school level. "Greeting Prelude" is included on the Columbia Record *Instrumental Miniatures,* a group of short pieces by Stravinsky. It is found in several music textbooks, with one suggesting that "Hot Cross Buns" be treated this way. Examples useful in exploring variation form include excerpts from variations Mozart wrote on a French folk tune we know as "Twinkle, Twinkle, Little Star,"* and the *Second Movement* of Haydn's *C Major* (Emperor) *Quartet,* which uses a familiar hymn tune.

The most popular approach in introducing the manipulation of melodies is by means of very simple and well-known songs. Some additional examples include "Baa, Baa, Black Sheep," "Three Blind Mice," "Are You Sleeping?" and "Mary Had a Little Lamb."

Thematic Development Familiar melodies comprise one successful approach to the study of symphonic music. When a song is well known by children, they thrill to its discovery in symphonic works and their interest in listening is stimulated. However, identifying the melody is only a first step. Because the essence of symphonic music is *thematic development,* the answer to the question, "What does the composer do with his or her tune?" can bring forth exciting explorations. How fully students are able to reply to the question will depend upon their stage of musical development. If they have a background of experience in composers' devices, they will identify many of them in their analyses of such compositions. Knowledge of variation form will assist such explorations.

Familiar melodies that appear in symphonic music are listed in Table 15.1 on pp. 346–347.

References on Form

GARY, CHARLES L., ed., *The Study of Music in the Elementary School—A Conceptual Approach.* Reston, Va.: Music Educators National Conference, 1967. Pp. 85–112. For teachers' lesson plans.

Films and Filmstrips *Discovering Form in Music,* BFA Educational Media, 2211 Michigan Avenue, Santa Monica, Calif. 90404 (phrases and sections)

Forms of Music: Instrumental, Coronet Instructional Films, 65 E. South Water St., Chicago, Ill. 60601 (sonata, concerto, symphony, and tone poem; for advanced students)

Let's Discover the Design, EMC Corporation, St. Paul, Minn. 55101. (Ages 10 and up)

The Metropolitan Opera Box for ages 11–18. Education at the Met, 1865 Broadway, New York, N.Y. 10023. Ten operas with teacher's manuals, recordings, filmstrips, and handouts.

* "Ah! Vous dirai-je Maman." Odyssey Y-30289.

Young People's Concert Series (Leonard Bernstein): *What Makes Music Symphonic? What Is a Concerto?; What Is Sonata Form?* McGraw-Hill Films, 1221 Avenue of the Americas, New York, N.Y. 10020. (60 min.) Ages 10–Adult. Also inquire at local Bell Telephone Office for possible free availability.

chapter sixteen

Part Singing

Part singing is a pleasurable activity that relates to the study of harmony and polyphony. It is a necessity for boys whose voices are beginning to change. Furthermore, every singer enjoys the aesthetic and social values of good part singing.

Traditionally, two-part singing is emphasized for ten-year-olds and three-part singing is introduced and worked with for eleven-year-olds. There are types of preparatory part singing in the primary grades that include ostinati and echo-type songs, discussed earlier, and simple rounds, canons, and descants.

Dialogue Songs Among the several theories about progressing toward comprehension of the vertical aspects of music (hearing more than one part at a time) is one that begins with the dialogue song, in which children are divided into two groups which take turns singing the sections. While this is not part singing in the harmonic sense, it is assumed that the singers will become accustomed to being assigned to groups responsible for singing their respective parts at the proper time in relation to the other parts. An example of a dialogue song for intermediate grades is "The Keeper."

Rounds and Canons The singings of rounds and canons* is believed to be a step toward the comprehension of harmony. Whether this opinion can be justified depends upon how such songs are taught. If children are taught to sing them in a manner

---

* Rounds and canons are similar. A round repeats (goes back to the beginning) whereas a canon does not. A round is a "circle canon" that is in unison; every performer

Old English
Dialogue Song

Unknown

The keep-er did a-shoot-ing go, And
un-der his cloak he car-ried a bow, All for to shoot at a
mer-ry lit-tle doe, A-mong the leaves so__ green, O!

Jack-ie boy! Sing ye well! Hey down,
Mas-ter! Ve-ry well! Ho down,

Der-ry der-ry down, A-mong the leaves so__ green, O! To my
A-mong the leaves so__ green, O!

hey, down, down! Hey down,
To my ho, down, down! Ho down,

der-ry der-ry down, A-mong the leaves so__ green, O!
A-mong the leaves so__ green, O!

sings the same part, but at different times. Canons may be more complex than rounds, with entrances at different pitch intervals.

that leads them to out-shout other parts, or to put their hands over their ears so that they cannot hear the other parts, then no real part singing is taking place. If, on the other hand, they are taught in a manner that leads the singers to hear how the other parts join with theirs, then the experience can justifiably be called a form of part singing. The teaching procedure may be outlined as follows:

1. The children learn the melody well.
2. The children learn to hear the harmony upon which the melody is based. The teacher chords this harmony on the Autoharp or piano, or uses a recording that provides a clear and simple harmonization. The children are told how many times they are to sing the song.
3. The hearing of the new part (second entrance) of the round is accomplished by the teacher singing or playing this part while the class is softly singing the first part and is listening to how the parts join together to make interesting music.
4. Some children join with the teacher on the new part. Listening to all the parts and how they join together in the harmonic setting is stressed. Balance of the parts so that all singers can hear all of the parts is essential.
5. If the round is of more than two parts, the new parts are added in the same general manner as above.
6. Rounds can be ended in three different ways: each part can finish separately, all parts can end on a chord together (each part stopping wherever it may be in the round), and each part can sustain the final note of that part until all parts are finished.

Remember that pentatonic melodies can usually be sung as rounds. Listening to a tape recording of the singing can focus attention on hearing both parts and how they relate vertically, as well as on tone quality and balance.

Rounds and canons are emphasized in fourth and fifth grades and are used less frequently in the primary grades because many of the children are not of sufficient musical maturity to be able to sing them well and to hear with understanding what they are doing. It is possible, however, for first-grade children to sing canons like "Old Texas" because they are *echo-type* songs.

Frequently sung rounds include "Are You Sleeping?", "Three Blind Mice," "Little Tom Tinker," "Row Your Boat," "Scotland's Burning," "Sweetly Sings the Donkey, "Kookaburra," and "The Canoe Song."

ROUND OF THANKS

OLD TEXAS

Canon

I'm goin' to leave _____ ol'_ Tex-as now _____ They've got no

I'm goin' to leave _____ ol'_ Tex-as now _____

use _____ for the long-horn cow. _____

_ They've got no use _____ for the long-horn cow.

PRAY GOD BLESS

Four-part round

Pray God bless all friends here, A

mer-ry mer-ry Christ-mas and a hap-py New Year.

Composing Chants

Chants (vocal ostinati) have been defined as recurring vocal patterns or figures. These added parts have value as creative and part-singing activities as well as being music that some immature singers can sing in tune.

Initial experiences in harmonic writing of simple chants may be gained through the use of well-known songs that can be accompanied by only one chord such as "Row Your Boat," "Are You Sleeping?" and "Little Tom Tinker." The first tone to be used would be the chord root. Using this tone, invent a rhythm pattern that contrasts with the melody. The regular recurrence of this rhythmic pattern is sung on the pitch of the chord root (i.e., the home tone, "1," or "do"). For example, in the case of "Row Your Boat" the patterns that can be composed to be sung in conjunction with the melody are myriad. A few of them are:

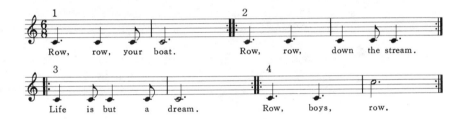

Row, row, your boat. Row, row, down the stream.

Life is but a dream. Row, boys, row.

Percussion instruments are frequently used to accentuate the rhythm of a chant, and melody instruments are sometimes of aid in keeping some children on pitch. For dramatic effect those children singing the chant often begin about four measures before the melody begins, thus adding an *introduction* to the song. They also may continue for a few measures after the melody is finished, thus adding a *coda*. "Row Your Boat" may be sung as a melody with an added chant. When sung as a two-part round, addition of the chant results in a form of three-part singing, and when extended to be a four-part round, the chant adds a fifth part. With such simple song material, three- and four-part singing of this type can be done in fourth grade. Furthermore, the chant itself can be extended so that still more parts result.

For example, the above chants are pitched on "1" (C) of the tonic chord. The chanters can be divided into two groups with one group singing on scale tone 3 at the same time the other sings on 1. When this is learned, the chanters can be divided further into three groups singing on scale tones 1, 3, and 5 respectively. This is an example of vocal chording done in the rhythm of a chant. The melody adds a part. If the chant now consists of three parts and the round is sung in four parts, a seven-part song results. The teacher is, of course, limited in the number of possible parts by the musical maturity and size of the group. However, the possibilities present in this simple music are surprising. Chording instruments can be a companion activity to this type of part singing (see Table 16.1). (See Piano Chording in Chapter Seventeen for an explanation of chords.)

Thus far we have been concerned with the one-note chant. There are other possibilities. For example, "Are You Sleeping?" could have chants as follows:

"Little Tom Tinker" could have these:

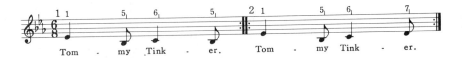

Multiple chants (two or more different ones) could conceivably be employed in the same song. However, if too many different words are sung at one time, the meaning is lost and the effect ceases to be very musical. Experimenting by substituting neutral syllables or melody instruments may be worthwhile.

When chants are sung with two-chord songs, the initial experiences are usually with scale tone 5 because that tone is common to two chords, I and V_7. This is the only tone of the scale on which it is possible to create a one-

Table 16.1. Chant Patterns for Simple Harmony

I-Chord Harmonization	V_7-Chord Harmonization
5 5 5	5 5 5
5 6 5	5 6 5
5 3 5	5 2 5, 5 4 5
3 5 3	2 5 2, 4 5 4
1 3 5, 5 3 1	5 4 2, 2 4 5
1 8, 8 1	5_1 5, 5 5_1
8 5 8	2 5 2, 7 5 7
8 7 6 5	7 7 6 5, 7 6 5 5
8 5 6 7	5 5 6 7, 7 6 5 5
8 5 6 5	7 5 6 5, 2 5 6 5
8 7 6 5, 5 6 7 8	5 4 3 2

pitch chant in such songs. Such rhythmic chants for "Three Blind Mice" might be:

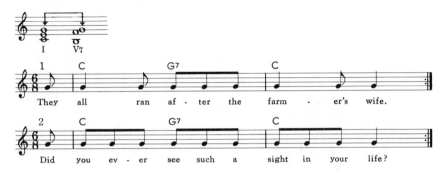

Children often alter the final repetition of such chants in order that the last pitch sung will be the home tone.

Another commonly used chant is one based on the scale tones 5 and 6. Scale tone 6 is a member of neither the I nor the V_7 chord, yet it has the unusual quality of not interfering with the harmony as long as it is placed on an unaccented part of the measure. This kind of a chant for "Looby Loo"* could be:

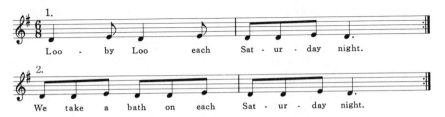

* This song describes an old American custom before the days of plumbing. The children are taking a bath in a washtub near the kitchen stove which burned wood or coal. They are testing the temperature before getting into the tub.

This 5–6–5 pattern works very well with songs like "Old Texas," "Ten Little Indians" and "Skip to My Lou"; children can invent many rhythmic variants of it.

LOOBY LOO

Lively

American Singing Game

Here we go loo - by loo_____ Here we go loo - by light_____

Here we go loo - by loo_____ all on a Sat - ur - day night_____ I

put my right hand in_____ I put my right hand out_____ I

give my right hand a shake shake shake and turn my - self a - bout._____

2. left hand   3. right foot   4. left foot   5. whole self

Although all good chants are essentially simple, slightly more complex chants can be written for songs like "Looby Loo." One way to proceed with writing such a chant is to analyze the harmony of "Looby Loo" and chart it to find what this harmony demands of a four-measure-long chant. Looking at the song, we find that it consists of four four-measure phrases. The problem is to find what chords harmonize each of the measures, and view this in a vertical fashion to find how to write a chant that will fit this harmonic arrangement. We find:

measure	1	2	3	4 (of each phrase)
phrase 1......	G	G	G	D$_7$
phrase 2......	G	G	D$_7$	G
phrase 3......	G	G	G	G
phrase 4......	G	G	G D$_7$	G
	G	G	G&D$_7$	G&D$_7$

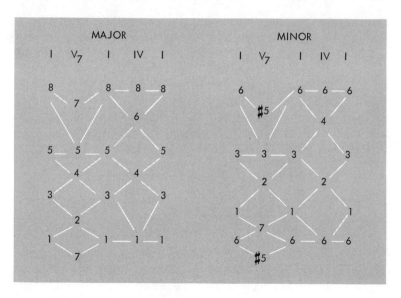

Figure 16.1. CHORD PATTERNS

Looking down the columns it can be seen that a chant for "Looby Loo" must be written in the following harmonic scheme: the first measure of the chant requires a pattern related to the G chord (I); the second measure requires a pattern related to the G chord; the third and fourth measures require patterns related to *both* G and D_7 (V_7) chords. This means that during measures three and four, the chant is restricted to patterns such as those made up of scale tone 5, or scale tones 5 and 6—simple patterns that sound well with *either* chord I or V_7.

The chart in Figure 16.1 is included for those who wish to pursue more fully the writing of chants and other added parts to songs. It endeavors to picture some of the simple movements of tones possible during common chord changes. It will assist in the writing of descants as well as chants.

Chants may become monotonous because of their constant repetition. Therefore it is desirable that they be omitted from sections of some songs. Chants for three-chord songs are necessarily more complex, since they are based upon the tones of three chords rather than two.

Counter-melodies and Descants Singing countermelodies and descants constitutes another of the many approaches. A countermelody is an added melodic part, usually lower than the original melody, which often *imitates* it and often moves in *contrary motion* to it. Ideally, a descant is a melody in its own right although written to accompany another melody. In practice, the descant is subordinate to the melody. It is usually higher in pitch than the melody; a small group of children sing it while the majority of the children sing the melody. The reason for this is that high pitches sound relatively louder than low piches when they are combined in part singing; therefore a small group on a high part balances with a larger group on a low part. When teachers understand the relation between countermelodies or descants, the chords and the original melodies, they can guide children to compose them. The first example is a countermelody to "Down in the Valley." In this case it is of such melodic nature in its own right that it is easier to sing than the real melody. Eight-year-olds can sing this simple polyphony.

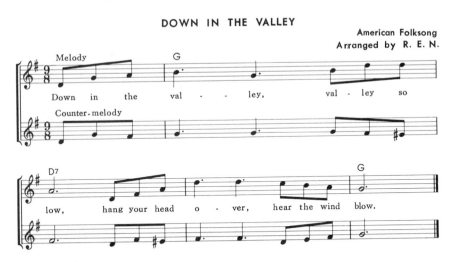

A beautiful traditional-type descant, higher than the melody, and therefore to be sung by a small group, is one composed by Ewald Nolte to "Silent Night." It is intended for sixth grade.

peace, _____   Sleep ____ in heav - en - ly   peace. _____

From Beattie, Wolverton, Wilson, and Hinga, *The American Singer, Combined Grades.* Used by permission of D. C. Heath and Company.

Ideally, countermelodies and descants should be learned in integral relation to the original melody, because when they are learned as separate songs and then combined, many students fail to hear the harmonic relationship of the two parts. The melody should be well learned first of all, and a feeling for the harmony should be established with guitar, Autoharp, or piano.

The elementary school chorus may learn a descant or countermelody to be sung while the others sing a melody; and these may be combined in an assembly program. Likewise, students who are musically advanced may prepare descants out of school to be used in class with the melody sung by the others. Another use for this type of added part is with certain melody instruments—from Melody Flutes, recorders, and bells to violins and flutes. If done with discretion, employing a melody instrument is a way of strengthening either or both parts.

Partner Songs   Some songs having identical harmonization can be sung simultaneously. A major value of this is recreational, because the attempt is fun. However, this has value in learning to sing in parts if it is taught in the same general manner suggested for rounds, remembering that the singers should hear both parts as they sing, and that aesthetic values should not be forgotten. "Three Blind Mice," "Row Your Boat," "Are You Sleeping," and "The Farmer in the Dell" can be combined with each other. Other combinations are "Bow, Belinda," "Sandy Land," "Paw Paw Patch," "Ten Little Indians" and "Skip to My Lou"; the choruses of "Blue-Tail Fly" and "Shoo Fly"; "Solomon Levi" and "A Spanish Cavalier"; "Darling Nellie Gray" and "When You and I Were Young, Maggie"; "Goodnight Ladies" and "When the Saints Go Marching In"; "Keep the Home Fires Burning" and "There's a Long, Long Trail"; "Humoresque," "Annie Laurie" and "Old Folks at Home"; and "Ring the Banjo" and "The Girl I Left Behind Me." Frederick Beckman has developed this idea in his two collections, *Partner Songs* and *More Partner Songs,* published by Ginn and Company. They can be used in intermediate grades.

Students should be guided to answer the question, "Why do these songs sound acceptable when they are sung at the same time?" The answer should be found by conducting experiments. "Let's try 'America' and 'The Star-Spangled Banner' to find out how they sound together." "What happened?" "Why don't they sound well in certain places?" "Let's write those notes on the board to see what they are and how they combine." "How many different aspects of music must be the same when two songs can be combined?" "Let's try to list them." Older learners may be able to make a generalization that when melodies have the same meter, tempo, and harmonic arrangement, they can be combined. An example of combining songs is the following, in which "Lone Star Trail" and "Leaving Old Texas" are arranged to "fit together."

THE LONE STAR TRAIL

(Descant: "Leavin' Old Texas") American Cowboy Songs
Arranged by R. E. N.

From *This Is Music,* Book V, by William R. Sur et. al. Copyright © 1971 by Allyn and Bacon, Inc. Used by permission.

Harmonic Endings   This simple and effective way to develop a feeling for harmony may be initiated in third grade, where two-part harmonic endings may be used, and expanded in the fourth grade to three-part endings. In this activity teachers add a part or parts to the final note or notes of a song. For example, "Three Blind Mice" ends with scale tones 3–2–1. The class would be told to sing or hum those tones softly while they listen to the teacher* sing the words on scale tones 3–2–3. Next, those who believe they can sing the new part will join with the teacher while the others continue singing the melody. It has been the experience of many teachers that some children may have never been conscious of their ability to hear two different pitches at one time in this fashion. These may ask to sing such a harmonic ending again and again in order that they may fully enjoy what is to them a new comprehension of beauty.

This idea can be expanded as follows:

Harmonic endings can be easily arranged by teachers and students. It is recommended that these be taught first by rote, since the aim is to concentrate on harmonic feeling. Perhaps this activity provides a helpful background for later improvising of parts (barbershop harmony) and for singing thirds and sixths. Eventually it can lead to an understanding and purposeful use of notation in part singing.

Chord Roots   Chord roots constitute one of the easiest parts to add to a song because of the harmonic strength of the root, which is the foundation tone of each chord. Although this activity is primarily for older students, it is possible for some younger ones to take part in it. The songs employed are those that are best harmonized by only two or three chords. The following example can be harmonized by G and D_7 (I and V_7). First, the melody is learned; then the harmony is experienced by chording an accompaniment or from a recorded accompaniment; finally, the chord roots are added. The words can be sung in melody rhythm on the pitch of the chord root. Numerals, note names, or syllables are sometimes sung on the pitch indicated.

Singing chord roots stresses the concept of chord change, and chord change is the essence of harmony. The singing or playing of melodies to

* A woman teacher is referred to here because the female voice has the same pitch as the unchanged child voice. A man teacher would probably play the new part on an instrument to avoid using his octave-lower voice, or sing falsetto.

which students "find" the roots by ear is another aspect of this study of harmony. It requires harmonic thinking without the aid of notation. Because this thin texture of melody and chord root is not always aesthetically satisfying, success with the activity quickly prompts the addition of more parts in order that a richer texture will make the harmony more complete.

To provide for individual differences and to support the new chord root part, some students can play this part on bells, piano, and small winds. The viola and cello can provide a bass effect. Let us assume that the students are going to build a score for the singing and playing of "Put Your Little Foot," a score that will reveal their ideas about rhythm and harmony as well as about melody. The teacher has placed the melody on the chalkboard and has also written the two chords that accompany this song. The first task is to find where in the song each of the chords is needed, if it is to be sounded on the piano or Autoharp to accompany the song. Since they have been taught that the note that receives the heavy accent or accents is ordinarily a tone of the required chord, they have an important clue on which to work. They know that the first beat of the measure in every meter signature is the most heavily accented beat, and that in 3/4 meter there is only one accent (the first beat) in each measure. (In 4/4 meter there are two—a primary accent on the first beat and a secondary accent on the third beat.) The students find that in the first three measures of "Put Your Little Foot" the note on the first beat is B. Looking at the chords, they notice that B is a member of the tones of the G (I) chord, but not of the D_7 (V_7) chord.

VARSOVIENNE
(Put Your Little Foot)

Traditional

Therefore, the chord needed for those three measures (or at least at the beginning of them) is the G chord. The note at the beginning of the fourth measure is A. They find A to be a member of the D_7 chord; therefore this is the chord needed in the fourth measure. They proceed in this manner to the end of the song, then "try out" their harmony with the melody to see if it is correct. In some songs, the note D may be on the first beat of a measure. In this case, the class will decide by listening which of the chords is the right one to use. They can also tell by analyzing all the notes of any measure to find to which chord most of the notes belong. This is an important clue whenever students are determining chords for songs for which chords are not designated.

Now that the students have found the chords, they may write these on a staff below the melody, later creating a more interesting piano part derived from these chords. If one knows the chord, he or she knows the note that is the chord root, because the note G is the root of the G (I) chord and the note D is the root of the D_7 (V_7) chord. These notes are placed on a staff below the other music already written. Next, they may invent rhythm patterns for the song, which they will play on suitable percussion instruments. There will be continuous experimenting which will involve singing and playing of parts, a use and understanding of harmony, and different ways of presenting the melody. The beginning of the score may look like this:

To add to this simple melody, harmony, and rhythm, students may create more parts in the form of chants and simple countermelodies:

Chant

Put your lit - tle foot, put your lit - tle foot, put your

Counter-melody

Put   your

lit - tle foot   right   there,   Put your lit - tle foot

foot   right   there,   Put

The opportunities for creative experiences are many in this approach to music. Creating and experimenting with such a score can provide a basic experience for understanding harmony. Singing chord roots contributes markedly to the further comprehension of harmony because they form the foundation tones of the harmonic structure that supports the melody. Since comprehending chord roots comes from understanding the chords (and chording) on the piano and Autoharp, it stimulates the addition of other harmonic parts. For older students, use of a currently popular tune for this activity can result in an inventive rhythmic orchestration of "their music."

Learning to Hear Chord Changes
The experience with chord roots is basically one in sensing and identifying chord changes. Teachers plan similar experiences with chording on the piano and Autoharp. They contrive situations in which the sounding chord is "wrong," and the students are to notice this and want it corrected. The wrong and right chords are played; the students choose the one that "fits" the melody best. The experience commonly includes the teacher's selecting a familiar two-chord song (I and V_7 or I and IV) and playing the tonic chord all the way through, or until the students show in some way that the harmonic accompaniment should be corrected. The students are motivated to search for the best sounding chord. The measures of some songs have alternate harmonizations. Teachers let the children select the Autoharp or piano chords which sound the best to them; they continue to help them be conscious of chord sounds and chord changes. After students have learned to play the Autoharp, they can let them improvise accompaniments to songs of simple harmonization "by ear"—listening to find when the melody demands a chord change, then choosing the chord that sounds best. With two-chord songs the problem is a simple one of deciding which of two chords should be used. When skill in this has been developed, teachers select three-chord songs for them to work with. Some can become expert in chord selection on the Autoharp and develop extreme sensitivity to chord changes when their

teachers have planned experiences which help them to develop this responsiveness to harmony.

The particular chords at the end of phrases form *cadences*. These pertain to a feeling of momentary or permanent conclusion. Students might analyze cadences, classify them accordingly, and apply them in their own compositions.

Thirds and Sixths

An approach older from the standpoint of general use than singing chord roots is the employment of thirds and sixths. As in other approaches to harmony, students are assumed to know the melody very well, and to have heard the song on a recording or accompanied in a manner that helps them comprehend the integral relation of the melody and harmony. The singing of thirds was introduced in the section on harmonic endings. This use of thirds can be expanded to include parts of songs and eventually entire songs, providing the melodies accommodate this. For example, "London Bridge" can be sung in thirds except for near the end, where a sixth is necessary.

LONDON BRIDGE

The music textbooks include songs that rely heavily on thirds to introduce part singing. A song that can be sung in its entirely in thirds is the well-known "Polly Wolly Doodle."

POLLY WOLLY DOODLE

An interval that sounds similar to the third is the sixth, which is the inversion of the third. After students have become accustomed to singing in parallel thirds, they can easily learn to sing in parallel sixths. Any song that can be sung in thirds can be sung in sixths. "Polly Wolly Doodle" illustrates this. However, when the interval is changed in this way the key must often change also to accommodate the voice range.

Songs such as "Lightly Row," "Goodbye My Lover, Goodbye," "Yankee Doodle," "Hand Me Down My Walking Cane," "To Puerto Rico" (page 254), "Catch a Falling Star," and the refrain of "Marching to Peoria" can be used to advantage in approaching part-singing through the use of thirds and sixths.

Older methods of teaching part singing include drilling on each part, then putting them together. Today the emphasis is upon helping learners to hear a new part in relation to the melody and the harmony so that they hear all of the music. This principle is applicable no matter what type of part singing is being done, whether it be round, descant, or traditional two- and three-part singing. The general outline of progress in part singing in grades four, five, and six is as follows:

1. The learning of the melody.
2. The comprehension of the harmony (chord structure) that accompanies the melody by use of Autoharp, piano, or guitar chording, or a suitable recording.
3. The introduction of the new part in a manner that permits the students to hear the integral relation of the two parts. (Learners hum the melody or sing it softly while the teacher sings or plays the new part.) Harmony must be *heard* before it is performed.

4. The singing of the new part by those who are ready for part singing, always working for a balance in volume that permits the hearing of both parts by all.
5. Introducing a third part by repeating Steps 3 and 4, adding the new part to the two parts previously learned.
6. When learners have learned to feel secure in part-singing activities, then the sight-reading of part songs can be an interesting and challenging activity. When this skill is developed, Steps 1, 2, and 3 are eliminated. Since sight-singing is a complicated skill, neutral syllables instead of words are generally used at first so that the students can concentrate on the notation. The words are added when they feel secure on the parts.

In general, the voices of fifth- and sixth-graders are unchanged and have approximately the same range, with the exception of boys in the first stage of the voice change whose ranges have dropped approximately a fourth. Technically, it is incorrect to call these immature voices "soprano" or "alto." It is more accurate to abandon these adult terms and to call the voice parts "high," "low," and "middle," rather than "first soprano," "alto," and "second soprano." It is the aim of the teacher that every learner sing each of these parts, changing from one to another according to the directions of the moment or by being assigned them in different songs.

In the fifth grade books will be found songs that stress parallel thirds. Following songs in thirds will be those that include both thirds and sixths. Every teacher of the older students should know the sequence of songs through which part-singing skills are expected to be learned in the particular books available in the school, and suggestions in the teacher's book must be studied carefully. Some two-part songs are included in the fourth-grade books in preparation for the emphasis on harmony in the fifth grade.

An interesting creative approach to singing thirds and sixths is one in which children compose songs confined within four pitches of the major scale, 3, 4, 5, and 6. After such a song has been composed and learned, a parallel third part can be added below. When this new part is transposed one octave higher, parallel sixths result. Try this with "Sleep, Baby, Sleep."

SLEEP, BABY, SLEEP

Traditional Words
Arranged

Slowly

Sleep, ba - by, sleep; Thy fa - ther guards the sheep, Thy

moth-er shakes the dream-land tree, And from it falls sweet dreams for thee;

Sleep, ba - by, sleep; Sleep, ba - by, sleep.

Older students may enjoy learning the song "You Are My Sunshine," then making it a two-part song by singing parallel sixths below the melody or parallel thirds above it. Adding chord roots will produce three parts. (Holt, Rinehart and Winston *The Music Book* 8)

The male teacher is at some disadvantage in teaching part singing, since his voice sounds one octave lower than the child voice. Therefore, it is necessary for him to use some melody instrument instead of his voice when he wishes to illustrate part singing of unchanged voices. His voice is excellent, however, in the singing of chord roots. There is seldom a changed voice among sixth-grade boys, but in case there should be, the singing of special parts, such as chord roots by the male teacher along with the boy, will help him adjust to his temporarily unique situation.

Improvising Harmony Parts   The improvising of harmony parts has often been overlooked as one practical approach to part singing. "Barber-shopping" or "singing harmony by ear" has a definite carry-over into the natural musical expression of boys and girls when they are on field trips or picnics, at camp and at home. The writers know of an elementary school where the improvising of parts by children's volunteer neighborhood quartets was an activity of importance, even affecting school and community programs. A list of songs that have had use in this activity includes "Home on the Range," "Down by the Old Mill Stream," "There's a Long, Long Trail," "Moonlight and Roses," "Let the Rest of the World Go By," "Eyes of Texas" ("I've Been Working on the Railroad"), "Red River Valley," "Oh My Darling Clementine," "A Bicycle Built for Two." This activity is usually most effective at sixth-grade level, where it develops into three-part singing, although some fifth grades can do well with it.

Vocal Chording   An example of one type of vocal chording was mentioned on page 354 in connection with I-chord songs. Usually, chording of the vocal type consists of the same tones that are often used for piano chording in the treble clef. The class may be divided into four groups, with one assigned the melody and the other three assigned the three chord tones. This activity would logically begin with one-chord melodies and progress to three-chord melodies. It may start in a simple way in third or fourth grade. It is sometimes emphasized in fifth and sixth grades as an approach to three-part singing. The ease with which students can learn to chord vocally will be determined by their ability to hear harmony; their ability to learn harmony will be favorably influenced by successful experiences in instrumental chording and by guided listening activities that aid the hearing of chord changes. A chord root part can be added if the range is appropriate.

The chords to be sung can be arranged in several positions. The chart in Figure 16.2 illustrates chord positions that are sometimes used as exercises to introduce children to this activity. Although numbers or syllables may be used to introduce this work, humming or the netural syllable "loo" is used in performance. The words of the song are sung on the chord tones in the same rhythm as the melody.

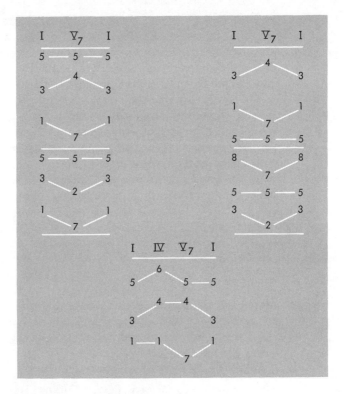

Figure 16.2. CHORD CHANGES

The following excerpts from "Silent Night" illustrate this activity:

Among the special interest groups in the elementary school are the orchestra, band, and chorus. The instrumental groups are generally the responsibility of special music teachers but the chorus is frequently taught either by a music teacher or a classroom teacher. Although some schools have a primary grades chorus which sings unison songs, the usual chorus is composed of ten- to thirteen-year-olds. Today's teachers are fortunate in having an improved selection of song materials to use, some of which are listed at the end of this chapter. Not only do the textbooks include chants, descants, and countermelodies in addition to the standard types of two- and three-part songs, but there are valuable supplementary materials. There is no standard seating arrangement for these choruses. However, it is best to have the lowest and highest parts seated so that each can hear the other well. In this way the group is able to keep more accurately on pitch. In chorus work which has a goal of public performance, the singers are more or less permanently assigned to one of the parts (high, middle, or low). Mention was made earlier of the excellence of choruses that follow Kodály principles.

Activities for Lesson Plans

Relating Melody and Harmony

Canon. The teacher creates simple canons and writes them in numbers or syllables for the class to sing. There will be two parts. Later, some of these should be notated and sung from notation. Examples:

1 1 2 3 4 5 – 5 4 3 2 1 –
    1 1 2 3 4 5 – 5 4 3 2 1 –

Hearing two pitches at once. One half of the class sustains one pitch, *do* or *1*, while the other half sings other pitches as indicated by the teacher's pointing to scale degrees written in numbers or syllables on the chalkboard, or by hand signs. Later, both *do* and *so,* and *la* and *mi* can be used as alternating sustained pitches.

Write the major scale vertically in numbers or syllables. Divide the class into two groups, left hand and right hand. Each group sings to the corresponding hand of the teacher as he or she points with it. The teacher points to scale degrees that will produce interesting two-pitch combinations. It is good to start with a unison and experiment from there. Later on, do the same with scales other than the major. For older, experienced students, this activity can progress until both groups are singing moving parts indicated by two-hand signs given by the teacher or an advanced student. From this they can proceed to a chart or chalkboard with notation.

Round. Write all or part of a traditional round with all parts fully notated on the chalkboard, or prepare this on a transparency. Children are asked to sing rounds and to listen to them, but they seldom see them notated in complete form so that they can obtain a visual image of what a round is. First, the class should learn to sing the round. This can be sung in from two to four parts; a new group enters two measures after the preceding group. Then after studying the score, questions such as the following can be asked. "What is the harmonic plan of this round?" (a two-measure phrase in which C and G_7 share the first measure with two beats each, while C harmonizes the second measure.) "Analyze this round vertically to be sure that this harmonic plan is really in operation." (The notes, viewed vertically, can be made into chords and played on bells or piano to show that harmonic plan is consistent—that the C and G_7 chords are really there.) Older students can be given manuscript paper and asked to write a round, using this same plan. Next, other rounds are studied and their harmonic plans revealed. Then rounds with other specified harmonic plans can be written by the students.

Examples for study: Let's Sing a Round, Bowmar Records. *Round and Round,* Franson YPR 431 (ages 6–10): from round to canon to fugue. Franck: *Violin Sonata,* last movement (a beautiful example).

JUNE, LOVELY JUNE

Descant, countermelody, and round. Sing and play songs that have descants and countermelodies. Ask the students to describe the difference between rounds and added parts of these types. Page 299 in *Singing With Children* lists songs with descants; also see indexes of music textbooks. Of the songs listed in *Singing With Children,* the following contain what could be termed countermelodies: "Mystic Number" (first half), "Streets of Laredo," "Ash Grove," and "O Give Me the Hills."

Polyphony. Sousa: *Semper Fidelis,* AM 3 v 1. Have children explore this march to discover the different melodies and how Sousa combines them.

Texture. Ask questions to help children develop a vocabulary of terms descriptive of texture such as light, heavy, thick, thin. Use recordings in which children can easily compare a thick texture with a thin texture. Compare the combining of melodic lines in polyphony with threads in weaving tapestry. Examples of contrasting textures:

Saint-Saëns: "The Swan" from *Carnival of the Animals,* AM 3 v 2 (homophonic texture)

Ligeti: "Atmospheres" from *Space Odyssey,* Columbia MS 6733

Bach: *Little Fugue in G Minor,* AM 6 v 1; BOL 86

Harmonic Part-Singing

Improvising harmony. Present the class with the task of improvising parts for "Streets of Laredo," using only scale tones 3, 4, and 5. This song has been selected because it is harmonized by only two chords, I and V_7. Scale tones 3 and 5 are members of the I-chord and scale tones 4 and 5 are members of the V_7-chord. In this particular song the chords alternate regularly; this makes it easy to think in terms of choices of chord tones the singers select to improvise their simple harmony parts. The class selects the pitches it wants for each of the measures of the song (which is either on the chalkboard or on a transparency), and writes them on the chalkboard. The class next sings the two parts (the melody and the new part) together until it performs it well and is satisfied with the added part. Next, the class adds another new part by writing it the interval of a third lower. Now the class has two new parts in parallel thirds. It then sings the three parts. The students evaluate the result and try to analyze what made it possible.

STREETS OF LAREDO

Cowboy Song

Wrapped	in white	lin - en	as cold	as the clay.
Shot	in the	breast and	I know	I must die."

3. "It was once in the saddle I used to go dashing,
   Once in the saddle I used to go gay;
   First down to Rosie's and then to the card-house;
   Got shot in the breast and I'm dying today."

4. "Get sixteen gamblers to handle my coffin,
   Let six jolly cowboys come sing me a song,
   Take me to the graveyard and lay the sod o'er me,
   For I'm a young cowboy, I know I've done wrong."

5. "Oh, beat the drums slowly and play the fife lowly,
   Play the dead march as they carry me along,
   Put bunches of roses all over my coffin,
   Roses to deaden the clods as they fall."

6. (Repeat Verse I.)

Chord root parts. Words of songs can be sung on the pitches of the chord roots—the "1" of a chord in root position (1 3 5). The letter names of the Autoharp chord designations placed above the song notation tell the reader the pitch to be sung or played.

Improvising part singing. Explore harmonizing parts "by ear," using songs such as "Goodbye, My Lover, Goodbye," "Good Night Ladies," "Kum Ba Yah," "Michael, Row the Boat Ashore," and "Sally Go Round." Others in *Singing With Children* are "Daisy Bell," "Golden Slippers," "Mary and Martha," "Hush, Little Baby," and "Sidewalks of New York."

Singing parallel thirds "by ear." There are some songs and parts of songs that can be sung and played in parallel thirds. *This is one of the easiest approaches to part singing.* Among these songs are "Hot Cross Buns," "Sally Go Round," "Polly Wolly Doodle," and "San Sereni." The last one is in *Singing With Children.* First review the melody thoroughly, with a strong harmonic accompaniment on Autoharp, piano, ukulele, or guitar. Oftentimes the teacher says to part of the class "Start singing the song on this pitch," and gives them the pitch that results in a third interval from the melody. Because the harmony has been well absorbed, automatic adjusments will take place in the new part, and the class may surprise itself by singing the song at once in two parts. The two parts should then be revealed on the chalkboard or transparency in order that the children see the related parts—"see what it looks like when it sounds that way." The interval of a third should be identified by sight and by sound. On the staff it is either line-line or space-space. In subsequent lessons the teacher can help students formulate the following ideas: (1) melody with harmonic accompaniment is *homophonic* music; (2) the interval of a third in this instance is a vertical or harmonic interval as compared to the horizontal or melodic interval that appears in melodies; (3) both types of intervals might be found in a two-part song.

Examples of harmonic intervals: thirds and sixths.

Tchaikovsky: *Italian Caprice* (a prominent theme is in thirds)
Mendelssohn: *Symphony No. 4,* First Movement (theme two has a two-part melody in thirds)
Charpentier: "On Muleback" from *Impressions of Italy,* AM 5 v 1 (theme three has a two-part melody in thirds and sixths)

Countermelody. After singing a song with a countermelody, select a familiar song requiring only I and V_7 chords for harmonization, and improvise a countermelody. Try having the class sing or hum the melody while one student attempts the improvisation. After several students have found successful ones, try combining two or three. Then discuss what seems necessary to produce a successful countermelody.

Dissonance. Experiment with singing as a round a known song that is not a round, having active harmonic changes of irregular nature. It should be a song that when sung this way will result in obvious dissonances (disagreeable sounds). Perform it this way, tape it, and let the class hear it. Ask the students to analyze the reasons for the dissonances, to try to define dissonance, and to evaluate their performance that examplified it. Since dissonance is one of the characteristics of contemporary music, students should have some experience with it and know what it is.

Nonharmonic music. Before asking young children to comprehend chord changes that are characteristic of harmonic music, they should have experienced a great deal of music in which there are no chord changes. This includes short tonal fragments and calls, pentatonic music, I-chord songs, and unaccompanied melodies that do not suggest harmonic changes. One chord played on the Autoharp suffices to accompany such music. Examples include "Old MacDonald" and "The Farmer in the Dell." More I-chord songs are listed in the Autoharp Accompaniments Index under the heading "Exemplary Songs," *Singing With Children,* p. 228, and on p. 395 in this book.

Bitonality. The class sings a familiar song such as "Twinkle, Twinkle, Little Star" while the teacher plays the accompaniment on the piano in another key. This could be done on the Autoharp if the instrument is amplified. In any event, the result should be taped and played back to the class for evaluation. Listen to recorded examples of bitonality and evaluate them.

References

Articles and Books

APFELSTADT, HILARY. "Children's Vocal Range: Research Findings and Implications for Music Education," *Update,* Fall 1982, 3–7.

COOPER, IRVIN, and KARL O. KUERSTEINER, *Teaching Junior High Music,* 2nd ed. Boston: Allyn and Bacon, Inc., 1970.

COOPER, IRVIN, and KARL O. KUERSTEINER, *Teaching Junior High School Music: General Music and the Vocal Program.* Conway, Ark.: Cambiata Press, 1973.

COOPER, MORTON, "Prescriptions for Vocal Health," *Music Educators Journal,* February 1983, 40–59.

FRANKLIN, ELDA, "Monotonism," *Music Educators Journal,* March 1981, 56–58.

FRANKLIN, ELDA, and A. DAVID FRANKLIN, "The Uncertain Singer," *Update,* vol. 1, number 3, Spring 1983, 3–5.

GARY, CHARLES L., ed., *The Study of Music in the Elementary School: A Conceptual Approach,* pp. 51–65. Reston, Va.: Music Educators National Conference, 1967. Helpful in writing lesson plans. Choral compositions, pp. 162–163.

MESKE, EUNICE B. and CARROLL RINEHART, *Individualized Instruction in Music.* Reston, Va.: Music Educators National Conference, 1975.

Music Educators Journal, "Sacred Music in the Schools: An Update," November 1979, 48–51.

NORDHOLM, HARRIET, *Singing in the Elementary School.* Englewood Cliffs, N.J.: Prentice-Hall, Inc., 1966.

SLAUGHTER, C. H., "Those Dissonant Boys," *Music Educators Journal,* February-March 1966, 110–12. Sociological factors relating to boy's disinterest in music.

TUFTS, NANCY P., *The Children's Choir,* Vol. 2. Philadelphia, Pa.: Fortress Press. The children's choir, the boy choir, the handbell choir.

Songs for Children

BAILEY, CHARITY, *Sing a Song with Charity Bailey.* New York: Plymouth Music Company.

BRADFORD, LOUISE, *Sing it Yourself.* Sherman Oaks, Calif.: Alfred Publishing Co., Inc., 1978. American pentatonic songs.

KERSEY, ROBERT, *Just Five.* Westminster, Md.: The Westminster Press. Pentatonic songs.

———. *Just Five Plus Two.* Westminster, Md.: The Westminster Press. *Fa* and *ti* are added.

LANDECK, BEATRICE, *Songs to Grow On; More Songs to Grow On.* New York: Marks and Sloane. Recorded by Folkways Records.

SCOTT, RICHARD, *Clap, Tap, and Sing Choral Method.* Minneapolis, Minn.: Handy-Folio Music Company. For grades 2–5. Beginning with rhythm, this 48-page book takes children through sightsinging to part singing. All songs are playable on small wind instruments.

SEEGER, RUTH CRAWFORD, *American Folk Songs for Children; Animal Folk Songs for Children; American Folk Songs for Christmas.* New York: Doubleday and Company, Inc.

Part Singing   BACON, DENISE, *46 Two-Part American Folk Songs*. Oceanside, N.Y.: Boosey & Hawkes, 1974.

BECKMAN, FREDERICK, *Partner Songs; More Partner Songs*. New York: Ginn and Company. Combinable songs for grades 5–7.

BELL, LESLIE, *The Festival Song Book One*. Melville, N.Y.: Belwin-Mills 11746. For unaccompanied voices.

BURKART, ARNOLD E., *Bicinia Americana Vol. 1*. Muncie, Ind.: Keeping Up With Music Education, 1976.

COOPER, IRVIN, *Songs for Pre-Teentime*. New York: Carl Fischer, Inc. For grades 6–7.

EHRET, WALTER, *The Youthful Chorister*. New York: Marks Music Corp. SA.

GEARHART, LIVINGSTON, *A Christmas Singing Bee*. Delaware Water Gap, Pa.: Shawnee Press.

JUREY, EDWARD B., *Mills First Chorus Album*. Melville, N.Y.: Belwin-Mills.

KENT, WILLYS PECK, *A Book of Descants*. New York: Vantage Press. For grades 5–8.

KRONE, BEATRICE, and MAX KRONE, *Our First Songs to Sing with Descants* (for upper primary); *Very Easy Descants; Songs to Sing with Descants; Descants for Christmas; Our Third Book of Descants; From Descants to Trios; Descants and Rounds for Special Days*. Park Ridge, Ill.: Neil A. Kjos Music Company.

MUSIC EDUCATORS NATIONAL CONFERENCE, *Music for Children's Choirs: A Selective Graded Listing*. Reston, Va.: The Conference, 1977. 44 pages.

PERINCHIEF, ROBERT, *Honor Your Partner Songs*. Whitewater, Wis.: Perry Publications, Inc.

SCOTT, RICHARD, *Sevenfold Choral Method*. Minneapolis, Minn.: Handy-Folio Music Company. For grades 5–7.

General Collections   ADES, HAWLEY, *One for the Melody*. Delaware Water Gap, Pa.: Shawnee Press. 26 unison songs by classic composers, with a story about each composer.

DALLIN, LEON, and LYNN DALLIN, *Heritage Songster*. Dubuque, Iowa: Wm. C. Brown Company Publishers. Traditional songs Americans sing.

HACKETT, PATRICIA, *The Melody Book*. Englewood Cliffs, N.J.: Prentice-Hall, 1983.

LEISY, JAMES, *The Good Times Songbook*. Nashville and New York: Abingdon Press, 1974. For informal singing.

NYE, ROBERT E., VERNICE T. NYE, NEVA AUBIN, and GEORGE KYME: *Singing With Children,* 2nd ed. Belmont, Calif.: Wadsworth Publishing Co., 1970. Selected songs for teaching music to elementary school children.

TOBITT, JANET E., *The Ditty Bag*. Pleasantville, N.Y.: P.O. Box 97.

Recordings   BOWMAR RECORDS, Belwin-Mills, Melville, N.Y. 11747. *Bowmar Records Catalog*. Lists approximately 20 albums for singing, including three for children "with special needs."

CHILDREN'S BOOK AND MUSIC CENTER, 2500 Santa Monica Blvd., Santa Monica, Calif. 90404.

CLASSROOM MATERIALS CO., 93 Myrtle Drive, Great Neck, N.Y. 11020. *Johnny Can Sing Too*. (K–3) Vol. 1, 2. For discovering singing voices and helping them develop.

You Too Can Sing! (4–6) For children with singing problems.

Classroom Sing Along (4–6) To aid the teacher in teaching songs.

FOLKWAYS RECORDS

You'll Sing a Song and I'll Sing a Song (Ella Jenkins) FC 7664

See the Folkways Catalog for many more.

FRANSON CORPORATION, 225 Park Ave. South, New York, N.Y. 10003. Children's Record Guild and Young People's Records.

Albums: *Let's Sing* (1–5)

Folk Songs (1–5)

Songs to Sing (1–4) activity songs

RCA MUSIC SERVICE, Educational Dept. A., 1133 Avenue of the Americas, New York N.Y. 10036. *The Singing Program* (albums).

STANLEY BOWMAR CO., INC., Valhalla, N.Y.

Records, Tapes, and Instructional Materials for the Classroom Catalog. Lists many records for singing activities.

Stage Productions

CARTER, JOHN, and MARY KAY BEALL, *Wheels.* Concerns invention of the wheel. For third grade through middle school. Jenson Publications, Inc.

GALLINA, JILL, *The Runaway Snowman.* A Christmas musical for all elementary grades. Jensen Publications, Inc., P.O. Box 248, New Berlin, Wis. 53151.

———, *The Wakadoo Zoo.* Involves outrageous animals that delight first through fourth graders. Wide World Music, Inc. P.O. Box B. Delaware Water Gap, Pa. 18327.

HAWTHORNE, GRACE, and JOHN F. WILSON, *The Electric Sunshine Man.* Thomas Edison is the leading character. Fifth grade through middle school. Somerset Press, Carol Stream, Ill. 60187.

———, *The Greatest Showman on Earth.* The story of P.T. Barnum. Fifth grade through middle school. Somerset Press.

———, *How the West Was Really Won.* For fifth grade through middle school. Somerset Press, Carol Stream, Ill. 60187.

ROSS, BEVERLY B., and JEAN P. DURGIN, *Junior Broadway.* Jeffeson, N.C.: McFarland, 1983. A guide to producing fully staged Broadway musicals with students aged nine to thirteen.

chapter seventeen

Melody and Harmony Instruments

Since developing music concepts by playing instruments has been considered in various settings in previous chapters, the reader has already given consideration to this activity as an integral part of a balanced music program. Musical instruments have been viewed as extensions of the body, as interpreters of actions and stories, as means of experimenting in sound for both aesthetic and scientific reasons, as aids in singing, as accompaniments to singing and dancing, and as a means of learning to read notation and to acquire music knowledges and skills. This chapter will consider playing instruments as a skill as well as a means of expanding music concepts.

The variety of possible instrumental experiences in the general music class can accommodate all the types of individual differences resulting from physical development in normal children that affect the manipulation of instruments, as well as variations in physical coordination resulting from deviant growth patterns or disease, and degrees of musical ability. For some children, manipulating an instrument is an important physical release, while for others it is an intellectual challenge. For those unable to sing well it is an opportunity to succeed in another area of music.

Melody Instruments

Children are characteristically interested in mechanical things. Making music by playing an instrument, no matter how simple the instrument, attracts them. It follows that if teachers guide this interest along the lines of learning both the skills of playing and the understanding of the elements of music, it can yield great benefits.

When melody instruments are employed to invent introductions, codas, interludes, and to play tone patterns, concepts of melody and form are being expanded. The concept of *interval* can be made clear by seeing intervals on keyboard instruments, by seeing and feeling them on blowing-type (small wind) instruments, and by comparing what is seen, felt, and heard with written intervals on the staff. The key signature is relatively unimpressive to the singer, but of undeniable significance to the player of pitched instruments. Note reading becomes clearly practical and functional when the player must relate notation to the keyboard or to fingerings on a wind instrument. Instruments are also useful in studying aspects of music such as scale line, chord line, legato, staccato, and a host of others related to analysis and performance. Flute-type instruments lend atmosphere to American Indian music; the individually plucked strings of the psaltery, Autoharp, guitar, and ukulele can produce imitation Oriental melodies; and the marimba contributes in an authentic manner to Latin American music. Children can use melody instruments to compose melodies. They are easy to play; they can be taught by the classroom teacher. Their use combines auditory, tactile, and visual perception to build music concepts. Some children will be more interested in trying to match tones with their voices when they produce pitches themselves on a melody instrument. Furthermore, the more experienced and gifted students can have additional musical experiences with instruments.

Water Glasses and Bottles Some teachers use water glasses and bottles as experiences introductory to keyboard instruments such as bells, xylophone, and piano. There are tuned glasses that can be used without water, obtainable from various sources on order, even from some variety stores. Other teachers employ glasses with water, knowing that this probably means some spilling and evaporation, both of which necessitate retuning because of the change in water levels. Some use bottles with water, often corked or capped to keep retuning at a minimum. By striking glasses and bottles when they are empty and when they contain water, children can make certain scientific observations. They discover that the pitch and tone quality are affected by size and thickness. They may also discover that decreasing the amount of water raises the pitch and increasing the amount of water lowers the pitch—except in some glasses and bottles that will not tune lower no matter how much water is added. They may also discover that striking glasses or bottles with soft objects such as felt-covered mallets produces soft tones. Let the children generalize from their experimentation that: The more water one pours into a glass or bottle, the lower the pitch is. The lowest pitch is made by filling glasses and bottles full of water. The highest pitch is produced when a glass or bottle is empty. The best tone quality is produced when a soft mallet strikes the glass as if pulling the sound out, not hitting it in.

After experimenting with glasses and bottles, children and teacher may decide that bottles are superior because if one can seal them, the pitch will remain stable. However, the most important element of comparison should be the beauty of the sound, which could be determined by the quality of the glass. Paint or paper strips can be placed on them to show the water level that produces the desired pitch. Numeral names, note names, or syllable names can be painted on or written on paper stickers. Some teachers put vegetable dyes or other coloring in the water to add interest. Placing glasses on a thick cloth will result in a better tone.

Interest in playing melodies on bottles may prompt the teacher or the children to make or obtain a rack from which to suspend the bottles. When this is done, each bottle is suspended by two loops of string, one on each side of the bottle neck, to help it to hang with more stability.

The first experience in playing songs on glasses or bottles is generally with only three pitches: 3–2–1 (mi-re-do). Known songs in the three-tone category are "Hot Cross Buns" and "Merrily We Roll Along." After this, the next step is to use four- and five-tone melodies. Teachers often devise their own three-, four-, and five-tone songs as examples, then encourage the children to compose others with scale tones 1–2–3–4–5. After this experience has been digested, more scale tones are added until melodies are created on all eight pitches of the major scale. A pentatonic tonal organization can be used also, beginning with songs based on scale tones 5–3, then 5–6–3, then 1–2–3–5–6. It is advantageous to transfer skills acquired on glasses and bottles to bells and xylophones; they provide a good introduction to the piano keyboard. Some teachers prefer to go directly to them rather than introduce them by means of experimental glasses and bottles.

Bells and Xylophones   When children have had opportunities to explore the bells (Figure 17.1) for themselves, they can make a number of discoveries:

Long bars sound low pitches.

Short bars sound high pitches.

The arrangement of white keys and black keys is the same as that of the piano except that the piano has more keys.

To play a scale going up, one plays from left to right.

To play a scale going down, one plays from right to left.

A five-note (pentatonic) scale can be played on the black keys.

White keys played from C to C sound the C major scale.

If a standard bell set can be stood on end, with large bars down, and held against the chalkboard or chart paper, staff lines can be drawn from the bars to relate the keyboard to the staff.

To produce the best tone, one strikes the middle of the bar and draws the tone out rather than hitting it in.

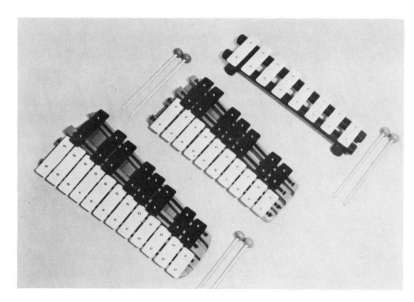

Figure 17.1. PENGUIN SONG BELLS. The World of Peripole Inc., Browns Mills, N.J. 08015

The same sequence of pitches described for glasses and bottles is used to initiate playing the bells. *Resonator bells* (Figure 17.2) are made of individual tone bars that can be taken from the carrying case if desired. For ex-

Figure 17.2. RESONATOR BELLS. Courtesy Ludwig Industries. Used by permission.

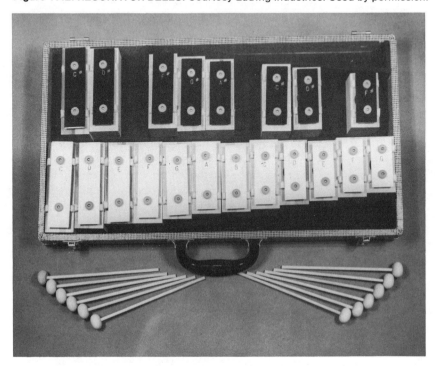

ample, if children are to compose tunes with only three or four pitches, those particular bars can be removed from the set, placed in order, and played apart from the other bars to prevent possible confusion of young children when they would try to play those bars in keyboard position among all the other bars.

Before children understand music notation, teachers guide them to play by ear and by numeral notation.* The scale-tone numbers can be written on the white metal keys with black crayon, or they can be placed on tagboard in back of the bells. Numeral notation could appear as follows. Notice that the "fast notes" are circled.

Hot Cross Buns	*Mary Had a Little Lamb*
3 2 1 – 3 2 1-	3212 333–222– 333–
⑪⑪ ②②②②3 2 1—	3212 3333 2232 1–

five-note tune:	six-note tune:
Jingle Bells	*Are You Sleeping?*
333- 333- 3512 3——	1 2 3 1 1 2 3 1 3 4 5 –3 4 5 –
4444 433 333 223 2-5–	⑤⑥⑤④3 1 ⑤⑥⑤④3 1 1 5₁ 1–1 5₁ 1–
333– 333– 3512 3——	
4444 433 33 5542 1—	

Use C major or G major to avoid black keys. Use F major to introduce one black key (B♭). *Hot Cross Buns* and *Mary Had a Little Lamb* can be played on the group of three black keys. Some teachers prefer to introduce the piano keyboard in this way to overcome possible hesitation about the black keys later. With guidance and careful listening, young children can play songs or parts of songs in keys such as F and G major where one black key is necessary. The general procedure at first is to learn a song well by rote before attempting to play it (*listen, sing,* then *play*).

Although children may begin playing songs with the aid of numerals, they are soon looking at notation the teacher has prepared for them that includes the numerals written beneath (or above) the note they represent. Later, teachers prepare notation in which the numerals appear only with the beginning note of each measure, then only with the beginning note of each phrase, and finally they are abandoned altogether because the children have made the transition from numerals to the notes on the staff.

The bells have many uses. If a classroom teacher has difficulty with his or her singing voice, the instrument can be used to teach rote songs. Difficult tonal patterns in songs can be isolated and studied by means of the bells. They are often employed to establish the pitch of songs by sounding the keynote, playing tones of the tonic chord (I), then playing the starting pitch. Special sound effects such as chimes, church bells, and sleigh bells can be produced to enhance songs. Children can play simple parts of songs involv-

* A well-known book that introduces numeral notation in kindergarten and first grade is *Timothy's Tunes* by Adeline McCall (Boston Music Company). The *Psaltery Book* by Satis Coleman (John Day Company) is another. *Fun with the Melody-bells* by Rj Staples (Follett) further expands the use of numeral notation.

ing a single tone up to an entire scale, and they can play complete songs. Introductions, codas, and interludes—all created on the bells—can be added. Older students can write descants and other added parts to songs and play them on the bells. Bells can assist part singing.

THE DRUNKEN SAILOR

Dorian mode

English Folksong

What should we do with a drun-ken sail - or? What should we do with a

drun-ken sail - or? What should we do with a drun-ken sail - or

ear - ly in the morn - ing? Cheers, cheers and

up she ris - es, Cheers, cheers and up she ris - es,

Cheers, cheers and up she ris - es, Ear-ly in the morn - ing.

2. *Into the longboat till he gets sober*
   Into the longboat till he gets sober
   Into the longboat till he gets sober
   Early in the morning

Bells accompaniment:

| d | a | d | a | c | g | c | g |

| d | a | d | a | c | g | a | a :|

The "suggestions to the teacher" in one of the music textbooks states that if children had access to keyboard instruments, many of the problems in teaching understanding of pitch differences, of the interval relationship of tones, and of music notation generally would be minimized. The reason is that the keyboard constitutes a highly significant *audiovisual* tool for learning. Children enjoy "picking out tunes" and in doing so on the bells or piano they *see* and *feel* and *hear* the interval relationships of tones. This can lead to a genuine comprehension of the meaning of the notes on the staff—a comprehension frequently lacking in children whose musical experiences have been confined to a singing approach. In every elementary classroom there should be a music corner that includes bells and easy music to play on them. Some teachers have a "song of the week" which children learn to play before school, after school, and during the school day. When played with a padded mallet or a pencil with a rubber eraser, this soft-toned instrument seldom disturbs other classroom activities.

The *xylophone* (Figure 17.3) is similar to the bells, but made of wood instead of metal. *Xylo* is the Greek word for wood. Because its wood strips do not vibrate as long as the metal bars of the bells, it has a more percussive quality. A more attractive xylophone is the *marimba,* which has resonators, usually metal tubes, beneath the wood strips. German music educators use the term xylophone, but prefer the terms *glockenspiel* or *metallophone* to bells. The metallophone is lower pitched than the glockenspiel.

Other forms of bells are the step bells, which are made in the form of stair steps illustrating the ascending and descending pitches of the scale, and the *glockenturm,* a German instrument which is played vertically and reveals visually the relationship of keyboard and staff.

The Piano As a Melody Instrument

The piano can be used in connection with songs in the same informal ways the percussion instruments and bells are used. Like the bells, the keyboard provides an audiovisual tool. The piano can be used as an instrument of percussion, melody, harmony, and in any combination of these. It is therefore a superior means by which to gain concepts in music study.

Classroom teachers do not need to be pianists to teach music through keyboard experience. They need only to be introduced to it so that they can proceed in the same way the children do. In the beginning a child can play a tone that sounds "one" when the clock strikes "one" in *Hickory Dickory Dock,* as he or she may have done earlier on the bells. In a song that has words of importance on one or two tones, children may play these at the time they occur in the melody. The same little three-note melodies played on

Figure 17.3. XYLOPHONE. Shawnee Press, Inc., Delaware Water Gap, Pa. 18327.

glasses, bottles, and bells can be played on the piano keyboard. As time goes on, four- and five-finger patterns can be used in an incidental way in both ascending and descending forms. Here are some examples of such usage:

One Finger   The child plays repeated single tones such as the beginning of *Jingle Bells.* A tone-matching game can be played by striking a pitch that is within his or her voice range, then trying to match it vocally.

Two Fingers   The child plays repeated motives in songs and can also match tones, playing as well as singing such scale tones as 5 and 3 ("so" and "mi").

Three Fingers   The scale tones 3–2–1 can be played whenever the words "three blind mice" occur in the song of that name. The tonal pattern 1–2–3–1 can be played with the words "Are you sleeping?" in the song of that name.

Four Fingers   Scale tones 4–4–3–3–2–2–1 in *Twinkle, Twinkle, Little Star* can be played when the following words appear: "How I wonder what you are," and "Twinkle, twinkle all the night." Scale tones 5–5–4–4–3–3–2 can be played along with the words, "Up above the world so high," and "Like a diamond in the sky."

Five Fingers   Scale tones 5–43–21 are used at the end of *Row Your Boat* with the words, "Life is but a dream," and the scale tones 5–443–2–1 are used with the words "Ten little Indian boys" at the end of that song. Songs requiring only five fingers can easily be played. Such songs are listed near the beginning of Chapter Fourteen.

Scales   Many songs are based on scales and parts of scales that can be played on the keyboard.

A natural outgrowth of such piano-song relationships is the composing of little songs within the limitations of three, four, and five scale tones—songs that children can both sing and play. Eventually this activity will lead to the use of more scale tones in song composition.

Another simple use of the piano is the playing of the notes according to the chord names to provide an easy added part to songs. Example: play F with the F chord, G with the G chord, and so on. Still more for children to do with the keyboard instruments include playing the rhythm of children's names with one tone or a series of tones; playing tones that illustrate the concepts of high and low pitch; playing short tone patterns for tone-matching purposes or to add interest to songs; playing octave intervals in songs that emphasize this interval; playing other intervals in songs that feature them; playing different note values and rhythm patterns for children to respond to; playing entire characteristic phrases such as the beginning of "The Caisson Song," and playing ostinatos.

Playing the bells, a small instrument, logically comes before playing the piano, a very large instrument. Whatever is done on the bells, however, applies directly to the piano.

Electric pianos, organs, and electronic keyboards are used in schools.

These vary in size from small two-octave instruments to the type people purchase for home use. Most can be played without disturbing others by use of earphones through which only the player can hear what is being sounded. The large ones can produce a number of different tone qualities. The organ's sustained and accurate pitch is an advantage. The older (nonelectric) reed organ often has a pleasant tone that blends well with voices.

The Recorder   The *recorder's* period of greatest popularity was between the fifteenth and eighteenth centuries. In recent years there has been a strong revival of interest in it because: (1) it is an adult instrument played by adults with pleasure; (2) there is a substantial amount of excellent solo and ensemble music available to play on it, including music by "name" composers of both the past and the present; and (3) it is comparatively inexpensive. See Figure 17.4.

Acceptance of the recorder for upper elementary and middle school use has been speeded by reductions in price when purchased by schools in quantity. The range of the soprano instrument permits sounding middle C as the lowest pitch and continuing upward to encompass the normal vocal range. (See Figure 17.5.) The soprano is widely used because it is built in the key of C, thus having immediate use in playing the music children sing directly from song books; also, it costs less than the larger recorders. Helpful information can be obtained from companies and music dealers that specialize in the recorder.

The baroque recorder is preferred to the German, despite the somewhat easier fingering of the latter, because of better pitch accuracy. The best recorders are made of wood, and the best of these are higher priced. Dolmetch and Schott are respected names among recorder manufacturers. Acceptable plastic instruments are available and are less expensive and more practical for elementary school use.

The Melodica and Melodica Piano (Figures 17.6a and b), which use metal reeds like the harmonica, are small wind instruments built in the form

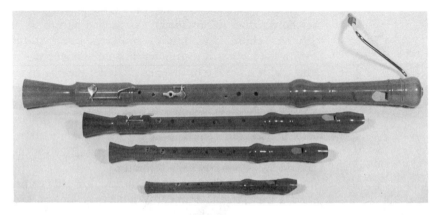

Figure 17.4. A FAMILY OF RECORDERS. Rhythm Band, Inc., Forth Worth, Texas 76101

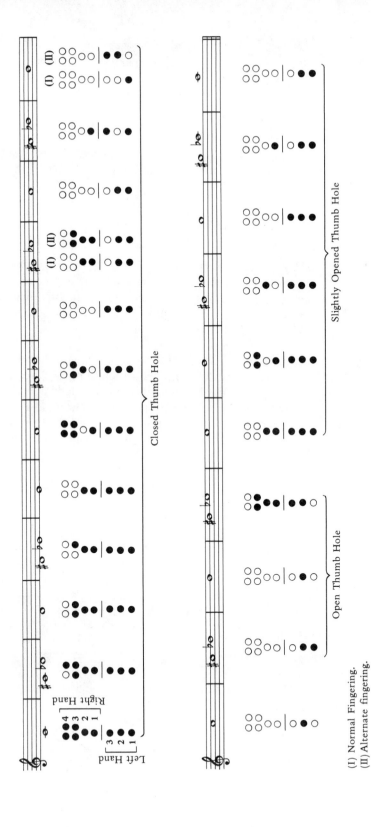

Figure 17.5. SOPRANO RECORDER FINGERING CHART. (ENGLISH OR BAROQUE FINGERING).

(I) Normal Fingering.
(II) Alternate fingering.

Figure 17.6a. MELODICA. M. Hohner, Inc., P.O. Box 15035, Richmond, Va. 23227.

Figure 17.6b. MELODICA PIANO. M. Hohner, Inc., P.O. Box 15035, Richmond, Va. 23227.

of a keyboard. Some teachers use them to play melodies to substitute for singing or to guard against overuse of their singing voices. A mouthpiece attachment permits the child to see the keyboard when he plays it to better understand intervals, note patterns, chords, and scalewise melodies. The instruments sound chords as well as melodies.

Teaching with Melody Instruments

Matching pitch. The use of individual resonator bars by children in relation to songs gives a helpful indication of pitch. Also, a game can be played in which each child plays his or her melody note each time it appears in the song. A pitch is *real* when held in the hand and struck with a mallet. There are many variations of this game. For example, "I Love the Mountains," a song used in middle and upper grades can be used with

I LOVE THE MOUNTAINS

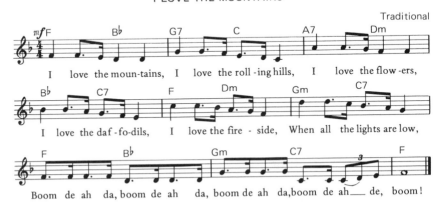

six resonator bars, F, G, A, B♭, C, and D, given to as many students. When their pitch is on the first beat of any measure, they play their resonator bar on that beat. Obviously, this can be done with other songs. See "adding simple parts" below.

Low-high. Relate low and high (vertical relationship of objects) with the keyboard left and right.

Experiment in composition. Have individual children select any four resonator bells. Arrange them in scale order and make up tunes on them.

Composition on black keys. Let children create pentatonic tunes and songs on keyboard black keys or on resonator bars representing a pentatonic scale on other keys.

Scale. Build the major scale concept (and later on, other scales) by means of children's playing them on keyboard instruments: bells, xylophone, Melodica, piano. Have them analyze scale patterns by examining the keyboard.

Tonal relationships. Have a large chart of the keyboard at the front of the room so that it can be used to answer questions and solve musical problems.

Ear training with bells. The teacher plays a few consecutive scale tones on the bells; a child is asked to reproduce the pitches on another bell set. A child can make up a short tune, then ask another to play what was heard. If this is done correctly, that child has the privilege of making up a tune and calling on another classmate to remember it and play it. If a child cannot remember the tune, another is called on. The group listens and judges. (This needs to be a game, not "pressure.") The teacher asks a child to play an easy, well-known song. At first the teacher will give the starting pitch. Later, as the game grows more demanding, the child will have to find that pitch. Later, older students can "take dictation" from the teacher's playing the bells. The teacher will give the name of the first note and the key in which the dictation will be given. Then the students will write the pitches they hear on the staff in notation, either individually on paper or collectively with a flannel or magnetic board. The chalk board could be used by a number of students, each working alone.

Adding simple parts. A simple bell or piano part can be added to songs by asking the player to sound only the note that is the first one in each measure. While technically any song can be used for this, songs that have each measure harmonized with one chord are obviously good. The Danish song "Han Skal Leve," sometimes titled "Birthday Song," is one. Parts of some songs, such as "Weggis Song," are good to use. Songs with melody lines that suggest scale patterns are also appropriate. The following are in *Singing With Children:* "Carrousel," "Clap Hands With Me," "Bow the Winds Southerly," "The Donkey," "Streets of Laredo."

Transposition. Help older students develop comprehension of this concept by playing a familiar song in several keys on a melody instrument. Ask the class what they think you did. Then ask the students to find easy tunes by ear, beginning on pitches selected by the teacher.

Key signature. This puzzle game relates to both ear training and tonal memory. The students will find that transposition demands different key signatures, which is another puzzle relating to the scale in which the song was played.

Improvising (pentatonic). Make up a melody with the right hand on the piano black keys. Then make up an accompaniment with the left hand on black keys.

Composing. Create a melody or song from playing on a xylophone or bell set. Notate it and perform it for a friend.

Improvising with bells or xylophone. Choose a child to improvise a free accompaniment to a pentatonic song. Have him or her experiment with accompaniments that use only two notes, only three notes, and so on until all five notes of the pentatonic scale are utilized.

Tonal memory. A game to be played by two recorder players is one in which the first player performs a short series of pitches to be imitated by the second player.

Tonal memory. Have individuals find on the black keys of the piano or bells pentatonic melodies they know such as "Goodbye, Old Paint," "Grandma Grunts," "The Riddle Song," "Nobody Knows the Trouble I've Seen," "Night Herding Song," "Old MacDonald," "All Night, All Day," "Get on Board," "Auld Lang Syne," "Land of the Silver Birch," "The Campbells Are Coming," and "Swing Low, Sweet Chariot."

Melody, playing. Compose short, three-note (G–A–B—*do-re-mi*) melodies on the recorder. Notate them on a staff with quarter, half, and whole notes.

Bitonality. Play a well-known song such as "Hot Cross Buns," using two keyboard instruments, each in a different key. "Farmer in the Dell" and "Mary Had a Little Lamb" are other candidates. Have the class judge the effect of hearing two keys at once. The effect can be altered somewhat by the tone qualities of the instruments used.

Exploration and practice. Provide for individual practice and experimentation on the keyboard by using a small classroom organ with head sets so that only the player hears the sound.

Less common intervals. For advanced students. Arrange to discover by means of the keyboard the two kinds of seconds, thirds, sixths, and sevenths (major or minor, or large or small). What might an *augmented* interval be? (Expand a major interval by another half step.) What might a *diminished* interval be? (Contract a minor interval by another half step.)

Use the keyboard, then notation to answer these questions so that the students see, hear, and feel these intervals.

Melody, phrase playing, stave. Compose a two-phrase piece for a small wind instrument using G–A–B–C–D, and write it on a two-stave staff. This can be extended to a three- or four-stave staff when appropriate, with more phrases.

Meter, coda. Compose a piece for recorder in either 2/4, 3/4, or 4/4 meter. Employ G–A–B–C–D. Add a coda.

Pentatonic mode. Improvise tunes on piano, bells, or xylophone using notes G–A–B–D–E. Relate selected Chinese songs that use this scale.

Improvising melody. Improvise what you believe could be an American Indian melody on a recorder, using four notes, middle C, D, E, and G.

Dorian mode. Individual students will compose a melody for recorder in the Dorian mode. Notate it on a transparency for class viewing, performance, and discussion. (The Dorian mode has an organization corresponding to a scale on piano white keys that begins and ends on D.)

Melody, chord-line or disjunct. Compose a melody of bugle-call type, based on a tonic chord (I-chord). Notate it and play it on recorder, bells, xylophone or piano.

Pentatonic mode, scale, phrase. Using recorders, improvise answers to given phrases, with tones of a pentatonic scale, either 1–2–3–5–6 or 6–1–2–3–5 of a major scale. Later, improvise both question and answer phrases.

Tone row, polyphony, canon. Listen to a recorded composition such as *Double Canon for String Quartet*, by Stravinsky, Columbia MS 6272. Analyze it to find that there is no tonic (home tone), that it is polyphonic, and that there is a canon. Then build a 12-tone row with resonator bells; the row must not suggest traditional tonal music; none of the pitches are repeated. Write the row on a staff, then write it in inversion. When the row is inverted, the pitch direction is reversed, but the intervals remain the same.

Improvise and play a short piece on the row and its inversions; utilize different rhythms, such as those of familiar songs. Write the composition on the staff. Then try playing it in canon form. Attempt to sing it and play it. Write and play it in retrograde (backwards). Write the row in retrograde inversion (backwards and upside down) by writing the inversion backwards. See *Macmillan Music*, Book Six, p. 106, for an example of how a textbook introduces the tone row.

Transposing instruments. When older children examine a band or orchestra score that they borrow from the instrumental music teacher, they will find that the music is written in a number of different keys. They may find that some instruments are built in different keys. By experimenting with notes on instruments and comparing the resulting pitch with the piano or bells, they can discover that when B♭ instruments play written C, the pitch is B♭, and when E♭ instruments play C, the pitch sounded in E♭. The teacher could plan a discrepant event by asking children who play instruments to all play the same song from a music textbook. This would be one way to discover which instruments are transposing instruments and which are not.

Harmony Instruments

Exploring Combinations of Pitches and Texture

Among the first experiences children have with harmony in the classroom are the accompaniments of songs they have learned as monophonic (unaccompanied) melodies. From this, the thinnest of textures, they are transported into a different world of sound by accompaniments played by the teacher on Autoharp, guitar, piano or by means of recordings. This is usually homophonic music (melody with accompaniment). Many different textures can be produced in accompaniments, and children should be guided to discern what types they are. Thin, thick, heavy, and light are simple descriptive terms for textures, but there should be a good many other adjectives in use as time goes by. As soon as they are able, students should be helped to find how music is organized to produce these various effects. An interesting question to ask when using the piano is, "What would happen if the melody (in the treble clef) and the harmony (in the bass clef) were inverted?" and then proceed to find out by experimenting. Older students can find chords in chord-line (disjunct) melodies and relate these to chords they can build on the bells and piano, or play on the Autoharp to accompany these melodies.

Some teachers make possible experimentation with combining all sorts of pitches and sounds, both as isolated "chords" and as a series of sound effects.

The Autoharp

The Autoharp is an instrument of ancient lineage which has come to be popular in elementary and middle schools, and is used by folk singers. The model most in favor today has 15 push-button bars with felts that prevent the vibration of strings other than those that sound the chord tones desired. The 21-chord model is growing in popularity. See Figures 17.7 and 17.8.

Although some children in primary grades are able to play the instrument satisfactorily, it is not until the fourth grade that most can do so. In early primary grades teachers often press the bars while children strum the strings. It is believed that guiding children to listen carefully to Autoharp chording assists the development of a feeling for harmony, which is part of the preparation for part singing. It is a substitute for the piano in situations

Figure 17.7. AUTOHARP. Oscar Schmidt-International, Inc., and Music Education Group. Northbrook, Ill. 60062

where no piano is available. Hearing chord changes and playing the correct chord at the proper time are valuable for ear-training purposes, and teachers should emphasize these as listening experiences in their efforts to develop children's musicianship. The act of chording is a rhythmic response. A child who is yet unable to sing beautifully may be able to make as beautiful music on the Autoharp as anyone else; thus success on this instrument can help children feel a sense of accomplishment. Chording on the Autoharp is an effective way to stimulate interest in the study of chords on the piano and on the staff. Another use of the Autoharp is to establish the tempo and key of a song by playing introductory chords in the desired rhythm.

The Autoharp is placed on a desk or table, with the corner between the two straight ends of the instrument pointing somewhat toward the player. Fingers of the left hand press firmly on the appropriate chord bar while the right hand strokes the full range of the strings from left to right with a pick. Sometimes the player may choose to stroke the strings on the left side of the bridge to produce a deeper-toned effect. *Finger forms* are important, and the player needs to analyze the chord progressions, then plan the most simple and efficient way to place the correct finger on the bar. In most of the music suggested for Autoharp chording there will be no more than three chords, the tonic (I), the dominant seventh (V_7), and the subdominant (IV). The finger form for these chords in the keys of C major, G major, F major, D minor, and A minor is as follows:

	IV	V_7	I
left hand	ring finger	middle finger	index finger

Try this finger form in the above keys, and find the straight position and the triangular position of the fingers in this basic finger form. See Figures 17.8 and 17.9.

The strings are stroked with a pick held in the right hand, unless the

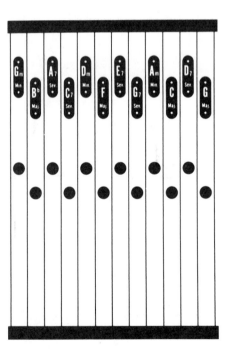

Figure 17.8. AUTOHARP, 21-CHORD MODEL. Music Education Group, Northbrook, Ill. 60062

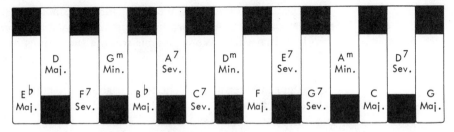

Figure 17.9. AUTOHARP BRIDGE (15-bar model)

player is left-handed. The loud tone produced with a plastic pick is needed for most classroom singing, while the soft tone produced with a felt pick is best for solo and small ensemble singing. Picks are made in different shapes and sizes. Some are worn on fingers while others are held between thumb and index finger. Plastic fasteners from bread wrappers are used as substitutes, and men often use their fingernails instead of a pick.

When teaching students to play the Autoharp, it is the usual practice to begin with songs that require only one chord to accompany, proceeding to those requiring two chords, then to songs in which three chords are necessary. It is desirable to play part of the time by rote to be sure that the students are *hearing* the chord changes, not simply pushing bars mechanically. Such songs follow:

	key:
One-chord songs:	
"Row Your Boat," "Little Tom Tinker"	C major
"Are You Sleeping?" "Farmer in the Dell," "For Health and Strength"	F major
"Canoe Song"	D minor
"Zum Gali Gali"	G minor
Two-chord songs:	key:
"Mary Had a Little Lamb, "Sandy Land," "Looby Loo"	G major
"London Bridge," "Ten Little Indians," "Hush Little Baby," "Polly Wolly Doodle"	F major
"Old Smoky," "Oats, Peas, Beans, and Barley," "Little Red Caboose"	C major
"Down in the Valley," "Long Ago," "Bow Belinda," "Shoo Fly," "Susie Little Susie"	F major
"Nobody Home"	G minor
"Lovely Evening" (I–IV)	F major
"Wayfaring Stranger"	D minor
Three-chord songs:	key:
"Silent Night," Brahms' "Lullaby," "Marines' Hymn"	C major
"My Bonnie," "Jingle Bells," "Camptown Races," "Old Brass Wagon"	G major
"Red River Valley," "Twinkle Twinkle, Little Star," "This Old Man," Hickory Dickory Dock," "Home on the Range"	F major
"Go Down, Moses"	A minor
"Old King Cole"	D minor

Since some two- and three-chord songs are not written in these common keys, using the Autoharp to accompany them requires *transposing* them into keys that will make it possible to play such songs on the instrument. This involves placing the fingers in the finger form of the key nearest to the original key of the song and following the I, V_7, and IV designations, or their equivalent in letter names. The teacher should be certain that the range of pitches in the new key is suitable for children's voices. The 15-bar model permits playing in B♭ and D major also.

A problem in the use of Autoharps is tuning them.* There is no universally accepted method. Ordinarily, one tunes to a piano that is in proper pitch, although a pitch pipe can be used. The strings sounding the C major chord may be tuned first (all of the C's, E's, and G's), then the strings of the G_7 chord (all B's, D's, and F's—the G's having been tuned as part of the C chord), and next the F major chord (all A's—the F's and C's having been tuned as pitches belonging to the other chords). These three chords should then be played slowly to hear whether any of the strings need further adjusting. After this, the other strings may be tuned as individual tones of the chromatic scale (all the half steps). Then every chord of the instrument is played slowly to determine possible need for further tuning. A child can play the pitches on the piano while the teacher adjusts the strings. As a general rule, the teacher must do the adjusting of the strings. The only cases the authors know where strings have been broken are those in which children tighten strings to the breaking point because they think they hear the pitch to which they are tuning one octave higher than it sounds. To keep the instrument in tune and to protect it, it should be kept either in the case it comes in or on a covered shelf, out of the sunlight and away from sources of heat, cold, or dampness. When the instrument is subject to changes in temperature, the expansion and contraction of the strings cause changes in their tension, hence changes in pitch.

Some European music educators do not look with favor on chording instruments such as the Autoharp at the primary level, claiming that children do not possess sufficient harmonic sense at this age to profit from it. However, many American educators believe that chording instruments can provide a valuable listening experience for this age group. Young children can learn to recognize the I-chord as the "home" chord, the V_7-chord as the "away-from-home" chord, and the IV-chord as the "longing-for-home" or "leaning" chord. They can identify them by appropriate motions: the "home" chord with folded arms, the "away-from-home" chord with outstretched arms, and the "leaning" chord by raising both arms to the left or to the right. Children can create other interpretations of the characteristic sound of each of these chords, and create their own related body responses.

Types of Autoharp accompaniments. Like any other musical instrument, the Autoharp should be played with good taste, and there should be logical reasons for the particular style of the accompaniment played. The mood of the

---

* The new Autoharps remain in tune much longer than the earlier models.

song indicates whether the player uses a slow relaxed stroke (as for lullabies and quiet songs), or a strong fast stroke (as for marches and rhythmic songs). For some waltzes, an ump-pah-pah style is called for. This can be made by strumming the first beat of each measure with low-pitched strings and the other two beats with high-pitched strings. A deeper, richer effect is obtained by playing on the left side of the bridge. This brings out the sound of the lower strings and omits a few of the highest pitches. The player can make an appropriate accompaniment for some Spanish-type music by chording in the rhythm of ♩. ♪♩ ♩ . A bagpipe or bourdon effect is made by holding down two bars at the same time; G major and G minor, D_7 and D minor, and A_7 and A minor. This effect is useful for pentatonic music, for some Scottish music, and for folksongs based upon the open fifth of the bagpipe or musette. Individual strings can be plucked to simulate Oriental-type music. A zither or tamburitza effect that characterizes some Eastern European folk music can be produced by two players on the same instrument. One player presses the bars while the other strokes the strings rapidly with wooden mallets. A metal bar or object placed across the strings will produce a steel guitar effect. Minor seventh chords can be sounded when two instruments are used. For example, G minor and B♭ major chords played simultaneously will sound the G minor seventh chord. A minor plus C major will sound the A minor seventh chord, and D minor plus F major sounds the D minor seventh chord. For songs of slow tempo, a skilled player can produce both the melody and the harmony. To obtain this effect, a chord is played for each tone of the melody, and the player strums the strings only as far as the melody pitch. A harp effect is obtained by reversing the usual stroke, the player beginning the stroke with the high strings and moving the pick toward the low strings.

A valuable teacher's guide to the Autoharp is *Teaching Music With the Autoharp,* Music Education Group, Northbrook, Ill. 60062. The book proceeds from beginning to advanced techniques for playing the instrument and includes a song collection of interest.

Ukulele and Guitar

If the desirability of chording experiences on the Autoharp has gained wide acceptance, it follows that there should be similar values in other chording instruments such as the ukulele and guitar. The ukulele has supporters from the fourth grade on, and chording on the guitar is done by some children who are ten and eleven years old.

Standard turning on the ukulele was once G–C–E–A from low to high strings. In recent years a preference for tuning the instrument one whole step higher, to A–D–F♯–B, has developed. Thus, the ukulele beginner finds two tunings in current use. Notice that if the teacher employs both tunings, the fingering for the common chords in G major and F major become the same, as does that for D major and C major.

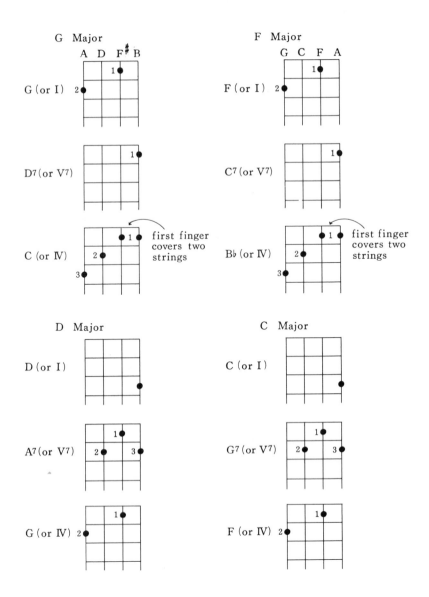

Most ukuleles are made of wood, and need the same protection against dropping, cold, heat, and sun that the Autoharp needs. Extreme dampness, dryness, or temperature changes will change the tuning and could crack the body of the instrument. Students need to be informed about how to strum the instrument or they may break strings by pulling them.

Experts in ukulele playing state that while the baritone ukulele is superior in tone quality and many teachers prefer it to the soprano (standard) instrument, the soprano is best for elementary school children in terms of student hand size; it is easier for them to play. It is easily retuned in C, when this is desirable for a whole-step lower singing range, and it costs less than the baritone. Wood is preferred to plastic. Some teachers introduce the ukulele in a way that relates to the guitar and string bass. The following describes this approach, which begins with the D tuning of the soprano ukulele: A–D–F♯–B.

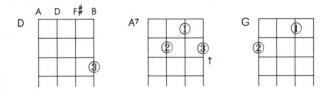

With these three primary chords one can play many folk songs.

When left-handed children play the soprano ukulele, the tuning should be changed to B–F♯–A–D or A–E–C–G so that when the fingerboard is held in the right hand, the left-handers will be able to use the tablature written for right-handers.

The baritone, which is becoming a popular instrument for adults, is tuned a 5th below the soprano ukulele. Its first string, however, is an octave and a 5th below the soprano's first string, making its strings the same as the top four strings of the standard guitar.

Baritone Tuning: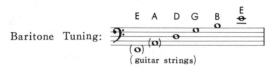

This makes it a good instrument for beginners who may want to transfer to a standard guitar later on. The chords will be formed in the same way but will sound in different keys.

If one is using both instruments simultaneously, it is possible to stagger the teaching of these fingerings, permitting the advantage of being able to practice together. A system one teacher* devised to teach seven fingerings on each instrument makes possible playing all primary chords in two keys in common plus one extra key for each. Directly below these are the keys in common plus one extra key for each. Directly below these are the added fingerings for the other two strings on the guitar. (See page 400.)

These seven fingerings are the easiest for the beginner to play. They comprise the primary triads of the keys of D, G, and C major for the ukulele, and G, C, and F major for the baritone ukulele.

Guitar chords that are easiest for the older child to play are those to follow. They are not easily learned.

The lower four guitar strings are the same as those on the string bass. The chord-roots are plucked with the index finger on the string bass. Since the bass does not have frets, small thin strips of masking tape can be used to mark the half steps for inexperienced players.

* Erma Kleehammer, University of Calgary, Alberta, Canada.

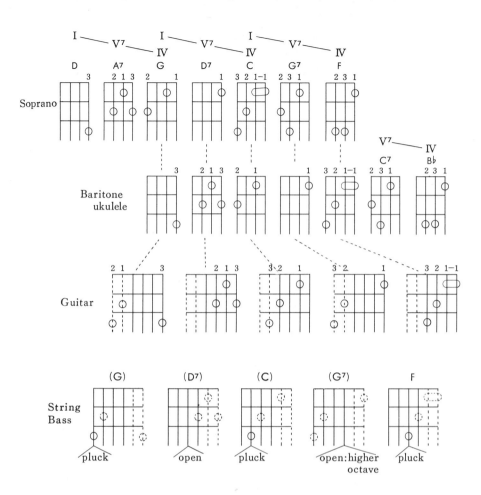

Some of the more common minor chords for the ukulele, baritone, and guitar are:

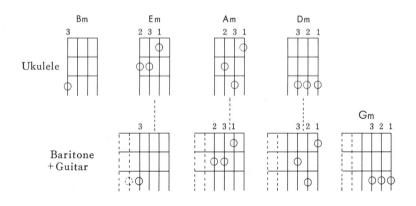

Piano Chording Since the 1–3–5 note pattern becomes a familiar one, being used both in songs and in the procedure that enables the class to have a feeling for the key before singing, this is a logical note combination to use in the initial teaching of chording. This 1–3–5 chord (a major *triad* in *root position*) is also a basic concept in the study of music theory.

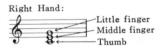

Should a learner be unable to exert equal pressure through these three fingers or in any way be unable to control them at first, the playing of the chord may be accomplished by using any combination of fingers of both hands or by playing only the two highest notes of a three-note chord. The teacher may help the child to play the chord in a steady walking tempo and as this playing of the chord on the beat continues, have the class sing "Row, row, row your boat." The discovery that an accompaniment can be provided for a well-known song in this way is thrilling. There are few standard songs that can be accompanied in their entirety by the lone 1–3–5 chord. Some were listed earlier in this chapter.

Songs that rightfully require two chords (I and V$_7$) but that might be usable as one-chord songs include "Old MacDonald," "Farmer in the Dell," "Three Blind Mice," "Goodbye Old Paint," "Swing Low, Sweet Chariot," "Taps," and "Shortnin' Bread."

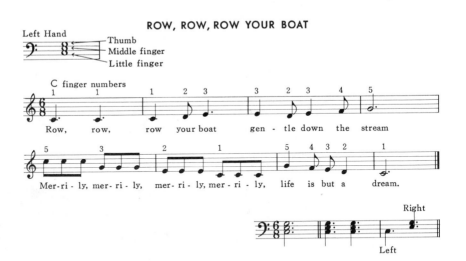

Summary of possibilities:

Play the melody with the right hand.
Play the melody with the left hand.
Play the chord with the left hand.

Play the chord with the right hand.

Play the chord with both hands.

Play the melody with the right hand and the chord with the left hand.

Play the melody with the left hand (in bass clef) and the chord with the right hand (in treble clef).

Play the chord in other forms, such as one note at a time.

How often the chord is sounded depends on how each student feels about the song. One may play a chord on every beat. Another may choose to sound the chord every other beat. Still another may alter the steady pattern of chord-sounding by a pause at the end of a phrase. Children should be free to be as individually creative as possible in this simple way.

When a child has learned how to build 1–3–5 chords on different pitches such as C, F, G, and has learned to recognize the distinctive sound of the major chord, the 1–3–5 chord in minor may be easily taught. A child can soon learn that the minor chord has its own characteristic sound and that major and minor chords can be built at will. Experience will expand the concept of the difference in sound between major and minor. The mechanical difference between major and minor 1–3–5 chords is merely that the middle finger, which plays scale tone 3, is placed one half step lower in minor than in major. Few commonly known songs can be accompanied by the lone minor 1–3–5 chord, but children can compose such songs easily. An example follows:

Piano chording:

Suggested rhythmic responses:

A piano part invented later which can be sung as a chant:

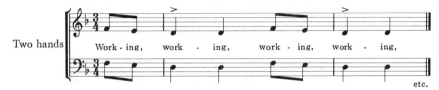

The students discovered that their song could be sung as a round.

A song of Israeli origin that can be accompanied by the G-minor chord is "Zum Gali Gali."

If students have used the Autoharp with songs requiring two or more different chords, the addition of the V_7 chord to permit improvising a piano accompaniment to many familiar songs is relatively easy. A simple form of the chord change from I to V_7 and back to I is as follows:

Using the hand position for the 1–3–5 chord as a starting point, the following directions apply in *all* major keys:

right hand: The little finger remains on the same key. The fourth finger is placed one half step higher than the third finger was. The thumb is placed one half-step lower than before.

left hand: The thumb remains on the same key. The index finger is placed one half step higher than the middle finger was. The little finger is placed one half step lower than before.

Many songs can be harmonized with the I and V_7 chords. Some of the most familiar were listed earlier for Autoharp chording.

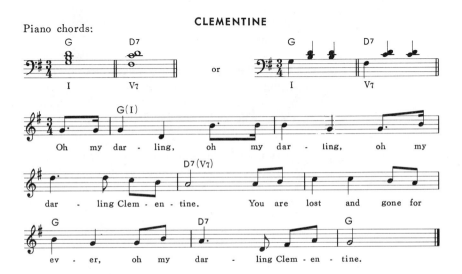

Since most songs in minor keys are based on a scale in which the seventh tone is raised one half step, practically all minor I-V$_7$ chord songs will have the V$_7$ chord played exactly the same as it is played in the major keys of the same name, i.e., the V$_7$ chord in G minor is the same chord as in G major. Thus, the only difference in chording would be in the I chord, which in minor would have its third (the middle note) one half step lower than in the major chord. It is a simple matter, then, to play "Nobody Home" in G minor.*

NOBODY HOME

Three-Part Round

Piano chording:

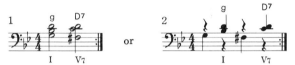

or yet another way:

Suggestion: Try making up an introduction using the style of Example 3. Also, improvise an ending for this round. Add suitable percussion instruments and hand clapping.

Other interesting songs in minor that use these same chords are the French carol "Pat-a-pan" and the English carol, "Dame, Get Up." Percussion instruments go well with "Pat-a-pan."

The hand position for the IV chord is easier than the hand position for the V$_7$ chord. The "rule" for the change from I to IV is as follows:

left hand: The little finger remains on the same key. The index finger is placed one half step higher than the middle finger was. The thumb moves up one whole step.

---

* Some musicians abbreviate G minor by writing "g," and G major by "G."

right hand: The thumb remains on the same key. The middle finger is placed one half step higher than before. The little finger moves up one whole step.

The round "Christmas Bells" provides a good introduction to this chord change. Use the above chords as marked.

The familiar round "Lovely Evening" and the cowboy song "The Railroad Corral" (*This Is Music: Book 6*) are other examples of songs that require only the I and IV chords for their harmonization.

The IV chord in minor is played by lowering the highest of the three tones of the major IV chord one half step. An American folk song that can be harmonized with only I and IV chords is "Wayfaring Stranger":

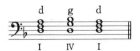

Examples of the many songs in major keys easily chorded with I, IV, and V₇ chords are "The Caisson Song, "Oh Susanna," "He's a Jolly Good Fellow," "The First Noel," "Night Herding Song," "Eyes of Texas (I've Been Working on the Railroad)," "All Through the Night," "Sing Your Way Home," "Deck the Halls," "Happy Birthday to You," "Old Oaken Bucket," "Auld Lang Syne," "Annie Laurie," "Old Folks at Home," "Reuben and Rachel," "Santa Lucia," and "The Muffin Man." Others were listed earlier for Autoharp chording.

CINDY

This use of the piano in the classroom can result in a teacher's learning to play comparatively well. Should any teacher desire to hasten this learning process, there are beginning piano books that employ and expand the method of chording used here.

Teachers should use the sustaining pedal of the piano sparingly. A common fault of piano players is overuse of this pedal, which results in a blur of tones rather than in the clarity and distinctness children need to hear.

If one can chord with I, IV, and V_7 chords in major keys, it is not difficult to chord in minor keys with I, IV, and V_7. Incidentally, minor keys are not as important as major keys as far as common usage in the United States is concerned. While peoples of Eastern Europe find in minor tonality a natural expression, the people of the United States lean rather heavily toward the major tonality. American children should be able to identify minor and major and to enjoy hearing the changes from minor to major and vice versa in songs such as "We Three Kings of Orient Are," "When Johnny Comes Marching Home," and "Minka."

Students sometimes ask the question, "From where do the V_7 and IV chords come, and why are our fingers in the positions they are on the keyboard?"

A 1–3–5 chord can be built on every step of the scale. We could chord by using only 1–3–5 chords, but it would be very awkward to do, and it would not sound well. What we are trying to do with our chord positions at the piano is to move our fingers as little as possible. It is something like being "intelligently lazy"—which in this case is also being efficient. Here are the I, IV, and V chords in the 1–3–5 position in the C-major scale:

These can also be called C, F, and G, because they have two names, one being the Roman numeral that corresponds to the Arabic number name of the scale tone on which the chord is built, and the other being the letter name of the note that is "1" when the chord is in the 1–3–5 (root) position. Here is the V_7 chord in root position:

We are still in the key of C major. Compare the V_7 with the V above. This chord is called V_7 because a note has been added that is seven lines and spaces above G. The notes from the bottom to the top in this chord are G, B,

D, and F, or 1–3–5–7. It is V_7 because G is the fifth step of the scale of C, and we are using that key in this illustration.

The following illustration shows where we obtain the simple three-finger hand position for chording:

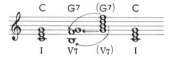

By rearranging the G 1–3–5–7 chord into another *position,* and by omitting the note D, which is the one we can most easily eliminate without injuring the sound of the chord, we can keep the hand in the same place as in playing the I chord and move only the fingers.

The IV chord that we use in piano chording is another position of original 1–3–5 arrangement of the notes:

Common chord positions are:

The first inversion is called 6–3 because if one counts from the lowest note to the highest, numbering the lowest note "1", the *interval* is found to be that of a *sixth.* Counting in similar manner, from the lowest note to the middle one, reveals that this interval is a *third,* hence this is a 6-3 chord. The origin of the name of the 6-4 chord can be counted out in the same way. The two intervals here are a sixth and a *fourth,* hence the name 6-4 chord. See "The Blacksmith," to find how these chords appear in a melody line.

THE BLACKSMITH

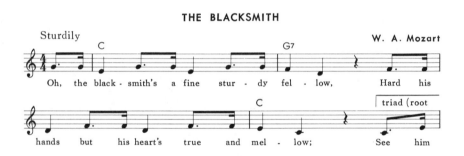

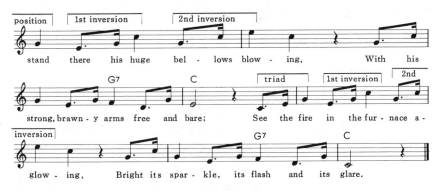

stand there his huge bel - lows blow - ing, With his strong, brawn - y arms free and bare; See the fire in the fur - nace a - glow - ing, Bright its spar - kle, its flash and its glare.

2. *Blow the fire, stir the coals, heaping more on,*
   Till the iron is aglow, let it roar on!
   As the smith high his hammer keeps swinging,
   Fiery sparks fall in showers all around;
   And the sledge on the anvil keeps ringing,
   Giving out its loud clanging sound.

These inversions appear in the melody of many songs. For most students, the names of the inversions are not particularly vital; the important factor is the comprehension that the same notes in these different positions form the same chord. Compare these horizontal chords with the vertical chords in piano chording, and plan similar experiences for children. Try using the chords indicated in the melody for accompanying those measures. Another song to use is "My Home's in Montana." The generalization resulting from a series of such experiments could be, "When tones of specific chords appear in melodies, those chords form a suitable accompaniment." Other possible conclusions might be, "A chord is a vertical arrangement of three or more tones," and "When there are distinct changes in a melody, there are usually changes in the harmony."

The relation of the I and V_7 chords to the major scale is as follows:

Seventh chords, or parts of them, are commonly found in melody lines. Find some in "The Blacksmith," "The Lone Star Trail," and "Down in the Valley." Children should rediscover that the I-chord yields a feeling of stability, whereas the V_7-chord is restless and seems to demand change (resolution). The IV-chord has the same pattern of inversions as the I-chord; its only difference is that it is constructed on the fourth degree of the scale while the I-chord is built on the first degree.

For studying chords in vertical position, some three-part songs in fifth- and sixth-grade series books are helpful. One of these is "Jarabe," in which *passing tones* and *nonchord* tones can be discovered.

JARABE

Spirited

Mexican Song

F
C7

Now the duck is in the stew pot, The bub-bles show that it is red - hot.
Ya el pa-to se está co-cien-do, En los her-vo-res de la o - lla,

C7
F

See he lifts his head to qua - ver, Put the on - ion in for fla - vor.
Sa - ca la ca-be-za y di - ce, Por-que no me e-chan ce-bo - lla.

F
C7

All the neigh-bors hun-gry look - ing, Come and watch while it is cook - ing,
Ven - gan por to-mar a - to - le, To - dos los que van pa - san-do,

C7
F

They would like so much to eat it, But it's bad, they say, and leave it.
Es que el a - to - li - to bue - no. El a-tote se está a - grian-do.

Melody and words from *Spanish-American Folksongs,* collected by Eleanore Hague; published by the American Folklore Society, Inc. Used by permission. *This Is Music For Today, Book V,* by William R. Sur et al. Copyright © 1971 by Allyn and Bacon, Inc. Used by permission.

The attention of older students can be drawn to songs in which there are key changes in order to solve the problem of how a composer *modulates* (changes) from one key to another. Two such songs are "The Erie Canal," and "We Three Kings of Orient Are," in which both major and minor tonalities occur. Relationships between the minor scales on which the songs are based and the minor chords used to accompany them can be examined, then compared with the relationships between major scales and major melodies. If there is sufficient interest, some questions might be, "What happens when triads are built on every degree of the major scale?" "What would happen if we build triads on every degree of the minor scale?" "Do you find any unusual chords?" "What might they be?" "How would you write them?" The harmonizations of "Ma Belle Bimba" and "We Wish You a Merry Christmas" require both major and minor chords; older children can create their own harmonizations, making aesthetic judgments as to which chords are the most pleasing.

The piano keyboard is a testing ground and experimental arena for hearing, seeing, and playing the chords extracted from songs and for trying out new harmonizations.

Chording with Bells

The "piano chords" can be played on resonator bells effectively. Teachers use these individual tone bars in many ways. The bars can be distributed among numbers of children, each having a bar and a mallet with which to strike it. In the key of C, for example, all children who hold bells marked C, E, or G will sound them when the C-major chord is needed, and when the F-major chord is required in the harmonization of the song, all children holding bars that sound F, A, and C will strike them. Of course, they must be struck at the same instant, and this demands the close attention of the players. To produce an interesting shimmering effect, the player needs two mallets, striking the bell in rapid alternation. Playing chords in this manner with appropriate songs can make truly beautiful music. Motivating a fourth-, fifth-, or sixth-grade class to harmonize a song in this way can initiate a study of chords and their relation to the staff and key signature.

Hand bells can be used also, and the Melodica was mentioned earlier as an instrument on which one can play both melody and harmony.

The Singing Classroom Orchestra

When students have learned to play recorders, to chord on the piano and Autoharp, and to play the bells and percussion instruments, the possibility of the singing classroom orchestra presents itself. When the teacher finds a melody line in the range of the wind instruments with the chords named, there are opportunities for combining various instruments with voices, or alternating instruments and voices. Here is a creative activity developing musical discrimination—the students and the teacher will orchestrate the song according to their own judgment. Students can also have experiences in conducting such orchestras. Songs that are not found in books at hand can be presented by means of a projector or can be drawn on large (two by three feet) sheets of heavy paper or light cardboard and placed where all can see. Music can be quickly drawn on such paper. A staff liner with chalk is used to mark the staff. These chalk lines are drawn over with black crayon, freehand. When two-part songs are written, the melody part may be in black crayon while the harmony part is in another color for easier reading. Examples follow:

Theme from NINTH SYMPHONY

Beethoven

The theme from Beethoven's Ninth Symphony is an example of the very simple beginning music a classroom orchestra may use. Ordinarily, themes from the great symphonies are not applicable to this type of work. This particular theme, however, has the simplicity of folk music. It can be extended to include more of the original melody than appears here. An interesting and thrilling event, after words have been set to it and the song is learned, is the teacher's playing a recording of a section of the last movement of the Ninth Symphony. The students will be fascinated listeners to "their song" and will be interested in what Beethoven does with it. Appreciation may be at an extremely high level at this point. The key of C was chosen because it is easiest for the playing of the instruments. The key of F is preferable as soon as the fingering of B♭ is learned, because it places the singing voice in a better range.

"Come, Ye Thankful People, Come" is more difficult and represents a later experience in the development of the classroom orchestra.

COME, YE THANKFUL PEOPLE, COME

While some classroom teachers will be able to write their own classroom orchestra arrangements and make their own charts, others may not be able to do so. In these cases the music specialist becomes the helper, the arranger, and perhaps the chart-maker who assists the room teacher.

Instrumental music activities in the general music program constitute not an end in themselves but an important aid in the teaching of better listening, singing, musical discrimination, creativity, part singing, and note reading, and serve as an introduction to simple music theory concepts, all in a setting that students enjoy, understand, and know to be purposeful.

I, V₇, IV chords. These chords are the *tonic, dominant seventh,* and *sub-dominant,* respectively. The teacher plays the chords slowly and repetitively on the Autoharp, piano, or guitar. The students are asked to describe, identify, and compare the chords in some inventive way. When this has been done, an identification game can be played. For example, some have identified the I-chord as the "at-home chord," and the V_7-chord as the "away-from-home chord." They sometimes identify the IV-chord as the "leaning chord" or the "yearning-for-home chord." The chords can be identified by arm motions. V_7 may be arms up; I may be arms down; IV may be arms at an angle or out in front.

Major, minor chords; Improvising harmony. Adding to the above activity, students can identify major and minor chords by palms up for major and palms down for minor. The teacher plays on the piano, or loudly on an Autoharp, a slowly changing succession of chords. The class will listen carefully to the chords and hum pitches to "fit" the harmony the teacher is playing.

Autoharp tuning. Recordings can assist Autoharp tuning:

Tuning the Autoharp, Rhythm Band, Inc., Fort Worth, Tex.
Tuning Your Autoharp, Oscar Schmidt—International, Northbrook, Ill.

Chord. Many students think of a chord as a triad of three notes, and they are correct. However, their concept of chord can be expanded by asking them to write on the grand staff the pitches of the C major chord as they are shown and sounded on the Autoharp. Ask them which chord tones are repeated at octave intervals, how this might affect their definition of "chord," and how this might relate to their future compositions. Have them try to play the Autoharp chord on the piano. How many hands will it require? Can the chord be extended to more pitches than are on the Autoharp?

Chording accompaniments. Arrange for children to create their own Autoharp, piano, or ukulele accompaniments for easy two- and three-chord songs. The songs are to have no chord designations to help the learners. The problem is to decide which chords to use. The solution can be done in groups, with reports being made back to the total group. The eye must be used to study the melody line for chord clues, and the ear must be used to test whether or not the chord "sounds right." The class may discover that some songs can be harmonized in several different ways.

Tone clusters. Another technique in contemporary composition is use of the tone cluster, a multiple pitch sound used by composers such as Charles Ives and Henry Cowell. To make a tone cluster, place the entire palm or forearm on the piano keys. (They can be made in other ways, too.) Young children use tone clusters to imitate the sound of a large animal walking.

Quartal chords. Traditional chords are constructed of thirds when in root position. Some chords used in contemporary music are constructed as a succession of perfect fourths—*quartal* chords. Have several students perform such chords at the piano. Discuss how they might be used in compositions and for sound effects.

Harmony. Listen to three selected recorded compositions and compare the element of harmony found in each of them.

Composition over an ostinato. Create a simple ostinato, then have individuals or small groups compose a melody over it. Teachers usually plan a pentatonic ostinato to begin with. Examples to learn from:

Pierné: *March of the Little Lead Soldiers,* BOL 54
McPhee: "Ostinatos" from *Tabuh Tabuhan,* Mercury MG 50103
Cowell: "Ostinato Pianissimo" on *Concert Percussion,* Time 8000

Accompaniment, ostinato, harmony. Improvise an accompaniment for "Row Your Boat" using G and E on bells, using two mallets. Is it an ostinato, or is it harmony?

Chords, harmony. Improvise chording accompaniments on Autoharp or ukulele for familiar songs requiring I and V_7 or I, IV, V_7 harmonization.

Quartal chords, round. Analyze the harmonic structure of a familiar round and generalize as to the structure of rounds. Then compose one based on quartal chords (chords made of fourths). Perform it and evaluate it. Example:

Try constructing chords in fifths.

Cadence. Write a piece to demonstrate complete phrase endings (end with a tonic chord), and incomplete phrase endings (end with V_7 or IV chord). The phrase ending is the cadence.

Blues. Compose a text and tune using a 12-bar blues chord progression in the key of C major. Be sure that you have a good rhythm pattern to accompany your three-phrase blues song. The chord sequence given below may be varied somewhat if this improves your song. Sing it with Autoharp accompaniment.

I	I	I	I_7
IV_7	IV_7	I	I
V_7	IV_7	I	I

Remember that the lowered third and seventh steps of the major scale are features of blues music.

Relating chords to scales. Dramatize the relation of chords to scales by forming a major scale of eight students standing before the class, each with a resonator bar representing the correctly-ordered notes of that scale from 1 through 8 (or 1'). The teacher asks students holding bars 1, 3, and 5 to step out in front of the scale and to play their tones together in tremulo style so that the chord can be sustained. "How can we make a minor chord?" "Can we make a minor chord based on scale step 2?" "How can we find the V_7 chord?" "Where are the notes belonging to the V_7 chord when we have only these eight pitches to work with?" "What does this look like in notation?" When notes are needed that are not in the eight scale tones, others from the class can be called upon, given the appropriate tone bar, and placed in keyboard position with the others. For example, a problem may be to act out the whole-tone scale. "What other bars will be necessary?" "What does it sound like?" "How can it be notated?"

Melodic improvisation based on chords. Use written chord sequences as the basis for melodic improvisation. Begin with I–IV–I–V_7–I sequence in familiar keys. One child can play the chords on Autoharp or piano while another improvises over the chords on bells, a small wind instrument, or with his or her singing voice.

F   B♭   F   C₇   F

References

GARY, CHARLES L., ed., *The Study of Music in the Elementary School: A Conceptual Approach,* Reston, Va.: Music Educators National Conference, 1967, pp. 67–81, harmony.

Autoharp   NYE, ROBERT E., and MEG PETERSON, *Teaching Music with the Autoharp.* Northbrook, Ill.: Music Education Group. Revised 1982. How to play it; how to use it in teaching.

Guitar   EISENKRAMER, HENRY E., *Strum and Sing: Guitar in the Classroom.* Evanston, Ill.: Summy-Birchard Co., 1969.

Guitar Magic. Atlanta, Ga.: Educational Productions, Inc., 454 Armour Circle, N.E. 30324. An audiovisual method.

Mel Bay's Guitar Class Method. Kirkwood, Mo.: Mel Bay Publications, Inc., 107 W. Jefferson Ave. 63122.

SILVERMAN, JERRY, *Graded Guitar Method.* New York: The Big Three Music Corp., 1970.

TIMMERMAN, MAURINE, and CELESTE GRIFFITH, *Guitar in the Classroom.* Dubuque, Iowa: William C. Brown Company Publishers, 1971.

Multiple Instruments   BURAKOFF, GERALD, and LAWRENCE WHEELER, *Music Making in the Elementary School,* Hargail Music, Inc., New York, N.Y. 10018. Student's and Teacher's Editions. Uses recorder, voice, bells, and rhythm intruments.

CHEYETTE, IRVING, and ALBERT RENNA, *Songs to Sing with Recreational Instruments,* Theodore Presser Company, Philadelphia, Pa.

SLIND, LLOYD H., *Melody, Rhythm, and Harmony; More Melody, Rhythm, and Harmony,* Belwin-Mills, Melville, N.Y. 11746.

SNYDER, ALICE M., *Sing and Strum.* Belwin-Mills, Melville, N.Y. 11746.

VANDRE, CARL, *Adventures in Harmony, Rhythm, and Song,* Handy-Folio Music Company, Minneapolis, Minn.

WIEDINMEYER, CLEMENT, *Play-Sing-Chord Along,* Shawnee Press, Delaware Water Gap, Pa.

Melody Flute and Tonette

BECKMAN, FREDERICK, *Classroom Method for Melody Flute,* Melody Flute Company, Laurel, Maryland. Contains melodies but no words to sing; a very good piano accompaniment book is available.

BURGETT, ELAINE, et al., *Modern Musical Fun for Singing and Playing with the Tonette.* Elkhart, Ind.: Lyons, 530 Riverview Ave., 46514

Organ

Adventure in Keyboard, Lowry Organ Company, Chicago, Ill. A ten-week program for elementary school students.

The Pointer System School Program, Pointer System, Inc., Winona, Minn. Includes instructional films.

Piano Books for Chording

EASY

ECKSTEIN, MAXWELL, *Play It Now.* Carl Fisher.

FRISCH, FAY TEMPLETON, *The Play-Way to Music, Book Two.* Amsco Music Publications, Inc.

GILBERT, GAIL, *Music Is for Everyone.* Mel Bay Publications, Inc.

NEVIN, MARK, *Tunes You Like,* Books 1, 2, 3, 4. Schroeder and Gunther, Inc.

NEVIN, MARK, *Repertoire Album,* Book 1. Belwin, Inc.

STEINER, ERIC. *One, Four, Five.* Mills Music, Inc.; *Repertoire Album Book I,* Belwin, Inc.

SLIGHTLY MORE DIFFICULT

BERMONT, GEORGES, *Play That Tune,* Books 1, 2, 3, 4. Musicord Publications.

115 Easy Piano Pieces and Folk Songs, Hansen Publications.

RICHTER, ADA, *Songs I Can Play.* M. Witmark and Sons.

STICKLES, WILLIAM, *Easy Hymns and Sacred Songs for the Piano.* Hansen Publications.

Recorder

BUCHTEL, FORREST, *Buchtel Recorder Method,* Book 1. Park Ridge, Ill.: Neil A. Kjos Music Company, 525 Busse Highway, 60068.

COX, HEATHER, and GARTH RICHARD, *Sing, Clap, and Play the Recorder,* Books 1 and 2. St. Louis, Mo.: Magnamusic-Baton, Inc. For ages seven to nine.

EARLE, FREDERICK, *Trophy Elementary Recorder Method, Baroque System.* Cleveland, Ohio: Trophy Music Co., 1278 W. 9th St. 44113.

LANAHAN, WALTER D., *Melody Method for the Recorder.* Laurel, Md.: Melody Flute Co.

NEWMAN, HAROLD, and GRACE NEWMAN, *Music Shall Live—Singing and Playing with the Recorder.* New York: Hargail Music Press, 28 W. 38th St. 10018. Hargail specializes in recorder.

Recorder Music Catalog. Melville, N.Y.: Belwin-Mills, 11746. Recorder music selected from many publishers.

RICHARDSON, ALLEN L., *The Breeze Easy One and All.* New York: Warner Brothers.

Sources of Classroom Instruments

CONTINENTAL MUSIC, Division of C. G. Conn, Ltd., 150 Aldredge Blvd., Atlanta, Ga. 30336.

LYONS, 530 Riverview Ave., Elkhart, Ind. 46514.

MAGNAMUSIC-BATON, INC., 10370 Page Industrial Blvd., St. Louis, Mo. 63132.

MUSIC EDUCATION GROUP, Northbrook, Ill. 60062. Autoharp and all other instruments.

PERIPOLE, INC., P.O. Box 146, Lewiston Road, Browns Mills, N.J. 08015.

RHYTHM BAND, INC., P.O. Box 126, Fort Worth, Texas 76101.

SCIENTIFIC MUSIC INDUSTRIES, INC., 525 N. Noble St., Chicago, Ill. 60622.

chapter 18

Exploring More Complex Analytical Concepts

Harmony and Texture The development of the harmonic sense follows the comprehension of rhythm and melody. This is characteristic of Western cultures. It is either not as evident or is absent in other cultures, although the mass audio media of our times is tending to produce a world music consisting of an amalgamation of the contributions of all peoples. While Western music evolved to emphasize harmony, music of Asia and Africa emphasized rhythmic and melodic developments more complex than those of the West. In the ethnic music of Asia and Africa, harmony is incidental to the interrelation of rhythm and melody, although the octave, the fifth, and the fourth appear vertically in much of it, as does some simple tonic-dominant harmony.

Polyphony is another word for counterpoint. Its earliest definition had to do with point against point (note against note). For our purposes we will regard it as a combining of melodic lines into a unified musical fabric. In traditional Western music, polyphony operates in accordance with certain harmonic principles. However, in some contemporary music it operates with disregard of traditional common practice harmony. Thus, there can be said to be two general types of polyphony, harmonic and nonharmonic. According to traditional standards, harmonic polyphony sounds well; it is consonant. Nonharmonic polyphony does not sound the same; it is apt to be dissonant. The music of Johann Sebastian Bach is polyphonic; it can be viewed as horizontal threads of melody moving along together. At the same time, when this music is viewed vertically, chords and chord changes appear at certain places. We find it is a texture woven of threads moving in both vertical and horizontal ways. A common example of this combination of the horizontal and vertical aspects of music is the round. Teachers should occasionally write a round in full on the chalkboard, each entry written on a staff beneath the previous entry. Students can then see, as well as hear, how the polyphony fits together harmonically.

Texture refers to the number and general effect of the horizontal and vertical lines in music. Adjectives commonly used to describe texture include, heavy, light, open, thick, and thin. Texture can be thick or thin according to the number of parts employed, their pitches, and their tone qualities. A two-part round is of thin texture while three- and four-part rounds have correspondingly thicker textures. Low pitches can influence textures toward heaviness while high pitches can produce an opposite effect. When the parts are close together, the texture is correspondingly thicker; when they are far apart, an opposite effect can occur. The terms monophonic, homophonic, and polyphonic refer to classification of textures.

Students first learn melody, the monophonic (one-voice) horizontal line. It is believed they are able to sense next the moving of two or more melody lines together. This is reflected in the classroom in the use of canons, rounds, chants, ostinati, and descants that they can perform after they have learned to sing in tune or to play a melody instrument with a group. For most students the ability to hear and sing harmonically develops between the ages of nine and thirteen. This growing harmonic sense is reflected by an emphasis on part singing for the ten and eleven-year-olds.

Among Western nations there are differences in the degree of emphasis given to harmonic music by music educators. In the United States it has been emphasized throughout all levels of instruction to a greater degree than in most other nations. It is possible that young children like the sound of harmony even though most of them cannot hear it analytically and, on the other hand, harmony may be overused; it can confuse some children who are trying to comprehend and sing melodies. Research is needed to determine the suitability of harmonic music for young children. It seems logical that the young child should first be helped to comprehend rhythm and melody and that this should be done with as little interference from other elements as possible. Second, the child should be assisted in developing the ability to comprehend two or more melodic lines functioning at once and relating to each other. Third, this interaction of melodic lines should lead rather quickly into learning about harmony. It should also develop a certain independence in thinking and composing melodic lines, which may or may not be harmonically related. Thus, the child will be able to deal both with traditional harmony and with some of the music of today which avoids such harmony; the eleven-year-old should be helped to understand both types of music.

Some conclusions for students to discover and develop in traditional harmony are:

Harmony is a vertical arrangement of pitches.

Tonality (key feeling) results when the harmony of a piece of music indicates a tonal center to which its other tones are attracted or related.

When two tones are on adjacent lines or spaces, they form the interval of a third.

Thirds (and other intervals) may be found vertically in harmonies and horizontally in melodies.

The tones of the dominant seventh chord (V_7) resolve naturally to the tonic chord; this fixes the tonality.

The tones of the subdominant (IV) chord resolve naturally to either the tonic chord or follow a progression to the dominant seventh chord followed by the tonic chord.

When at the end of a succession of chords in a phrase a feeling of repose is suggested, the chords which communicate this feeling comprise a cadence.

The IV–1 cadence sounds like "Amen."

Contemporary Harmony

One possible approach to contemporary harmony would take place after students have found that chords in traditional harmony are constructed in thirds. The teacher could ask, "What would happen if chords were built of fourths rather than thirds?" and let the students find out by their experimenting with fourths. Then the teacher might ask the same question about fifths, sevenths, and seconds. Another beginning could be in response to the question, "What kinds of chords are needed to harmonize a composition written in the whole-tone scale? Write one and be ready to tell the class about those chords."

Music of today is in a period of unlimited experimentation. It is described by some as involving deliberate violation of the traditional harmonic system of chords and chord resolutions by the employment of parallel chords, chords built with fourths, other arrangements leading to abandonment of former restrictions, and toward the absence of tonal centers. This does not mean that the music of the future is necessarily what the results of experimental composition seem to indicate, but it is likely that some of this will be a part of it. It appears that music educators have the responsibility of helping children think musically in the two generally defined areas of traditional harmony and its opposite, and in the great area in between these two extremes. This area in between the extremes may be the most important when the future reveals itself.

In *tone row* composition tones of the row are combined as chords. In tonal polyphony the chords "happen" when horizontal lines of melody sound at one time. The pen of the less talented experimenter is likely to produce less artistic music; the more talented will use new harmonic resources with discretion and taste. The composers most likely to live in the history of music will do what the great ones have always done—find some way to integrate the new with the old in a pleasing way. In the schools our duty is to expose students to all types of music. Experience with the tone row and its type of harmony can begin as early as the third grade. The fifth and sixth grades can sing a folk song in one key while chording it in another, record this bitonality on tape, play it back and evaluate the effect. They can also sing songs in parallel fourths and fifths for experimental purposes and evaluate them the same way. *Students like to experiment* and to evaluate what happens—and this seems to be one of the best times in history to do it. They can experiment with traditional harmony by finding different harmonizations for the same song. Improvisation can be done on the black keys while chording in the key of C major. Authentic recorded music of Africa and Asia can be listened to, studied, and its harmonic qualities can be examined and compared to Western harmony. In some of this music, harmony may be absent, in some it may be present but different from Western harmony, and in some the harmony may resemble that of the West.

Recordings useful in exploring contemporary harmony include:

Bartók: "Bear Dance" from *Hungarian Sketches* AM 3 v 2
Bartók: *Concerto for Orchestra.* Quartal harmony (chords built in fourths)
Milhaud: "Laranjeires: from *Saudades do Brazil,* AM 4 v 2 (dissonance, bitonality)
Milhaud: "Copacabana" from *Saudades do Brazil,* AM 4 v 2 (bitonality, dissonance)
Hindemith: *Mathis der Maler,* Columbia (harmony constructed of fourths and fifths)
Harris: *Folk-Song Symphony,* Vanguard (contemporary harmonizations of U.S. folksongs)
Honneger: "March from *King David,* Vanguard (polytonality: three keys at one time)
Ives: "Putnam's Camp" from *Three Places in New England,* BOL 75; Columbia; Mercury (bitonality; describes two bands playing in different keys). Also "Fourth of July," Columbia MS-6889 and *Variations on America,* Columbia MS-7269 and Victor LSC-2893.
Copland: "Circus Music" from *The Red Pony,* AM 3 v 1 (tone clusters, polytonality)
Webern: *The Complete Music,* Columbia K4L 232 (tone row music)
Sounds of New Music, Folkways FX 6160 (electronic music) tone clusters: see music of Charles Ives and Henry Cowell

Students' exploration of harmony and polyphony should deepen their insight into how melody and harmony interrelate. There is no better way to learn about music than to compose it. Although few students will become professional composers, every child can benefit from writing his or her own melody and harmony, regardless of how modest the level may be. Music paper should be standard equipment in the classroom.

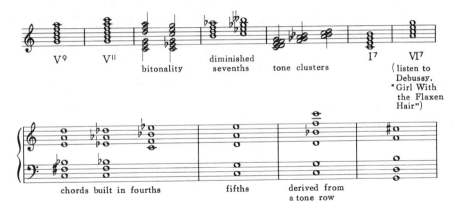

Electronic music is bringing about a reexamination of current definitions of harmony, polyphony, form, and other musical elements. In electronic music, the simultaneous sounding of two tone qualities, whether these have definite pitch or not, can be considered to be a type of harmony. Polyphony of electronic sounds may consist of simultaneous sounding of different streams or bands of sounds that produce a contrapuntal effect. When one finds that some of the recorded examples of "new" music listed in this book are from the 1950s and 1960s, the urgency of keeping abreast of this rapidly-moving thrust in music becomes evident. Some radio and television programs utilize electronic and other types of contemporary music. These can be tape recorded and brought into the classroom for analysis.

References and Materials

Recordings MAJOR AND MINOR

Mussorgsky: "Bydlo" from *Pictures at an Exhibition.* AM 2 v 1

Bizet: "Farandole" from *L'Arlésienne* Suite. AM 6 v 1 (also form)

Lecuona: "Andalucia" from *Suite Andalucia,* AM 4 v 1 (includes a canon)

Mozart: "Romanze" from *Eine kleine Nachtmusik,* AM 4 v 1

Charpentier: "On Muleback" from *Impressions of Italy,* AM 5 v 1

de Falla: "Spanish Dance" from *La Vida Breve,* AM 6 v 1

COMMON CHORDS

Brubeck: "Unsquare Dance" on *Time Further Out.* Columbia CS 8490

Mozart: "Romanze" from *Eine kleine Nachtmusik,* AM 4 v 1 (I, V_7, and IV chords can be heard and identified)

Ginastera: "Wheat Dance" from *Estancia,* AM 4 v 1

Milhaud: "Copacabana" from *Saudades do Brazil,* AM 4 v 2

TEXTURES

Sousa: *Semper Fidelis,* AM 3 v 1. Have children explore this march to discover the melodies and how the composer combines them.

Saint-Saëns: "The Swan" from *Carnival of the Animals,* AM 3 v 2 (homophonic texture)

Ligeti: "Atmospheres" from *Space Odyssey,* Columbia MS 6733

Bach: Little Fugue in G Minor, AM 6 v 1; BOL 86

Britten: *Young Person's Guide to the Orchestra,* London 6671 (polyphony, theme and variations)

Benjamin, *Jamaican Rhumba,* BOL 56 (homophony, polyphony)

TONE QUALITIES

Cage, Cowell, Ussachevsky, *Sounds of New Music,* Folkways FX 6160. For stimulating sound exploration on piano and Autoharp.

Kraft, *Theme and Variations for Percussion Quartet,* BOL #83

The Science of Sound, Folkways FX 6007.

LEGATO, STACCATO
Gretry, "Ballet Music" from *Cephale et Procris,* Tambourin, AM 2 v 1. Also useful
for major, minor, and loud-soft concepts.

MELODY
Shostakovitch, "Petite Ballerina" from Ballet Suite No. 2, AM 2 v 1

Bartók, "Jack-in-the-Box" from *Mikrokosmos* Suite No. 2, AM 2 v 1

Schuller, "Twittering Machine" from *Seven Studies on Themes of Paul Klee,* AM 2 v
2. (12 tone music)

Schubert, "First Movement" from Symphony No. 5, AM 5 v 1

OSTINATO
Cowell, *Ostinato Percussion,* Mainstream 5011.

Kabalevsky, "Pantomime" from *The Comedians,* AM 1 v 1.

IMPROVISATION
Brubeck, *Dialogue for Jazz Combo and Orchestra,* Columbia CL 1466.

Bernstein, "Improvisation I" from *Four Improvisations for Orchestra,* Columbia MS
6733

CHANGING AND LESS COMMON METERS
Brubeck, *Time Out* (2/4, 3/4, 4/4, 4/4 : ||) Columbia CL 1397

————, *Time Further Out* (7/4, 5/4) Columbia CL 1690

Tchaikovsky, "Second Movement" from Symphony No. 6 (5/4 meter)

INTERVALS
Bartók, "Second Movement" from *Concerto for Orchestra,* Pairs at Play (bassoons in
6ths, oboes in 3rds, clarinets in 7ths)

Hanson, "Bells" from *For the First Time* on *The Composer and His Music,* Mercury
MG 50357 (5ths)

WHOLE-TONE SCALE
Debussy, "Voiles" from *Preludes,* Book 1.

Hanson, "Mists" from *For the First Time* on *The Composer and His Orchestra,* Vol.
III, Mercury MG 50357

TWELVE-TONE MUSIC
Schoenberg and others, piano music (Gould) Columbia ML 5336

Schoenberg and others, orchestral pieces, Columbia ML 5616

Stravinsky, Double Canon for String Quartet, Columbia MS 6272

ELECTRONIC MUSIC
Mimaroglu, "Prelude XI" on *Electronic Music III* Turnabout VOX TV 34177. The
sound of a rubber band on manipulated tape recorder.

Powell, *Electronic Setting,* Son Nova 1

Stockhausen, *Gesang der Jünglinge,* Deutsche Grammophon 138811

Ussachevsky, *Piece for Tape Recorder,* CRI 112

Varèse, *Poem Electronique,* Columbia ML 5478

Cage, Cowell, others, *Sounds of New Music,* Folkways FX 6160

FORM
Pinto, *Memories of Childhood,* BOL #68 (ABA, meter)

Vaughan-Williams, "March Past of the Kitchen Utensils" from *The Wasps,* AM 3 v 1 (phrase, repetition, contrast)

Menotti, "March of the Kings" from *Amahl and the Night Visitors,* AM 1 v 2 (rhythm pattern, form based on repetition and contrast of two melodies, coda)

McDonald, "Third Movement" from *Children's Symphony,* AM 2 v 1 (introduction, coda, contrast, interlude)

Delibes, "Swanhilde's Dream" from *Copelia,* AM 2 v 2

Prokofiev, "Waltz on Ice" from *Winter Holiday, AM 3 v 2 (ABACA rondo)*

Pinto, "Run, Run" from *Memories of Childhood,* BOL #68 (ABA sections, meters)

Haydn, "Andante" from Symphony No. 94, BOL #62 (theme and variations)

Sousa, *Stars and Stripes Forever,* AM 4 v 1

Mozart, Overture to *The Marriage of Figaro,* BOL #76 (overture)

El-Dabh, *Leilya and the Poet,* Columbia MS 6566 (form in tape processes)

Halloween Listening and Analyzing

Halloween provides an exceptionally promising time to analyze recorded music to determine how a composer employs the various musical elements to produce the effects desired. The following compositions are among those studied in relation to Halloween:

Berlioz: "Witches' Sabbath" from *Symphonie Fantastique*

Cowell: "Banshee" on *Sounds of New Music,* Folkways FX 6160

Dukas: *The Sorcerer's Apprentice,* BOL #59

Grieg: "In the Hall of the Mountain King," from *Peer Gynt* Suite, BOL #59
March of the Dwarfs, BOL # 52

Humperdinck: "Witches' Ride" from *Hansel and Gretel*

MacDowell: "Villain" from *Marionettes,* RCA Basic Library 45-5032
"Witch," RCA Listening III
"Witches' Dance," RCA Listening V

Mussorgsky: *Night on Bald Mountain,* BOL #82

Reinheld: *Dwarfs,* RCA Basic Library
Gnomes, RCA Rhythm Album One

Saint-Saëns: *Danse Macabre,* BOL #59

Stravinsky: "Infernal Dance of the Kastchei" from *Firebird* Suite, BOL #69

Films

Elements of Composition (New York Wind Ensemble), NET Film Service, Bloomington, Ind. 47401 (melody, harmony, rhythm, and counterpoint)

Discovering Melody and Harmony, BFA Educational Media, 2211 Michigan Ave., Santa Monica, Calif. 90404. (Harmony is added to melody through use of descant and thirds and by playing instruments.)

Harmony in Music, Coronet Instructional Films, Chicago, Ill. 60601 (introduces harmony and chords, ages 10–13)

Let's Get Together EMC Corporation, St. Paul, Minn. 55101 (harmony, ages 10–adult)

Music, The Expressive Language, Sutherland Productions, 201 N. Occidental Blvd., Los Angeles, Calif. 90026 (rhythm, melody, harmony, reading music, for ages 9–11)

Music: Churchill Films, 662 N. Robertson Blvd., Los Angeles, Calif. 90069. From a popular series of music education films.

Two-Part Singing, Johnson Hunt Productions, Hollywood, Calif. 94105 (ages 9–11)

Refer to *Film Guide for Music Educators,* Music Educators National Conference.

Analyzing Ethnic and Intercultural Music

Black and Chicano music are of high importance today, and not only in communities that have large black and Chicano populations. As is true of all music, much can be learned from them. Many state departments of education, county and city school systems have compiled collections of Latin American music that reflect the Spanish or Mexican-American cultures, one example being *Cancionero Alegre,* published by the Department of Public Instruction, State Capitol, Phoenix, Arizona. Probably because this music has long been considered to be a traditional part of Western culture, sessions devoted to the teaching of it at the conferences and conventions of music educators have been too few.

The music of former Africans in many Latin American nations has resulted in a merging of musical styles that has produced much popular music, folk music, and dance. The following are in large part of African origin:

country	dance
Argentina	Tango
Brazil	Samba, Maxixe
Cuba	Habañera, Rhumba, Congo, Mambo, Cha-Cha
Haiti	Merengue (French and African influences)
Mexico	Huapango
Trinidad	Limbo

In addition to the above, the calypso, part of the popular music of Trinidad and the Bahamas, combines European melody and harmony with African rhythm. American composers who have utilized musical ideas from these sources include:

Benjamin	*Jamaican Rhumba*
Copland	*El Salon Mexico*
Gould	*Latin-American Symphonette*

Characteristics of black music from which all can learn include the use of music in all phases of daily living, antiphony (call and response), use of pentatonic and gapped scales and flatted scale tones 3, 5, and 7, complex rhythms with syncopation and shifting meters, improvisation, alteration of melody, harmonies using I, IV, and V chords, storytelling in song, and performance techniques that include hand clapping, rhythmic movement, stamping, shouting, percussive vocal effects, ostinato effects, and falsetto singing. These elements of black or African music are found in blues, jazz riffs, and in rock-and-roll music. Black folksongs are a vital element in

American musical culture. They have been classified by John W. Work under the following headings:

Call-and-response chant	Storytelling
Slow, sustained, long-phrase melody	Trial and tribulation
Syncopated, segmented melody	Faith and inspiration

Sessions in black music at conferences and conventions stress repeatedly that rhythm is the primary element in performing African-American music, thus active physical movement is a necessity.

One of the strong trends in music education is an interest in music of the world. While there have been songs from Western Europe and Latin America in music textbooks, Africa and Asia, where the majority of the people on the earth reside, have been less well represented. Efforts are now being made to learn more about the indigenous music of all peoples. We become involved with generalizations such as:

1. The early history of the development of music in any country has a direct influence on the present and future types of music in that country.
2. The music of any country is undergoing more or less constant change.
3. The music of any country reflects the people's concerns in every aspect and area of life—social, esthetic, religious, political, and economic.
4. The music of most cultures has been altered and influenced by music from another or other cultures.
5. Folksongs in all societies undergo constant change which reflects the changes taking place in those societies; both words and melodies may change over the years (Example: Songs about "choo-choo" trains are not written today because the modern diesel engine does not make that sound.)
6. The music of a particular culture has a distinctive style that differentiates it from all other cultures.
7. Every society has found a need for music, and has created its own types of music to serve its purposes.
8. The music, art, language, literature, architecture, recreation, food, clothing, and political and social customs of a people serve to bind them together into a national or cultural unit.

Music is sometimes considered solely as an art to be studied, and sometimes considered solely as an art that reflects humanity. This implied division is in many respects artificial, since music as an art is rooted in the lives of people. Both social studies and ethnomusicology demand that music be studied *in the context* of the society and times of which it is an expression. An example is the minuet, which became an official French court dance in 1650, and eventually became an expression of a courtly and aristocratic society. Its restraint and sophisticated artificiality reflected the patterned dignity and courtesies of the eighteenth-century ruling class. As this aristocratic society began to weaken, the minuet began to decline in importance as a dance, but became a movement in symphonies of Haydn and Mozart at a faster tempo, not danceable. This finally evolved to become the *scherzo* (literally "joke") movement of Beethoven symphonies. Music is always communicating something, whether it is feelings of restraint or of freedom, a folk singer's reaction to the environment, aspects of a specific culture, or a sophisticated reflection of that culture by a professional composer.

Songs, dances, and instruments yield data about people's beliefs, values, and how they live or lived. Through the music of various people and times, children can discover *who they are,* and can find their places in the cultural stream that began in the past and will flow into the future. New songs explain the concerns of the present day, while old songs are a means of understanding the past and its influence on the present. The historian and the anthropologist find music an ingredient of a culture, society, or tribal organization; thus it is one of the essentials of a civilized state of being. Music is not necessary for mere physical survival, but it helps make survival worthwhile; it is a quality factor for living which reflects degrees of cultural sophistication.

The school music of Japanese children is similar to that of American children, while the original, authentic Japanese music occupies a minority position. The native Japanese music stems historically from Chinese culture, causing the Japanese children to find themselves amid two cultural streams of music. The excellent film, *Folk Songs of Japan,* useful for age eight and up, can be obtained from the nearest Japanese consulate (color, 29 min.). It portrays the beauty of the Japanese countryside while taking the listener through examples of all types of folk music including a contemporary popular song performed by young people at a ski resort. The combination of Japanese and American influences in this song encourages students' analyses of the music.

The Japanese haiku poem can be created, then set to music using a Japanese scale. Accompanying instruments can be added rather delicately, with gong, bells, woodblocks, finger cymbals, and a light rattle being appropriate in many cases. The poem includes a central idea, a suggested or inferred location, reference to seasons of the year, and seventeen syllables in three lines, although the latter is not always held to. An example might be:

The late poppy bloom
Withers in the cold.
Orange petals are falling.

Japanese scales (pentatonic scales with half-steps) :

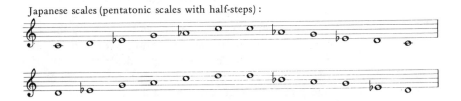

As students explore Asiatic music by means of television, recordings, films, and books, they will discover that concepts of music which differ from ours have a utility, charm, and worth of their own. Rhythm and melody, often accompanied by a simple drone, characterize the music of India. The scale and melodic structure is found in the *raga,* of which there are hundreds. Each of these has from five to seven pitches and one or two secondary pitches. The performer elaborates and improvises on the raga. Each raga has nonmusical implications which could be some feeling or emotion, a season, or a time of day. This music is horizontally conceived; there is no harmony as we know it—only the drone. Both melody and rhythm are more sophisticated than their counterparts in Western music; our composers are being increasingly influenced by Indian concepts of melody and rhythm. The *tala* is the rhythmic structure, organized into a number of beats with recurring accents. Approximately thirty talas are in common use. Some are regular in meter, such as 4 + 4 + 4 + 4 beats, while others are irregular, such as the eleven-beat 7 + 2 + 2. The musician improvises rhythmically on the basis of the tala. Three popular instruments are the *sitar,* a many-stringed fretted instrument, the *tabla,* a double drum, and the *tamboura,* a long-necked unfretted instrument with drone strings.

The mixing of Eastern and Western music took place in the popular music field with the raga-rock concept. Arabic music is a worthy study, as is the *gamelan* music of Indonesia which influenced Debussy and other composers. Something to avoid is thinking of non-Western music as stereotypes. It is infinitely varied. For example, there are many differences in the music of one section of a country like Nigeria from that of other sections; the same is true of China and almost every country. The music of Africa has been influenced by music of Asia, Arabia, and of the West, with Central Africa providing music more indigenous than other sections of that continent. American Indian and Hawaiian music are of special interest to people of the United States. American Indian music, generally speaking, utilizes steps smaller than our half steps, uses a percussion accompaniment of drums, rasps, and rattles, employs the flute as a solo instrument, has no structured harmony, and has chant-like melodies which do not conform to the European scales. Original Hawaiian music has been practically destroyed by European musical influence, but researchers have manged to reconstruct some of it.

Native Hawaiian music was largely chant, centered about one pitch. Harmony was absent; the form was mainly of short repeated chants with instrumental interludes to provide contrast. The modern Hawaiian style resulted when missionary hymns and the Portuguese guitar were introduced. The guitar evolved to become the modern ukulele.

Recordings are a necessity when studying the music of the world, but listening to fascinating authentic music can have its problems when students are called upon to analyze it and to describe it. One problem is that of identifying the meter. The solution is a mathematical one; identify the two-beat and three-beat segments. While this can become a complex study, an easy introduction can begin with 5/4 meter, one that is used to some extent in the folk music of the West. Children accept this meter readily. While a few songs written in it are found in the music textbooks, a creative approach can be made by students composing their own percussion scores and songs in that meter. *The important principle is that the beats in this and the meters to follow are organized in groups of two's and three's.*

5/4 = 3 plus 2 *or* 2 plus 3

Examples:

In Latin American music we find occasional measures in fast 6/8 meter that are performed differently than those in traditional North American music. Traditional American music usually has this meter divided into two-beat measures. South of the border one finds a three-beat measure among the predominant two-beat measures.

Traditional North American — or 3 plus 3

Occasional measures in Latin-American music — or 2 plus 2 plus 2

Leonard Bernstein's "America" from *West Side Story* is an example:

In Eastern Europe, the Middle East, and Asia are found 7/8, 8/8, 9/8 and other meters. Measures in those meters can be divided by beat-count as follows:

7/8, 7/4 = 3 plus 2 plus 2
        2 plus 2 plus 3
        2 plus 3 plus 2
8/8, 8/4 = 2 plus 2 plus 2 plus 2
        3 plus 3 plus 2
9/8, 9/4 = 2 plus 2 plus 2 plus 3
        3 plus 3 plus 3

Writing music in these rhythmic groupings can be a fascinating task.
Learning the Greek folksong *Gerakina* (page 242) will help one to become oriented to a less common meter. The tempo is fairly fast. When the song is learned, it will be found that counts 1, 4, and 6 mark the beats.
Another problem is identifying instruments. Because there are probably thousands of standard folk instruments, this becomes virtually impossible. Yet, the ear can classify the instruments heard so that class discussion about them can take place. The following classification has proved to be helpful:

string	Membrane (drum-type)
plucked	pitched
struck	unpitched
bowed	percussion
stroked	metal
wind	wood
open hole	stone
(flute-type)	body sounds
single reed	
double reed	
brass	

Other headings to assist analysis are:

vocal sounds	pitch
rhythm	straight (true and unwavering)
regular beat	bent (swooping up or dropping down; unsteady)
flexible	harmony, if any
melody, type of	form (unity-contrast)

One can expect varying tonal (scale) organizations. Tempo and dynamics should be easily described. Acceptable tone qualities are different in various cultures.

The October, 1972 issue of the *Music Educators Journal* concerned music in world cultures. It contained nineteen articles on world musics, a glossary, a bibliography, discography, and filmography. It affords the reader greatly more than is possible to include in this textbook, so the authors refer to that publication for books, recordings, and films for use in this interesting area of emphasis.

The final Contemporary Music Project *Newsletter,* dated Spring, 1973, contains a recommended list of recordings of Asian and African music thought to be useful for teaching purposes. Those preceded by one asterisk are especially recommended; a second asterisk indicates that extensive notes are provided to help orient the listener.

JAPAN
Bell Ringing in Empty Sky, Solo Flute (Shakuhachi) music. Nonesuch 72025

Music from the Kabuki. Nonesuch 72012

Music from the Kabuki. Nonesuch 72012

Japanese Koto Classics. Nonesuch 72008

Gagaku, Ancient Japanese Court Music. Everest 3322

SOUTHEAST ASIA
**Traditional Music of Thailand.* Institute of Ethnomusicology, UCLA, Los Angeles, 90046. Includes an excellent booklet by David Morten.

Music from Cambodia. UNESCO Anthology, Bährenreiter 30L 2002

Music from Vietnam I. UNESCO 30L 2022

INDONESIA
*Golden Rain (Bali). Nonesuch 72028

*Gamelan Music of Bali. Lyrichord LLST 7179

The Jasmine Isle (Java). Nonesuch 72031

Gamelan Semar Pegulingan (Gamelan of the Love God) (Bali). Nonesuch H-72046

Music for the Balinese Shadow Puppet Plays, Gender Wayang. Nonesuch H-72037

CHINA
Shantung Folk Music and Traditional; Instrument Pieces. Nonesuch H-72051

AFRICA
**Mbira Music of Rhodesia.* University of Washington Press, Seattle

The African Mbira. Nonesuch 72043

**Music of the Dan Territory.* Ocora, OCR 17

**Music of Central Africa (Musique centrafricaine).* Ocora, OCR 43

**Black Africa, Panorama of Instrumental Music (Afrique noire, Panorame de la musique instrumentale).* BAM LD 409A

**Nigeria—Hausa Music I.* UNESCO 30L 2306

INDIA
Sarangi, Voice of a Hundred Colors. Nonesuch 72030

**The Anthology of Indian Music, Vol. I.* World-Pacific WDS 26200 (three records and extensive notes)

Drums of North and South India. World Pacific WPS 21437

Indian Drums. Connoisseur Society CS 1466

West Meets East, Ravi Shankar and Yehudi Menuhin. Angel 36418

The Sound of Subbudlakshmi. World Pacific WPS 21440

The Music of India (South). Nonesuch 72003

**Ustad Ali Akbar Khan, Raga Chandranandan.* Connoisseur Society

Bhavalu/Impressions, South Indian Instrumental Music. Nonesuch 72019

PERSIA (IRAN), THE MIDDLE EAST
The Persian Santur, Nonesuch 72039

The Living Tradition: Music from Iran. Argo ZFB 51

Music from Turkey. Living Tradition, Argo ZRG 561

Music from the Middle East (Syria, Iraq, Palestine). Living Tradition, Argo ZRG 532

TIBET
**Anthology of Asian Music: Tibet.* AST 4005 (Anthology Record Corp.), 135 West 41 St., N.Y. 10036

AFGHANISTAN
Music of Afghanistan. UNESCO 30L 2003

In addition to the above, the educator can consider twelve long-playing records or cassettes produced by UNICEF. In them one hears native groups, soloists, and children performing music, songs, and dances of 48 different nations, 43 of them non-European. The music series provide some helpful recordings of ethnic music.

Ethnic Music   After listening to a recording of some specific ethnic music, have your students analyze it in terms of types of instruments and voices used, types of melody, harmony, rhythm, tone qualities and texture. Then have them compose music that has similar sounds.

The term "ethnic" should be applied to every person because all people have ethnic roots whether they be African, American Indian, Mexican Indian, Chinese, Irish, Spanish, Arabic, English, Polish, Swedish, "American," or Portuguese. Children can learn about their cultural origins through the music of their people's heritage. Music can assist the understanding of other cultures, and the commonalities and differences of people everywhere can be illustrated through the music of those cultures.

References for Ethnic Music

AMOAKE, W. K., *African Songs and Rhythms for Children.* Mainz, W. Germany: B. Schott's Söhne, 1971. Belwin-Mills, agent.

BALLARD, LOUIS W., "Put American Indian Music in the Classroom." *Music Educators Journal,* March 1970.

COOPERATIVE RECREATION SERVICE, *World Around Songs,* Burnsville, N.C. Inexpensive songbooks concerning states, nations, and peoples of the world.

CROOK, ELIZABETH et al.: *Afro-American Music and Its Roots, Country Music and Its Roots, Music of North American Indians, Spanish-American Music and Its Roots.* Morristown, N.J.: Silver Burdett Co., Inc., 1975. Booklets with recordings. For middle school students.

CURTISS, MARIE JOY, "India." *Music Educators Journal,* September 1969.

DEITZ, BETTY W., and MICHAEL OLATUNJI, *Musical Instruments of Africa.* New York: John Day, Inc., 1965. Grades 7–12.

HAUSMAN, RUTH L., *Hawaii: Music in Its History.* Rutland, Vt.: Charles E. Tuttle, 1968.

INNISS, CARLETON, "A Practical Introduction to African Music.: *Music Educators Journal,* February 1974.

KARPELES, MAUD, ed., *Folk Songs of Europe.* London: Novello, 1956. Authentic folksongs edited for the International Folk Music Council.

KEBEDE, ASHENAFI, *Roots of Black Music.* Englewood Cliffs, N.J.: Prentice-Hall, Inc., 1982.

KELLY, JOHN M., JR., *Folk Songs Hawaii Sings.* Rutland, Vt.: Charles E. Tuttle, 1963.

LANDECK, BEATRICE, *Echoes of Africa in Folk Songs of the Americas.* New York: Marks Music Corporation, 1973.

LOMAX, ALAN, *Folk Songs of North America.* New York: Doubleday & Company, 1960. Includes historical backgrounds.

LYONS, JOHN H., *Stories of Our American Patriotic Songs.* New York: Vanguard Press, Inc., 1942.

MCNEIL, ALBERT J., "The Social Foundations of the Music of Black Americans," *Music Educators Journal,* February 1974. Includes a bibliography.

MALM, WILLIAM, *Japanese Music and Musical Instruments.* Rutland, Vt.: Charles E. Tuttle, 1959.

MALM, WILLIAM P., *Music Cultures of the Pacific, the Near East and Asia,* 2nd ed. Englewood Cliffs, N.J.: Prentice-Hall, Inc., 1977.

MARSH, MARY VAL, et al., *The Spectrum of Music with Related Arts: Afro-American Music, Music of the Orient, Music of Latin America.* New York: Macmillan Publishing Co., Inc., 1975. Booklets with recordings for group and individual instruction for middle school students.

MAY, ELIZABETH, ed. *Music of Many Cultures: An Introduction.* Berkeley: University of California Press, 1981. Twenty essays by as many authors. Music, photography, recording. A scholarly, expensive book.

Music Educators Journal. November 1971, Music and Black Culture issue. October 1972, Music in World Cultures issue; includes glossary. May 1983, The Multiculture Imperative issue; includes Africa, Hawaii, Samoa, the Philippines; bibliography and recordings sources pp. 69–70.

NKETIA, J. H. KWABENA, "Music Education in Africa and the West: We Can Learn from Each Other," *Music Educators Journal,* November 1970.

PETERSON, FREDERICK A., *Ancient Mexico.* New York: G. P. Putnam's Sons, 1959. Chapter 9 describes ancient instruments and dance.

PHILLIPS, ROMEO E., "Black Folk Music: Setting the Record Straight," *Music Educators Journal,* December 1973.

RECK, DAVID, *Music of the Whole Earth.* New York: Charles Scribner's Sons, 1977.

REEDER, BARBARA, "Afro Music: As Tough as a Mozart Quartet," *Music Educators Journal,* January 1970.

REEDER, BARBARA, and JAMES A. STANDIFER, *Source Book of African Materials for Music Educators.* Reston, Va.: Music Educators National Conference, 1972.

SEALEY, JOHN, and KRISTER MALM, *Music in the Caribbean.* London: Hodder and Stoghton, 1982. 44 pp. Can be read by middle school students.

SEIDEMAN, LAURENCE I., "Teaching About the American Revolution Through Folk Songs," *Social Education,* November 1973, 653–64.

SOUTHERN, EILEEN, *The Music of Black Americans: A History.* New York: Norton, 1971.

SUR, WILLIAM R., et al., *This Is Music,* Book Five. Boston: Allyn & Bacon, Inc., 1967. Pages 18–161 reflect United States history in song.

WARRICK, MANCEL, J. R. HILLSMAN, and ANTHONY MANNO, *The Progress of Gospel Music: From Spirituals to Contemporary Gospel.* New York: Vantage Press, 1977.

WHITE, FLORENCE, and KAZUO AKIYAMA, *Children's Songs from Japan.* New York: Marks Music Corporation, 1965. Fifty songs that tell American children how Japanese boys and girls live.

WHITING, HELEN, *Negro Art, Music and Rhyme.* Washington, D.C.: Associated Publishers, 1967.

WIANT, BLISS, *The Music of China.* Hong Kong: Chung Chi Publications, 1965.

Films and Filmstrips with Recordings

See city and county school repositories.

Read catalogs of companies such as BFA Educational Media, Keyboard Publications, National Geographic Society, Society for Visual Education, Bowmar Records, Prentice-Hall Media (including Jam Handy Organization), National Educational Television, McGraw-Hill Films and others.

The American Music Conference, 1000 Skokie Blvd., Wilmette, Ill. 60091 provides a free brochure "Film Review Service" in which current music education films are reviewed.

.

chapter nineteen

Infusing the Arts into General Education

Many years ago John Dewey said, in effect, that the arts were the cement that joined the curriculum. It has taken many years for American education to come to grips with this idea, but currently it has gained strength. In Part 1 of this book the reader was introduced to the effort made through music to develop students' cognitive process skills. A growing number of educators have found that music is a superior vehicle with which to accomplish this, and may be the school subject best suited for the task. The many "hands-on" (psychomotor) experiences in music provide data from which conceptual thinking results. Muscle, voices, ears, and eyes work in combination with the brain. The skill of arriving at generalizations was emphasized in lesson plans and pointed out as a highly important aspect of learning to think at higher levels. The arts contain prerequisites to cognition such as interpreting symbols, coordinating muscles, stimulating imagination, and refining perceptions. It stands to reason that if teachers of music could prove this in their daily teaching, music might become the last subject to be removed from the curriculum rather than one of the first, as often happens in financial crises. Thus, music and other subjects unite in the mutual goal of elevating the level of thought processes in the nation, with the possibility that music can become the leading discipline in that effort.

Another view says that when arts are integrated into the general school curriculum, all education in that school is enhanced. (In this arrangement, it is essential that the arts maintain their integrity.) When this is accomplished, all subject areas benefit, students are happier, the school becomes a more inviting place in which to live, and truancy and vandalism diminish.

The aesthetic, emotional, and cultural qualities of music point toward their use for adding interest, meaning, and enjoyment to other areas of the curriculum. It is also true that the subject matter of other areas can make music study more interesting, meaningful, and enjoyable. Neither the learning of music nor learning in other areas can, in many instances, approach completeness without each aiding the other. Music has always been one of the most natural mediums of human expression, and through its use, individuals continually interpret civilizations, past and present. When music assumes its rightful place in the curriculum, marked emphasis is given to it because of its real functions. On the other hand, relationships with other areas of instruction can assist the formulation of music concepts and generalizations. Ways must be found to reduce or eliminate the barriers traditional education has erected separating subject areas.

Relating the Arts

Many generalizations can be made in relating the arts:

Any work of art has a plan or form.

The arts are a source of pleasure for people.

When people work creatively with the arts they arrange their materials in various combinations—words in literature; color, forms, and spaces in painting; elements of music in creating music; tempos and movements in dance.

Combinations of the materials of art provide interest and variety.

Everyone can experiment with original expressions by arranging and combining the materials of the arts.

Application of artistic principles can affect daily living in a great many ways.

An artist may view topics in special ways.

Humanity expresses universal and unique concerns through the arts

The arts have some common elements.

The arts have some marked differences.

Certain principles are common to all of the arts: *repetition* (including design, poetry, architecture), *contrast* (clearly evidenced in music by means of contrasting melodies, rhythms, tone qualities, dynamics, and textures), *unity* (by varied uses of repetition), and *balance* (the A B A type of design—a statement, a contrasting section, and return to the statement). Anderson (1982) expands on the above and tells of the common theme approach (subjects such as seasons and other aspects of nature, religion, emotions) and the historical era approach in which the arts reflect humanity at a given time. The two approaches are easily related to other subject fields, and from the students' point of view music and other subjects are all pieces to be assembled to gain better comprehension of such topics. There are also works that combine the arts, such as opera and other stage works, including puppet theater and ballet. Here the elementary-middle school musical stage work is a good example.

Basic Education   Fowler (1978) says that when one tries to identify the "basics" in terms other than describing subject areas, basic education refers to "skills that are prerequisite to learning, such as the ability to distinguish and interpret symbolism, to organize words into expression, to coordinate muscles, to harness imagination, to hone perception, and to grasp the essentials of cultural history." He further states that the infusion of the arts into *all* subject matter is mutually beneficial. The movement toward a new view of basic education and the crucial place of the arts in it requires new or revised college courses in education and the subject fields, and makes in-service education for all teachers necessary. Fowler continues, "To move from the periphery of the curriculum to its center means that the arts are no longer a separate realm but are woven into the fabric of daily life. When students see that most subjects have aesthetic components, they begin to see and accept the import of aesthetic considerations in the world about them—the decisions about the clothes they select, the way they furnish their homes, and the need for urban landscaping. The arts suddenly take on real importance; they have significant practical value . . . ."

Where We Are Now   Much of the above consists of projections into the future of arts education. There has been evidence for years that the social sciences, for example, need the arts, and that the arts need social sciences in order to combine data into a meaningful whole.

Consider the study of the Civil War period, in which the slave song is an important source of information and understanding. By analyzing the words and tonal communication of such songs, students can reach back into the minds of slaves and find double meanings. "The Blue-Tail Fly" contains clues to a murder mystery, and its words are a tongue-in-cheek description of how a slave caused an "accident" that eliminated old massa. The tune is flippant, which is another strong clue. The clever slaves created songs that held one meaning for blacks and another for whites. Blacks understood certain code names in the songs and most whites did not. Examples are "Go Down Moses," "Follow the Drinking Gourd," "I've Got Shoes," "Take This Hammer," "This Train," "Who's That Calling?" "I'm On My Way," "Cotton Field at Home," "Elisha Rock," and many others. The slaves were singing about going north to escape slavery. The approach to learning using these and many other slave songs is that of inquiry. Students are called upon to exercise their imaginations, and the teacher will expect many interpretations of the words. Surely, with this type of experience the social studies class is greatly enriched by music (Lord, 1971), and the music class is enriched by enhanced comprehension of songs they sing. To know the peoples of the world one must know their arts; to attempt to comprehend recent and contemporary world situations, one must study the arts that reflect them. The arts are humanity's voice, thus indispensable to comprehending the world of yesterday and today.

The use of art in understanding the nations and peoples of the world is well known and need not be elaborated upon here. The closing part of the preceding chapter discussed some of the world's music from the "music"

point of view with one major exception, the relating of the minuet to historical times. Consider what is omitted: virtually all relationships to other subject areas that would enrich the study of the music. Again we are reminded
of the problem of how to make the transition to a better educational environment in which departmentalization exists only where it is clearly essential. Mary Helen Richard's *Education Through Music* is one attempt to
bring subject areas into fusion.

Many music materials suppliers offer recordings that assist in relating
music and other subject areas, and their catalogs have sections classified in
this way. When such music is authentic and performed well, there can be
nothing "wrong" in using music to enhance another subject. Usually such
use enhances the music as well.

EXPLORATORY ACTIVITIES

Analyze the defense of music in the curriculum stated by the authors in Chapters
One and Nineteen. Then write your own.

References

Alliance for Arts Education, John F. Kennedy Center for the Performing Arts,
Washington, D.C. 20566. For information about arts in general education projects.

ANDERSON, WILLIAM M., and JOY E. LAWRENCE, "Approaches to Allied Arts,"
Music Educators Journal, September 1982, 31–35.

CEMREL, Aesthetic Education Program. Write to The Viking Press, Lincoln Center for the Performing Arts, 625 Madison Ave., New York, N.Y. 10022.

FOWLER, CHARLES B., "Integral and Undiminished: The Arts in General Education," *Music Educators Journal,* January 1978, pp. 30–33.

JDR 3rd Fund, 50 Rockefeller Plaza, New York, N.Y. 10020. Information to encourage administrators and teachers to adopt an arts in general education approach.

LEWIS, ADEN G., *Basic Skills through Music.* Sherman Oaks, Calif.: Alfred Publishing Company. For nursery school through third grade.

LORD, DONALD C., "The Slave Song as a Historical Source," *Social Education,* November 1971, 763–767, 821.

PALMER, HAP, various song books and recordings. Publishers include Educational
Activities, Baldwin, N.Y., and Alfred Publishing Company, Sherman Oaks,
Calif.

WILSON, FRANK R., "The Full Development of the Individual through Music," *Update,* Spring 1984, 3–7.

appendix a

Books for Elementary School Children* 1979 Edition

Legend
IL = Interest Level by Grade
RL = Reading Level by Grade

Biographies   Selections preceded by an asterisk are especially recommended.

CONE, MOLLY. *Leonard Bernstein.* Crowell, 1970. IL 2-3/RL 2-3
Well-written biography describing the life and career of this contemporary composer and conductor.

CORNELL, JEAN GAY. *Louis Armstrong: Ambassador Satchmo.* Garrard, 1972. IL 3-6/RL4
Biography conveys the exuberance of Satchmo's trumpet and the vitality of his contribution to jazz.

———. *Mahalia Jackson: Queen of Gospel Song.* Garrard, 1974. IL 3-6/RL 4
The moving story of Mahalia Jackson's rise from poverty to renown. Includes her activities in the civil rights movement, and emphasizes how she sang about her beliefs from the heart.

EVANS, MARK. *Scott Joplin and the Ragtime Years.* Dodd, Mead & Co., 1976. IL 4-up/RL 4-up

* Courtesy of the Oregon State Department of Education, Delmer Aebischer, Music Consultant.

A thorough account of Joplin's involvement in the development of ragtime. Joplin's pieces are traced historically from early compositions to the release of the film "The Sting." (SLJ)

*GREENFIELD, ELOISE. *Paul Robeson.* Crowell, 1975. IL 3-6/RL 4-6
Reflects the dynamic spirit of Robeson's life and accomplishments in his fight for freedom.

IVERSON, GENIE. *Louis Armstrong.* Crowell, 1976. IL 3-6/RL 3-4
Explains jazz through "Satchmo's" life story. (BL, CC, SLJ)

KRISHEF, ROBERT K. Various titles listed below. Lerner, 1978. each IL 3-up/RL 5-up
Series tracing the development of country music. Straightforward accounts of entertainers' lives illustrated with excellent photographs. Each includes table of contents and index. (BL, SLJ)

The Carter Family—Country Music's First Family

Comedians of Country Music

The Grand Ole Opry

Hank Williams

Jimmie Rodgers

Loretta Lynn

The New Breed

Western Stars of Country Music

MATHIS, SHARON BELL. *Ray Charles.* Crowell, 1973. IL 3-6/RL 4
Clearly written biography of this world-famous blues, gospel, and jazz entertainer.

McDERMON, KAY. *Mahalia: Gospel Singer.* Dodd, Mead & Co., 1976. IL 3-6/RL 4-6
The life of Mahalia Jackson, a voice for freedom and an inspiration for people of all races.

MONTGOMERY ELIZABETH R. *Duke Ellington: King of Jazz.* Garrard, 1972. IL 3-6/RL 4
A lively account of Ellington's dedication to music; years of practice, his work with jazz, success, and his honor at being named "Musician of Every Year."

SCHAAF, MARTHA E. *Duke Ellington: Young Music Master.* Bobbs-Merrill, 1975. IL 3-6/RL 3-6
Beautifully told story of Duke's life; his early interest in sports, art and music, and his success as a conductor and composer

SILL, HAROLD D. *Misbehavin' With Fats.* Addison Wesley, 1978. IL 5-up/RL 6-up
The life story of singer, organist, pianist and composer Fats Waller, who wrote over 400 songs before his death at 39.

TERKEL, LOUIS. *Giants of Jazz.* Crowell, 1975. IL 5-up/RL 5-up
Details the lives of many jazz musicians. The final chapter sums up the history of jazz to the present.

TOBIAS, TOBI. *Marian Anderson.* Crowell, 1972. IL 3-5/5L 3-5
A look at the emotions and feelings of Marian Anderson in a way that young children can understand. Beautifully illustrated.

Folk Music   AGAY, DENES. *Best-Loved Songs of the American People.* Doubleday, 1975. IL 3-up/RL 3-up

An anthology of popular songs from "Yankee Doodle" to "The Impossible Dream." Piano arrangements, guitar chords and historical notes are included in this spiral bound volume.

BERGER, MELVIN. *The Story of Folk Music.* Phillips, 1976. IL 5-up/RL 5-up

Songs and information about folk music and instruments, the role of folk music in politics, and how folk music relates to young people today. (BL, CC)

BIERHORST, JOHN. *Songs of the Chippewa.* Farrar, Straus and Giroux, 1974. IL 3-6/RL 3-6

Beautiful songs of the Chippewa Indians arranged for piano and guitar. (CC, ESLC)

*BRYAN, ASHLEY. *Walk Together Children: Black American Spirituals.* Atheneum, 1977. IL 1-6/RL 1-6

A collection of spirituals (melody only), complemented with striking woodcut illustrations. (CC, ESLC)

CROFUT, WILLIAM. *The Moon on the One Hand.* Atheneum, 1975. IL 3-6/RL 3-6

Poems by well-known poets set to music. Useful for language arts and music teachers. (CC)

*DISNEY, WALT. *The Walt Disney Song Book.* Golden, 1971. IL 1-6/RL 2-6

Thirty-four Disney songs illustrated by Disney Productions. Simple piano arrangements and large type make it particularly useful with younger children.

*FOWKE, EDITH. *Sally Go Round The Sun.* Doubleday, 1969. IL 1-4/RL 3-4

A collection of 300 singing games, fun songs and jumping rhymes. Guitar chords and some piano arrangements. (ESLC)

GLASS PAUL. *Songs and Stories of the North American Indians.* Grossett and Dunlap, 1968. IL 5-up/RL 5

Songs of many Indian tribes: sacred, dream, legends, games. History of each tribe included. (ESLC)

HOFMANN, CHARLES. *American Indian Sing.* Day, 1967. IL 4-up/ RL 4)up

An extensive study of American Indian music and how it was a part of everyday life.

HOUSTON, JAMES. *Songs of the Dream People; Chants and Images from the Indians of North America.* Atheneum, 1972. IL 4-up/RL 4-up

Songs, chants, and poetry of the Eskimos and North American Indians. (CC, ESLC)

JOHN, TIMOTHY. *The Great Song Book.* Doubleday, 1978. IL 1-up/RL 4-up

A large collection of folk tunes ranging from nursery rhymes and lullabies to Christmas songs. All include guitar chords, many piano accompaniment.

LANGSTAFF, JOHN. Hot Cross Buns and Other Old Street Cries. Atheneum, 1978. IL 1-4/RL 2-up

An illustrated collection of short street cries. Some arranged as rounds and part songs. (BL)

―――. *The Season for Singing: American Christmas Songs and Carols.* Doubleday, 1974. IL 3-up/RL 3-up

A collection of American Christmas songs. All arranged for piano and guitar. Notes on history included. (CC, ESLC)

————. *Shimmy Shimmy Coke-A-Pop! A Collection of City Children's Street Games and Rhymes.* Doubleday, 1973. IL 2-5/RL 2-5

Games and chants under eleven headings: name calling, ball bouncing, sidewalk drawing games, circle games, who's it?, tag games, jump rope, action games, follow the leader, hand clapping, dramatic play. (CC, ESLC)

————. *Sweetly Sings the Donkey: Animal Rounds for Children to Sing or Play on Recorders.* Atheneum, 1976. IL 1-5/RL 2-5

Collection of thirteen ancient and modern rounds with music, each printed on a double-page illustration of medieval life. (BL, CC, ESLC, SLJ)

LEWIN, OLIVE. *Dandy Shandy: 12 Jamaican Folk Songs for Children.* Oxford, 1975. IL 3-6/RL 3-6

Twelve folk songs from Jamaica arranged in two-part harmony.

POSTON, ELIZABETH. *The Baby's Song Book.* Crowell, 1972. IL 1-4/RL 1-4

Eighty-four nursery songs and Mother Goose Rhymes from all over the world, each with simple piano arrangement. English translations with foreign language songs. (ESLC)

ROBINSON, ADJAI. *Singing Tales of Africa.* Scribner, 1974. IL 1-6/RL 3-6

Seven African tales with active parts for listeners, and a moral. Chants introduce each tale. Woodcut illustrations. (CC, ESLC)

*SACKETT, S. J. *Cowboys and the Songs They Sang.* Scott, 1967. IL 3-up/RL 4-up

Collection of authentic cowboy songs with notes on history (1870–1890). Illustrated with period photographs. (CC, ESLC)

SEEGER, RUTH CRAWFORD. *American Folk Songs for Christmas.* Doubleday, 1953. IL 1-6/RL 3-6

A collection of American folk songs celebrating Christmas. Three sections: Stars and Shepherds, Mary and the Baby, Praise and Festivity. Arranged for piano. (CC, ESLC)

————. *American Folk Songs for Children in Home, School and Nursery School; A Book for Children, Parents and Teachers.* Doubleday, 1948. IL 1-6/RL 1-6

Ninety selections for singing and acting out. Introductory chapters explain how to use the music, and its value as an activity. (CC, ESLC)

*SERWADDA, W. MOSES. *Songs and Stories from Uganda.* Crowell, 1974. IL 1-6/RL 5-up

A collection of songs and stories in Luganda, the language of Uganda, with English translations. Red and black woodcuts enhance the East African flavor. (CC, ESLC)

YURCHENCO, HENRIETTA. *A Fiesta for Folk Songs from Spain and Latin America.* Putnam, 1967. IL 2-6/RL 2-6

Collection of singing games, songs about people, animals, nature and Christmas from Spain and Latin America. English translations, guitar/piano chords included. (CC, ESLC)

History and Origin

DAVIS, MARILYN K. AND ARNOLD BROIDO. *Music Dictionary.* Doubleday, 1956. IL 3-up/RL 5-up

Excellent format and illustrations. Easy to read and use. (CC, ESLC)

DAVIS, MAY AND ANITA DAVIS. *All About Music.* Oxford University Press, 1975. IL 3-6/RL 3-6

Excellent explanation of basic music theory. Good for individualized music stations.

*GILDER, ERIC. *The Dictionary of Composers.* Paddington, 1978. IL Adult/RL Adult
Excellent resource publication.

INGMAN, NICHOLAS. *The Story of Music.* Taplinger, 1976. IL 5-up/RL 5-up
A comprehensive history of music. Colorfully illustrated. (BL)

SCHOLES, PERCY A. *The Oxford Junior Companion to Music.* Oxford University
Press, 1954 (reprinted 1977). IL 6-up/RL 6-up
Short articles about composers, instruments, musical terms, etc. Well illustrated. (CC, ESLC)

Instruments *DIAGRAM GROUP. *Musical Instruments of the World.* Paddington, 1976. IL 4-up/RL 6-up
Informative and well-illustrated book describing instruments from around the world. Excellent reference.

BAILEY, BERNADINE. *Bells, Bells, Bells.* Dodd, Mead, 1978. IL 4-UP/RL 5-up
History of bells, casting, tuning, handbell ringing, and carillon playing. Stories of famous bells, such as Big Ben and the Liberty Bell, generously illustrated with photographs.

ETKIN, RUTH. *Playing and Composing on the Recorder.* Sterling, 1975. IL 4-6/RL 4-6
An excellent "how-to" book, information about music theory, composition, notation, rhythm bands, and how to make a recorder case. (ESLC)

KETTLEKAMP, LARRY. *Drums, Rattles and Bells.* Morrow, 1960. IL 4-up/RL 4-up
Descriptions of four types of percussion instruments: rattles, drums, keyboard, and bells. Includes history of use, how they are made and played. (CC)

———. *Flutes, Whistles and Reeds.* Morrow, 1962. $4.81 IL 4-up/RL 4-up
Contains information on production of sound, history of sound, directions for making a whistle, pipe, reed mouthpiece, and oboe.

SURPLUS, ROBERT W. *The Beat of the Drum.* Lerner, 1963. IL 4-up/RL 6-up
History and cultural significance of drums, with specific information on percussion instruments used today. Special section on South American percussion.

WHEELER, TOM. *The Guitar Book.* Harper and Row, 1974. IL 5-up/RL 8-up
Although this book may be too difficult for elementary grade students, it's an excellent teacher resource. Contains many illustrations, complete information about guitars, performers, history, and styles of playing.

YOLEN, JANE. *Ring Out! A Book of Bells.* Seabury, 1974. IL 6-UP/RL 6-up
Historic information on bells sacred and secular, their significance, and usage. (CC, ESLC)

Opera BULLA, CLYDE ROBERT. *More Stories of Favorite Operas.* Crowell, 1965. IL 5-up/RL 5-up
Simply told stories of twenty-two operas including *Hansel and Gretel, Cosi fan tutte, Fidelio.* (CC)

BULLA, CLYDE ROBERT. *Stories of Favorite Operas.* Crowell, 1964. IL 5-up/RL 5-up
Simply told stories of twenty-three operas including *Marriage of Figaro, Barber of Seville, Magic Flute.*

MONTRESOR, BENI. *Cinderella.* Knopf, 1965. IL 2-5/RL 3-5
Montresor's beautiful illustrations enliven this retelling of Rossini's opera *Cenerentola.* (CC, ESLC)

SPENDER, STEPHEN. *The Magic Flute.* Putnam, 1966. IL 2-5/RL 3-5
A retelling of Mozart's opera with impressionistic illustrations by Montresor.

Sound and Music

BRANLEY, FRANKLYN M. *High Sounds, Low Sounds.* Crowell, 1967. IL 1-3/RL 3
Experiments using spoons, strings, and straws help the young reader understand sound.

FAULHABER, MARTHA AND JANET UNDERHILL. *Music: Invent Your Own.* Whitman, 1974. IL 3-6/RL 3-6
Basic musical concepts of rhythm, timbre, melody, and dynamics inventively presented. (ESLC)

HAWKINSON, JOHN AND MARTHA FAULHABER. *Music and Instruments for Children to Make.* Whitman, 1969. IL K-3/RL 3-up
Rhythm and sound experiments and how to make rhythm instruments. (CC)

HAWKINSON, JOHN AND MARTHA FAULHABER. *Rhythms, Music and Instruments to Make.* Whitman, 1970. IL 3-6/RL 4-up
How to make wind, string, and percussion instruments; good teacher resource for upper grades. (CC)

KIRSHEF, ROBERT K. *Playback: The Story of Recording Devices.* Lerner, 1974. IL 4-7/RL 6
A history of recording equipment from Thomas Edison's first phonograph to the record player of today.

Stories

BRAND, OSCAR. *When I First Came To This Land.* G. P. Putnams, 1974. IL 2-4/RL 2
Song-story of an American homesteader. Musical score included. (ESLC)

*CHILD, LYDIA MARIA. *Over the River and Through the Wood.* Coward, McCann and Geoghegan, 1974. IL 1-4/RL 2
Beautiful illustrations help tell the story of a trip to grandparents' house for Thanksgiving. (CC)

*Disney, Walt. *Peter and the Wolf.* Random House, 1974. IL 1-4/RL 3
Beautifully illustrated version of Prokofiev's famous adaptation of the story of a boy and a wolf.

Fantasia Pictorial. Various titles listed below. Gakken, 1971. IL 1-5/RL 3
Stories of famous musical compositions, with unusual illustrations combining many textures and materials.

Carnival of the Animals	*The Nutcracker*
Coppelia	*Peter and the Wolf*
Hansel and Gretel	*The Sorcerer's Apprentice*
Invitation to the Dance	*Swan Lake*
A Night on Bald Mountain	*William Tell*

GALDONE, PAUL. *The Star-Spangled Banner.* Crowell, 1966. IL 1-6/RL 3-4
This colorfully illustrated book brings to life the writing of the national anthem.

KROSKE, ROBERT. *America The Beautiful.* Garrard, 1972. IL 3-up/RL 4
Stories about patriotic songs and why they were written. Includes America the Beautiful, Yankee Doodle, Star-Spangled Banner, God Bless America, and America.

LANGSTAFF, JOHN. *Frog Went A-Courtin.* Harcourt, Brace, 1955. IL 1-3/RL 1-3
Beautifully done Caldecott Medal book telling the story of the frog who courts a mouse. (CC, ESLC)

LANGSTAFF, JOHN. *Oh, A-Hunting We Will Go.* Atheneum, 1977. IL 1-3/RL 2
Piano and guitar arrangements accompany this story of this old folk song. (CC, ESLC)

LANGSTAFF, JOHN. *Over in the Meadow.* Harcourt, Brace, 1967. IL 1-2/RL 1-2
Story of ten meadow families in folk song. Melody arrangement included. (CC, ESLC)

L'ENGLE, MADELEINE. *Prelude.* Vanguard, 1968. IL 5-up/RL 5-up
Fictional story of a young girl's struggles to become a concert pianist.

LENSKI, LOIS. *Blue Ridge Billy.* Lippincott, 1946.
A boy in the mountains of North Carolina dreams of becoming a fiddler. Illustrations by author.

LYONS, JOHN HENRY. *Stories of our American Patriotic Songs.* Vanguard, 1942. IL 3-up/RL 4
The histories of ten of America's most popular patriotic songs. (CC, ESLC)

PECK, ROBERT NEWTON. *King of Kazoo.* Knopf, 1976. IL 2-4/RL 3
Fun book to read, can also be performed. With lyrics, scores, and staging suggestions.

QUACKENBUSH, ROBERT. *Old MacDonald Had A Farm.* Lippincott, 1972. IL 1-2/RL 2
End result of this add-on song book is a barnyard full of animals! (CC)

SCHICK, ALICE AND JOEL. *Viola Hates Music.* Lippincott, 1977. IL 1-4/RL 2-3
Viola, the dog, doesn't like music, but then becomes a music lover when she learns to play the bagpipes. (SLJ)

SPIER, PETER. *The Erie Canal.* Doubleday, 1970. IL 1-6/RL 2-3
Watercolor illustrations enliven this old folk song. History and music included. (CC, ESLC)

SPIER, PETER. *London Bridge Is Falling Down.* Doubleday, 1967. IL 1-3/RL 2
History, lyrics, and score, complemented by colorful illustrations. (CC)

SPIER, PETER. *The Star-Spangled Banner.* Doubleday, 1973. IL 1-4/RL 3
Spier's outstanding illustrations dramatize the first four stanzas of the American national anthem. Score and historical information included. (CC, ESLC)

VAN LAMSWEERDE, JOYCE. *Ziggy and His Music.* Ideals, 1968. IL 1-3/RL 2-3
Introduces music in terms of everyday sounds. Beautifully done in rhyme.

appendix b

Alphabetical Listing of Composers in ADVENTURES IN MUSIC

Anderson: Irish Suite—"The Girl I Left Behind Me," GR. 5, Vol. 2

Arnold: English Dances—
Allegro Non Troppo, GR. 2, Vol. 2
Grazioso, GR. 1, Vol. 2

Bach:
Cantata No. 147—Jesu, Joy of Man's Desiring, GR. 5, Vol. 1
Little Fugue in G Minor (arr. by L. Cailliet), GR. 6, Vol. 1
Suite No. 2—Badinerie, GR. 3 Vol. 1
Suite No. 2—Rondeau, GR. 2, Vol. 2
Suite No. 3—Gigue, GR. 1, Vol. 1

Bartók:
Hungarian Sketches—"Bear Dance," GR. 3, Vol. 2
Hungarian Sketches—"Evening in the Village," GR. 5, Vol. 2
Mikrokosmos Suite No. 2—"From the Diary of a Fly," GR. 1, Vol. 2
Mikrokosmos Suite No. 2—"Jack-in-the-Box," GR. 2, Vol. 1

Beethoven: Symphony No. 8—Second Movement, GR. 6, Vol. 1

Berlioz: The Damnation of Faust—Ballet of the Sylphs, GR. 1, Vol. 1

Bizet:
Arlésienne Suite No. 1, *L'*—Minuetto, GR. 4, Vol. 2
Arlésienne Suite No. 2, *L'*—Farandole, GR. 6, Vol. 1
Carmen—"Changing of the Guard," GR. 3, Vol. 2

Carmen—"The Dragoons of Alcala," GR. 2, Vol. 2

Children's Games—"The Ball"; "Cradle Song"; "Leap Frog," GR. 1, Vol. 1

Borodin: *On the Steppes of Central Asia,* GR. 6, Vol. 1

Brahms: *Hungarian Dance* No. 1, GR. 5, Vol. 2

Cailliet: "Pop! Goes the Weasel"—Variations, GR. 4, Vol. 1

Carpenter: *Adventures in Perambulator*—"The Hurdy-Gurdy," GR. 5, Vol. 2

Chabrier:
España Rapsodie, GR. 5, Vol. 1
Marche Joyeuse, GR. 4, Vol. 1

Charpentier: *Impressions of Italy*—"On Muleback," GR. 5, Vol. 1

Cimarosa: *Cimarosiana*—Non Troppo Mosso, GR. 2, Vol. 2

Coates: London Suite—"Knightsbridge March," GR. 5, Vol. 2

Copland:
Billy the Kid Ballet Suite—"Street in a Frontier Town," GR. 6, Vol. 1
The Red Pony Suite—"Circus Music," GR. 3, Vol. 1
The Red Pony Suite—"Dream March," GR. 2, Vol. 2
Rodeo—"Hoe-Down," GR. 5, Vol. 2

Corelli-Pinelli: Suite for Strings—Sarabande, GR. 6, Vol. 2

Debussy:
Children's Corner Suite—"The Snow is Dancing," GR. 3, Vol. 1
La Mer—"Play of the Waves," GR. 6, Vol. 2

Delibes:
Coppelia—"Waltz of the Doll," GR. 1, Vol. 1
Coppelia—"Swanhilde's Waltz," GR. 2, Vol. 2
The King Is Amused—"Lesquercarde," GR. 1, Vol. 2

Dvořák: Slavonic Dance No. 7, GR. 4, Vol. 2

Elgar:
Wand of Youth Suite No. 1—"Fairies and Giants," GR. 3, Vol. 1
Wand of Youth Suite No. 1—"Sun Dance," GR. 2, Vol. 2
Wand of Youth Suite No. 2—"Fountain Dance," GR. 2, Vol. 1

Falla: *La Vida Breve*—Spanish Dance No. 1, GR. 6, Vol. 1

Fauré: *Dolly*—Berceuse, GR. 2, Vol. 1

German: *Henry VIII* Suite—"Morris Dance," GR. 1, Vol. 2

Ginastera: *Estancia*—"Wheat Dance," GR. 4, Vol. 1

Gliére: *The Red Poppy*—"Russian Sailors' Dance," GR. 6, Vol. 2

Gluck:
Armide Ballet Suite—Musette, GR. 2, Vol. 2
Iphigenie in Aulis—"Air Gai," GR. 1, Vol. 1

Gottschalk-Kay: *Cakewalk* Ballet Suite—"Grand Walkaround," GR. 5, Vol. 1

Gould: *American Salute,* GR. 5, Vol. 1

Gounod: *Faust* Ballet Suite—Waltz No. 1, GR. 3, Vol. 1

Grainger: "Londonderry Air," GR. 4, Vol. 2

Gretry:
Cephale et Procris—Gigue (Arr. by Mottl), GR. 1, Vol. 1
Cephale et Procris—Tambourin (Arr. by Mottl), GR. 2, Vol. 1

Grieg:

Lyric Suite—"Norwegian Rustic March," GR. 4, Vol. 1

Peer Gynt Suite No. 1—"Anitra's Dance," GR. 1, Vol. 2

Peer Gynt Suite No. 1—"In the Hall of the Mountain King," GR. 3, Vol. 2

Griffes: *The White Peacock,* GR. 6, Vol. 1

Grofé: *Death Valley* Suite—"Desert Water Hole," GR. 4, Vol. 1

Guarnieri: Brazilian Dance, GR. 6, Vol. 2

Handel:

Royal Fireworks Music—Bourrée, Minuetto No. 2, GR. 3, Vol. 2

Water Music—Hornpipe, GR. 2, Vol. 1

Hanson:

For the First Time—"Bells," GR. 1, Vol. 2

Merry Mount Suite—"Children's Dance," GR. 3, Vol. 1

Herbert:

Babes in Toyland—"March of the Toys," GR. 2, Vol. 1

Natoma—"Dagger Dance," GR. 3, Vol. 1

Holst: *The Perfect Fool*—"Spirit of the Earth," GR. 6, Vol. 2

Howe: "Sand," GR. 2, Vol. 2

Humperdinck: *Hansel and Gretel*—Prelude, GR. 5, Vol. 2

Ibert:

Divertissement—"Parada," GR. 1, Vol. 1

Histories No. 2—"The Little White Donkey," GR. 2, Vol. 1

Kabalevsky:

The Comedians—March, "Comedians Galop," GR. 3, Vol. 1

The Comedians—"Pantomime," GR. 1, Vol. 1

The Comedians—Waltz, GR. 1, Vol. 2

Khachaturian:

Gayne Ballet Suite—"Dance of the Rose Maidens," GR. 1, Vol. 2

Masquerade Suite—Waltz, GR. 4, Vol. 2

Kodály:

Háry János Suite—"Entrance of the Emperor and His Court," GR. 4, Vol. 2

Háry János Suite—"Viennese Musical Clock," GR. 2, Vol. 1

Lecuona: *Suite Andalucia*—"Andalucia," GR. 4, Vol. 1

Liadov: Eight Russian Folk Songs—Berceuse, GR. 1, Vol. 2

Lully: Ballet Suite—March, GR. 3, Vol. 2

MacDowell: *Second (Indian) Suite*—"In Wartime," GR. 5, Vol. 1

Massenet: *Le Cid*—"Aragonaise," GR. 1, Vol. 1

McBride:

Pumpkin Eater's Little Fugue, GR. 2, Vol. 2

Punch and the Judy—"Pony Express," GR. 1, Vol. 2

McDonald:

Children's Symphony (1st Movement)—*"London Bridge," "Baa, Baa Black Sheep,"* GR. 3, Vol. 2

Children's Symphony (3rd Movement)—*"Farmer In the Dell," "Jingle Bells,"* GR. 2, Vol. 1

Menotti:
Amahl and the Night Visitors—"March of the Kings," GR. 1, Vol. 2
Amahl and the Night Visitors—"Shepherds' Dance," GR. 4, Vol. 2

Meyerbeer: *Les Patineurs*—Waltz, GR. 2, Vol. 1

Milhaud:
Saudades do Brazil—"Copacabana," GR. 4, Vol. 2
Saudades do Brazil—"Laranjeiras," GR. 2, Vol. 1
Suite Provencale—"Modere No. 1," GR. 1, Vol. 2

Moore: Farm Journal—"Harvest Song," GR. 1, Vol. 2

Mussorgsky:
Pictures at an Exhibition—"Ballet of the Unhatched Chicks" (Orchestrated by Ravel), GR. 1, Vol. 1
Pictures at an Exhibition—"Bydlo" (Orchestrated by Ravel), GR. 2, Vol. 1
Pictures at an Exhibition—"Promenade" (Orchestrated by Ravel), GR. 1, Vol. 2

Mozart:
Divertimento No. 17—Menuetto No. 1, GR. 5, Vol. 2
Eine kleine Nachtmusik—Romanze, GR. 4, Vol. 1
The Little Nothings, No. 8, GR. 1, Vol. 2

Offenbach: *The Tales of Hoffmann*—Barcarolle, GR. 3, Vol. 1

Pierné: *Cydalise* Suite No. 1—"Entrance of the Little Fauns," GR. 2, Vol. 2

Prokofiev:
Children's Suite—"Waltz on the Ice," GR. 3, Vol. 2
Lieutenant Kije—Troika, GR. 2, Vol. 2
Summer Day Suite—March, GR. 1, Vol. 1
Winter Holiday—"Departure," GR. 2, Vol. 1

Ravel:
Mother Goose Suite—"The Conversations of Beauty and the Beast," GR. 5, Vol. 1
Mother Goose Suite—"Laideronnette, Empress of the Pagodas," GR. 4, Vol. 2

Respighi:
The Birds—Prelude, GR. 2, Vol. 2
Brazilian Impressions—Danza, GR. 5, Vol. 2
Pines of Rome—"Pines of the Villa Borghese," GR. 4, Vol. 1

Rimsky-Korsakov:
Le Coq d'Or Suite—"Bridal Procession," GR. 4, Vol. 1
The Snow Maiden—"Dance of the Buffoons," GR. 2, Vol. 2

Rossini: *William Tell* Overture—Finale, GR. 3, Vol. 1

Rossini-Britten:
Matinees Musicales—Waltz, GR. 1, Vol. 2
Soirees Musicales—Bolero, GR. 2, Vol. 2
Soirees Musicales—March, GR. 1, Vol. 1

Rossini-Respighi:
The Fantastic Toyshop—Can-Can, GR. 2, Vol. 1
The Fantastic Toyshop—Tarantella, GR. 3, Vol. 2

Saint-Saëns:
Carnival of the Animals—"The Elephant," GR. 1, Vol. 2
Carnival of the Animals—"The Swan," GR. 3, Vol. 2

Scarlatti-Tommasini: *The Good-Humored Ladies*—Non Presto ma a Tempo Di Ballo, GR. 4, Vol. 2

Schubert: Symphony No. 5—First Movement, GR. 5, Vol. 1

Schuller: Seven Studies on Themes of Paul Klee—"The Twittering Machine," GR. 2, Vol. 2

Schumann: *Scenes from Childhood*—Traumerei, GR. 4, Vol. 2

Shostakovich:

Ballet Suite No. 1—"Petite Ballerina," GR. 2, Vol. 1

Ballet Suite No. 1—"Pizzicato Polka," GR. 1, Vol. 1

Sibelius: *Karelia* Suite—Alla Marcia, GR. 5, Vol. 1

Smetana: *The Bartered Bride*—"Dance of the Comedians," GR. 6, Vol. 2

Sousa:

Semper Fidelis, GR. 3, Vol. 2

Stars and Stripes Forever, GR. 4, Vol. 2

Strauss, R.: *Der Rosenkavalier*—Suite, GR. 6, Vol. 1

Stravinsky:

The Firebird Suite—Berceuse, GR. 1, Vol. 1

The Firebird Suite—"Infernal Dance of King Kastchei," GR. 5, Vol. 2

Petrouchka—"Russian Dance," GR. 1, Vol. 2

Taylor: *Through the Looking Glass*—"Garden of Live Flowers," GR. 3, Vol. 2

Tchaikovsky:

Nutcracker Suite—"Dance of the Sugar Plum Fairy," "Dance of the Reed Pipes," GR. 1, Vol. 2

The Sleeping Beauty—"Puss-in-Boots and the White Cat," GR. 3, Vol. 1

The Sleeping Beauty—Waltz, GR. 4, Vol. 1

Swan Lake— "Dance of the Little Swans," GR. 1, Vol. 1

Symphony No. 4—Fourth Movement, GR. 6, Vol. 2

Thomson:

Acadian Songs and Dances—"The Alligator and the 'Coon,' " GR. 3, Vol. 2

Acadian Songs and Dances—"Walking Song," GR. 1, Vol. 1

Vaughan-Williams:

Fantasia on "Greensleeves," GR. 6, Vol. 2

The Wasps—"March Past of the Kitchen Utensils," GR. 3, Vol. 1

Villa-Lobos: *Bachianas Brasileiras* No. 2—"The Little Train of the Caipira," GR. 3, Vol. 1

Wagner: *Lohengrin*—Prelude to Act III, GR. 6, Vol. 1

Walton: *Facade* Suite—Valse, GR. 6, Vol. 2

Webern: Five Movements for String Orchestra—Sehr Langsam, GR. 2, Vol. 2

appendix c

Compositions in the
BOWMAR ORCHESTRAL
LIBRARY

Series 1 ANIMALS AND CIRCUS (BOL #51)

CARNIVAL OF THE ANIMALS, Saint-Saëns. (Introduction, Royal March of the Lion, Hens and Cocks, Fleet Footed Animals, Turtles, The Elephant, Kangaroos, Aquarium, Long Eared Personages. Cuckoo in the Deep Woods, Aviary, Pianists, Fossils, The Swan, Finale)

CIRCUS POLKA, Stravinsky

UNDER THE BIG TOP, Donaldson. (Marching Band, Acrobats, Juggler, Merry-Go-Round, Elephants, Clowns, Camels, Tightrope Walker, Pony Trot, Marching Band.)

NATURE AND MAKE-BELIEVE (BOL #52)

MARCH OF THE DWARFS, Grieg

ONCE UPON A TIME SUITE, Donaldson. (Chicken Little, Three Billy Goats Gruff, Little Train, Hare and the Tortoise)

THE LARK SONG (*Scenes of Youth*), Tchaikovsky

LITTLE BIRD, Grieg

DANCE OF THE MOSQUITO, Liadov

FLIGHT OF THE BUMBLE BEE, Rimsky-Korsakov

SEASON FANTASIES, Donaldson. (Magic Piper, The Poet and his Lyre, The Anxious Leaf, The Snowmaiden)

TO THE RISING SUN (Fjord and Mountain, Norwegian Suite 2), Torjussen

CLAIRE DE LUNE, Debussy

PICTURES AND PATTERNS (BOL #53)

PIZZICATO (*Fantastic Toyshop*), Rossini-Respighi

MARCH—TRUMPET AND DRUM (*Jeux d'Enfants*), IMPROMPTU—THE TOP (*Jeux d'Enfants*), Bizet

POLKA (*Mlle. Angot* Suite), GAVOTTE (*Mlle. Angot* Suite), Lecocq

INTERMEZZO (*The Comedians*), Kabalevsky

GERMAN WALTZ-PAGANINI (*Carnival*), Schumann-Glazounov

BALLET PETIT, Donaldson

MINUET, Mozart

A GROUND, Handel

CHOPIN (*Carnaval*), Schumann-Glazounov

VILLAGE DANCE, Liadov

EN BATEAU (In a Boat), Debussy

HARBOR VIGNETTES, Donaldson (Fog and Storm, Song of the Bell Buoy, Sailing)

MARCHES (BOL #54)

ENTRANCE OF THE LITTLE FAUNS, Pierné

MARCH, Prokofiev

POMP AND CIRCUMSTANCE #1, Elgar

HUNGARIAN MARCH (*Rakoczy*), Berlioz

COL. BOGEY MARCH, Alford

MARCH OF THE LITTLE LEAD SOLDERIS, Pierné

MARCH (*Love for Three Oranges*), Prokofiev

CORTEGE OF THE SARDAR (*Caucasian Sketches*), Ippolitov-Ivanov

MARCHE MILITAIRE, Schubert

STARS AND STRIPES FOREVER, Sousa

THE MARCH OF THE SIAMESE CHILDREN (*The King and I*), Rodgers

DANCES, PART I (BOL #55)

DANCE OF THE CAMORRISTI, Wolf-Ferrari

DANCA BRASILEIRA, Guarnieri

GAVOTTE, Kabalevsky

SLAVONIC DANCE #1, Dvořák

HOE-DOWN (Rodeo), Copland

FACADE SUITE, Walton (Polka, Country Dance, Popular Song)

HUNGARIAN DANCE #5, Brahms

SKATER'S WALTZES, Waldteufel

MAZURKA (*Masquerade* Suite), Khatchaturian

GALOP (*Masquerade* Suite), Khatchaturian

DANCES, PART II (BOL #56)

FOLK DANCES FROM SOMERSET (*English Folk Song* Suite), Vaughan-Williams

JAMAICAN RHUMBA, Benjamin

BADINERIE, Corelli

DANCE OF THE COMEDIANS, Smetana

CAN CAN (*Mlle. Angot* Suite), Lecocq

GRAND WALTZ (*Mlle. Angot* Suite), Lecocq

TRISCH-TRASCH POLKA, Strauss

TARANTELLA (*Fantastic Toyshop*), WALTZ (*Fantastic Toyshop*), Rossini-Respighi

ESPAÑA WALTZES, Waldteufel

ARKANSAS TRAVELER, Guion

RUSSIAN DANCE (*Gayne* Suite #2), Khatchaturian

FAIRY TALES IN MUSIC (BOL #57)

CINDERELLA, Coates

SCHERZO (*Midsummer Night's Dream*), Mendelssohn

MOTHER GOOSE SUITE, Ravel (Pavane of the Sleeping Beauty, Hop o' My Thumb, Laideronette, Empress of the Pagodas, Beauty and the Beast, The Fairy Garden)

STORIES IN BALLET AND OPERA (BOL #58)

SUITE FROM AMAHL AND THE NIGHT VISITORS, Menotti (Introduction, March of the Three Kings, Dance of the Shepherds)

HANSEL AND GRETEL OVERTURE, Humperdinck

NUTCRACKER SUITE, Tchaikovsky (Overture Miniature, March, Dance of the Sugar-Plum Fairy, Trepak, Arabian Dance, Chinese Dance, Dance of the Toy Flutes, Waltz of the Flowers)

LEGENDS IN MUSIC (BOL #59)

DANCE MACABRE, Saint-Saëns

PEER GYNT SUITE #1, Grieg (Morning, Asa's Death, Anitra's Dance, In the Hall of the Mountain King)

SORCERER'S APPRENTICE, Dukas

PHAETON, Saint-Saëns

UNDER MANY FLAGS (BOL #60)

THE MOLDAU, Smetana

LAPLAND IDYLL (Fjord and Mountain, Norwegian Suite #2), Torjussen

FOLK SONG (Fjord and Mountain, Norwegian Suite #2), Torjussen

LONDONDERRY AIR, Grainger

FINLANDIA, Sibelius

LONDON SUITE, Coates (Covent Garden, Westminster, Knightsbridge March)

AMERICAN SCENES (BOL #61)

GRAND CANYON SUITE, Grofé (Sunrise, Painted Desert, On the Trail, Sunset, Cloudburst)

MISSISSIPPI SUITE, Grofé (Father of Waters, Huckleberry Finn, Old Creole Days, Mardi Gras)

Series 2 MASTERS IN MUSIC (BOL #62)

JESU, JOY OF MAN'S DESIRING, Bach

BOURRÉE FROM FIREWORKS MUSIC, Handel

VARIATIONS (from *Sunrise* Symphony), Hadyn

MINUET (from Symphony #40), Mozart

SCHERZO (from Seventh Symphony), Beethoven

453 COMPOSITIONS IN THE BOWMAR ORCHESTRAL LIBRARY

WEDDING DAY AT TROLDHAUGEN, Grieg

RIDE OF THE VALKYRIES, Wagner

TRIUMPHAL MARCH (*Aïda*), Verdi

HUNGARIAN DANCE #6, Brahms

THIRD MOVEMENT, SYMPHONY #1, Mahler

CONCERT MATINEE (BOL #63)

CHILDREN'S CORNER SUITE, Debussy. (Doctor Gradus ad Parnassum, Jumbo's Lullaby, Serenade of the Doll, The Snow is Dancing, The Little Shepherd, Golliwog's Cakewalk)

SUITE FOR STRING ORCHESTRA, Corelli-Pinelli (Sarabande, Gigue, Badinerie)

MINUET (from *Surprise* Symphony), Haydn

ANVIL CHORUS (*Il Trovatore*), Verdi

NORWEGIAN DANCE IN A (#2), Grieg

TRAUMEREI, Schumann

MINIATURES IN MUSIC (BOL #64)

CHILDREN'S SYMPHONY, Zador

THE BEE, Schubert

GYPSY RONDO, Haydn

WILD HORSEMEN, Schumann

HAPPY FARMER, Schumann

LITTLE WINDMILLS, Couperin

ARIETTA, Leo

MUSIC BOX, Liadov

FUNERAL MARCH OF THE MARIONETTES, Gounod

DANCE OF THE MERRY DWARFS (*Happy Hypocrite*), Elwell

LITTLE TRAIN OF CAIPIRA, Villa-Lobos

MUSIC, USA (BOL #65)

SHAKER TUNE (*Appalachian Spring*), Copland

CATTLE & BLUES (*Plow that Broke the Plains*), Thompson

FUGUE AND CHORALE ON YANKEE DOODLE (*Tuesday in November*), Thomson

PUMPKIN EATERS LITTLE FUGUE, McBride

AMERICAN SALUTE, Gould

POP! GOES THE WEASEL, Cailliet

LAST MOVEMENT, SYMPHONY #2, Ives

ORIENTAL SCENES (BOL #66)

WOODCUTTER'S SONG, Koyama

THE EMPEROR'S NIGHTINGALE, Donaldson

SAKURA (folk tune), played by koto and bamboo flute

FANTASY IN MUSIC (BOL L#67)

THREE BEARS, Coates

CINDERELLA, Prokofiev (Sewing Scene, Cinderella's Gavotte, Midnight Waltz, Fairy Godmother)

MOON LEGEND, Donaldson

SLEEPING BEAUTY WALTZ, Tchaikovsky

CLASSROOM CONCERT (BOL #68)

ALBUM FOR THE YOUNG, Tchaikovsky. (Morning Prayer, Winter Morning, Hobby Horse, Mamma, March of the Tin Soldiers, Sick Doll, Doll's Burial, New Doll, Waltz, Mazurka, Russian Song, Peasant Plays the Accordion, Folk Song, Polka, Italian Song, Old French Song, German Song, Neapolitan Dance Song, Song of the Lark, Hand-organ Man, Nurse's Tale, The Witch, Sweet Dreams, In Church)

OVER THE HILLS, Grainger

MEMORIES OF CHILDHOOD, Pinto (Run, Run; Ring Around the Rosie; March; Sleeping Time; Hobby Horse)

LET US RUN ACROSS THE HILL, Villa-Lobos

MY DAUGHTER LIDI, TEASING, GRASSHOPPER'S WEDDING, Bartók

DEVIL'S DANCE, Stravinsky

LITTLE GIRL IMPLORING HER MOTHER, Rebikov

Series 3 MUSIC OF THE DANCE: STRAVINSKY (BOL #69)

FIREBIRD SUITE (L'Oiseau de Feu) (Koschai's Enchanted Garden, Dance of the Firebird, Dance of the Princesses, Infernal Dance of Koschai, Magic Sleep of the Princess Tzarevna, Finale: Escape of Koschai's Captives.)

SACRIFICIAL DANCE from "The Rite of Spring" (*Le Sacre du Printemps*)

VILLAGE FESTIVAL from "The Fairy's Kiss" (Le Baiser de le Fée)

PALACE OF THE CHINESE EMPEROR from *The Nightingale* (*Le Rossignol*)

TANGO, WALTZ AND RAGTIME from *The Soldier's Tale* (*L'Histoire du Soldat*)

MUSIC OF THE SEA AND SKY (BOL #70)

CLOUDS (Nuages), Debussy

FESTIVALS (Fêtes), Debussy

MERCURY from *The Planets,* Holst

SEA PIECE WITH BIRDS, Thomson

OVERTURE TO "THE FLYING DUTCHMAN" (*Der fliegende Holländer*), Wagner

DIALOGUE OF THE WIND AND SEA from *The Sea* (*La Mer*), Debussy

SYMPHONIC MOVEMENTS, NO. 1 (BOL #71)

FIRST MOVEMENT, SYMPHONY No. 40, Mozart

SECOND MOVEMENT, SYMPHONY No. 8, Beethoven

THIRD MOVEMENT, SYMPHONY No. 4, Tchaikovsky

SECOND MOVEMENT, SYMPHONY No. 4, Schumann

THIRD MOVEMENT, SYMPHONY No. 3, Brahms

FOURTH MOVEMENT, SYMPHONY No. 3, Saint-Saëns

SYMPHONIC MOVEMENTS, NO. 2 (BOL # 72)

FIRST MOVEMENT, SYMPHONY No. 9 (*From the New World*), Dvořák

FIRST MOVEMENT, SYMPHONY No. 5, Beethoven

FIRST MOVEMENT (Boisterous Bourrée), A SIMPLE SYMPHONY, Britten

SECOND MOVEMENT, SYMPHONY No. 2, Hanson

FIRST MOVEMENT, SYMPHONY No. 2, Sibelius

SYMPHONIC STYLES (BOL #73)

SYMPHONY No. 99 (*Imperial*), Haydn (Adagio: Vivace Assai, Adagio, Minuetto, Vivace)

CLASSICAL SYMPHONY, Prokofiev (Allegro, Larghetto, Gavotte: Non troppo allegro, Molto vivace)

TWENTIETH-CENTURY AMERICA (BOL #74)

EL SALON MEXICO, Copland

DANZON from *Fancy Free,* Bernstein

EXCERPTS, SYMPHONIC DANCES from *West Side Story,* Bernstein

AN AMERICAN IN PARIS, Gershwin

U.S. HISTORY IN MUSIC (BOL #75)

A LINCOLN PORTRAIT, Copland

CHESTER from NEW ENGLAND TRIPTYCH, Schumann

PUTNAM'S CAMP from *Three Places in New England,* Ives

INTERLUDE from FOLK SYMPHONY, Harris

MIDNIGHT RIDE OF PAUL REVERE from Selections from McGuffey's Readers, Phillips

OVERTURES (BOL #76)

OVERTURE TO "THE BAT" (*Die Fledermaus*), Strauss

ACADEMIC FESTIVAL OVERTURE, Brahms

OVERTURE TO "THE MARRIAGE OF FIGARO," Mozart

ROMAN CARNIVAL OVERTURE, Berlioz

OVERTURE TO "WILLIAM TELL," Rossini (Dawn, Storm, Calm, Finale)

SCHEHERAZADE BY RIMSKY-KORSAKOV (BOL #77)

The Sea and Sinbad's Ship, Tale of the Prince Kalendar, The Young Prince and the Princess, The Festival at Bagdad

MUSICAL KALEIDOSCOPE (BOL #78)

ON THE STEPPES OF CENTRAL ASIA, Borodin

IN THE VILLAGE FROM CAUCASIAN SKETCHES, Ippolitoff-Ivanov

EXCERPTS, POLOVETSIAN DANCES FROM "PRINCE IGOR," Borodin

RUSSIAN SAILORS' DANCE FROM "THE RED POPPY," Glière

L'ARLÉSIENNE SUITE No. 1, Bizet (Carillon, Minuet)

L'ARLÉSIENNE SUITE No. 2, Bizet (Farandole)

PRELUDE TO ACT 1, "CARMEN," Bizet

MARCH TO THE SCAFFOLD, from *Symphonie Fantastique,* Berlioz

MUSIC OF THE DRAMA: WAGNER (BOL #79)

LOHENGRIN (Overture to Act 1, Prelude to Act 3)

THE TWILIGHT OF THE GODS (*Die Götterdämmerung*) (Siegfried's Rhine Journey)

THE MASTERSINGERS OF NUREMBERG (*Die Meistersinger von Nürnberg*) (Prelude, Dance of the Apprentices and Entrance of the Mastersingers)

TRISTAN AND ISOLDE (Love Death)

PETROUCHKA BY STRAVINSKY (BOL #80)

COMPLETE BALLET SCORE WITH NARRATION

ROGUES IN MUSIC (BOL #81)

TIL EULENSPIEGEL, Strauss

LIEUTENANT KIJE (Birth of Kije, Troika), Prokofiev

HÁRY JANÓS, Kodály (Viennese Musical Clock, Battle and Defeat of Napoleon, Intermezzo, Entrance of the Emperor)

MUSICAL PICTURES: MUSSORGSKY (BOL #82)

PICTURES AT AN EXHIBITION (Promenade Theme, The Gnome, The Old Castle, Tuileries, Ox-Cart, Ballet of Chicks in Their Shells, Goldenberg and Schmuyle, The Market Place at Limoges, Catacombs, The Hut of Baga Yaga, The Gate of Kiev)

NIGHT ON BALD MOUNTAIN

ENSEMBLES, LARGE AND SMALL (BOL #83)

YOUNG PERSON'S GUIDE TO THE ORCHESTRA, Britten

CANZONA IN C MAJOR FOR BRASS ENSEMBLE AND ORGAN, Gabrieli

CHORALE: AWAKE, THOU WINTRY EARTH, Bach

FOURTH MOVEMENT, "TROUT" QUINTET, Schubert

THEME AND VARIATIONS FOR PERCUSSION QUARTET, Kraft

THEME AND VARIATIONS from SERENADE FOR WIND INSTRUMENTS, Mozart (K361)

CONCERTOS (BOL #84)

FIRST MOVEMENT, PIANO CONCERTO, Grieg

FOURTH MOVEMENT, PIANO CONCERTO No. 2, Brahms

THIRD MOVEMENT, VIOLIN CONCERTO, Mendelssohn

SECOND MOVEMENT, GUITAR CONCERTO, Castelnuovo-Tedesco

THIRD MOVEMENT, CONCERTO IN C FOR TWO TRUMPETS, Vivaldi

MUSICAL IMPRESSIONS: RESPIGHI (BOL #85)

PINES OF ROME (Pines of the Villa Borghese, Pines Near a Catacomb, Pines of the Appian Way)

FOUNTAINS OF ROME (The Fountain of Valle Giulia at Dawn, The Triton Fountain at Morning, The Trevi Fountain at Midday, The Villa Medici Fountain at Sunset)

THE BIRDS (Prelude)

FASHIONS IN MUSIC (BOL #86)

ROMEO AND JULIET (Fantasy-Overture), Tchaikovsky

LITTLE FUGUE IN G MINOR, Bach

SUITE NO. 2 FROM "DAPHNIS AND CHLOË," Ravel

ROMANZE FROM A LITTLE NIGHT MUSIC (*Eine kleine Nachtmusik*), Mozart

PERIPETIA FROM FIVE PIECES FOR ORCHESTRA, Schoenberg

appendix d

Copyright Law

A concern of every teacher when gathering materials of instruction is the copyright law, which protects copyrighted materials. Under Section 107 of the Copyright Act, unfair use is determined if the photocopied material is used commercially and for profit, if more than a portion of the work is copied, or if it reduces the copyright owner's market for the material. In an MENC *Newsbrief* dated July, 1983, guidelines state that a single copy for research, teaching, or preparation to teach may be made of a chapter from a book; a periodical or newspaper article; a short story, essay, or poem; or a diagram or picture. Allowed are multiple copies, not more than one copy per pupil in class, of a 250-word poem, a 2,500-word article, a 1,000-word excerpt, and special works shorter than 2,500 words. Not allowed are more than one piece or two excerpts from the same author, more than nine multiple copies for one course during one term, and copying that replaces collective works. The above refers primarily to words; the music teacher is concerned primarily with making photocopies of music. Incidentally, most music series publishers and some other sources offer materials that can be reproduced freely; this fact is stated clearly in the materials and no teacher need worry about these. In an emergency situation, a teacher may reproduce copyrighted songs or instrumental music if such copies will be promptly replaced with those purchased from the copyright owner or agent thereof. This refs to music for performance. For academic (nonperformance) purposes multiple copies of *excerpts* of works may be made, provided that such excerpts do not comprise a part of the whole that would be considered a performable unit such as a section, movement, or aria, but in any case more than 10 percent of the whole work. The number of copies shall not exceed one copy per pupil. Printed copies that have been purchased may be edited or simplified provided that the fundamental character of the work is not distorted or the lyrics altered or lyrics added if none exist. Thus, teachers may not write new versions of a copyrighted song and photocopy them for classroom use without permission from the copyright owner. A single copy of recordings of performances by students may be made for evaluation or rehearsal purposes and may be retained by the school or individual teacher. A single copy of a sound recordings such as a tape, disc, or cassette of copyrighted music may be made from sound recordings owned by the teacher for the purpose of constructing aural exercises or examinations and may be retained by the school or teacher. (This pertains only to the copyright of the music itself and not to any copyright which may exist in the sound recording.) Prescott and Gary (1982) state that the following are prohibited:

> Copying to create or replace or substitute for anthologies, compilations, or collective works.
>
> Copying of or from works intended to be "consumable" in the course of study or of teaching, such as workbooks, exercises, standardized tests, and answer sheets and like material.
>
> Copying for purpose of performance, except as in the above emergency for public performance.
>
> Copying for the purpose of substituting for the purchase of music, except as stated above in emergency situations.
>
> Copying without inclusion of the copyright notice, which appears on the printed copy.

Because the copyright law is complex, it is urged that an informed person (such as a librarian) be appointed as one who keeps records and through whom permission to copy is sought, and who keeps copies of correspondence relating to obtaining permissions. The purpose of this is to protect teacher and school districts from lawsuits.

References

Copyright Basics. Washington, D.C.: Copyright Office, Library of Congress, 1981.

Highlights of the New Copyright Law. Washington, D.C.: Copyright Office, Library of Congress, 1981

PRESCOTT, MICHAEL P., and CHARLES L. GARY, "Copyright in the Legal Spotlight," *Music Educators Journal,* March 1982, 25–27.

The United States Copyright Law: A Guide for Music Educators. Reston, Va.: Music Educators National Conference. Single free copies available.

Index of Songs

General Index

A

Activities, general, for music learning, 118–22
  categorized, 121
Adventures in Music recordings, 446–50
American Indian, music of, 428
Arts, relationships, 436
Augmentation, 245
Autoharp, 392–97

B

Band, 196–97
Barbershop harmony, 368
Basic education, 437
Beer, Alice, 5, 35
Behavior, *see* Classroom management
Bells, 380–84, 411
Black music, 425–26
Blues, 414
Books, music series, 50–52
Books for children, 439–45
Bordun, 204
Boston Academy of Music, 2

Bowmar Orchestral Library, 451–57
Brain, research on, 29
Bruner, Jerome, 8, 27–28
  structure of a subject, 43–44

C

Canon, 350–53
Cary, Sylvia E., 73
Chant, 353–57
Child development, 7–31
  norms of, 9–22
Chording, piano, 401–8
  with bells, 411
  vocal, 368
Chord inversions, 408–9
Chord roots, 361–64
Chorus, 369–70
Classroom, self-contained, 53
Classroom management, 65–71
  factors affecting behavior, 67–69
  individualized instruction, 78–80
  minority students, 65–66
  self-control, 66

National music convention, 2
Norms, developmental, 9–22
Note reading, 299–300, 319

O

Oberlin Conservatory, 3
Objectives, 99–102, 113–18
    behavioral, 99–100
    content areas, relation to, 101–12
    four areas of, 101–2
Octave displacement, 345
Opera, 344
Orchestra, 196–97
    singing classroom, 411–12
Orff, Carl, 1, 3, 203–7, 215
    instruments, 205–6
Orff Schulwerk, 63, 236, 281–93
Organizational plans, 52–54
    alternative schools, 53
    departmental, 53
    middle school, 54
    self-contained classroom, 53
    6-3-3, 4-4-4, 5-4-4 plans, 53
Ostinato, 204, 206, 353–57

P

Partner songs, 359–60
Part singing, 350–74
    chants, 353–57
    chord roots, 361–64
    countermelodies, 357–58
    descant, 358–59
    dialogue songs, 350
    harmonic endings, 361
    improvising, 368
    partner songs, 359–60
    rounds and canons, 350–53
    thirds and sixths, 365–68
    vocal chording, 368
Patschen, 206
Percepts, 33
Phrase, 335–37
Piaget, Jean, 8, 23–26
    stages of cognitive development, 24–26
Piano, 384–85
    chording, 401–8
Pitch, establishing, 285
Play-party games, 213
Polymetrics, 265
Polyphony, 107, 418

Q

Questioning and learning, 40–42

R

Recorder, 386–98
    fingering, 387
Rhythm, 105 (*see also* Concepts, rhythm-related)
    individual differences, in, 247–48
    normal expectations, 248–50
    songs for classwork, 250–55
Rhythm syllables, 227
Richards, Mary Helen, 207–8, 224
Root, George, 3
Round, 350–53

S

Scales, 307–18, 427
    chromatic, 316
    ethnic, 317
    Japanese, 427
    major, 309–10
    minor, 312, 313, 315
    modal, 315
    pentatonic, 310–11, 314, 427
    tone row, 317–18
    whole-tone, 316
Schwadron, Abraham A., 40
Sequence, 335
Singing, 271–88
    boys and, 272
    out-of-tune singing, 278–85
    pitch discrimination in, 277–85
Smith, Robert B., 272
Solfège, 203
Songs, 286–306
    activities with, 321
    creating, 301–6
    echo-type, 286–87, 295
    one-, two-, and three-chord, 399
    partner, 359
    recordings of, 300
    rote songs, teaching of, 293–98
    in symphonic music, 346–47
Sounds, 108–9
Sound sources:
    conventional, 172–201
    science of, 187–89
    unconventional, 153, 171
Special learner, 89–95
    culturally and economically different, 94
    educable retarded, 93–94
    gifted, 95
    hearing impaired, 92–93
    parents of, 91
    perceptually handicapped, 94
    staff for, 89
    visually impaired, 92
Spiral curriculum, 26
Staccato, 232–33
Structure, of a subject, 43–44